WOMEN OF COLOR
AND THE MULTICULTURAL
CURRICULUM

WOMEN OF COLOR AND THE MULTICULTURAL CURRICULUM

Transforming the College Classroom

Edited by

LIZA FIOL-MATTA and MARIAM K. CHAMBERLAIN

THE FEMINIST PRESS
at The City University of New York
New York

Published 1994 by The Feminist Press at The City University of New York,
311 East 94 Street, New York, NY 10128

98 97 96 95 94 5 4 3 2 1

Library of Congress Cataloging-in-Publication Data

Women of color and the multicultural curriculum : transforming the college classroom
  / edited by Liza Fiol-Matta and Mariam K. Chamberlain.
      p. cm.
  Includes bibliographical references.
  ISBN 1-55861-082-0 (hard : acid-free paper) : $35.00 — ISBN
1-55861-083-9 (pbk. : acid-free paper) : $18.95
      1. Universities and colleges—United States—Curricula. 2. Curriculum change—
United States. 3. Minority women—Study and teaching (Higher)—United
States. 4. Multiculturalism—Study and teaching (Higher)—United States.
I. Fiol-Matta, Liza. II. Chamberlain, Mariam.
LB2365.5.W65 1994
378.1'99—dc20   94-8242
                                                                      CIP

The preparation and publication of this volume was supported by the Ford Foundation
through a subcontract under a grant to the National Council for Research on Women
for coordination of the Mainstreaming Minority Women's Studies Program. The
Feminist Press would also like to thank Sallie Bingham, Eleanor T. Elliott,
Helene D. Goldfarb, Jane S. Gould, Dorothy Hart, Deborah Ann Light,
Joanne Markell, Daphne Patai, and Genevieve Vaughan for their genorosity.

Text and cover design by Paula Martinac

Cover art: *The Library* by Jacob Lawrence, 1960, tempera on fiberboard, 24 × 29 ⅞
in. Courtesy of the National Museum of American Art, Smithsonian Institution, gift of
S. C. Johnson & Son, Inc. © Jacob Lawrence

Typeset by Creative Graphics

Printed in the United States of America on acid-free paper by McNaughton & Gunn,
Inc.

CONTENTS

PREFACE

Women's Studies and the Evolution of Mainstreaming

Women's studies as a formal area of teaching and research first appeared in higher education in 1969 and is now in its third decade. Fueled by the women's movement and the growth in the number of female students and faculty members in colleges and universities, the field has burgeoned and is now an established part of the curriculum. Well over a thousand institutions, including two thirds of all universities, half of all four-year colleges, and a quarter of two-year colleges, offer women's studies courses.[1] Of these, over six hundred have coordinated interdisciplinary programs offering a concentration in women's studies. From its origins in the United States women's studies has also spread across national boundaries, first to Europe and then, with the advent of the United Nations Decade for Women, in 1975, to developing countries as well.

The widespread introduction of women's studies courses and programs as part of the curriculum of higher education, important as it is, does not in itself fully represent the impact of the new scholarship on the academy. As a field that is cross-disciplinary in nature, women's studies and feminist perspectives have a bearing on the mainstream curriculum and its various disciplines. The world of feminist scholars not only enlarged but also challenged the assumptions of the traditional disciplines, and it did not take long before efforts were made to measure the impact of women's studies on the core curriculum.

The first such effort was undertaken by a group of faculty members at Princeton University in 1976. Their project, which was funded by the Ford Foundation, focused on an examination of introductory courses in four disciplines—history, sociology, psychology, and English. The staff of the project collected and analyzed 355 course syllabi from 172 departments in a variety of institutions. Supplementary information was gathered through questionnaires sent to department chairs, directors of women's studies programs, and publishers of textbooks. It was found that, with few exceptions, little or no attention was being given to women in the mainstream curriculum. Department chairs reported that the presence of women in their departments and the existence of women's studies programs on campus were important factors in determining whether individual faculty members were taking heed of the new scholarship on women and incorporating it into their courses. Yet unless male as well as female faculty members did so, as the report noted, most undergraduate men and many undergraduate women would leave college without an understanding of women's roles in society or the influence of sex stereotyping on their daily lives. Based on these findings, the Princeton Project concluded that special efforts were called for to introduce faculty members to the new scholarship on women and its implications for the curriculum.[2]

Since that time there have been numerous curriculum integration projects designed to do just that. By the end of 1991, a period of fifteen years, there were no less than two hundred curriculum integration projects completed or under way.[3] These have encompassed a variety of techniques, including the preparation of monographs and guides to relevant topics and source material, workshops, summer institutes, conferences, faculty development grants, consultations, and curriculum development programs. For the most part these projects have been funded by foundations and government agencies, although in some instances colleges and universities have allocated internal resources for campuswide programs. To date, the principal sources of external funding have been the Ford, Rockefeller, and Andrew W. Mellon foundations, the Fund for the Improvement of Postsecondary Education (FIPSE) of the U.S. Department of Education, and the National Endowment for the Humanities (NEH). Significant support has also been provided by a variety of national and regional foundations as well as other government agencies such as the federally funded Women's Educational Equity Act Program.[4] There have also been some state-supported programs, the most outstanding of which is the New Jersey Project, a statewide attempt to foster the integration of gender scholarship into the curriculum. Since 1986 the New Jersey Department of Higher Education has provided a total of over $1.5 million in forty grants to nineteen institutions for support of campus-based curriculum integration projects.[5]

One of the earliest and most influential of the curriculum integration efforts was a four-year, cross-disciplinary project conducted by the women's studies program at the University of Arizona. This program, initiated in 1981, was the forerunner of the integration movement and served to demonstrate the magnitude and importance of the task as well as some of the challenges. Directed toward senior faculty, including department chairs, in the social sciences and humanities, the project developed integration strategies that included summer seminars, colloquia, and lectures by visiting scholars. Later programs benefited from the Arizona experience, particularly in confronting the resistance of male faculty members to feminist scholarship.[6]

These projects have resulted in a spate of publications about mainstreaming. Notable among them are: *The Prism of Sex* (1977), edited by Julia Sherman and Evelyn Torton Beck; *Changing Our Minds* (1988), edited by Susan Hardy Aiken et al.; and *Transforming Knowledge* (1990), by Elizabeth Kamarch Minnich.[7]

MAINSTREAMING MINORITY WOMEN'S STUDIES

In 1985 the Ford Foundation hosted a meeting of scholars and leaders in the movement to integrate women's studies in the curriculum, assess the progress of curriculum reform, and identify areas requiring further support. An important conclusion that emerged from the meeting was that inadequate consideration was being given to the roles, contributions, and perspectives of women of color. As a result, the Ford Foundation turned its attention more specifically to the growing body of scholarship on that subject and the increasing number of scholars active in its production. In 1986 Ford awarded grants to Spelman College and Memphis State University, which house two of the principal centers for research on black women. These laid the groundwork for a more comprehensive program to mainstream minority women's studies.

The broader program was launched in 1988 with grants to four institutions. A second round of grants in 1989 extended the program to seven additional institutions, and two further grants in 1990 raised the total number of participating institutions to thirteen. Overall, the Ford Foundation committed nearly $1.7 million to the program. Institutions were selected on the basis of projects submitted by campus-based centers for research on women which were also affiliated with women's studies programs. The program's mission was to enable these centers, many of which were already engaged in curriculum integration efforts, to collaborate with women's studies and racial-ethnic studies programs and scholars in planning and implementing projects to incorporate research and teaching about women of color into the undergraduate curriculum.

All participating institutions were members or affiliates of the National Council for Research on Women, which represents over seventy research centers nationwide. With that in mind, the Ford Foundation designated the Council to coordinate the overall program. Its functions were to facilitate communication and cooperative exchange among the program grantees, to assist projects in generating and distributing resource materials, and to disseminate information, material, and strategies for mainstreaming minority women's studies widely. As part of the dissemination activities of the Council, specific provisions were made to prepare a resource volume following the conclusion of the program, consisting of course syllabi and other curriculum material emanating from the program. *Women of Color and the Multicultural*

Curriculum: Transforming the College Classroom, prepared in collaboration with The Feminist Press, represents that volume.

MAINSTREAMING AND WOMEN'S STUDIES INTERNATIONAL

Although women's studies is now widespread and continues to expand throughout the world, mainstreaming, or curriculum development, is not yet a visible part of the movement abroad, as it is in the United States.[8] There are several reasons for this. In most other countries, unlike the United States, women's studies programs tend to be peripherally related to higher education institutions. With some exceptions, such as Canada, the United Kingdom, and the Netherlands, such programs are more often located within research institutes or special training programs. This structure limits the access of women's studies programs to the mainstream curriculum. Another deterrent to curriculum integration efforts abroad is the lack of financial support. In the United States, as we have seen, such support has usually come not from the university itself but from external sources—private foundations and government agencies. Elsewhere local support from private foundations is largely absent, and support from public sources is limited to a few countries.

In some instances there is an additional reason for the absence of curriculum integration programs; it is the ideological view that women's studies must remain separate in order to flourish. Those that adhere to this view believe that mainstreaming leads to co-optation and a loss of identity of women's studies. The U.S. experience suggests otherwise. Indeed, every indication is that successful curriculum integration goes hand in hand with the existence of a strong women's studies program. In other words, it is not necessarily a question of either/or; curriculum integration is a process of, not a substitute for, women's studies.[9]

MAINSTREAMING AS A STRATEGY FOR CURRICULUM DEVELOPMENT

Although the term *mainstreaming* is usually applied to women's studies, curriculum integration programs as such are not unique to women's studies. New development seminars and faculty institutes have long been held and continue to be held in numerous other fields. During the 1950s and 1960s, for example, they were conducted with great success by the Ford Foundation as part of its program to strengthen management education by integrating quantitative and social science methods. Summer institutes for faculty members are also regularly offered in the humanities disciplines with support from sources such as the National Endowment for the Humanities. What they are designed to do is to accelerate the application of new knowledge and ideas into the curriculum of higher education.

Curriculum change is part of the normal process of higher education, responding in part to the advancement of knowledge in the various disciplines and in part to the changing composition and needs of the student body. In the absence of strong external forces, the change takes place in incremental steps, as successive generations of scholars enter the faculty ranks. In these terms the past twenty-five years have been anything but "business as usual." Women's studies and ethnic studies have grown at an exponential rate. At the same time, the enrollment of women and minorities in higher education has reached record highs. Women now represent 54 percent and minorities 19 percent of the overall student body of colleges and universities in the United States. Also adding to the diversity of the student population is the growing enrollment of foreign students of all races.

To enable educational institutions to be more responsive to these changes than would otherwise be the case, foundations and public agencies have provided support for special programs of curriculum development. Women's studies, ethnic studies, and mainstreaming programs are all part of the overall effort. Given the scope and nature of the changes involved, it is not surprising that these programs have encountered resistance. In the case of mainstreaming programs, there is direct confrontation with entrenched faculty members who have their own agendas and do not welcome new ideas coming from unexpected sources. It is particularly difficult to make headway in the introductory courses of the disciplines in which available textbooks reflect accepted doctrine and require a long lead time to incorporate new concepts. The outcomes of the mainstreaming minority women's studies program are illustrative. The greatest gains have been made in upper-division and other specialized courses, women's studies courses, and new courses, rather than in the basic courses of the traditional disciplines.

Thus, while mainstreaming has made some progress, it has been slow, and much remains to be done. We hope that this resource volume will be helpful on the road ahead.

Mariam K. Chamberlain

NOTES

1. Elaine El-Khawas, *Campus Trends: 1984*, Higher Education Panel Report no. 65 (Washington, D.C.: American Council on Education, February 1985).

2. Princeton Project on Women in the College Curriculum, Final Report, 1 March 1977 (MS).

3. Betty Schmitz, "Diversity and Collegiality in the Curriculum," *Liberal Education* 77, no. 4 (September–October 1991): 19.

4. For a directory of projects with brief descriptions, commentary, and sources of funding, see Betty Schmitz, *Integrating Women's Studies into the Curriculum: A Guide and Bibliography* (New York: The Feminist Press, 1985).

5. *Transformations: The New Jersey Project Journal* 2, no. 1 (Winter 1991): 1.

6. For an account of the Arizona experience, see "Trying Transformations: Curriculum Integration and the Problem of Resistance," by Susan Hardy Aiken, Karen Anderson, Myra Dinnerstein, Judy Lensink, and Patricia MacCorquodale, in *Signs: Journal of Women in Culture and Society* 12, no. 2 (Winter 1987): 255–75.

7. Julia A. Sherman and Evelyn Torton Beck, eds., *The Prism of Sex* (Madison: University of Wisconsin Press, 1977); Susan Hardy Aiken, Karen Anderson, Myra Dinnerstein, Judy Lensink, and Patricia MacCorquodale, eds., *Changing Our Minds* (Albany: SUNY Press, 1988); Elizabeth Kamarch Minnich, *Transforming Knowledge* (Philadelphia: Temple University Press, 1990). See also Dale Spender, ed., *Men's Studies Modified* (Oxford: Pergamon Press, 1981); Ellen Carol DuBois, Gail Paradise Kelly, Elizabeth Lapovsky Kennedy, Carolyn W. Korsmeyer, and Lillian Robinson, *Feminist Scholarship: Kindling in the Groves of Academe* (Urbana and Chicago: University of Illinois Press, 1985); Elizabeth Langland and Walter Gove, eds., *A Feminist Perspective in the Academy* (Chicago: University of Chicago Press, 1983); and Christie Farnham, ed., *The Impact of Feminist Research in the Academy* (Bloomington: University of Indiana Press, 1987).

8. For an international portrait of women's studies research, teaching, and strategies, see *Nairobi and Beyond*, ed. Aruna Rao (New York: The Feminist Press, 1991).

9. For a concurring view, see Schmitz, *Integrating Women's Studies*, 8.

ACKNOWLEDGMENTS

The editors of this volume are indebted to Alison Bernstein of the Ford Foundation for her inspiration and support of this volume and the Mainstreaming Minority Women's Studies Program on which it is based. We are indebted also to Florence Howe for her wisdom and guidance and to her associates at The Feminist Press for their unflagging efforts to bring the volume to fruition, especially to Julie Malnig and Neeti Madan for in-house editing and for assistance in expediting the completion of the manuscript. For generously sharing their knowledge, we are grateful to various individuals who are at the forefront of curriculum transformation: Johnnella E. Butler, Sara Coulter, Angela Ginorio, Dorothy O. Helly, Deborah Rosenfelt, Paula Rothenberg, Betty Schmitz, and Susan Searing. Our thanks go also to all who contributed essays and shared course syllabi, making this volume possible.

WOMEN OF COLOR AND THE MULTICULTURAL CURRICULUM

INTRODUCTION

Liza Fiol-Matta

This volume documents the results of a unique experiment in higher education curriculum transformation, the Ford Foundation's Mainstreaming Minority Women's Studies Program. The curriculum transformation projects that produced these seminar models and syllabi addressed the shortsightedness of an exclusive curriculum by concentrating specifically on the issues, learning, research, and achievements of women of color in the United States.[1]

Curriculum reform is a continuous process; critiquing exclusions is not without historical antecedents. The reform of American language and literature studies is a primary example. It revolutionized the study of English and English literature by pointing out the devaluing of writing and criticism by authors from the United States. Yet it was, until recently, shaped by the same standards of the literature it sought to open up. In other words, the authors that were included were the American counterparts to those of the previous canon: white, male, and middle-to-upper class. Furthermore, similar to the discipline on which it modeled itself, the women included not only had to be white but also had to be some combination of doomed or damaged, or brilliant but somehow limited. The restricted sphere of influence and knowledge of Jane Austen's parlor has its parallel in Emily Dickinson's garden, Virginia Woolf's madness in Sylvia Plath's despair. By widening the areas of knowledge and research to include the many realities of gender, women's studies has made significant contributions to pedagogy in higher education, but one of its most significant achievements has been the influence it has exerted on other disciplines and fields of research. It was not so long ago that, primarily through the efforts of women's studies, Woolf, Austen, Dickinson, and Plath began to be accepted for English program reading lists, comprehensive examinations, and dissertations. Racial and ethnic studies for their part helped to open department doors ever so slightly to a few black men, while women's studies again played a significant role in opening the canon to include black women. Harriet Jacobs joined Frederick Douglass; Zora Neale Hurston took her place alongside Richard Wright.

Once these gains were made, the lessons taught and learned were inevitably different; thus, the projects that teach how change takes place—and what change means—are becoming increasingly important. Perhaps most significant for faculty members engaged in the actual curriculum work, the transformation projects created spaces and times, forums and strategies, for professors to talk about teaching and to become acquainted with new materials and knowledge within their fields. The projects designed various types of disciplinary and interdisciplinary faculty development workshops, seminars, and conferences to facilitate just that kind of interaction, to talk not as experts but as learners. Curriculum transformation projects are stimulating and vital because they tackle concrete objectives; they provide the opportunity for university and college faculty to talk about methodology as well as content, pedagogy, and research. Successful workshops and seminars have addressed both *what* the new knowledge is and *how* to incorporate into current curricula the materials about women of color that are being discovered. This emphasis on teaching the new material provides the faculty with a means of renewal and an opportunity to engage the new knowledge themselves. With the emphasis on integration into the curriculum, syllabi and course revisions are major tangible products that programs such as these generate, but faculty development is itself a productive, innovative component of education, and several teacher-training models have evolved from transformation projects. In short, it is possible to change the ways we teach and learn, and the models provided here attempt to show how.

Peggy McIntosh's, and Marilyn Schuster and Susan Van Dyne's work on phase theory, in particular, was instrumental in laying the foundation for a methodology of feminist curriculum reform and transformation. From the beginning their findings were expanded on by African-American women, whose early work has since informed that of other women of color. Early on, for example, Beverly Guy-Sheftall, Elizabeth Higginbotham, and Johnnella E. Butler pointed out the exclusionary patterns in women's studies and feminist pedagogy. Butler's "Transforming the Curriculum: Teaching about Women of Color," one of the key readings in the faculty seminars, shows how identity and knowledge create connected thinking and visibility.[2] Gloria T. Hull, Patricia Bell Scott, and Barbara Smith's *All the Women Are White, All the Blacks Are Men, but Some of Us Are Brave: Black Women's Studies*, published in 1982, is still a useful model and resource.[3]

The work by these women is in turn being broadened by the Chinese, Puerto Rican, Native American, Chicana, Japanese, Indian, and Korean women and women of African descent whose work is largely responsible for the workshops that produced the materials in this book. The transformation projects detailed in this volume illustrate some of the dialogues created by and creating the new teaching, thinking, and learning. Increasingly, there is an awareness that these voices from the various borderlands, tribal lands, islands, and mainlands are neither marginal nor irrelevant. As women of color in the academy establish themselves within a changing curriculum, they give back to their disciplines a knowledge of the complexity of identity, of the fluid boundaries of class, race, ethnicity, and sexuality.

Phase theory and other theories of curriculum integration remain useful as tools to name the exclusion of certain groups from course content and textbooks. While many may optimistically think that the "womanless curriculum" no longer exists,[4] too many of us can name instances in which the continuing total exclusion of women, and particularly women of color, from the content of a course can still be found.

As women's studies has explored the possibilities of an inclusive curriculum, it has stumbled, quite naturally, upon its own exclusions. While feminism and feminist research continue to expand "traditional" academic disciplines, the transformation of women's studies curricula has also been necessary. The last few years have brought important new critiques of the racial and ethnic dimensions of feminist knowledge to its already established work of uncovering power relations and systems of oppression based on gender. What is missing in the women's studies curriculum, these critiques point out, are the multiple racial, ethnic, and class realities of women—as well as their diversity based on sexual preference, age, physical ability, and other often overlooked categories used to marginalize them. The thirteen transformation projects involved in the Ford Foundation's Mainstreaming Minority Women's Studies Program addressed precisely these areas of exclusion, both in the undergraduate curricula of their institutions and in their ongoing women's studies research.[5]

The Ford program forced women's studies to look within its own course offerings, programs, and research to address its white-privileged structures. This required the recognition of those scholars whose work within their disciplines has opened new doors on the realities of women of color in this country. Neglected and emerging scholars were identified and new information and approaches to the various disciplines unearthed. In addition to providing resource lists and delivering interesting talks on women of color, scholars who are women of color challenged, questioned, and modified the ways in which the disciplinary areas have traditionally constituted knowledge. The projects provided a variety of forums for women of color scholars to share their experiences and knowledge with other colleagues and with one another. Through informal and formal meetings these scholars had the opportunity to contribute new knowledge on pedagogy and research from a multiple-context perspective, and, as a result, these projects were often at the forefront of cultural diversity and other campus-based curriculum transformation initiatives. The excitement and affirmation that faculty felt in being at these conferences and workshops were mirrored in the women of color teachers-scholars-activists themselves as the seminars brought them together, enabling them to network and plan collaborative projects. Furthermore, the expertise of women of color, speaking for themselves, helped shape the projects and fill many of the existing exclusionary gaps.

One of the first critiques of the program concerned its name. Mainstreaming Minority Women's Studies was conceptually awkward, since "mainstreaming" was neither the actual objective of the projects nor the basis of the thinking behind the program's formation. Transformation of the curriculum, which reflects replacing fragmentation with wholeness, and isolation with community, was more properly its goal; mainstreaming is just one method that can result in transformation. Challenging the name, then, was a product of finding and redefining the words as the work went along—an example, in fact, of the process in which the participants were engaged. Evidence of this are the varied names of the individual projects: A University for Everyone (University of Oregon), Infusing Material on Minority Women into the Liberal Arts Curriculum of the CUNY Senior Colleges (City University of New York), Integrating Women of Color into the Liberal Arts Curriculum (Duke University / University of North Carolina), Incorporating Feminist Scholarship concerning Gender and Cultural Diversity into the Curriculum (Metropolitan State University), and Toward a Gender Balanced Liberal Arts Core Curriculum (University of Puerto Rico–Cayey).

Anticipating the impact that awareness of our cultural diversity is having on our campuses, the program acknowledged that to understand and properly value that diversity we need to educate responsibly and accept the need to reformulate our own knowledge. By foregrounding women of color, and race and gender analysis, these projects addressed the gaps that traditional approaches to knowledge and teaching have created. They remind us that curriculum balancing cannot happen by simply subsuming the variety of experiences by people of color under words like *Asian, black, Hispanic,* and *Native American,* for these, as we all know, do not even begin to name the diversity of ethnicities, the multiplicity of nations, the myriad combinations of class and race represented—not submerged—in the term *women of color.* Putting the knowledge of and about women of color at the center of this curriculum reform (in the disciplines and in the classroom) is necessary to complete the pictures of the society we live in which we present in our classrooms. This is possible and, indeed, was achieved in these projects.

The Ford program was far-reaching and ambitious. Among its achievements was the creation of an opportunity for racial ethnic studies and women's studies faculty at the participating campuses to break bread and engage in dialogue. Equally important was the validation and rewarding of faculty involved in producing materials and revising syllabi or courses to reflect the experience and the new knowledge of women of color in the curriculum. These certainly should be incorporated into other projects and by campus committees charged with looking at diversity and curriculum issues—but with a few caveats.

First, for several reasons, it was naive to assume a ready-made alliance between racial and ethnic studies and women's studies. Relying on women of color to serve as the primary bridge across that gap is placing far too great a burden on them and far too little on others. It is asking women of color in the academy to choose loyalties between race and gender, or to be engaged in a struggle on two fronts, educating and confronting the largely white women's studies programs, on the one hand, and the mostly male, and often sexist and homophobic, racial and ethnic studies programs, on the other. Many women of color in this position find themselves asserting, as Cherríe Moraga does, "I am a woman with a foot in both worlds. I refuse the split. I feel the necessity for dialogue."[6] In short, programs like these must address clearly the issue of how to theorize about race, ethnicity, and gender while fostering the connections and coalition work between women's studies and the various racial and ethnic studies programs in the academy.[7]

Second, the dialogues that need to take place across race and class within the women's studies community itself cannot be underestimated. It was neither comfortable nor easy, for example, for women of color to challenge the National Women's Studies Association (NWSA) to address structural racism in its organization at its annual conference in June 1990. Understanding that this shifting of position, this progression in addressing the stages and manifestations of racism beyond the personal, is a necessary step did not make it any easier for them or for the white women who were in leadership positions. Most of the women's research centers involved in the Ford program were directed by white women. They, in turn, needed the expertise, authority, and cooperation of women of color to meet the objectives of the projects. But as the confrontation with NWSA clearly showed, women of color cannot be expected to wade in the waters of women's studies without stirring them up.

Another fact that became readily apparent once the initiatives were under way was that women of color (and most especially the newly recognized groups of Latina, Asian, and Native American women in the academy) need to talk, need to meet one another as well as with one another, and not just move into roles as individual facilitators or experts. Funding for this type of activity is needed, and projects that build this kind of opportunity into their faculty development activities should be rewarded. A particularly good model for this was State University of New York (SUNY)–Albany's three-day symposium on Puerto Rican women, which brought together leading Puerto Rican women researchers from the island and from the continental United States.

Finally, outright support must also be provided for initiatives planned, conceived, and proposed by women of color themselves. The importance of appointing women of color to play central, not peripheral, roles in directing and planning transformation initiatives cannot be stressed enough. We must recognize that for too long the experience and knowledge of women of color has been segregated from the mainstream, its humanizing potential ignored. Despite their shortcomings, however, the Ford program and curriculum projects like it have demonstrated that it is possible to change the ways we teach and learn; it is possible to create a curriculum that encompasses the complexity of contemporary American reality in all its diversity.

Higher education in the late-twentieth-century United States is at a peculiar place. While we are every day integrating cutting-edge technology into our lives and learning, we are paradoxically still struggling with some of the basic questions of living together on this planet. Pitting the right of all to be educated against the responsibility of educating about all is a particularly American dilemma. In the media diversity on campus is portrayed as a battle, the root of unrest. Reactionary curricular agendas, wrapped in the cloak of basic values and intellectual conservatism, have tried to argue that diversity itself is the problem. What the efforts of projects like the Ford program offer both the campus as well as the academy is the opportunity to think creatively about diversity.

When students were found "deficient" in basic skills, English, reading, and mathematics departments searched for ways to teach these skills. Indeed, basic skills programs have transformed much of the way learning is viewed. Much work on ways of learning and thinking has found its way into the academy and into the needs assessments of colleges and universities because these departments and disciplines responded when they were called upon to deal with the academic "problem" of these student populations. The same transformations that have occurred in learning theories, however, must be questioned about how they address gender and race diversity. Just as "the First-Year Experience" is not uniformly similar for all "First-Year Learners," an essentialist conceptualization of "women's ways of knowing" is only as descriptive as the diversity of women represented in a given sample.

Now, as students are being found "socially deficient," women's studies and ethnic studies programs similarly have much to offer the university. Date rapes, fraternity party gang rapes, gay bashing, and anti-Semitic and racist incidents are social realities on our campuses which mirror the violence of our society. Young men and women, white and of color, must learn to live with one another just as much as they must learn the research and technological methodologies of their disciplines. Projects such as those presented here propose that diversity is addressed effectively by weaving the excluded experiences and achievements of all members of the global society into the fabric of knowledge, course content, and campus climate. The educators involved in the seminars that produced these syllabi models prove that there are, indeed, ways to accommodate change and renewal into our disciplinary and institutional structures.

This is not to say, of course, that all faculty embraced these initiatives with open minds and willing spirits. Much transformation work naturally has had to address faculty resistance. This is easier to understand if we consider the difficulty and scope of what we are asking college instructors to do. They are being asked to value new areas of knowledge both in their work with their students and in their fields as well as be willing to address their own race, class, ethnicity, and gender assumptions. To do this work faculty members must reassess their ideas of what the academic community is, of who it (and their own work within it) includes and who it excludes. Faculty must be willing to recommit to a different, diverse community.

Inclusion of the scholarship on women of color is not only working against ignorance and apathy; it is also overtly antiracist, anticlassist, antisexist work. Furthermore, we cannot overlook that the necessary internal and difficult antiracist and antisexist work begins with the instructor. One cannot teach or ask others to teach about class and ethnic difference (which inclusion of minority women will inevitably bring up) without having explored one's own class and ethnic background. This is a prelude to consciously connecting to how our language, our choice of words, our interests, our assumptions—even when we think we are the most conscientious and conscious of people— reverberate in the shared space that we create in a classroom, laboratory, or mentoring relationship. Thus, because the objectives of the program could not be achieved without transforming the teacher, this was also a program of faculty education. Successful projects do not assume that those we are asking to transform, revise, integrate, balance, or infuse specific courses will have the language and experience of self-critique.

The higher media profiles in the closing decade of the twentieth century of the incidence of racist and sexist clashes and struggles on our campuses underscore one very important thing: antiracist work has to be done over and over again. Just as the higher education curriculum is one of the most visible arenas of exclusion in our society, our colleges and universities must also be among the most visible arenas of engagement and change. Despite the increasing reliance on corporate and business models in higher education administration, there are still two essential components in the learning process—teacher and student, facilitator and learner. Working in diverse communities requires methodologies and philosophies that must be rethought, taught, learned, and fostered. Ignoring this is tantamount to wishing to turn back the calendar to "comfortable" days when certain people were "college material" and others were not, when students and teachers who were victimized by attacks and slurs would take it quietly and disappear. The college campus and the college classroom are, by virtue of their diversity, community scenarios for transformation.

* * *

"Change comes," Elizabeth Kamarch Minnich reminds us, "when thinking is released from old tangles of errors that have locked it into the past *and* when we learn to analyze the potential for real change in our very specific contexts."[8] We cannot cynically believe the old, reactionary adage that the more things change the more they remain the same. Understanding diversity and its strengths is an occasion for shifting relationships and perceptions of many kinds. Change—in this case the shifting of academic and intellectual power—is in turn an occasion for fear, and some colleagues and policymakers are going to be seriously resistant. Further, because most of us were not educated in a curriculum that challenged canons or power and the construction of power relationships, the types of faculty and administrative resistance will be as multifarious as the diversity we are trying to understand. Although part of a tradition of curricular renewal and transformation, these projects are just the beginning of a conversation that includes the voices of an increasingly diverse scholarship.

The projects described in this volume, generously shared for our scrutiny and learning, offer a glimpse of what a truly multicultural curriculum would look like. Educating the college student of the early twenty-first century will mean taking on the antiracist, antisexist work of educating the whole person. The Mainstreaming Minority Women's Studies Program helped focus on positive measures to influence the quality of campus life at a time of growing dissension and increased problems of racial and diversity disharmony on U.S. campuses.

As the projects drew to a close, finding alternative ways to institutionalize the ongoing types of faculty renewal and curriculum reform projects begun by the program became a major concern. One thing is clear: there are many faculty who wish to become agents of change. When presented with new material and the opportunity to engage in debate, they become involved in and connected by new ways of thinking and teaching. The faculty seminar models that follow, and the syllabi produced by participants in these seminars, should at the very least remind us that the curriculum models of exclusion, despite their existence in our lives as a historical fact, do not need to be embedded forever as a standard, nor do their inherent inequities need to be replicated as if we are powerless to change them.

Designed in 1988, the Ford program explicitly encouraged women's research centers to collaborate with racial and ethnic studies programs to design and implement projects incorporating research and teaching about women of color (specifically, according to the original guidelines of the grants, black, Hispanic, Native American, and immigrant Asian women) into the undergraduate curricula at several colleges and universities. Twenty-one centers of research on women were invited to submit proposals; eleven were funded in the first round, and two more were added subsequently. They were given one- and two-year grants ranging from $50,000 to $100,000 to implement faculty training and syllabi revision projects.[9] In some cases faculty education involved full-day conferences on teaching and the new scholarship on women of color. For example, the Metropolitan State project sponsored major symposia on the four major racial-ethnic groups named by the grant. These were open to faculty from the eleven colleges and universities participating in their consortium. Extensive bibliographies and required readings were distributed to faculty before the event, and teaching and scholarship were addressed hand in hand. SUNY-Albany, whose project was codirected by women's studies and Latin American and Caribbean studies, sponsored an invitational conference for SUNY faculty on incorporating materials by and about Puerto Rican women into the curriculum. At this conference, as in those of other projects, faculty members had the opportunity to hear transforming scholars such as Margaret Anderson, Elizabeth Kamarck Minnich, and Patricia Hill Collins speak on knowledge-based concerns as well as Puerto Rican scholars such as Virginia Sánchez Korrol, Altagracia Ortiz, and Clara Rodríguez, who are researching the Latina reality in the United States.

Just as the projects represented diverse ways of approaching curriculum integration, they were also marked by the different characteristics and realities of their institutions. Some were based at private institutions, others at public; some were at small colleges, others at large research universities. The development of resources or databases to facilitate future research about women of color was the major concern of several projects. SUNY-Albany, for example, compiled an annotated bibliographic database of materials on Puerto Rican women. Memphis State continued to expand its well-known pioneering database and resource center on women of color in the social sciences and enhanced its successful yearly curriculum transformation workshops for faculty.

In the consortium projects at the University of Arizona, University of Wisconsin, and Metropolitan State, hundreds of faculty members from affiliated colleges and universities participated in project-sponsored colloquia and workshops. Other projects, notably at Barnard College, Columbia University, George Washington University, and the University of Puerto Rico, were designed to foster intensive ongoing seminars attended by a smaller number of faculty working on syllabi and course revision and reading the new scholarship in their disciplines and on curriculum integration. All the projects intended to impact system- or campuswide curriculum reform, anticipating that faculty members would return to their campuses and departments and share their ideas with colleagues.

Thus, the types of faculty development activities from which the syllabi in this volume are drawn varied according to the type of institution and the goals of the projects. Barnard, a small liberal arts college, revised its required First-Year Seminars. The University of Puerto Rico–Cayey project focused on revising a cluster of high-enrollment first-year courses, initiating the first curriculum revision of these courses in decades. In the Metropolitan State,

SUNY-Albany, and City University of New York (CUNY) projects large groups met by disciplines to revise courses. Some of the projects (notably University of Wisconsin, University of California–Los Angeles [UCLA], and CUNY) included graduate students, particularly those employed as teaching assistants or adjunct faculty, in order to train them in developing courses, syllabi, and strategies that they will carry on into their future teaching assignments.

All told, because some of the projects included multicampus university systems or consortiums of colleges, over sixty campuses benefited from the faculty development and the curriculum transformation efforts of the program. The number of faculty that applied for these seminars and ongoing projects varied, depending on the size of the university or college and the scope of the individual projects. At CUNY, for example, approximately eighty faculty members from the various senior colleges applied for a week-long intensive workshop in the summer of 1991. At UCLA sixty-five to seventy faculty members took part in ongoing workshops. Some four hundred faculty members took part in some form of active syllabi revision projects, while outreach via the various additional activities that accompanied the projects (seminars, databases, library resources, film and video screenings, reports at departmental meetings, and so on) affected many more.[10]

Along with the thirteen projects the Northwest Center for Research on Women at the University of Washington was awarded a grant to evaluate the projects, and the National Council for Research on Women (NCRW) received a grant to coordinate the work of participating projects by facilitating communication and cooperative exchange among the centers and dissemination of information, materials, and strategies for curriculum transformation. The council also published an information booklet describing the projects and organized three meetings of project directors.

The representative models included in this volume underscore that curriculum transformation for inclusion of women of color cannot prioritize elements of identity. Instead, it addresses the whole experience as well as the intersections, as Leslie I. Hill points out in her essay, "Transition in Curriculum Transformation: Some Trends and Challenges." The faculty development model syllabi presented in part 1 are drawn from the UCLA Ford Ethnic Women's Curriculum Transformation Project (FEW). Each is accompanied by an introductory essay by the seminar facilitators. The UCLA seminars are a good example of what was done in the institutes, colloquia, or conferences sponsored by the other projects. Apparent in these models is that the process involves more than creating reading lists. The conceptualizing of the discipline itself, the ways terms are used, the chronology of events, and the structural paradigms of knowledge fundamentally change when weighing the experiences of women of color. Karen E. Rowe details the stages of designing and redesigning the various seminars at UCLA in her essay, "Shifting Models, Creating Visions." Paula Ries reports on her findings about faculty perceptions at one of the projects of how transformation of a course comes about and how to gauge the success of transformation projects.

The undergraduate syllabi offered in the middle section of the volume are representative of the course revisions produced by the seminars. They are useful in answering the inevitable dilemma of course revision: if I include X in my syllabus, will it be at the expense of Y? Syllabi transformation and course revision, however, calls not for mere addition or subtraction of material but for reconceptualizing the lessons, research problems, methods of study, and outcomes. Many of the syllabi are accompanied by short essays by the instructors explaining their process in revising the course. We hope that these will help overcome the uncomfortable feeling of ignorance when first naming, placing, and validating new knowledge. The Barnard College First-Year Seminars, for instance, show how various canonical texts can be studied with texts by white women and women of color for fuller thematic context. Yet revising a course for inclusion is not exclusively about content revision, as Maxine Clair's essay on creative writing demonstrates. By using the African-American oral tradition of storytelling, valuing the spoken as well as the written word, she conceptualizes her class in a fundamentally different way. We should keep in mind, however, that evaluating a course syllabus in isolation from other factors is not necessarily the best way to gauge transformation. Because pedagogy, classroom dynamics and techniques, and how and what the instructor values or emphasizes in research and discussion are often not reflected in a syllabus, a better indicator might include a self-assessment of the process of, and intentions underlying, course revision.

Finally, the complete faculty seminar curriculum from the SUNY-Albany project, *An Interdisciplinary Guide for Research and Curriculum on Puerto Rican Women*, is included as a model for focused faculty development. The units demonstrate how resources and materials across the disciplines can enhance the subjects of study. Reviewing oral histories, for example, may augment quantitative research in economics, and reading fiction may round out the "facts" of history. While similar group-focused seminars were part of other projects, the SUNY-Albany project was the only one to use its entire resources on one group. It is not difficult to see how other racial-ethnic groups can be approached in a similar manner. For some institutions this may be the most feasible model, depending on available expertise and resources.

The projects whose work follows demonstrated how essential it is to bring racial and ethnic analysis to women's studies and gender analysis to racial and ethnic studies. While both have traditionally studied systems of oppression, the former's emphasis on gender analysis and the latter's on race analysis, even when intersecting with other categories such as class, have not necessarily led to overlap or integration of the two. Thus, for many years what Elizabeth Spelman has called the "ampersand problem" (e.g., being Chicana *and* female, black *and* female)[11] was perceived as a polarized duality and not the interwoven whole experience of women of color. A transformed curriculum acknowledges the need to integrate these two areas along with the other categories of difference.

NOTES

1. Here I join so many of my colleagues in footnoting the term *women of color.* I find myself usually using this term, and not *minority women* or *Third World women,* when I am referring in general to myself and the women of whom I am writing here. Otherwise, I use the appropriate ethnicity or race reference. The problematics of naming, like so many other concerns of women of color, is one of the areas of ongoing dialogue.

2. In *Multicultural Education: Issues and Perspectives,* ed. James A. Banks and Cherry M. Banks (New York: Allyn and Bacon, 1988), 145–63.

3. New York: The Feminist Press.

4. Peggy McIntosh, "Interactive Phases of Curricular Re-Vision," in *Toward a Balanced Curriculum: A Sourcebook for Initiating Gender Integration Projects,* ed. Bonnie Spanier, Alexander Bloom, and Darlene Boroviak (Cambridge, Mass.: Schenkman, 1983), 25–34. See also Marilyn R. Schuster and Susan R. Van Dyne, "Stages of Curriculum Transformation," in *Women's Place in the Academy: Transforming the Liberal Arts Curriculum,* ed. Schuster and Van Dyne (Totowa, N.J.: Rowman and Allenheld, 1985), 13–28; Maxine Baca Zinn, Lynn Weber Cannon, Elizabeth Higgingbotham, and Bonnie Thornton Dill, "The Costs of Exclusionary Practices in Women's Studies," *Signs* 11:2 (Winter 1986): 290–303; and Betty Schmitz, *Integrating Women's Studies into the Curriculum: A Guide and Bibliography* (New York: The Feminist Press, 1985). For other resources, see also the bibliographies on curriculum transformation and pedagogy included in the faculty development seminar models of this volume.

5. These projects are listed on pages 19–21 in this volume. For a description of each project, see *Mainstreaming Minority Women's Studies Program* (New York: National Council for Research on Women, 1991).

6. *Loving in the War Years/Lo que nunca pasó por sus labios.* Boston: South End Press, 1983, 58.

7. For more on how this can be done, see Johnnella E. Butler and John C. Walter, *Transforming the Curriculum: Ethnic Studies and Women's Studies* (Albany: SUNY Press, 1991). Butler's "The Difficult Dialogue of Curriculum Transformation: Ethnic Studies and Women's Studies," (1–19), in particular, addresses these points.

8. *Transforming Knowledge* (Philadelphia: Temple, 1990), 190.

9. Alison Bernstein, then program officer at the Ford Foundation, initiated the call for proposals and is largely responsible for the program's focus on women of color. For the history of how the program emerged, see Mariam K. Chamberlain and Alison Bernstein, "Philanthropy and the Emergence of Women's Studies," *Teachers College Record* 93, no. 3 (Spring 1992): 556–68;

and Leslie I. Hill, "The Ford Foundation Program on Mainstreaming Minority Women's Studies," *Women's Studies Quarterly* 18, nos. 1–2 (Spring–Summer 1990): 24–38.

10. To get an idea of the number of students who potentially will be the beneficiaries of these projects, approximately 1,150 students were enrolled in the first-semester course sections taught by the faculty trained at the University of Puerto Rico project alone. Because for the most part the program targeted large-enrollment classes (e.g., anthropology, sociology, economics, political science, psychology, history, and English) and the participating faculty members will probably teach these courses over a period of many years, it is obvious that large numbers of students will be exposed to the revised courses.

11. "Gender and Race: The Ampersand Problem in Feminist Thought," chap. 5 of *Inessential Woman: Problems of Exclusion in Feminist Thought* (Boston: Beacon Press, 1988) 114–32.

TRANSITION IN CURRICULUM TRANSFORMATION: SOME TRENDS AND CHALLENGES

Leslie I. Hill

Curriculum transformation is a process that has been unfolding and expanding for more than twenty years. In that time work to incorporate women into the curriculum has yielded a wealth of materials, deepened the conceptual tasks curriculum reform set for itself, used new methodological tools to connect students with course subject matter, and spurred a serious reassessment of the epistemological and pedagogical consequences of traditional curricula in liberal arts education.

In this expansion and enrichment of curriculum transforming activities new challenges have emerged. Some, entrenched in standard academic structures, were made more apparent by the work under way, while others arose from the manner in which curriculum transformation efforts themselves were being carried out. First, it is useful to turn our attention to a few of the more significant trends and changes in curriculum reform efforts. I focus here on efforts to integrate women and gender issues into the curriculum. While there is no doubt that analysis of race and class as well as gender is fundamental to any hope for a balanced curriculum, only gender has received consistent and systematic attention in curriculum reform activities nationally.

Initial attempts to change academic offerings focused on content; the concern was to uncover and reclaim women and their work, which had been rendered invisible by disciplines that regarded them as neither valuable, legitimate subjects nor significant contributors to the knowledge base in those disciplines. The search for women earnestly sought to add those exceptional

Leslie I. Hill served as project coordinator during the first phase of the Mainstreaming Minority Women's Studies Program. She is currently an instructor in the Department of Political Science at Bates College.

female figures and, in doing so, left largely undisturbed the academic standards already in place, which were rooted in the experience and perspectives of men who were economically and racially privileged.

As scholarship explored the parameters of gender "difference," curriculum change included materials and perspectives that examined experiences heretofore undervalued or wholly invisible in the shadow of male norms of thought and behavior. The affirmative nature of Carol Gilligan's research or of a work such as *Women's Ways of Knowing* was significant for empowering many women and giving intellectual import to women's experiences. While such materials positively value women's gender difference, they neither focus on nor fully apprehend the institutional mechanisms through which both the academy and society continue to marginalize the "other."

Responding to such criticism, faculty engaged in curriculum reform efforts began to generate courses and began materials that examine power relations as they are produced and reproduced in our institutional life. A view of system wide processes that routinely confer dominance and extend privilege to some groups while generating disadvantage for others shifts attention away from individual chauvinism and bigotry to the manner in which institutions allocate access to and use and control of a society's material and ideological resources. In the classroom analysis of power relations challenges myths of individual merit as the basis for power and success and helps to dismantle internalized notions of race, class, and sex inferiority and incapacity.

In emphasizing the systematic, interconnected nature of institutionalized oppression and the pervasiveness of the social constructs and practices that support systems of hierarchy, oppressed people sometimes appeared as victims, without agency and without active resistance to exploitation, discrimination, and marginalization. Efforts to reveal the agency, participation, and resistance of white women, women and men of color, and subordinate classes involve the presentation of their experiences in their own words and through their own eyes. Examination of social and cultural phenomena through multiple perspectives decenters the interpretive views and interpretive power of dominant groups and makes possible the exploration of the realities of people variously positioned in gender, race, and class relations. Shifting away from the constricting dichotomy of domination-subordination permits students and teachers to record and consider multiple experiences. Thus, they perceive the full range of humanity as subjects making choices, continually contesting boundaries, and creating and revising the central images and meanings of hierarchical social systems.

Over the years curriculum transformation efforts have shifted from adding "exceptional" women to integrating scholarship on gender, and in some projects have given substantive attention to race and class. Primary concern with content has been combined with faculty efforts to attend to classroom dynamics and pedagogical strategies as well as content. Furthermore, the academic climate has changed from one that was hostile to curriculum reform efforts.

Where once administrations often impeded such work, now college and universities support—financially and in other ways—curriculum change projects. Now work takes place in increasing measure, according to Elizabeth Higginbotham, in a context of still-tentative and controversial reassessments of the content, central issues, and self-definitions of disciplines, majors, and general education programs.

For all this, however, U.S. students are still far more likely—with minimal maneuvering in some schools, more in others—to obtain an undergraduate degree with little more than a parenthetical or supplemental look at the life of generic (read: white, economically privileged, heterosexual) "Woman," an unshakable faith in the existence of race as a biological fact, and uncritical assumptions that all wealth is earned and that a "middle-class life" is the norm, the standard, and the ideal. Middle-class life is believed to be the norm because it is supposedly shared by almost all Americans. Middle-classness is the standard by which normality and deviance are judged. It is the ideal because it is believed to be the main source of worthwhile and enduring social values in American life.

For an increasing number of students, however, such a myth-full journey through higher education is both less likely than before and unsatisfying. Efforts to balance the curriculum or merely to add what or who has long been absent make it difficult to learn and teach about the world as if women don't matter, as if race itself is a problem, and as if class is a subversive concept. Given the successes and the vast potential of curriculum balancing, there are at the same time outstanding challenges, which present both dangers, if not addressed, and opportunities for enhanced advancement in the ability of higher education curricula to apprehend, examine, and engage students in thinking about a much more complete picture of human experience and creativity.

One of the enduring issues in women's studies scholarship and curriculum transformation work is the treatment of difference. Race, class, and sexual preference profoundly shape the experiences of being female and, thus, constitute critical categories of lived social reality that are the rightful subjects of education. How are differences to be handled substantively and pedagogically in our classrooms? If, as Elizabeth Spelman notes, the door one walks through shapes what one sees, is it possible to engage curriculum transformation on grounds of gender and satisfactorily deal with race? Or vice versa?

Deborah King points out that the intersections—the amplifications, modifications, linking mechanisms, that is, the multiplicative and transformative effects—of gender with race and with class operate in ways that need to be explored both for the sake of more accurate knowledge construction and for the building of more effective coalitions and struggles for social justice. One of the difficulties of this work is that, while there is a rich literature on the concept of class and models for use in teaching about class, race is less well understood. Women's studies has explored the social construction of gender, yet our understanding of race as a socially constructed concept, whose meaning is derived from power relations and social and political struggle, is fledgling. The conflation of race with ethnicity needs to be untangled so that race as an ideology and as a lens through which we make sense of the world can be viewed as shifting, contextual, and contested—over time, in different contexts of gender and class, and with respect to different racial-ethnic groups. Race for the Puertorriqueña garment worker, for example, will not be interpreted by her or with regard to her in the same manner as it would for an African-American domestic laborer. Such an approach to race, moreover, may facilitate clarity about how race and gender ideologies combine, for example, in the dominant culture to render females in one racial-ethnic group as "women" and those in other groups as "girls" (less than "womanly").

Significant categories of social experience—gender, race, ethnicity, class, and sexuality—constitute multiple parts of identity. Students and those of us who work with them must acknowledge that everyone has a racial identity, that both men and women have a gender, that all people have a class identity, and that each of us has a sexuality. Our multiply constituted identities generate complex positioning in the various social and political hierarchies of U.S. society. The shifting significance of any of those identities under various circumstances needs to be understood as reflecting the fluid interconnections of racism, classism, and sexism. For example, clearly gender is foregrounded in the incidence of rape, but a woman's vulnerability will differ depending upon her class, race, and perceptions of her sexual identity. Under other circumstances race may be more salient in determining that same woman's access to power or her ability to protect herself.

Thus, difference—diversity, if you prefer—challenges those of us attempting to transform courses and balance the curriculum to treat gender, race, and class as sources of social stratification rather than as mere difference. Adequately doing so requires that we understand the social meanings attached to those constructions and treat them as categories for analyzing social experience rather than as ascriptive characteristics distinguishing between individual human beings. Race, gender, and class, then, become analytical categories rather than merely empirical variables.

These alternative treatments are illustrated easily in my own discipline, political science. In graduate school I was frustrated by studies of voting behavior which sought to compare black voters with white voters, explaining black differences with reference to norms of political behavior based on "Political Man," a prototype of white, (unconsciously) middle-class, male experience. Applications of this model produced assessments of black distance from the norm as deviance. I recognize now that using race as a descriptive variable renders traditional analysis unable to grasp the full meaning of political action by African Americans and thoroughly inadequate to explain political behavior endemic to the experiences of racial oppression.

I have focused mainly on conceptual issues in curriculum transformation and want to add that the clearest analysis, the most inclusive thinking, will mean little if we do not find effective and empowering ways of engaging students in critical thinking and constructive dialogue about science, art, psychology—the substance of the liberal arts education. The tasks before us include dismantling the hierarchies that often are replicated in the classroom, generating interactive and student-centered learning, and shifting power away from instructors while enhancing students' responsibility for their own learning. Being effective requires that we interrupt racism, sexism, and heterosexism in our classrooms and continually work to reveal and to subvert hierarchical, oppressive ideologies. These are elements of what bell hooks refers to as "critical pedagogy," through which students can view themselves as fully capable and having significant choices to make along with others whom they recognize as fully human. Democratic practice, in fact, requires no less if students-citizens are to enact together, in public and private ways, alternative social relations through which to engender social justice.

NOTES

This paper was presented at the 1991–92 City University of New York Faculty Development Colloquium, "Transforming the Curriculum: The Next Five Years," on 8 May 1992 at Baruch College.

1. Mary Field Belenky, Blythe McVicker Clinchy, Nancy Rule Goldberger, and Jill Mattuck Tarule, *Women's Ways of Knowing: The Development of Self, Voice, and Mind* (New York: Basic Books, 1986).

PARTICIPATING PROJECTS

Integrating Minority Women into the Liberal Arts Curriculum
Project Codirectors: Karen Anderson and John Garcia
Southwest Institute for Research on Women
University of Arizona
Douglas Building 102
Garden Level
Tucson, AZ 85721

> A consortium project including Arizona State University, Metropolitan State University–Denver, Northern Arizona University, Northern Colorado University, University of Arizona, University of Colorado–Boulder, and University of Colorado–Colorado Springs

Ford Ethnic Women's Curriculum Transformation Project (FEW)
Project Director: Karen E. Rowe
UCLA Center for the Study of Women
276 Kinsey Hall
University of California–Los Angeles
402 Hilgard Avenue
Los Angeles, CA 90024

Infusing Material on Minority Women into the Liberal Arts Curriculum of the CUNY Senior Colleges: A Collaborative Outreach Project
Project Director: Sue Rosenberg Zalk
Center for the Study of Women and Society
City University of New York
33 West 42d Street
New York, NY 10036

The Integration of Scholarship on Minority Women in the Undergraduate Curriculum
Project Director: Martha Howell

Institute for Research on Women and Gender
Columbia University
763 Schermerhorn
New York, NY 10027

Integrating Women of Color into the Liberal Arts Curriculum
Project Director: Christina Greene
Center for Research on Women
Duke University / University of North Carolina
207 East Duke Building
Durham, NC 27708

Women of Color in the Liberal Arts Curriculum
Project Director: Phyllis Palmer
Women's Studies Program and Policy Center
George Washington University
217 Funger Hall
Washington, DC 20052

Integrating Women of Color into the Curriculum
Project Director: Elizabeth Higginbotham
Center for Research on Women
Memphis State University
College of Arts and Sciences
Memphis, TN 38152

Incorporating Feminist Scholarship concerning Gender and Cultural Diversity into the Curriculum
Project Director: Marsha Neff
Women's Program
Metropolitan State University
Suite 121, Metro Square Building
121 Seventh Place East
St. Paul, MN 55101-2189

> A consortium project including Augsburg College, College of St. Catherine, Macalester College, Metropolitan State, St. Cloud State, and University of Minnesota

A University for Everyone
Project Director: Barbara Corrado Pope
Center for the Study of Women in Society
University of Oregon
Eugene, OR 97403

Toward a Gender-Balanced Liberal Arts Core Curriculum
Project Director: Yamila Azize
Proyecto de Estudios de la Mujer
Universidad de Puerto Rico
Cayey, PR 00633

Incorporating Puerto Rican Women into the Curriculum and Research
Project Codirectors:
Edna Acosta-Belén, Director, Center for Latin America and the Caribbean
Chris Bose, Director, Institute for Research on Women
State University of New York–Albany
1400 Washington Avenue
Albany, NY 12222

Women of Color in the Curriculum Project
Project Director: Cyrena Pondrom
Project Coordinator: Alejandra Elenas
Women's Studies Research Center
University of Wisconsin–Madison
209 North Brooks Street
Madison, WI 53715

FACULTY
DEVELOPMENT

SHIFTING MODELS, CREATING VISIONS: PROCESS AND PEDAGOGY FOR CURRICULUM TRANSFORMATION

Karen E. Rowe

In 1988–89 the UCLA Center for the Study of Women initiated the Ford Ethnic Women's Curriculum Transformation Project (FEW). The challenge was twofold: to identify the rapidly increasing research by and about ethnic women and to make the new perspectives central more to the undergraduate liberal arts curriculum. Earlier, UCLA's historically strong relationships among four ethnic and women's studies programs and centers had provided the substantive basis for responding to the Mainstreaming Minority Women's Studies Program's call for proposals from the Ford Foundation. Simultaneously, Chancellor Charles E. Young's policy commitment to "excellence through diversity" had provided a campus catalyst for integrating new scholarship on ethnicity and gender within traditional disciplines and departments. FEW offered a unique opportunity, therefore, to respond *proactively* not only to clear demographic shifts within UCLA's undergraduate student body to an ethnic majority of more than 60 percent, but also to core disciplines that were seeking redefinitions of research and curricular content and methods.

With additional support from the College of Letters and Science and the Chancellor's Committee on Instructional Improvement Programs (CCIIP), the FEW project launched its three-year effort. The primary goal was to transform syllabi and pedagogy for existing courses and to create new courses that incorporated new research by and about African American, Chicana/Latina, American Indian, and Asian American women. The second goal was to develop resource materials, a bibliographic database, and innovative pedagogies for changed classroom dynamics resulting from a transformed curriculum. Seven curriculum development seminars enabled faculty to participate in an intensive eleven weeks of three-hour sessions. Between spring 1989 and spring 1991 FEW sponsored seminars in American and Related Literatures, Sociology, Psychology and Cognate Fields, History, Interdisciplinary Studies, and American Ethnic Studies, culminating with the spring 1991 offering entitled "The Americas: Crossing Borders, Crossing Cultures," which brought together faculty from geography, urban planning, and women's studies. With seventy-five participating faculty (including two facilitators per seminar) and forty graduate students, FEW seminars yielded nearly ninety transformed or new syllabi (ten to fifteen general education courses), twenty bibliographies, and ten other projects, including textbook revisions, teaching packets, and departmental guidelines for teaching and course content. Even if courses were taught only once, the number of students affected would be fourteen thousand. More significant than numerical outcomes, however, has been a new faculty awareness of how a seminar *process* that fosters discussion, debate, and absorption *over time*, and is reinforced by a demand for a *product* and by *peer* support, is vital to the integration of ethnic women's studies with the existing curricula and provides an institutionally viable model for curriculum transformation.

Seminar Planning and Process

From the generating of a proposal to final implementation of seminar designs, ethnic and women's studies leaders and faculty worked together to create FEW. Not only was the steering committee that initiated the proposal composed of long-standing directors of ethnic and women's studies centers and programs, but key faculty with ethnic and/or gender research expertise were also selected to become facilitators. Project coordinators for the first year included the directors of Women's Studies, Asian American Studies and the Center for Pacific Rim Studies, and the Center for Afro-American Studies in addition to the FEW principal investigator, who was the founding director of UCLA's Center for the Study of Women. This coordinating group established initial procedures for the project's organization, but its functions became less necessary as seminar facilitators took increasingly active ownership of specific seminars. The fourteen facilitators, each receiving one course release from CCIIP, worked collaboratively with a multiethnic FEW staff composed of the project manager Norma Rice, bibliographer Bhagirathi Subrahmanyam, and research assistants, as well as the director, to create the seminar syllabi (based upon faculty applications).

Since all facilitators were members of departments, the work of integrating new research on ethnicity and gender within disciplines was significantly enhanced. Facilitators and the project director undertook early planning by soliciting advice from departmental chairs and vice chairs of undergraduate studies, in order to identify likely faculty participants, to mesh the seminar's work with departmental priorities, and to provide support resources that enabled the release and compensation of participants without undue disruption of the academic program—but with the benefit of bringing to the department opportunities for curriculum innovation which had not formerly existed. What have been issues of divisiveness for other curriculum projects, therefore, were not in evidence at UCLA. Continuously collaborative relationships among ethnic and women's studies faculty, programs, and centers and between these entities and traditional departments were negotiated successfully by astute, highly skilled, and deeply committed facilitators and strengthened by an increasingly clear university perception of the complementarity of departmental curricular revision needs and the FEW faculty development model.

Of particular concern for many such curriculum integration projects and academic institutions is the often hidden issue of exploitation of younger faculty, often the most vulnerably junior members—people of color and women. In selecting facilitators, therefore, the director enlisted input from departmental chairs and worked closely with facilitators to minimize any detrimental impact on the junior faculty's advancement or research. Of the fifteen project and seminar facilitators five were untenured assistant professors, one was a lecturer, five were tenured associate professors, and four were full professors. With one exception ("The Americas: Crossing Borders, Crossing Cultures"), all seminars included a senior facilitator together with a junior faculty member, assisted and backed up by regular attendance and, where necessary, intervention of the FEW director and project manager. All untenured assistant professors who participated as facilitators or seminar members were given preferential choice of receiving available course release, if they so requested.

UCLA is fortunate in having an extensive faculty in ethnic and women's studies from which to draw facilitators, ones who (whether tenured or untenured) commanded the respect and attention of participants and were selected because of their skills as teachers, negotiators, and moderators and their rich knowledge of ethnic and gender scholarship. Virtually all facilitators were active participants in interdisciplinary programs, and had, therefore a particularly useful vantage point from which to understand curriculum integration and new research methodologies and theories. Among the assistant professors three have subsequently received tenure (all had outside tenured offers as well), and two others have several more years before their tenure reviews. Contrary to conventional wisdom, active leadership and participation by junior faculty in the FEW project has been incorporated into the center/program, departmental, and university reviews; has enhanced not detracted from advancement; and has frequently given other faculty members a broader and deeper understanding of new research in the fields of ethnic and gender studies, theories, and methods.

Faculty members were invited to submit applications for the seminars. Eight to ten participants were chosen by facilitators and the project director to reflect a distribution of junior and senior faculty with different bases of knowledge about ethnicity and gender, with high curricular impact because of the courses they regularly taught, and whose applications reflected specific goals and a coherent, even if only preliminary, sense of what and how they would think about course transformations. In order institutionally to validate the faculty commitment, seminar members received a $1,500 stipend (from the Ford grant) or a course release (from UCLA's College of Letters and Science). As the seminars progressed, a few key faculty participated in more than one seminar, were enlisted doubly as FEW facilitators, or helped to develop later seminars (e.g., in Asian American studies and Chicano studies) modeled on the FEW project. Although many faculty members began with minimal exposure to research by and about women of color, others were chosen specifically for their expertise in ethnic or women's studies. Such persons became important catalysts and models, those within women's studies often more willing to express their limited understanding of ethnic women's experiences, and those within ethnic studies their inadequate command of gender issues.

Most participating faculty had lacked both time and opportunity to undertake systematic reading in new areas of research on ethnicity and gender, even within their own disciplines. Furthermore, they felt uncomfortable and overwhelmed in attempting to communicate research on cultures with which they shared no racial or gender identification. Hence, the seminars always began with faculty spread out along a broad spectrum of interest in, ideological and psychological tolerance for, and accessibility to change; widely varying degrees of knowledge about ethnicity and gender; deeply personal and professional concerns about their authority and position in the classroom; and strong commitments to ingrained methodological and field-specific protocols about objective and subjective research. Faculty members were also intrigued by, yet often fearful of, the need to examine pedagogical strategies that meet the needs of an ethnically diverse undergraduate population and to rethink how their own ethnicity and gender worked for and against them. The deliberate design of the application and selection process, however, was both to make the activity institutionally desirable and to create a faculty commitment to the collegial group process. That collegiality did, in many instances, generate and nurture the transformative core and curriculum within a department as well as a cadre of fifteen trained facilitators (director included) and sixty participating faculty, whose active service on university tenure and senate committees and within other programs had a still broader institutional impact.

Because of new critical masses of faculty within departments and the ethnic and women's studies programs and centers, which had led national research efforts for two decades, UCLA has an increasingly diverse graduate student body. Graduate students serve in nearly all departments as teaching assistants, frequently within discussion sections for large introductory courses or, in the case of English, as primary instructors for English composition courses required of all UCLA students for graduation. From the original proposal and throughout project implementation graduate students were included in the FEW process. Thus, the project made an important commitment not simply to revitalizing its existing professoriate but also to preparing graduate students to be faculty of the future. Moreover, the steering committee and facilitators recognized that many graduate students were pushing forward new theoretical models for research on ethnicity and gender, often in more radically transformative ways than faculty trained in older methodologies and eras. With the same criteria as that governing faculty selections, the facilitators selected four to seven graduate participants, each of whom received four units of "Directed Individual Study" credit for the seminar. Priority was given to advanced graduate students, often with several years of teaching experience and with related dissertation or master's thesis topics, who would benefit from the seminar. In addition to regular seminar participation students were paired with faculty members with whom they formulated projects, such as new course designs, teaching packets for discussion sections, recommended textbook revisions in psychology, and annotated bibliographies of research on women of color.

Seminars varied considerably in the degree to which graduate students became integral members, dependent upon faculty receptivity, the students' assertiveness and position, and skillful facilitation. Despite initial inhibitions, however, the seminar process usually yielded increasingly freer and more active engagement as the quarter progressed. In many instances the experiential sharing of pedagogical dilemmas in the classroom united the graduate students and faculty alike, and graduate students boldly challenged misassumptions and misperceptions, rooted in their own sense of the diverse student populations, with whom they frequently worked more closely than faculty. Moreover, the graduate students often raised issues that forced a radical rethinking of research methods and orientations, sometimes by way of staking out new subjects for analysis, sometimes simply by virtue of having fewer set (and outmoded) intellectual frameworks. Within American and Related Literatures, for example, graduate students pushed for materials on Afro-American lesbian writers, for analyses of contemporary Chinese women writers in comparison with Asian American women, for attention to emerging theories of postcolonial discourse, and for feminist analysis of "the body" in comparative and Third World literatures. Although many graduate students do not have the opportunity to teach advanced courses in the major, their ability to imagine and generate such syllabi also led to innovative reconstruction, for example, of a "Social Problems" model in sociology which could be implemented at UCLA and elsewhere. By becoming actively engaged with faculty and often struggling together with the same issues of research integration and classroom pedagogical strategies, graduate students obtained an increasingly clearer perception of the obstacles that bedevil any innovative field of research and the strategies and struggles faculty members experience in moving forward institutional agendas for curricular change and ethnic diversity.

Within the seminars themselves the push of such new research, newly articulated from within the experiences often of younger as well as older ethnic faculty, engendered predictable tensions, often resistances, and occasionally outright conflicts and verbal confrontations. Debates often centered on the apparent lack of methodological rigor, the assumed "experiential subjectivity," or the more radically politicized viewpoint articulated in the readings and by consultant speakers and/or resident participants. For instance, while a white male theorist could comfortably quote Heidegger and Hegel, he might find inconceivable an African American woman's assertion of belief in ghosts as part of the legacy of New Orleans voodoo, an inspiration for her poetry, and a vehicle for entering into the world of Toni Morrison's *Beloved*. Or, while a feminist sociologist could accept the premises of Marxist analysis of oppressions of the working class, she could also deny the validity of research on Chicana/Latina domestics presented by ethnic women sociologists using a participant-observer analysis that studied employer-employee interactions. Moments of painful insensitivity—some blatant, some unintentional or uninformed—were inevitably a part of the seminar dynamic. Such moments became perhaps the most productive sites of transformation, making clear the conflicts of ideology, culture, experience, and academic training. But these dramatic conflicts also forced seminar members to examine more closely their own analytic and personal assumptions and to think creatively about how "eruptions" within the classroom can be permitted, reconstructed, molded, and potentially transformed into epiphanies.

SHIFTING MODELS AND SEMINAR DESIGN

The conceptual model of the seminars also shifted over the course of the FEW project, and this created markedly different transformational experiences. Because of both a short lead time between receipt of Ford funding and implementation and the explicit mandate to integrate research on women of color, the initial seminar designs for American and Related Literatures, Sociology, and Psychology and Cognate Fields tended to showcase, or "display," new research on discrete groups of ethnic women, usually by devoting one or two weeks each to African American, American Indian, Asian American, and Chicana/Latina issues. All the seminars opened with at least two weeks of discussion, whether about theoretical models of canonicity and the contemporary debates over "American" literature, the exclusions of women of color from sociological research, or psychological constructs, such as "locus of control," which displayed most clearly the normative experimental models and recent controversies in psychology. Frequently the seminars invited outside consultants (as required by Ford) to present historical and/or theoretical overviews of recent research on an ethnic group. Those presentations were vehicles for launching debate and discussion about assigned articles, a second week of text-specific analysis with accompanying criticism, or an examination of research being undertaken by ethnic women scholars. Pedagogical discussions were stimulated by asking visiting speakers to bring sample bibliographies and course syllabi, by including presentations by campus ethnic and women's studies librarians and centers about available bibliographic resources, and by scheduling sessions specifically with readings on feminist and ethnic studies pegagogies. For example, Barrie Thorne led a lively discussion that drew from participants' experiences of "being silenced" in the classroom. Thorne also used existing syllabi from participants to make recommendations about changed readings that might integrate new women's studies research into a wide variety of traditional sociology courses, responsive to both the guidelines from the American Sociological Association and to critiques of sociology (and other disciplines) by Margaret Anderson, Judith Stacey, and Barrie Thorne, bell hooks, Paula Rothenberg, and Johnnella Butler, among others. All FEW seminars ended with two weeks of presentations of transformed syllabi and projects, often with accompanying pedagogical or final theoretical readings, often with extensive critique and group commentary, and always with a feminist-ethnic "potluck" supper following the final session.

Though this seminar design promoted the visibility of ethnic women scholars and their research, it nonetheless also had inherent drawbacks, which, as early as the fall 1989 seminar in Psychology, led to a rethinking of integrative strategics. The initial model usefully provided background introductions to culture-specific research from mainstream journals, faculties, professional organizations, and existing curricula. But differentiating ethnic women's research by group also reinforced stereotyping and separatism, making it less possible to envision transformative analytic models within disciplines which would actually alter the landscape of contemporary scholarship. In other words, the margins were still marginal. Participants could discern more discretely the histories, cultures, ideologies, and degrees of disciplinary acceptance and rejection or denial which differentiated research on African American women from that on Asian American women. But many faculty members could too comfortably retain a "show me" stance. The structure itself "invited" speakers, in essence, to prove the coherence, value, and worth of including "their" literature and research. Hence, the paradigms of judgment which often led to exclusions could be easily replicated, often because the "outsider" perspective and methodological approaches did not conform to preexisting and internalized models of aesthetic judgment, psychological method, or sociological field parameters.

The burden of breaking through boundaries and into disciplines, even when undertaken by scholars within the field and when assisted by internal catalysts, still reinscribed the power inequalities and often the standards of objectivity versus subjectivity upon which scholars more subtly base resistances to methodological and curricular change. The ease with which challenges could be mounted by faculty comfortable with shared disciplinary assumptions testified to both the resistances and the privileged superiority (i.e., the insider-outsider dichotomy) which continues to marginalize ethnic and gender research and practitioners. In part, the structure of the seminars replicated systemic and institutional models of protective boundary maintenance. Nevertheless, the cumulative effect—in short, the process of exposure, revisualizing, challenging back and forth at the contested borderlands of scholarship enacted weekly—resulted in often surprisingly bold curricular remodeling. Although some scholars created "add-ons," whether by including a text or two or inserting a section, many faculty members jettisoned old syllabi and designed entirely new courses, a transformative act that began with conceptually different starting points and frameworks, within which research by and about women of color became a central locus rather than a nonnormative experience.

The FEW project model shifted with the History, Interdisciplinary, American Ethnic Studies, and Crossing Borders–Crossing Cultures seminars to emphasize a more faculty-engaged process of discovery, ownership, and mentoring. Rather than a superimposed, somewhat prescriptive syllabus designed by the project director and seminar facilitators and then presented to the faculty–graduate student group, a basic seminar framework of topics of immediate interest to participating members was created. With substantially more time for planning, it became possible to work with faculty to identify weekly readings on different topics, such as the focus in the history seminar on colonial settlement or nineteenth-century plantation culture, or on the rise of gospel music and jazz in twentieth-century Los Angeles to be discussed in the interdisiplinary seminar. Faculty (and occasionally graduate students), sometimes working alone but more often in pairs, were designated as facilitators for a given week, for which readings were jointly determined, often assisted by staff searches of the bibliographic database and by inclusion of materials drawn from bibliographies and texts known to the faculty member.

Consultant speakers were identified and invited to work with the departmental member. This provided both an implicit sponsorship and a direct collaborative linkage that lessened the distance between "departmental insiders" and "ethnic women outsiders." Although the number of invited consultants from outside UCLA decreased, the integration of resident scholarly expertise, particularly new research being conducted by junior ethnic and women scholars, was intensified and more fully understood as part of the expanding boundaries of scholarship within the discipline and institution rather than as a direct assault upon existing analytic models. Rather than permitting a comfortable displacement of ownership—by making ethnic and gender studies faculty and their research into something "other," to be invited in, observed, and then accepted or not by the rules of conformity to disciplinary standards—such a model engendered a greater sense of collective ownership. It reduced the gulf between senior and junior faculty, often by opening up discussions about different perspectives from which analyses might be undertaken, by making the "Subjects" within the seminar owners of the "subject matter," and by reducing considerably (though not without acknowledgment) the fear of misrepresentation of a voice and vision different from one's own.

Not only did the structuring of the seminar become a more collaborative enterprise, but the content changed to a thematic, ethnically integrated model. Although introductory weeks might still raise questions about inclusive and exclusive dynamics within disciplines, more frequently the seminars examined texts about curriculum integration processes, about specific discipline critiques, and about the "construction" of gender and ethnicity as a multivalent process. The notion of construction—rooted in more contemporary theories from Fredrik Barth to Werner Sollors as well as feminist analyses of difference—reduced the participants' impulse to stereotype groups. Instead, an interactive model of ethnic and gender formations and the cultural negotiations that cut across societal groups provided a more flexible conceptual framework, which broke down boundaries of protected territoriality in thinking about ethnic women's experiences and about the discipline's way of creating analytic categories.

Such shifts to faculty-centered syllabi development as well as concepts of ethnic and gender construction were accompanied by a movement to seminars formulated around thematic topics rather than ethnic-specific groups. For example, in American Ethnic Studies, ethnic women's writings in relationship to landscape and space dominated the first half, while the latter sequence of texts and criticisms focused on the literature of spirituality. By also focusing more comparatively, the seminar brought to the forefront similarities and differences among the cultures of ethnic women, reflected not just in the written word but also in storytelling, ritual, and song. The themes of landscape, space, ancestors, spirituality, memory, and silence, which span the writings of ethnic women, created vital new connections—between Paula G. Allen's *The Woman Who Owned the Shadows* and Gloria Anzaldúa's *Borderlands / La Frontera: The New Mestiza,* between Toni Morrison's *Beloved* and Anna Walters *Ghost Singer,* between Harriet B. Jacobs's *Incidents in the Life of a Slave Girl* and Ronyoung Kim's *Clay Walls.* A far richer understanding of border identities, remembered histories, (in)visibility, and "unspeakable things (un)spoken" emerged.

In the history seminar the syllabus emerged as a semichronological progression from early colonization to contemporary U.S. urban history, while the topic areas focused on debates within current historiography, wherein ethnicity and gender are focal points for generating new analytic methods. Thus, women's roles or positions within Indian cultures as power brokers, trade negotiators, participants in interracial marriages, and cultural translators provided a lens for understanding Spanish conquests, the Southwest mestizo culture, the colonial fur trade, and cultural differences in defining land ownership, property, inheritance, and social or tribal organization. Such themes also permitted a variety of readings on any given week about different ethnic women's experiences. In order to maintain focus we usually considered no more than two groups, often by using theoretical articles as departure points and more specialized studies of research about ethnic women as exemplary models of analysis.

Predictably, the tendency to stereotype or isolate ethnic groups was significantly diminished, while the necessary complexity of studying intersections of cultures as conflictual and contested as well as negotiated and fluid was heightened. Similarly, the reliability of using methods that ignored intersections of race, class, and gender was constantly questioned, thereby stimulating faculty recognition of their need for more complicated, more ethnically and gender-sensitive, approaches to the disciplines, and the need for innovative interdisciplinary methods and models. The syllabi produced in such a seminar may still range from "add-on" to transformative reconstructions, but there is greater likelihood that they will also map out new intellectual terrain, that topics will be more thematic than chronological or merely topical, and that polarized concepts such as "centers" and "margins," "normative" and "deviant," "canonical" and "noncanonical" will become less useful for analysis.

NEW VISIONS FOR A TRANSFORMED CURRICULUM

What became exciting for FEW staff was the enthusiasm with which faculty, departments, and the college itself participated in the process. What we learned is the extensive hunger among faculty for new materials, leading to the development of a 4,000-item bibliographic database and a filmography by O.Funmilayo Makarah of *Films and Videos by and about American Ethnic Women*. But it is the more fundamental issues that provoked the greatest debate and learning, because curriculum change demands a transformation of both method and mind. Whether in the social sciences or literary studies, conflictual dialectics often emerged between the claims of female experience, cultural modes of expression, and values and the "dominant" paradigms of a discipline, whether expressed as a literary canon, a chronological narrative of history, a normative experimental model, or privileged, often nongendered, categories of analysis. By unraveling some of the knotted assumptions that led to exclusions, marginalizations, and devaluations of ethnic women's experience and voices, all seminars questioned how knowledge enters the academy, is published, and becomes "mainstream," and they challenged faculty members to imagine and engender alternative ways of knowing.

Shared across all FEW seminars was a struggle to comprehend the cultural politics of naming and intraethnic variations, which demand a complicated tracing of historical alienation and empowerment that shifts over time.

Who names? Who claims a name? How and when does a name confer group identity? What does it mean to be a "hyphenated American"? These questions became critical for understanding southwestern history and literature, for instance, in which the terms *Hispanic, Latina, Chicana, Tejana,* and *mestiza* signify resonant and charged distinctions. In the fall of 1990 the CARA exhibit of "Chicana Art: Resistance and Affirmation" also illuminated the issues of representation and political movements through art as well as language. But group identity, whether a result of slavery systems of migrant labor, immigration and settlement patterns, or indigenous histories reinforced the need to determine still more complex intraethnic variations, for example, which distinguished among Pacific Islander, Thai, Vietnamese, Chinese, Japanese, Korean, and East Asian groups; which reflected generational shifts; and which informed debates over assimilation, biculturalism, and acculturation.

Furthermore, FEW enabled us firsthand to identify the sequence of challenges that faculty confront in rethinking curricular models and research paradigms: "There isn't any scholarly research!" "There isn't any *good* scholarly literature!" "How can I fit it all into a course?" Examining these resistances often opened up ways of envisioning curricular design less as an inevitability of what is authoritative than as a process that involves constant choices of subject, approach, works, assignments, and places to start, intervene, and end. Beginning American history and literature with Indian myths, Cortés, La Malinche, women in the fur trade, and agricultural and cultural dislocations repositions the lens of vision, for example, away from the more traditional model of New England's providential destiny. Transformation begins when the questions change, when the perceiving vision shifts to Dorinne Kondo's concept of the "Eye/I" or Trinh Minh-ha's *Woman, Native, Other* and when linear history and theories give way to matrix models for understanding intersecting cultures, ethnic women's multiple identities, the interplay of self and other. When we reposition the Other in the center rather than on the margins, as bell hooks urges, and when women of color become the Subject of their own discourses, analytic categories that previously defined the "normative," "classical," and "canonical" must be redefined.

As the syllabi in this volume illustrate, and as the preceding seminar models indicate, FEW necessarily focused on multi ethnic and multicultural approaches to integrating research by and about women of color into the undergraduate liberal arts curriculum. Models of analysis, of faculty development seminar structures, and of individual course syllabi that reinforce strictly bipolar oppositions, that too often set an ethnic-specific group against a Euro-American norm, or that use an academic measuring stick rooted in Western assumptions of culture, are neither possible nor desirable. But the April 1992 riots in Los Angeles remind us that the process by which interracial, interethnic negotiations proceed in order to create a more integrated society and a less fragmented sense of consciousness is not an easy one.

Neither is curriculum transformation a simple bringing in from the margins to the mainstream the consciousness, culture, history, arts, perspectives, and knowledge of separate groups, as if to homogenize it all into a common American experience or else a hyphenated biculturalism. Profoundly rooted in a mestizo culture from its earliest periods of Aztec and Hispanic encounter to the most contemporary encounters through immigration, Los Angeles and UCLA provide a site in which transformations and new discourses of interethnic communication must and can develop. In a Los Angeles defined by Edward Soja as a "postmodern geography," because of the fluid diversity of its urban populations, there can be no more fertile intellectual endeavor than to transform a curriculum that sets aside easy stereotyping of cultural groups in favor of more complex visions of difference within and among peoples and of coexistence that creates change.

Curriculum integration is neither an easy nor a comfortable process because it calls into question many of the fundamental assumptions of traditional academic methods, values, and hierarchies. All of our planners from the women's studies and ethnic studies centers stressed that this project's success has been its ability to force reconceptualizations of how we think about difference, and how we question differently, and how we teach from *within* ethnicity and gender. Although we anticipated that some participants would simply "tinker" with syllabus transformations, most faculty chose to undertake far more rigorous and difficult tasks. They began to learn how to reconceive history, periods, and borders; how to value experience differently; how to question the frames of references or voices at work when we speak of a dominant culture or a tradition; and how to think in terms of heterogeneity even within seemingly homogeneous "ethnic" and "women's" cultures.

In the Ford Ethnic Women's Curriculum Transformation Project the emphasis has been on an intensive, collegial, collaborative, conflicted process, in which change is engendered and in which the effects of change expand and ripple beyond the boundaries of individual courses or faculty to create an institutional impact that is evolutionary and transformative. The FEW process included many moments of recognition; startled, sometimes painful confrontations with new terminology and ideas; the naming and sharing of differences; the exploration of what it means for ethnic women to be doubly marginalized in academic discourse; and the affirmation of how necessary it is to perceive individuals rather than color-coded groups or census-designated categories of human beings. Differences—cultural, racial, gendered differences—all too often make us feel that we are a minority within a majority society. It is hoped that what FEW helped faculty and students to understand better is that the few *are* the many. Our goal is to create a multicultural education that gives all students new opportunities to know differently about their own lives and cultures and new visions of how ethnicity and gender shape what we learn and teach.

UNDERSTANDING OUTCOMES OF CURRICULUM TRANSFORMATION

Paula Ries

Despite nearly twenty years of experience, the process of curriculum transformation is not yet fully understood. My own experience working with a curriculum transformation project was simultaneously intriguing and frustrating and left me with more questions than answers: What does it really mean to transform courses, to make them more inclusive of race, gender, and ethnicity? Why do some courses change and others not? What issues emerge for faculty when they engage in such projects? And why does this type of change occur so slowly?

Fortunately, I had the opportunity to study a curriculum transformation project at a large public university to answer some of these questions. The study sample consisted of three seminars and twenty-two faculty participants representing four departments (English, psychology, sociology, and Spanish) and two interdisciplinary programs (comparative literature and communication studies). Each seminar met for three hours a week, over the course of ten weeks, with the goal of increasing faculty members' knowledge of scholarship on women of color and facilitating the use of this scholarship in their courses. The outcomes I explored were the revision of undergraduate courses with scholarship on women of color; I observed faculty who participated in the three project seminars and interviewed them regarding their seminar experiences as well as their research training, perspectives, and interests.

This essay focuses on some of the problems involved in the classification of course revisions, the factors that facilitate or inhibit these revisions, and the issues that emerged in the process of curriculum transformation.

Faculty members who participate in these projects are engaged in an incredibly complex task. Revising a course to include scholarship on women of

Paula Ries is currently manager of the Doctorate Records Project of the National Research Council in Washington, D.C.

color does not occur in a vacuum. Rather, it takes place within the context of extant disciplinary knowledge. Consequently, faculty members are not merely revising their courses; they are also rethinking the very content of their disciplines. In addition, because of the nature and relative newness of these projects, few models of curriculum transformation exist. Thus, these faculty have few maps or compasses to guide them through this uncharted terrain.

CLASSIFICATION OF REVISED COURSES

Initially, curricular transformation was measured using "Feminist Phase Theory" (McIntosh 1983; Schuster and Van Dyne 1985; Tetreault 1985). But the difficulties inherent in using a heuristic device to measure concrete change led me to develop my own classification scheme based on Feminist Phase Theory. A continuum of course revisions emerged from the analysis of the seminar observations and faculty interviews which reflect the different ways faculty incorporated scholarship on women of color into their courses: "Adding," "Shifting," and "Transforming." In Adding revisions, faculty either made no revisions or inserted information on women of color where it fit into preexisting course topics. In Shifting revisions, faculty began to alter the structure of their courses as they considered how to address ethnicity and gender in their courses. In Transforming revisions, faculty restructured their courses so as not to minimize or marginalize the experiences, lives, and works of women of color. Based on the type of course transformation, each participant was assigned to one of these three categories. Then, within each of these three categories of course revision, participants' seminar perceptions and experiences, their disciplinary training and research interests, and their social location were analyzed to assess whether a pattern of facilitators or inhibitors emerged in relation to these types of course revisions.

Because the purpose of this study was to gain an understanding of the process of a single curriculum transformation project, the findings must be considered "working hypotheses" (Lincoln and Guba 1985) which need to be tested in similar contexts (e.g. in research universities) and with different and larger samples of participants.

THE EXTENT OF COURSE CHANGE

Almost all of the targeted courses did, in fact, change. Five of the twenty-two "revised" courses were actually new courses that faculty created as a result of their seminar participation. Of the seventeen "existing" courses that were targeted for revision only two remained unchanged. To what degree do courses change? Ten of the twenty-two revisions were classified as Adding, six were classified as Shifting, and six were classified as Transforming.

It is important to bear in mind the enormity of such a task as one attempts to assess outcomes—any amount of change is welcome. That over one half of the participants made either Transforming or Shifting revisions indicates substantial change; one half of the courses now seriously consider and discuss the lives and experiences of women of color. In addition, eight of the ten participants who made Adding revisions did change their courses in some way to include scholarship on women of color. Thus, this curriculum transformation project stimulated a great deal of course revision.

Furthermore, change is not limited to targeted courses. What faculty learned in these seminars about women of color will almost certainly filter into other courses. In fact, during the interviews several faculty who made Shifting and Transforming revisions stated that their newly heightened awareness of gender and ethnicity will extend to other courses.

The type and amount of change that occurred in this project also has implications for the body of disciplinary knowledge on which courses are based. It is hoped that participants' own scholarship will change as a result of experimenting with new ways of presenting course content and thus contribute to the general knowledge base. Although such an outcome was not the focus of the study, there is evidence that this may well be a likely consequence of curriculum transformation efforts. For example, one psychologist related that he had never before considered gender as a factor in psychological outcomes in his research. During the course of the seminar this participant decided to use gender as an independent variable in a study he was conducting. Because he found some significant gender differences, he plans to pursue this in his research:

> I've never used gender as an independent variable, and because of the seminar I did for the first time . . . and got some enormous sex differences . . . which I don't understand because I've never run gender on any of this before. . . . I probably never would have done this if I hadn't been in the seminar. So we're going to continue this and look at it a little more systematically. It was interesting.

THE LIMITATIONS OF CLASSIFYING COURSE CHANGE

Although issues involved with classifying course change are not the primary focus of this essay, a few observations on this subject are necessary. My own experience using Feminist Phase Theory and conversations with some of the scholars who developed it have led me to conclude that phase theory is a heuristic device to facilitate thinking about knowledge change rather than a concrete measure of curricular revision. As a result of the difficulties I encountered in trying to classify pre- and postseminar courses into these phases, I developed a set of questions, based on phase theory, to apply to course revisions to measure change. These questions include: If there are women in the course, how are they presented? Are they presented as female versions of male standards? Are they discussed as problems or anomalies? Are all women represented or are white, middle-class women used as the norm?

How are race, class, and gender attended to? If men and women are presented together, how is it done? Are men's experiences used as the norm? What priority is information on women of color given? Is it used to introduce a course, presented throughout the course, or tacked onto the end of a course?

The continuum of course change (Adding, Shifting, and Transforming revisions) which emerged in this study has its limitations. First, the reliability of this classification system is uncertain. The next step to take regarding reliability is to have several "judges" apply the questions utilized in this study to a sample of courses to determine whether they classify revisions in a similar fashion. If some consensus is reached on the classification of course revisions, then this continuum of course change may be said to be a reliable measure of curricular transformation.

Second, the static nature of this (or any) classification system captures only a tiny portion of the process of curriculum transformation. Even if the reliability of this continuum is established, I would hesitate to use it as a concrete measure of project outcomes. It should be emphasized that this study provides a window into a single moment or point in time in an otherwise dynamic and changing process. Thus, these participants may have already altered their thinking about their revised courses: those classified as Adding today might be classified as Shifting or Transforming tomorrow. In addition, the judges' evaluation or classification of course revisions may change over time. This continuum was explicitly developed for the purpose of this study—to gain an understanding of the process of and issues involved in curriculum transformation projects. Classifying dynamic change(s) into static categories is useful only to gain a rough measure of change in order to begin to understand the complex nature of knowledge change.

Further, faculty should be interviewed over time in order to capture the evolutionary nature of knowledge change. It would be ideal to interview faculty before, during, and after their participation in these seminars to illuminate the process of curriculum transformation projects. A successive interview schedule such as this would allow the researcher to establish rapport with her participants and provide an enormously rich database to chart the evolution of participants' thinking about curriculum transformation.

Finally, both syllabi and faculty interviews should be used to evaluate course revisions. Because syllabi are one-dimensional, when used alone they provide limited information regarding course change. Although several participants' pre- and postseminar courses appeared the same, their thinking about and plans for addressing women of color in course lectures had in fact changed, but if only syllabi had been examined, this would not have been apparent. Thus, it is vital to interview faculty members to really understand how they view their courses and revisions.

FACILITATORS AND INHIBITORS TO CURRICULUM TRANSFORMATION

Three broad factors were proposed as potentially facilitating or inhabiting faculties' ability to revise courses with scholarship on women of color: their actual experience in the seminar; their disciplinary training; and their social location (rank, gender, race, etc.). The rationale for this conceptual model is based on the cultural view of curricula (Gumport 1988), which posits that faculty members' intellectual, political, and social lives influence what they consider as legitimate knowledge to study and teach.

The data from this study suggest that Transforming revisions require some kind of outsider status (outsider status refers to some kind of experience which places individuals outside of a particular group and its norms) as well as either an interdisciplinary perspective or an ethnic research focus. Shifting revisions are facilitated by either a qualitative methodology, an interdisciplinary perspective, or an ethnic research focus. In the absence of these conditions and if faculty members' seminar experience is either negative or uninspiring, participants are more likely to make Adding revisions. These are working hypotheses and need to be tested in similar settings (e.g., in research universities) and in other departments. In particular, the hypotheses concerning disciplinary issues are tentative because they are based on only one department's expression of that particular discipline.

OUTSIDER STATUS   The fact that outsider status appears to facilitate Transforming revisions has interesting theoretical as well as practical implications. Outsider status was not a single or uniform experience but, rather, was manifested differently in each individual who made Transforming revisions. For example, one faculty member is an outsider because she does not conform to the academic norms of separating political and intellectual interests. Another faculty member is an outsider because he is a white male teaching an ethnic literature that has become increasingly dominated by female writers. A third participant's outsider status comes from a combination of being a female administrator in a university in which male administrators predominate and teaching an "experimental" course in which she relinquishes her expert status in the classroom. Thus, these faculty members' outsider status or experience covers a wide range of definitions and experiences.

The finding that individuals, all with some kind of outsider experience, made Transforming revisions supports the contention of sociologists of science that outsider or marginal status facilitates a scholar's receptivity to innovation (Coser 1958; Gumport 1987; Hagstrom 1965; Kuhn 1970; Merton 1973; Mulkay 1972). What are the implications for practitioners and administrators that being an outsider facilitates Transforming changes? Administrators who are committed to diversifying their faculty as well as the curriculum can seize this as an opportunity to bring "marginalized" faculty members into the center of the organization by supporting curriculum transformation projects with financial and other resources and by utilizing these individuals as leaders (e.g., seminar facilitators) of such efforts.

INTERDISCIPLINARY PERSPECTIVE An interdisciplinary perspective facilitated both Transforming and Shifting revisions, and its absence partially contributed to Adding revisions. In particular, all of the participants from comparative literature and communication studies—both interdisciplinary programs—made either Shifting or Transforming revisions. It seems that faculty who are trained in interdisciplinary programs are not constricted by the weight of what traditional disciplines have defined as core, or legitimate, disciplinary knowledge. The hegemonic nature of knowledge has been described as "those categories of knowledge that disciplines . . . have established historically and carried into the present, producing an inertia that powerfully prefigures the future" (Clark 1987, 268).

This suggests that the success of curriculum transformation projects depends, partially, upon academe's willingness to value and perceive interdisciplinary research and academic programs (such as ethnic studies, women's studies, American studies, etc.) as legitimate and important avenues of inquiry. This is no small task given the dominant position that departments (and, by extension, disciplines) hold on most colleges and universities. Small steps can be taken, however, toward legitimizing multidisciplinary perspectives on traditionally organized campuses by funding interdisciplinary research and granting interdisciplinary programs departmental status.

TYPE OF COURSE The type of course—new versus existing courses—also seems to affect curricular transformation. Three of the six Transforming revisions were new courses, suggesting that it is easier to make these types of revisions with "a clean slate," so to speak. In addition, only three of the seventeen courses targeted for revision were introductory-level courses, which are designed to introduce students to a particular discipline through a broad survey of the field. The remaining courses were upper division and focused on specific issues or topics within a given discipline.

That none of the three introductory courses was classified as a Transforming revision has several theoretical and practical implications. Theoretically, it supports the notion that curriculum transformation encompasses not only specific courses but the larger disciplines as well. Faculty had trouble revising introductory-level courses because they were unwilling to omit core disciplinary paradigms, theories, and methods. This suggests that disciplines must be transformed before, or at least simultaneously with, introductory courses.

Practically, this highlights the difficulties facing projects that target lower-division survey courses rather than upper-division courses. This does not mean that projects should avoid lower-division survey courses but, rather, that project managers and administrators should be aware of the potential obstacles they face in attempting to revise these types of courses. Lower-division courses will probably become easier to transform if and when disciplines begin to change as a result of incorporating scholarship on women of color, in particular, and gender, class, and race, in general.

DEPARTMENTAL AND DISCIPLINARY DIFFERENCES As a group, the literature seminar participants revised more courses, in quantity and degree, than either the psychology or sociology seminar participants. Most of the sociology revisions clustered in the Adding category and the psychology revisions were distributed rather evenly among the three categories of change. These data support what other scholars (Gumport 1987; Stacey and Thorne 1985) have found regarding the variable response of different disciplines to feminist scholarship (and, by extension, scholarship on women of color)—that disciplines such as literature tend to be more receptive than psychology or sociology. The data also indicate that these differences may be related to the perceived legitimacy of the scholarship on women of color in the different disciplines represented by these departments.

Women of color have gained preeminent positions in the field of contemporary literature, while scholarship on women of color is still perceived as marginal or within very narrow specializations in psychology and sociology. Many psychology and sociology seminar participants felt that the research on women of color did not address core disciplinary concerns or questions. Some stated that they wanted scholars to show if, where, and how scholarship on women of color makes a difference to the frameworks and paradigms of the discipline. Still others felt that this scholarship was descriptive rather than theoretical.

Such views might be responsible for the relatively small body of research on women of color. Because scholarship on women of color is not perceived as legitimate, only a few scholars pursue it. As a result, the growth and development of research on women of color is slow, which in turn contributes to its specialized, or marginal, status within the discipline. In addition, many scholars who pursue this area of inquiry seek to study the lives, experiences, and work of women of color within their own context; they hesitate to use existing disciplinary paradigms or theories because many of the traditional theoretical frameworks have rendered women of color invisible or have portrayed them as deviants. Possibly because this scholarship has labored under the burden of "illegitimacy" and has received very little support (financial as well as intellectual), it has remained more at the descriptive level and less at the analytical and theoretical levels. A critical mass of this type of scholarship may be necessary before it can be used to challenge extant paradigms and create new theories.

A related issue involves the difficulty that most of the psychologists and sociologists in the study encountered in considering ethnicity, gender, and class simultaneously. This difficulty may explain why women of color have largely been ignored as a topic of research in these disciplines. The sociologists in this study tended to privilege either race over gender, gender over class, or class over race when studying society. Few could envision how to study these three factors. Similarly, the psychologists who did consider ethnicity or gender in their research (which many psychologists do not) tended, as did the sociologists, to study these factors separately. This suggests that there may be formidable theoretical and epistemological barriers to placing the lives and experiences of women of color (in whom we see most clearly the intersection of race, class, and gender) at the center of these disciplines. Perhaps scholars can only begin to study one or the other as a preparatory step toward studying the three together. Clearly, more research needs to be done which examines how these three facets of social life and experience conform to or challenge different paradigms, theories, and methodologies of a given discipline.

INTRADEPARTMENTAL DIFFERENCES In addition to departmental differences regarding the types and numbers of course revisions made by participants, there were also differences within departments.

Literature Seminar Although the literature seminar participants revised more courses than the psychology or sociology seminar participants, this study provides some evidence that literary theory may act as a barrier to scholarship by women of color (Kolodny 1981; Sherman and Beck 1979). The three literature seminar participants interested in literary theory were all very disappointed with the "atheoretical" nature of the seminar discussions, and the one participant who did revise a theory course made very limited changes. The women of color in the literature seminar stated repeatedly that theories derived from the traditional literary canon do not apply to most ethnic literatures and that theories for these literatures are continually evolving. Literary scholars may need to go to the ethnic literatures in question to determine whether theories emanating from these literatures converge with or challenge traditional literary theory. In this way theory can be discussed in seminars, which will in turn facilitate course revisions.

Psychology Seminar The data from this study indicate that a familiarity with the concept of "culture" facilitated Shifting and Transforming psychology revisions.[1] This obviously needs to be tested with a larger and more varied group of psychologists, but it suggests that psychologists trained in areas of psychology which encompass culture (e.g., social psychology) may find it easier to revise their courses with scholarship on women of color. If further research confirms this, then the next step is to see how and if culture can be used in other areas of psychology which do not explicitly focus on the relevance of contextual factors to human behavior, in order to help these faculty members to revise their courses.

Sociology Seminar   For the group of sociologists in this study a qualitative and interpretive methodology facilitated Shifting revisions, while research on various ethnic groups contributed to Transforming revisions. Because only two of the eight sociologists employed either this methodology or research focus, any trend needs to be verified by a larger sample of sociologists. It does, however, support the notion that interpretive methodologies facilitate curricular transformation. It may be that interpretive methods resonate with the reflexive, or standpoint, methodologies proposed by many feminist scholars, which acknowledge the social, political, and historical context in which knowledge develops. More research is required with a larger and wider range of faculty who employ interpretive methods to determine whether and why interpretive methods facilitate curricular transformation.

Obviously, for faculty members who study ethnic populations the scholarship presented in the seminars was clearly pertinent and more easily incorporated into their courses than it was for those unfamiliar with the study of ethnic groups and minority populations.

As the above discussion of intraseminar/disciplinary issues indicates, a great deal more research is necessary to substantiate these hypotheses. In fact, future research on curriculum transformation may well want to focus on a single discipline, and using several sample departments within it, in order to verify and deepen our understanding of how disciplines differentially affect the process of curricular transformation.

SEMINAR PROCESS AND FORMAT

The data from this study suggest that the departmental climate within which seminars take place may be an important factor to the seminar dynamics, which, in turn, affects course revisions. Departmental climate refers to the perceived legitimacy of feminist and ethnic scholarship within the department.

For most of the sociology seminar participants the seminar was a very tense, political, and conflicted experience. An unfortunate disagreement among three participants prior to the seminar seems to reflect the contested nature of feminist as well as ethnic scholarship within this department. In addition, the often angry reactions of the women of color graduate students to faculty members' attempts to separate ethnicity and gender in seminar discussions about women of color suggest that this conflict may be endemic to the department (and perhaps even to the whole discipline). As a result of their seminar experience, many sociology participants stated that the seminar did not demonstrate to them how they might reconceptualize their courses to be more inclusive of ethnicity and gender.

The English department, from which most of the literature seminar participants were drawn, was more receptive to scholarship by women of color. This is partially due to the preeminent status of women of color writers in contemporary literature, but it may also reflect the department's positive stance toward literature by people of color. The latter was manifested in the department's active recruitment of faculty with expertise in these literatures during the two years preceding the seminar.

The psychology department seemed to be somewhat receptive to gender and ethnic research, at least as "specialties" within psychology. One of the seminar participants was recruited by the department specifically to teach psychology of gender courses. Another participant conducts his research on Asian Americans through an Asian-American research center, which he directs within the department. During the interviews neither of these scholars indicated that they had encountered difficulties in conducting their research. This relatively receptive departmental climate may partially account for the calm and pleasant atmosphere that prevailed in the psychology seminar.

Although there is little data to support these speculations regarding departmental climate (because it was not the primary focus of the study), it does suggest interesting theoretical as well as practical avenues to pursue. Future studies of curriculum transformation may well want to explore the notion that the perceived legitimacy of feminist and ethnic scholarship within a given department will affect the seminar dynamics. If this is supported, then project directors would be well advised to assess a particular department's climate or ethos concerning ethnic and gender scholarship before organizing a seminar within it. Or they may want to mix people from different departments in order to get a range of views regarding the legitimacy of feminist and ethnic scholarship.

POLITICAL AND EMOTIONAL FACETS OF ETHNIC AND GENDER SCHOLARSHIP As the sociology seminar experience indicates, research on women of color can be emotionally and politically charged. Aiken et al. (1987), who consciously tried to avoid it, could not keep the emotional subtext of feminist scholarship from surfacing in the project they facilitated. This occurred several times in the sociology seminar during discussions of the effects of racism and sexism on the lives of women of color. When faculty members attempted to explain a given situation or experience of women of color with existing theories, the graduate students (the majority of whom were women of color) would object, and often a heated argument ensued. In some cases the faculty and graduate students ended up polarized—with the faculty feeling that the graduate students were being political and emotional rather than intellectual and the students feeling that faculty members were being racist under the guise of being intellectual. Discussions of groups that have been kept on the margins of society are bound to take on emotional as well as political overtones. Although this is probably unavoidable, it does present problems given the norms governing the academic profession, which require that emotions and politics remain separate from intellectual discussions. This problem could be ameliorated somewhat if project directors take the lead of feminist theory seminars in which the potential political and/or emotional nature of the issue at hand is acknowledged at the outset, in order to create a "safe space" for discussions.

THE SEMINAR FORMAT Many of the faculty participants did not like the "lecture format" of the seminars, in which speakers presented their research, because it did not always address faculty members' research interests. This issue may be partially eased if scholars are funded to examine the existing body of literature on women of color, synthesize it with respect to disciplinary theories and frameworks, and demonstrate to seminar participants where and how it fits or deviates from disciplinary paradigms or theories. This could then provide a context for faculty members to discuss, with the presenter and with their colleagues, how the consideration of gender, ethnicity, and class may or may not require rethinking a given discipline.

PEDAGOGY Faculty members in this study expressed a very strong desire and need to discuss the pedagogical implications of curriculum transformation. They wanted to know how to present this material to their classes and how to respond to students' ignorance of and reactions to scholarship on women of color. This raises interesting theoretical issues given the nature of research universities, which value research over teaching. Clearly, if research universities continue to engage in such projects, they will have to address these pedagogical issues. One way would be to offer a separate seminar devoted to pedagogy during the term that faculty members teach their revised courses. In this seminar faculty members could discuss with their colleagues any problems they encounter and collectively devise solutions. This implies that the reward structure of a university must shift to accord pedagogy the same value as research, to insure the success of a project with an explicit pedagogical focus.

CONCLUDING REMARKS

This study highlights the very complex task facing higher education organizations and individuals as they embark on curriculum transformation projects. The challenge to faculty members who engage in these projects is not confined merely to revising their courses to be more inclusive of race, class, and gender. They are also being confronted with the formidable task of rethinking the ways they have been trained to view the world through their respective disciplinary lenses. As this study suggests, curriculum transformation (especially concerning women of color) may well require a fundamental reconceptualization of disciplines in order to better reflect the experience and lives of all people.

If the working hypotheses regarding outsider status and an interdisciplinary perspective (as facilitators of course revisions) are supported in further research, then colleges and universities undertaking such projects may well have to engage in some fundamental restructuring themselves. If these institutions are committed to diversifying the curriculum, then faculty who do not conform to expected norms (outsiders) will have to be brought back to the center of the organization and involved in integral ways in curriculum transformation projects.[2] Scholarship on various ethnic groups and minority populations will also have to be encouraged in order to achieve the "critical mass" necessary for it to challenge extant disciplinary paradigms and create its own theories. In addition, higher education, if it wants to succeed in diversifying its curricula, will have to renew its support for interdisciplinary programs (such as women's studies and ethnic studies) by giving them departmental status and ample resources. Finally, research universities must rethink their approaches to teaching and pedagogy. As the data from this study indicate, faculty members who engage in curriculum transformation projects require support and a context within which to discuss the pedagogy of teaching a transformed curriculum.

NOTES

1. For the purpose of this discussion *culture* is defined as the social context within which human behavior occurs.

2. I realize the paradox of this suggestion—as these faculty are brought to the center of the organization they may no longer experience being outsiders, which in turn may affect their receptivity to change.

REFERENCES

Aiken, S. H., K. Anderson, M. Dinnerstein, J. Lensink, and P. MacCorquodale. 1987. "Trying Transformations: Curriculum Integration and the Problem of Resistance." *Signs* 12, no. 2: 255–75.

Clark, B. R. 1987. *The Academic Life*. Princeton: Carnegie Foundation for the Advancement of Teaching.

Coser, L. A. 1958. "Georg Simmel's Style of Work: A Contribution to the Sociology of the Sociologist." *American Journal of Sociology* 63: 635–41.

Gumport, P. J. 1987. "The Social Construction of Knowledge: Individual and Institutional Commitments to Feminist Scholarship. Ph.D. diss., Stanford University.

———. 1988. "Curricula as Signposts of Cultural Change." *Review of Higher Education* 12, no. 1: 49–61.

Hagstrom, W. O. 1965. *The Scientific Community*. New York: Basic Books.

Kolodny, A. 1981. "Dancing through the Minefield: Some Observations on the Theory, Practice and Politics of Feminist Literary Criticism." In *Men's Studies Modified*, ed. D. Spender, 23–42. Oxford: Pergamon Press.

Kuhn, T. S. 1970. *The Structure of Scientific Revolutions.* Chicago: University of Chicago Press.

Lincoln, Y. S., and E. G. Guba. 1982. "Epsitemological and Methodological Bases of Naturalistic Inquiry." *Educational Communications and Technology Journal* 4, no. 30: 311–33.

———. 1985. *Naturalistic Inquiry.* Beverly Hills, Calif.: Sage.

McIntosh, P. 1983. "Interactive Phases of Curricular Re-Vision." Wellesley College. Center for Research on Women.

Merton, R. K. 1983. *The Sociology of Science: Theoretical and Empirical Investigations.* Chicago: University of Chicago Press.

Mulkay, M. J. 1972. *The Social Process of Innovation: A Study in the Sociology of Science.* London: Macmillan.

Schuster, M. R., and S. R. Van Dyne. 1985. *Women's Place in the Academy: Transforming the Liberal Arts Curriculum.* Lanham, Md.: Rowman and Allanheld.

Sherman, J. A., and E. T. Beck. 1981. *The Prism of Sex.* Madison: University of Wisconsin Press.

Stacey, J., and B. Thorne. 1985. "The Missing Revolution in Sociology." *Social Problems* 32, no. 4: 301–16.

Tetreault, M.K. 1985. "Feminist Phase Theory: An Experience-Derived Evaluation Model." *Journal of Higher Education* 56, no. 4: 363–83.

FACULTY SEMINAR MODELS

PROCESS IN CURRICULUM TRANSFORMATION

Phyllis Palmer Women's Studies Program
George Washington University
Washington, DC 20052

Faculty curriculum transformation seminars need feminist pedagogy as much as good readings, speakers, and other information resources. The syllabus describing the seminar at George Washington University outlines a framework and reading assignments for a successful faculty seminar. Like most syllabi, it gives little idea, however, about how participants interacted during three-hour sessions. This essay describes *how* faculty worked together to absorb new theories and information about women of color.

The planning for the integration seminar relied on two theoretical approaches to seminar process. Using Nancy Schniedewind's "Teaching Feminist Process" for women's studies as a reference,[1] the planner took as the seminar's goals to enable faculty members (1) to integrate emotion and intellect, (2) to listen to one another attentively, and (3) to engage in cooperative learning. The seminar leader used one theory of group dynamics from experiential education: ICA (for Inclusion, Control, Accommodation), the idea that groups develop through three stages. People coming to a new group worry first about Inclusion. Each person asks, "Who is here, and do I belong to this group?" Second, participants ask (unconsciously) about Control. "Who is running things, and do I have some say in decisions?" Third, members wonder, "Can I like some people in the group and not others? Can the group accommodate personal likes and dislikes and still function?"[2] Each session of the seminar drew on this complex theory to produce an apparently simple design.

To feel comfortable and ready to work in a new endeavor participants need to be informed about basic subsistence requirements. The syllabus, sent out two weeks before the first seminar meeting, told faculty members how and when they would receive stipends, how long the seminar meetings would last, what food and drink would be supplied (low on sugar and high on health), how much preparation was required for seminar meetings, what materials they needed, and what clothes were appropriate. This may seem juvenile, but all new activities make emotional demands similar to those encountered on one's first day of school. When participants don't need to worry about the basics they can more easily concentrate on curriculum work.

All six seminar sessions opened with a welcome and a review of the day's agenda for our three hours of work. Agendas fill a basic need; everyone can plan stretching, food, bathroom, and phone call desires around the schedule. Agendas also initiate power sharing between the seminar leader(s) and participants; everyone becomes responsible for keeping track of time and getting the necessary work done.

An innovation in this framework was "check-in." During this opening activity every person in the room responded to a common question, such as, "What were your feelings and your thoughts on leaving the first session?" This activity usually lasted about thirty minutes, as each person simply gave her or his response, without query or criticism. In theoretical terms check-in aided feelings of Inclusion because every person spoke and received some affirmation. Check-in also allowed participants to express negative feelings and anxieties as well as positive ones; it clarified that participants could find acceptance for their genuine feelings and not just for being "nice"—and it vented anger.

In women's studies terms check-in gave faculty the instruction to speak about feelings and thoughts and to integrate emotion and intellect. Faculty also spoke for the "I" and not for the department or the discipline. This exercise legitimated discussions that included feelings, which was helpful, since a lot of faculty members' doubts about curriculum change is based in incompletely conscious anger, doubt, guilt, or fear and then rationalized.

Brief lectures (fifteen to twenty minutes) to supplement assigned readings followed check-in and provided the formal feminist theory portion of each meeting. Often questions followed, and discussion by faculty ensued. The agenda helped focus time, however, so that faculty members were willing to carry questions from the discussion into work sessions. The brevity of the lectures derived from the group dynamics Control principle. Taking all the time for oneself to talk establishes the seminar leader as the person in control; other participants have only a modest chance to intervene and must fight for time. In this seminar lectures did not function to establish the seminar leader's control of content or authority. That faculty spent most of their time in small work groups, preparing reports for the large group, gave most participants relatively equal time to present their thoughts, interests, and critiques.

About an hour and a half of the seminar was spent in work groups of five to ten people, which had a clearly defined task. At the first meeting, for example, each person explained the design of the course syllabus being revised. In the second faculty participants described examples they had brought for "show and tell" to illustrate how their respective disciplines depicted women of color. This kind of exercise revealed how the discipline's assumptions denigrated or rendered invisible these women. Such tasks required that every person have some time and share control of the essential information needed for the group's task.

In women's studies terms the task groups functioned to familiarize faculty with cooperative learning. The groups were instructed to select facilitators and recorders to enable every participant to present materials and to report results to the larger group. The work groups were given general questions, which required them to pool results of individual presentations to discern patterns; to paraphrase Schniedewind each person's participation was essential to the group's completion of its task ("Teaching Feminist Process," 23). Faculty learned from the patterns that emerged from discussions that generalizations about "women," for instance, often do not connect with generalizations about "race." *Women* typically means "white" women, and those women who are not white become, by default, an inferior or archetypal version of womanhood or else simply absent.

How a group works together when some participants have longtime friendships and shared interests and others do not is especially complicated in a faculty seminar that brings together a group diverse in race, gender, status, and discipline. It helped that there were no "tokens": every person in the room had a "like" person, if we define *like* by gender, race, religion, class, and faculty status, so no one had to be friendly just to prove that these characteristics don't matter.

Providing good food and having regular break times seemed to act as a valve to release the dual tensions of liking and disliking. People who felt frustration found others with whom to vent their feelings. Friends could chat. New friendships formed around newly discovered and shared interests in children, computer communication, exercise, music—the gamut of human interests that underlie our social behavior. Webs of affection allowed faculty members to disagree with one another, take pleasure, and feel annoyance without fearing the breakup of the group.

Let me note that, as part of the course integration effort, many faculty devised new student assignments that required students to interview someone different from themselves in race, gender, class, religion, sexuality, or nationality. Though I have not investigated their motives, one might be that they had positive experiences of difference within the seminar.

In conclusion, we need to document the *processes* of change as adequately as new course *content*. Curriculum integration demands hard intellectual and emotional work from faculty and students. Women's studies and group dynamics offer well-developed techniques to encourage the emotional risks that accompany intellectual growth, and they provide skills and information for faculty members who must lead their students through similarly difficult transformations. Faculty seminars should embody the most relevant lessons of the women's movement and feminist theory: the means determine the quality of results, and process always affects content.

NOTES

1. *Women's Studies Quarterly* 15, nos. 3–4 (Fall–Winter 1987): 15–31.
2. This group theory offers almost an organizational schema of Bernice Johnson Reagon's feminist essay "Coalition Politics: Turning the Century," in *Home Girls: A Black Feminist Anthology*, ed. Barbara Smith (Latham, N.Y.: Kitchen Table, 1983), which ponders, appropriately for this work, whether or not feminists can tolerate differences of background, race, class—of not finding a comfortable "home"—enough to work together for a shared political purpose. All groups of diverse people must face the same question.

Seminar Objectives

The following agenda was designed by five of the participants. The emphasis is on doing and discussion. We intend for this to be fun, to rely on active engagement by all participants, and to be experimental; we do not expect anyone to come with every question answered, every issue explored. *Exploration is what the seminar is for.* Research assistance will be provided by the library staff and by a research assistant to the project. Mainly we want participants to have time to reflect, to listen to one another, to receive some new information, to read some new materials, and to formulate and try out some new ways to think about the content in the courses being revised. The seminar is to be a springboard for work during the summer; we do not expect to complete the large and probably lifelong tasks envisioned by the project.

Syllabus

Session 1

Introduce ourselves to one another. Reflect on course to be revised as we currently teach it. Each participant should bring syllabus from course they intend to revise and books they use in course. Participants will talk in work groups divided into humanities and social sciences and science about why they currently teach the course the way they do, how they learned to organize the class this way, and what means they use to revise courses and to incorporate new information. After this discussion each group will report to the whole about what patterns describe our thinking about course design and course revision.

Session 2

In order to begin answering the question "How does my discipline, how do I, currently conceive women of color?" participants will each bring something, some artifact, which illustrates how and where their disciplines make visible African-American, Hispanic, Native American, or Asian-American women. The artifacts may be objects, photographs, literary texts, academic articles, quantitative data, government reports—whatever the faculty member "sees" when mentally envisioning a woman of color within the discipline. Much of this session will be spent with participants explaining their artifacts to see what are our existing disciplinary images and data and texts.

Session 3

Each participant will formulate goals for revising a course syllabus during this session. These will be written up in notebooks, which will then be copied and distributed to the entire seminar for Session IV. After people state their goals we will brainstorm what help participants need to meet these goals. This information will also be compiled to serve as a resource request list for the seminar. In preparation for this meeting each participant will be given a basic reading about the state of scholarship on women and/or women of color in the participant's discipline. We will each be learning about and reporting to the group how our discipline conceives racial difference and gender.

Reading Assignments: Margaret L. Andersen, "Changing the Curriculum in Higher Education," *Signs* 12, no. 2 (Winter 1987): 222–54; Jill Nelson and respondents, "Race, Rudeness, and Revenge: When Whites Treat Blacks as Invisible, We All Lose," *Washington Post*, 2 April and 7 April 1989; and discipline-specific essays for appropriate faculty.

Session 4

Three scholars who have moved their work toward grappling with new questions that grow from considering the experiences and institutional/legal status of women of color will give brief talks about *how they formulated new questions in their disciplines*. These brief presentations will be used as the basis for a general discussion about what new questions we can ask in our disciplines. The seminar will also have been given four readings that represent cultural experiences of African-American, Asian-American, Native American, and Hispanic women, so that we can discuss how each of our disciplines makes sense of, responds to, these accounts. What do each of us do with these accounts? How do our disciplines enlighten or draw on them?

Reading Assignments: Nellie Wong, "When I Was Growing Up"; Mary Hope Lee, "on not being"; Cherríe Moraga, "For the Color of My Mother";

Rosario Morales, "I Am What I Am"; Naomi Littlebear, "Dreams of Violence"; Chrystos, "He Saw"; Mitsuye Yamada, "Invisibility Is an Unnatural Disaster: Reflections of an Asian American Woman"—all in Cherríe Moraga and Gloria Anzaldúa, eds., *This Bridge Called My Back;* Audre Lorde, "Man Child: A Black Lesbian Feminist's Response," *Sister Outsider;* Leslie Marmon Silko, "Lullaby," *Storyteller;* Alice Walker, "Zora Neale Hurston: A Cautionary Tale and a Partisan View," *In Search of Our Mothers' Gardens;* and Gloria Anzaldúa, "The Homeland, Aztlán," *Borderlands / La Frontera: The New Mestiza.*

Session 5

Participants will bring tentative course redesigns to the final session, and we will discuss these designs, with explanations and suggestions. Participants will describe why they redesigned the course as they did, first in social sciences and science / humanities group divisions and then across these lines in order to get cross-fertilization of concepts. I am especially interested in encouraging faculty to think about both culture and institutional frameworks as explanations of gender- and race-based patterns of experience and social organization.

Reading Assignments: bell hooks, "Men: Comrades in Struggle," *Feminist Theory from Margin to Center;* Nancy Schniedewind, "Teaching Feminist Process," *Women's Studies Quarterly* 15, nos. 3–4 (Fall–Winter 1987): 15–31.

The seminar will meet again formally as participants begin to teach redesigned classes.

AMERICAN AND RELATED LITERATURES

King-Kok Cheung English and Asian American Studies
Brenda Marie Osbey English, Afro-American Studies, and
  Women's Studies
University of California
Los Angeles, CA 90024

"American and Related Literatures" was one of the first two seminars (spring 1989) in the multiyear Ford Ethnic Women's Curriculum Transformation Project (FEW) at UCLA. The syllabus was based largely on a graduate seminar I taught in the fall of 1988 entitled "Fiction by Women of Color in the United States." As a specialist on Asian American literature, I felt the need to go beyond the dominant-minority or white-nonwhite binary opposition in approaching American literature by people of color and to explore some of the common themes and narrative strategies in literature by women of Native American, African American, Mexican American, and Asian American descent.

I was by no means an authority on these diverse ethnic groups.[1] Quite the contrary: in the graduate seminar I had been teaching works by Native American, African American, and Mexican American writers for the first time. I told my class that I too was groping my way through most of the texts assigned, that I hoped to learn as much from them as they could expect to learn from me, and that all of us would take turns being seminar leaders. In each class one person would make a brief presentation and then raise questions about a text assigned; then the rest of the class would intervene. The quality of the presentations far exceeded my expectations: I learned more from that class than from any other I had taught up to that point.

Cofacilitating the Ford seminar gave me another opportunity to deepen my knowledge about ethnic women writers. I particularly welcomed the idea of *co*facilitating with visiting professor Brenda Marie Osbey, an accomplished poet and a scholar in African American literature. The fact that the reading list was based largely on the one used in my graduate seminar on fiction explains the preponderance of prose works in the "Required Texts." Thanks to Professor Osbey, there is a substantial poetry component in the African

The facilitators of these seven UCLA faculty development seminars gratefully acknowledge the central role played by FEW Director Karen E. Rowe, as a collaborator and coauthor, in the conceptual framing, development, and editing of the following syllabi and in facilitating the seminars. They also acknowledge FEW Project Coordinator Norma W. Rice, whose research, editorial, and administrative support made these seminars and syllabi possible, and the research and bibliographic assistance of Angela James (Sociology), Shu Mei-Shih (American and Related Literatures), Grace Wang (Psychology), Margaret McMillen (History, Interdisciplinary), Alycee Lane (American Ethnic Studies, FEW Project), Kimberly Slaughter (American Ethnic Studies), Susie Wirka (Crossing Borders, Crossing Cultures), Celia Naylor (FEW Project), and Bhagirathi Subrahmanyam (FEW Bibliographer).

American segment. The Ford grant also allowed us to invite speakers from other institutions: Paula Gunn Allen, Angie Chabram, and Teresa McKenna. They, along with faculty participants Kenneth Lincoln and Abena Busia, suggested some of the readings incorporated into the syllabus.

The seminar was organized according to ethnic groups. Since most of the sessions were facilitated by teachers with expertise on a particular group of female writers, that format seemed quite logical. But there were both pros and cons to such an organization. On the positive side, it allowed the primary speaker to give a historical and literary overview of each ethnic group before launching into a discussion of a particular text. Given that many of the participants were reading works by writers from several ethnic groups for the first time, such background information was desirable and even indispensable. On the negative side, such an organization could distract participants from seeing connections among the various groups of writers; it might also run the risk of essentializing these writers according to face and gender and of overshadowing the fluid identities and vast differences within each group.

One of the recurrent concerns expressed in the seminar had been who could "legitimately" teach words by ethnic women. None of the participants would claim mastery over the divergent cultural texts. Most of us, however, agreed that as long as teachers could be honest about their limitations, they should not hesitate to introduce texts by authors whose gender and ethnic backgrounds differ from their own. The important thing is to avoid approaching those texts from a predominantly Eurocentric perspective and to guard against presenting a single text as representative of the ethnic culture to which the writer belongs. (See my essay "Reflections on Teaching Fiction by American Women of Color" for further discussion of this and other pitfalls.)

The content of the Ford seminar was more substantial and challenging than the graduate seminar I had taught. The interaction in the classroom, however, was not always smooth. Of the fifteen participants about two thirds were faculty, and one third were graduate students. While there were both white and nonwhite, female and male, faculty members, all but one of the graduate students were women of color. Needless to say, the participants' degrees of sophistication vis-à-vis the works studied were not necessarily proportional to their academic status. Because of the power asymmetry, the gender and racial diversity, the highly uneven levels of preparation, and the textual material itself, which was all too close to the lived experience of some participants, there were tense moments of confrontation. Instructors and students of "minority" literature, often expected to know most canonical works, were not always willing to put up with ignorance on the part of faculty members regarding writing by women of color.

In retrospect I realize that those moments were also important learning moments. I myself was too personally engaged and relatively powerless (as an assistant professor at that time) to be a clear-headed and effective mediator, but the experience has equipped me—albeit the hard way—to handle similar situations in subsequent courses. When a conflict erupts in my classroom these days I avoid the temptation to glide over it or to change the subject. Instead, I try to get to the root of the disagreement by dwelling on it, by analyzing the strengths and limits of each perspective, and by teasing out the underlying assumptions. In short, I force the disputants to listen to one another, to see the extent to which certain remarks might be shaped by the gender and race of the speaker and, conversely, the extent to which some angry responses could be provoked by the gender and race and perhaps also sexual orientation of a speaker, rather than by what that person has said. My goal is not to arbitrate who is right and who is wrong but, instead, to encourage everyone to hear rather than ignore the differences. If the disagreement arises over a text, I will also use the clashing perspectives to explode the myth of a universal text or a universal reader. When I, as the instructor, am being challenged, I remind myself how much courage it takes for a student to disagree with a teacher. Instead of being defensive, as I previously was wont to be, I have learned to admit my own mistakes or biases.

Cofacilitating "American and Related Literatures" was not an easy experience, but it made a more thick-skinned teacher out of me.

King-Kok Cheung

NOTE

1. I use the terms *minority, race,* and *ethnicity* more or less interchangeably to refer to persons of color, even though I am dissatisfied with all three. People of color are numerically no longer "minorities" in many parts of the United States; *race,* when applied to Asian Americans, homogenizes highly distinctive national groups; *ethnicity* obscures the charged differences due to race.

Syllabus

Week 1: Race and Gender Intersections

Homans, Margaret. "Feminist Criticism and Theory: The Ghost of Creusa." *Yale Journal of Criticism* 1 (1987): 153–82.

Joseph, Gloria I., and Jill Lewis. "Introduction." *Common Differences: Conflicts in Black and White Feminist Perspectives,* 1–15. Garden City, N.Y.: Anchor-Doubleday, 1981.

Lauter, Paul. "Race and Gender in the Shaping of the American Literary Canon: A Case Study from the Twenties." In *Feminist Criticism and Social Change: Sex, Class, and Race in Literature and Culture,* ed. Judith Newton and Deborah Rosenfelt, 19–44. New York: Methuen, 1985.

Sollors, Werner. "Beyond Ethnicity." *Beyond Ethnicity: Consent and Descent in American Culture*, 20–39. New York: Oxford University Press, 1986.

———. "Introduction." *Beyond Ethnicity: Consent and Descent in American Culture*, 3–19. New York: Oxford University Press, 1986.

Yarborough, Richard. "Breaking the 'Codes of Americanness.' " Review of *Beyond Ethnicity: Consent and Descent in American Culture*, by Werner Sollors. *American Quarterly* 38 (1986): 860–65.

Week 2: Native American Literature (I)

Guest Lecturer: Kenneth Lincoln, English and American Indian Studies, UCLA

Allen, Paula Gunn. "The Sacred Hoop: A Contemporary Perspective." *The Scared Hoop: Recovering the Feminine in American Indian Traditions*, 54–75. Boston: Beacon Press, 1986.

Dearborn, Mary V. "Introduction: Gender and Ethnicity in American Culture." *Pocahontas's Daughters: Gender and Ethnicity in American Culture*, 3–11. New York: Oxford University Press, 1986.

———. "Pocahontas's Sisters: A Case Study of American Indian Women Writers." *Pocahontas's Daughters: Gender and Ethnicity in American Culture*, 12–30. New York: Oxford University Press, 1986.

Erdrich, Louise. *Love Medicine*. New York: Holt, 1970.

Lincoln, Kenneth. " 'Bring Her Home': Louise Erdrich." *Indi'n Humor: Bicultural Play in Native America*, 192–236. New York: Oxford University Press, 1991.

Handouts:

Lincoln, Kenneth. "American Indian Studies M200B and English 266: Cultural World Views of Native Americans." Syllabi. UCLA, Winter 1988.

———. "Selected Bibliography." *Native American Renaissance*, 285–300. Berkeley: University of California Press, 1983.

Week 3: Native American Literature (II)

Guest Lecturer: Paula Gunn Allen, Native American Studies, UCLA

Allen, Paula Gunn. "Grandmother of the Sun: Ritual Gynocracy in Native America." *The Sacred Hoop: Recovering the Feminine in American Indian Traditions*, 13–29. Boston: Beacon Press, 1986.

———. "Introduction." *The Sacred Hoop: Recovering the Feminine in American Indian Traditions*, 1–7. Boston: Beacon Press, 1986.

———. "Introductory Courses in American Indian Literature" and "Survey

Courses." In *Studies in American Indian Literature: Critical Essays and Course Designs*, ed. Paula Gunn Allen, 225–39. New York: MLA, 1983.

———. "Kochinnenako in Academe: Three Approaches to Interpreting a Keres Indian Tale." *The Sacred Hoop: Recovering the Feminine in American Indian Traditions*, 224–44. Boston: Beacon Press, 1986.

———. "Teaching American Indian Women's Literature." In *Studies in American Indian Literature: Critical Essays and Course Designs*, ed. Paula Gunn Allen, 134–44. New York: MLA, 1983.

———. "Teaching the Indian in American Literature." In *Studies in American Indian Literature: Critical Essays and Course Designs*, ed. Paula Gunn Allen, 273–77. New York: MLA, 1983.

Baker, Houston A., Jr. "Introduction: English as a World Language for Literature." In *English Literature: Opening Up the Canon*, ed. Leslie A. Fiedler and Houston A. Baker, Jr., ix–xiii. Selected papers from the English Institute, 1979, n.s. 4. Baltimore: Johns Hopkins University Press, 1981.

Silko, Leslie. *Ceremony*. New York: Viking Press, 1977.

———. "Preface" and "Language and Literature from a Pueblo Indian Perspective." In *English Literature: Opening Up the Canon*, ed. Leslie A. Fiedler and Houston A. Baker, Jr., vii–viii, 54–72. Selected papers from the English Institute, 1979, n.s. 4. Baltimore: Johns Hopkins University Press, 1981.

Handouts:

Allen, Paula Gunn. "Selected Bibliography." *The Sacred Hoop: Recovering the Feminine in American Indian Traditions*, 287–95. Boston: Beacon Press, 1986.

Week 4: Chicana Literature (I)

Guest Lecturer: Angie Chabram, Spanish and Classics, University of California–Davis

Cisneros, Sandra. *The House on Mango Street*. Houston: Arte Público, 1984.

Herrera-Sobek, María. "The Acculturation Process of the Chicana in the *Corrido*." *De Colores: Journal of Chicano Expression and Thought* 6 (1982): 7–16.

Leal, Luis. "Mexican American Literature: A Historical Perspective." *Modern Chicano Writers: A Collection of Critical Essays*, ed. Joseph Sommers and Tomas Ybarra-Frausto, 18–30. Englewood Cliffs, N.J.: Prentice-Hall, 1979.

Ordóñez, Elizabeth. "Sexual Politics and the Theme of Sexuality in Chicana Poetry." In *Women in Hispanic Literature: Icons and Fallen Idols*, ed. Beth Miller, 316–39. Berkeley: University of California Press, 1983.

Paredes, Américo. "The Folk Base of Chicano Literature." In *Modern Chi-*

cano Writers: A Collection of Critical Essays, ed. Joseph Sommers and Tomas Ybarra-Frausto, 4–17. Englewood Cliffs, N.J.: Prentice-Hall, 1979. This essay appeared in more extensive form as "El folklore de los groupos de origen mexicano en Estados Unidos," *Folklore Americano* 14 (1964): 146–63.

Sánchez, Marta. "Bibliography." *Contemporary Chicana Poetry: A Critical Approach to an Emerging Literature,* 361–66. Berkeley: University of California Press, 1985.

————. "Gender, Ethnicity, and Silence in Contemporary Chicana Poetry." *Contemporary Chicana Poetry: A Critical Approach to an Emerging Literature,* 1–23. Berkeley: University of California Press, 1985.

Sommers, Joseph. "From a Critical Premise to the Product: Critical Modes and Their Applications to a Chicano Literary Text." *New Scholar* 6 (1977): 51–80.

Yarbro-Bejarano, Yvonne. "The Female Subject in Chicano Theatre: Sexuality, 'Race,' and Class." *Theatre Journal* 38 (1986): 389–407.

Week 5: Chicana Literature (II)

Guest Lecturer: Teresa McKenna, English and Chicano Studies, University of Southern California–Los Angeles

Alarcon, Norma. "Chicana's Feminist Literature: A Re-Vision through Malintzin; or Malintzin: Putting Flesh Back on the Object." In *This Bridge Called My Back· Writings by Radical Women of Color,* ed. Cherríe Moraga and Gloria Anzaldúa, 182–90. Watertown, Mass. Persephone Press, 1981.

Castillo, Ana. *The Mixquiahuala Letters.* Binghampton, N.Y.: Bilingual Press / Editorial Bilingue, 1986.

Cervantes, Lorna de. *Emplumada,* 44–45. Pittsburgh: University of Pittsburgh Press, 1981.

Chávez, Denise. *The Last of the Menu Girls.* Houston: Arte Público, 1984.

McKenna, Teresa. " 'Immigrant in Our Own Land': A Chicano Literature Review and Pedagogical Assessment." *ADE Bulletin* (Winter 1988): 30–38.

Vigil, Evangelina. *Thirty an' Seen a Lot.* Houston: Arte Público, 1985.

Handouts:

Hernández-Araico, Susana. "Spanish C197/C290: Contemporary Latin American Women Writers and the Revision of History." UCLA summer session.

McKenna, Teresa. "Chicano Literature." In *Redefining American Literary History,* ed. A. LaVonne Brown Ruoff and Jerry W. Ward, Jr., 363–72. New York: MLA, 1990.

————. "Chicano Studies P81 and English 1635: Third World Women in Literature." University of Southern California, Winter 1986.

————. "English 448a: Chicano Literature." University of Southern California, Spring 1989.

————. "English 470: Women in British and American Literature." University of Southern California, Spring 1989.

————. "English 254xg: Women Writers in English." University of Southern California, Spring 1988.

————. "English 442g: American Literature 1900–Present." University of Southern California, Fall 1988.

————. "English 260xg: British and American Literature since 1900." University of Southern California, Fall 1988.

Week 6: African-American Literature (I)

Guest Lecturer: Brenda Marie Osbey, English, Afro-American Studies, and Women's Studies, UCLA

Christian, Barbara. "The Race for Theory." *Cultural Critique* 6 (1987): 51–63.

————. "Shadows Uplifted." In *Feminist Criticism and Social Change: Sex, Class, and Race in Literature and Culture,* ed. Judith Newton and Deborah Rosenfelt, 181–215. New York: Methuen, 1985.

Davis, Angela Y. *Women, Race, and Class.* New York: Vintage, 1983.

Marshall, Paule. *Praisesong for the Widow.* New York: Dutton, 1984.

Osbey, Brenda Marie. *Ceremony for Minneconjoux.* Charlottesville: University Press of Virginia, 1985.

Selected Poems:

"Madhouses," 3–8.

"Ceremony for Minneconjoux," 9–21.

"Eliza," 51–57.

"The Fefe Women," 85.

————. "Faubourg Study No. 3: The Seven Sisters of New Orleans." *Callaloo* 11 (1988): 464–76.

————. *In These Houses.* Middletown, Conn.: Wesleyan University Press, 1988.

Selected Poems:

"The Wastrel-Woman Poem," 12–13.

"Elvena," 20–23.

"House of Bones," 50–51.

Tate, Claudia. "Sherley Anne Williams." *Black Women Writers at Work,* 205–13. New York: Continuum, 1983.

Taylor, Clyde. "Black Writing as Immanent Humanism." *Southern Review* 21 (1985): 790–800.

————. "Salt Peanuts: In Sound and Sense in African-American Oral/Musical Creativity." *Callallo* 5, no. 2 (1982): 1–11.

Williams, Sherley Anne. "Letters from a New England Negro." *Some One Sweet Angel Chile*, 13–65. New York: Morrow, 1982.

Week 7: African American Literature (II)

Guest Lecturer: Brenda Marie Osbey

Carby, Hazel. " 'Women's Era': Rethinking Black Feminist Theory." *Reconstructing Womanhood: The Emergence of the Afro-American Woman Novelist*, 3–19. New York: Oxford University Press, 1987.

McKay, Nellie. "An Interview with Toni Morrison." *Contemporary Literature* 24 (1983): 413–29.

Morrison, Toni. *The Bluest Eye*. New York: Holt, 1970.

———. "Unspeakable Things Unspoken: The Afro-American Presence in American Literature." *Michigan Quarterly Review* 28 (1989): 1–34.

Smith, Barbara. "Toward a Black Feminist Criticism." In *Feminist Criticism and Social Change: Sex, Class, and Race in Literature and Culture*, ed. Judith Newton and Deborah Rosenfelt, 3–18. New York: Methuen, 1985.

Stepto, Robert B., "Teaching Afro-American Literature— Survey or Tradition: The Reconstruction of Instruction." In *Afro-American Literature*, ed. Dexter Fisher and Robert Stepto, 8–24. New York: MLA, 1979.

Tate, Claudia. "Toni Morrison." *Black Women Writers at Work*, 117–31. New York: Continuum, 1983.

Willis, Susan. "Eruptions of Funk: Historicizing Toni Morrison." *Specifying: Black Women Writing the American Experience*, 83–109. Madison: University of Wisconsin Press, 1987.

Week 8: Asian American Literature (I)

Guest Lecturer: King-Kok Cheung, English and Asian American Studies, UCLA

Chin, Frank, Jeffrey Paul Chan, Lawson Fusao Inada, and Shawn Hsu Wong. "An Introduction to Chinese- and Japanese-American Literature." In *Aiiieeeee!* ed. Frank Chin, Jeffrey Paul Chan, Lawson Fusao Inada, and Shawn Hsu Wong, 3–36. Garden City, N.Y.: Anchor-Doubleday, 1975.

Kim, Elaine, H. "Defining Asian American Realities through Literature." *Cultural Critique* 6 (1987): 87–111.

Kingston, Maxine Hong. "On Discovery." *China Men*, 3–5. New York: Knopf, 1980.

———. *The Woman Warrior: Memoirs of a Girlhood among Ghosts*. New York: Knopf, 1976.

Yamada, Mitsuye. "Invisibility Is an Unnatural Disaster: Reflections of an Asian-American Woman." In *This Bridge Called My Back: Writings by*

Radical Women of Color, ed. Cherríe Moraga and Gloria Anzaldúa, 35–40. New York: Kitchen Table / Women of Color Press, 1981.

Yang, Eun Sik. "Korean Women of America: From Subordination to Partnership, 1903–1930." *Amerasia* 11 (1984): 1–28.

Handouts:

Cheung, King-Kok, and Stanley Yogi. *Asian American Literature: An Annotated Bibliography.* New York: MLA, 1988.

Hsu, Kai-Yu, and Helen Palubinskas, eds. *Asian American Authors.* Boston: Houghton Mifflin, 1972.

Excerpts:

"Chinese-American Literature," 7–14.

"Japanese-American Literature," 90–93.

"Filipino-American Literature," 126–29.

Iwata, Edward. "Hot Properties: More Asian Americans Suddenly Are Winning Mainstream Literary Acclaim." *Los Angeles Times,* 11 September 1989, 5:1+.

———. "Word Warriors." *Los Angeles Times,* 24 June 1990, E:1+.

Klein, Dianne. "Monkeying with Myths: Maxine Hong Kinston Takes Glee from Mischief of Her First Novel." *Los Angeles Times,* 11 May 1989, 4:1+.

"The Ballad of Mulan." In *Chinese Poems,* ed. Arthur Waley, 113–18. London: George Allen, 1976.

Week 9: Feminist Theories / Faculty Presentations

Carby, Hazel. "On the Threshold of 'Woman's Era': Lynching, Empire, and Sexuality in Black Feminist Theory." *Critical Inquiry* 12 (1985): 262–77.

hooks, bell. "Black Women and Feminism." *Ain't I a Woman,* 159–96. Boston: South End Press, 1981.

———. "Racism and Feminism: The Issue of Accountability." *Ain't I a Woman,* 119–58. Boston: South End Press, 1981.

Smith, Valerie. "Gender and Afro-American Literary Theory and Criticism." In *Speaking of Gender,* ed. Elaine Showalter, 56–70. New York: Routledge, 1989.

Spivak, Gayatri Chakravorty. "Can the Subaltern Speak?" In *Marxism and the Interpretation of Culture,* ed. Cary Nelson and Lawrence Grossberg, 271–313. Urbana: University of Illinois Press, 1988.

Week 10: Ethnic Lesbian Literatures / Faculty Presentations

Guest Lecturer: Alycee Lane, Graduate Student, English, UCLA

Allen, Paula Gunn. "Lesbians in American Indian Cultures." *Conditions* 7

(1981): 67–87. Reprinted in *Women-Identified Women*, ed. Trudy Darby and Sandee Potter, 83–96. Palo Alto, Calif.: Mayfield, 1984.

Browning, Christine. "Changing Theories of Lesbianism: Challenging the Stereotypes." In *Women-Identified Women*, ed. Trudy Darby and Sandee Potter, 11–30. Palo Alto, Calif.: Mayfield, 1984.

Lane, Alycee. "Saving *Sula* from 'Lesbianism': Heterosexual Privileging in African American Feminist Criticism." Seminar on Studies in Criticism, UCLA, Spring 1989.

Shockley, Ann Allen. "The Black Lesbian in American Literature: An Overview." *Conditions* 5 (1979): 133–42.

Week 11: Women's World Ethnic Literatures

Guest Lecturer: Abena Busia, English, Rutgers University, and Postdoctoral Fellow in Afro-American Studies, UCLA

Busia, Abena P. B. "Words Whispered over Voids: A Context for Black Women's Rebellious Voices in the Novel of the African Diaspora." In *Black Feminist Criticism and Critical Theory*, vol. 3 of *Black American Literature*, ed. Joel Weixlmann and Houston A. Baker, Jr., 1–41. Greenwood, Fla. Penkevill, 1988.

————. "Towards a Global Herstory of Women's Images in Myth and Literature." In *Global Interdependence and New Jersey Education: Part I Case Studies for the Humanities*, ed. Patricia F. Morrissey, 147–72. Princeton: Woodrow Wilson National Fellowship Foundation, 1985.

SOCIOLOGY SEMINAR

Melvin L. Oliver Sociology and Center for Afro-American
Studies
University of California
Los Angeles, CA 90024

The faculty development seminar in sociology was one of the first two seminars created in spring 1989 under the Ford-sponsored initiative—the Ford Ethnic Women's Curriculum Transformation (FEW)—to integrate ethnic women into the undergraduate liberal arts curriculum at the University of California–Los Angeles (UCLA). A few faculty members within sociology had participated in a previous initiative, the Fund for the Improvement of Post-Secondary Education (FIPSE) Project, to transform two general education courses, Introduction to Sociology and The Sociology of Everyday Life. But sociology, both as a discipline and a department, presented a formidable challenge to any efforts at curriculum transformation for gender and ethnic inclusiveness. As a discipline, sociology is characterized by multiple paradigms whose adherents are frequently engaged in contentious debates over the "soul," or "center," of the discipline. Issues of gender and ethnicity are most often viewed as "marginal" to these paradigmatic debates, often reduced to one among many demographic variables in empirical studies or treated as epiphenomenon of larger structural forces or cultural processes.

Selected from nearly twenty applicants, the seminar members reflected the diversity of paradigms and subfields in the discipline. Participants brought to bear micro and macro perspectives as well as divergent theories and methods to such substantive interests as stratification, race and ethnic relations, organizational analysis, work and occupations, social psychology, and social demography. Each participant proposed one to two courses (a total of fourteen) for transformation, ranging from The Sociology of Everyday Life, Ethnic and Status Groups, and Collective Behavior, to Social Psychology, Urban Sociology, Sociology of Education, and Organizations in Society, or new courses on Gender and Work, Sociological Theories of Race, Class, and Gender, and Latinas in the United States.

Together with the facilitator and FEW coordinators, the eight faculty and seven graduate student participants represented three unique groups, each limited in its approach to combining sociology, ethnicity, and gender. Among the feminist scholars there was little depth or breadth of knowledge concerning the diversity of ethnic women's experiences; the ethnic (for the most part male) scholars were likewise unaware of and more critical of feminist and gender issues in sociology; the remaining members, while predisposed to new materials, were resistant to significant challenges to their preferred paradigms and existing bases of knowledge. The differential power between graduate students and faculty complicated an already complex intersection of agendas and needs because many graduate students represented the perspectives of women of color. The significant leadership provided by senior ethnic and female faculty members, including well-known sociologists Lucie Cheng, Vilma Ortiz, and Julia Wrigley, however, assisted the facilitator in shaping the seminar content and in negotiating often contentious, yet productive, debate and discussion.

As one of the first seminars in the UCLA FEW project, we began with limited time for faculty engagement in preplanning and extensive bibliographic research, both of which became hallmarks of all later seminars. Moreover, given sociology's multiparadigmatic structure and the project's emphasis on the experiences of women of color, we felt that the seminar should examine new sociological research on each of the four ethnic groups identified by the Ford Foundation: African American, Hispanic, American Indian, and Asian American. First, we focused on a critique of traditional sociological approaches. This discussion allowed for a self-reflexive critique of our existing courses and a reconceptualizing of the project of feminist theory and women of color within sociology as a professional discipline and as a classroom practice. Second, we introduced the participants to a wide range of available campus resource materials, including a wealth of available data and secondary studies housed in the libraries of UCLA's four ethnic studies centers. Throughout the seminar we also maintained a cumulative supplementary bibliography on the major topics within sociology as well as feminist and ethnic studies scholarship in related fields. Third, the seminar featured distinguished guest lecturers, who were invited to present their new research on women of color. We concluded with two sessions in which faculty presented revised syllabi and engaged in collective problem solving for the construction of new courses.

Barrie Thorne's early session presented an overview of how to incorporate new materials on ethnicity and gender into different sociology courses. More provocatively, by asking faculty to recall and retell their own experiences of marginalization within the classroom, she assisted seminar participants in repositioning themselves as "students" confronted with both new materials and professional stances of authority which often disempower ethnic students. Both the ethnic women faculty members and sociologists within the seminar as well as the guest speakers introduced new materials, and, more important, new perspectives that challenged conventional sociological paradigms of analysis. Marta Lopez Garza and Mary Romero, for example, opened up the complex relationships between migration, labor force participation, and domestic service. Belinda Tucker used national and Los Angeles–based demographic studies to challenge stereotypical notions of marriage formation among African Americans, pointing to the significance of low sex ratios and how these are related to changing educational and employment patterns for African American men and women. Dana Takagi reviewed the research on Asian American women, pioneered by Lucie Cheng and Evelyn Nakano

Glenn, and demonstrated the use of innovative methods in uncovering the lives of Japanese Americans during the internment through archival research on primary, but previously unstudied, documents.

The seminar brought into focus how ethnicity, class, and allegiance to discipline-based paradigms enable scholars to discount or explain away aspects of ethnic women's concrete contemporary and historical experiences that challenge and confront conventional sociological understandings. When the social and personal experiences of ethnic women which do not conform with, or do not validate, standard theories of social and cultural organization were presented in the seminar, several sociologists were quick to reinterpret, negate, or even disbelieve these experiences. For example, in the discussion on the relationship of employers to employees in the informal sector, new research that examined the experiences of Chicana domestics led to extended debate and discussion. This was an area that practically all seminar participants felt comfortable discussing because the issue was close to their personal lives. Los Angeles, the new American "Ellis Island," has integrated hundreds of thousands of immigrant Asian and undocumented Chicana / Latina domestics into the households of middle- and upper-middle-class Anglo families. The perception of "exploitation" in the experiences and voices of the Latina respondents which were reported by our outside research experts was responded to in a number of surprising ways. First, many participants discounted these experiences by reinterpreting them through larger theoretical arguments that "normalized" the exploitation as part of a "world systems" approach. Second, other participants emphasized the way in which "informal" wages (i.e., cast-off clothing, Christmas bonuses, and emergency help) mediated the relationship of exploitation by aiding in the transnational networks of support between kin in the United States and those left behind in poverty in war-torn nations. Third, participants were quick to point out that many domestics become "members of the family" and are aided in their adjustment to the United States through employers' "helping them to learn English" and/or assisting them in negotiating the bureaucracies and red tape of U.S. society (i.e., immigration).

These interpretations were not so much wrong as they were, in this context, attempts to deflect or discount the experiences of women of color. Even "Marxist"-oriented scholars were adamant in insisting that the contemporary "domestic" relation was not a classic case of exploitation. This startling assertion was made with the knowledge that the domestic employer-employee relationship is not formalized or protected by a contract and due process, wages are often below minimum wage, and the employees receive no health, vacation, disability, or retirement benefits. While willing to admit that this kind of relationship is one of exploitation for the U.S. working class, or workers and peasants in the Third World, the exploitative experiences of women whose work is central to the maintenance of a middle- and upper-middle-class life-style in the United States was dismissed or reconceptualized in a more benign way. Armed with the vocabulary and concepts of one of several paradigms in American sociology, class and ethnic biases were easily accommodated in seemingly "objective" explanations that did not give credence to, or acknowledge, the voices and experiences of women of color.

Despite and because of this tension throughout the seminar, we are convinced that the fruits of this daunting challenge were well worth the effort. Several indicators suggest this. First, this was one of the first times in the history of the sociology department in which ethnic and female faculty members were able to broach issues of ethnicity and gender in a serious and organized forum. The silence of many ethnic and female faculty was broken as a consequence of the seminar. This was not accomplished easily nor without trepidation. But the result has been the forging of some significant lines of communication in the department and growth in the courage and conviction of the younger ethnic and female faculty that their voices are important and need to be heard—and will be heard. Second, faculty and graduate students responded sincerely, and with considerable effort, to the transformation of existing courses and the construction of new ones. Faculty members transformed existing courses by proposing new readings or adding sections that reflected issues and concerns introduced in the seminar. Some were much braver, devising new courses that integrated perspectives introduced by the new scholarship on women of color. An example of this approach was a new course on Latinas in the United States developed by Professor Vilma Ortiz. What is exciting about this course is that it is now part of a three-quarter introduction to Chicano Studies which has just been inaugurated at UCLA. In addition, the graduate students were able to free themselves most from conventional thinking and produced several bibliographies and courses that portend a bright future for transforming the curriculum, such as Kristine Zentgraf's creative reformulation of the classic Social Problems class. Finally, despite the problems of being one of the first seminars to be organized and the unique character of sociology, sociologists in the department seem genuinely excited about the prospect of curriculum integration in reference to ethnic women. Many sociologists, several who had been members of this seminar, applied to enroll in the interdisciplinary seminar on curriculum integration. And because of a perceived need, rooted in part in this experience, the department is now poised to hire a woman of color with expertise in precisely this area.

Syllabus

Weeks 1–2: Moving Our Minds: Taking Stock in Our Thinking about Women of Color

Andersen, Margaret L. 1988. "Moving Our Minds: Studying Women of Color and Reconstructing Sociology." *Teaching Sociology* 16:123–32.

Baca Zinn, Maxine, Lynn Weber Cannon, Elizabeth Higginbotham, and Bonnie Thornton Dill. 1986. "The Costs of Exclusionary Practices in Women's Studies." *Signs: Journal of Women in Culture and Society* 12:290–303.

Collins, Patricia Hill, and Margaret L. Andersen, eds. 1987. *An Inclusive Curriculum: Race, Class and Gender in Sociological Instruction*. Washington, D.C.: American Sociological Association.

Committee on the Status of Women in Sociology. 1985–86. "The Treatment of Gender in Research." Washington, D.C.: American Sociological Association.

Course Critique: Sociology 3: Sociology of Everyday Life. Robert Emerson. Handout.

Rothenberg, Paula. "Integrating the Study of Race, Gender, and Class: Some Preliminary Observations." *Feminist Teacher* 3:37–42.

Week 3: The Relationship of Feminist Theory to Women of Color

hooks, bell. 1989. "Black Women: Shaping Feminist Theory," 1–15; "Changing Perspectives on Power," 83–93; "Men: Comrades in Struggle," 67–81; "Re-Thinking the Nature of Work," 95–105; "Sisterhood: Political Solidarity between Women"—all in *Feminist Theory: From Margin to Center*. Boston: South End Press.

Stacey, Judith, and Barrie Thorne. 1985. "The Missing Feminist Revolution in Sociology." *Social Problems*. 32:301–16.

Week 4: The Pedagogy of the Women's Studies Classroom

Guest Speaker: Barrie Thorne, Sociology, University of Southern California–Los Angeles

Klein, Renate D. 1987. "The Dynamics of the Women's Studies Classroom: A Review Essay of the Teaching Practice of Women's Studies in Higher Education." *Women's Studies International Forum* 10:187–206.

McIntosh, Peggy. 1987. "Understanding Correspondences between White Privilege and Male Privilege through Women's Studies Work." Paper presented at the National Women's Studies Association annual meeting.

Thorne, Barrie. 1989. "Rethinking the Ways We Teach," in *Educating the Majority*, ed. Carol Pearson, Donna Shavlik, and Judith Touchton, 311–25. New York: Macmillan.

———. "A Very Selective Bibliography and Set of Suggestions." From UCLA Sociology Department's Curriculum Integration Workshop for Everyday Life, 3 February 1989.

Week 5: Resources on Women of Color at UCLA

Guest Speakers: Richard Chabran, Librarian, Chicano Studies Research Center, UCLA; Lucie Cheng, Sociology, UCLA; O. Funmilayo Makarah, Graduate Student, School of Theater, Film, and Television, UCLA; and Oscar Sims, Afro-American Collection Librarian, University Research Library, UCLA

Hirschfelder, Arlene B., Mary Gloyne Byler, and Michael A. Dorris. 1983. "Social Organization." *Guide to Research on North American Indians*, 222–25. Chicago: American Library Association.

Salabiye, Velma. 1980. "American Indian Library Resources at UCLA." Los Angeles: UCLA Institute of American Cultures.

Handouts:

"American Indians: A Pathfinder—Guide to Resources at the American Studies Center Library, UCLA." Native American Bibliography from the Library of Congress.

Chabran, Richard. "Selected Reference Sources in Chicana Studies." Prepared for the Women. Culture, Conflict, and Consensus Conference, UCLA, 21 February 1986.

Garol, Miki, and Oscar Sims. "Afro-Americana: Selected Resources Available in the University Research Library, UCLA." 25 February 1984.

Makarah, O. Funmilayo, Norma Rice, and Karen Rowe, eds. 1989. "Films and Videos about Ethnic Women." Los Angeles: Ford Ethnic Women's Project / UCLA Center for the Study of Women.

Salabiye, Velma. "Publications Available from the American Indian Center at UCLA."

"Women's Studies, Chicano Studies, Black Studies, Asian American Studies and Women's History." University of California–Irvine, library reference guides.

Week 6: Pedagogical Issues on Teaching Gender and Ethnicity

Carroll, Constance M. 1983. "Three's a Crowd: The Dilemma of the Black Woman in Higher Education." In *All the Women Are White, All the Blacks Are Men, but Some of Us Are Brave: Black Women's Studies*, ed. Gloria

Hull, Barbara Smith, and Patricia Bell Scott, 115–28. Old Westbury, N.Y.: The Feminist Press.

Collins, Patricia Hill. 1986. "Learning from the Outsider Within: The Sociological Significance of Black Feminist Social Thought." *Social Problems* 33:814–32.

Crenshaw, Kimberle Williams. "Forward: Toward a Race-Conscious Pedagogy in Legal Education." *National Black Law Journal* 11:1–14.

Handouts:

Timberlake, Andrea, Lynn W. Cannon, Rebecca F. Guy, and Elizabeth Higginbotham, eds. 1988. Excerpts from *Selected Bibliography of Social Science Readings on Women of Color.* Memphis: Center for Research of Women at Memphis State University.

"Women in Latin American: A Research Guide." Compiled by Joan Ariel, Women's Studies Librarian, University of California–Irvine.

Week 7: Sociology of La Chicana

Guest Speakers: Marta López-Garza, Postdoctoral Fellow, Chicano Studies Research Center, UCLA; and Mary Romero, President's Fellow and Visiting Scholar, University of California—Berkeley

Baca Zinn, Maxine. 1982. "Mexican-American Women in the Social Sciences." *Signs: Journal of Women in Culture and Society* 8:259–72.

López-Garza, Marta. 1988. "Migration and Labor Force Participation among Undocumented Female Immigrants from Mexico and Central America." In *Defense of the Alien: Volume X Proceedings of the 1987 Annual National Legal Conference on Immigration and Refugee Policy,* ed. Lydio F. Tomasi, 157–70. Washington, D.C.: Center for Migration Studies.

Romero, Mary. 1987. "Domestic Service in the Transition from Rural to Urban Life: The Case of La Chicana." *Women's Studies* 13:199–222.

———. 1988a. "Chicanas Modernize Domestic Service." *Qualitative Sociology* 11:319–34.

———. 1988b. "Sisterhood and Domestic Service: Race, Class and Gender in the Mistress-Maid Relationship." *Humanity and Society* 12:318–46.

Handouts:

Romero, Mary, and the National Association for Chicano Studies, eds. 1988. *Syllabi and Instructional Materials for Chicano Studies in Sociology.* Washington, D.C.: Teaching Resources Center.

Week 8: Sociology of African American Women

Guest Speaker: M. Belinda Tucker, Assistant Director, Center for Afro-American Studies, UCLA

Baca Zinn, Maxine. 1987. "Transforming the Sociology of the Family: New Directions for Teaching and Texts." Paper presented at the Third Workshop on Women in the Curriculum. Center for Research on Women, Memphis State University.

Dill, Bonnie Thornton. 1986. "Our Mothers' Grief: Racial Ethnic Women and the Maintenance of Families." Research Paper no. 4. Center for Research on Women, Memphis State University.

Ehrenreich, Barbara. 1986. "Two, Three, Many Husbands." *Mother Jones* 11:8+.

Ferber, Marianne A., and Helen M. Berg. 1987. "Labor Force Participation of Women and the Sex Ratio: A Cross-Country Analysis." Paper presented at the Annual American Economics Association Convention.

"Paradigms and Prejudice." 1983. *Quarterly Newsletter of the Laboratory of Comparative Human Cognition* 5:87–92.

Rollins, Judith. 1985a. "The Women." *Between Women: Domestics and Their Employers,* 91–152. Philadelphia: Temple University Press.

———. 1985b. "Deference and Materialism." *Between Women: Domestics and Their Employers,* 153–206. Philadelphia: Temple University Press.

———. 1985c. "Invisibility, Consciousness of the Other, *Ressentiment."* *Between Women: Domestics and Their Employers,* 207–32. Philadelphia: Temple University Press.

Schoen, Robert, and James R. Kluegel. 1988. "The Widening Gap in Black and White Marriage Rates: The Impact of Population Composition and Differential Marriage Propensities." *American Sociological Review* 53:895–907.

Tucker, M. Belinda, and Robert Joseph Taylor. 1989. "Demographic Correlates of Relationship Status among Black Americans." *Journal of Marriage and the Family* 51:655–65.

Week 9: Sociology of Asian American Women

Guest Speaker: Dana Takagi, Sociology, University of California–Santa Cruz

Cheng, Lucie. 1984. "Free, Indentured, Enslaved: Chinese Prostitutes in Nineteenth-Century America." In *Labor Immigration under Capitalism: Asian Workers in the United States before World War II,* ed. Lucie Cheng and Edna Bonacich, 402–34. Berkeley: University of California Press.

Glenn, Evelyn Nakano. 1980. "The Dialectics of Wage Work: Japanese-

American Women and Domestic Service, 1905–1940." *Feminist Studies* 6:432–71.

————. 1981. "Occupational Ghettoization: Japanese-American Women and Domestic Service, 1905–1970." *Ethnicity* 8:352–86.

Handouts:

Takagi, Dana. "Sociology 1: Introduction to Sociology." Syllabus and bibliography.

————. "Sociology 128C: Introduction to Social History of Asian Americans."

————. "Sociology 171M." Exercises and mid-term examination.

Weeks 10–11: Participants' Presentations

"Sociology of Everyday Life."
"Social Psychology: Sociological Approach."
"Color, Ethnicity, and Gender: Clarifying the Concepts."
"Gender and Work."
"Sociology of Education."
"Ethnic and Status Groups"; "Organizations and Society."
"A Bibliography of Black Feminist Thought and Theory."
Winifred Nombulelo-Ndulo, "Annotated Bibliography on Single Parents in the United States."
"Chicanas in the Labor Force."
"Ethnicity and Status Groups."
"Social Problems."

Handouts:

Cheung, King-Kok. 1989. Contents for "Reader on Asian American Women" used in Asian-American Studies 105. Asian American Studies Program, UCLA.

"Bibliography on Sociological Studies of Ethnic Women." 1989. Los Angeles: Ford Ethnic Women's Project, UCLA Center for the Study of Women.

PSYCHOLOGY AND COGNATE FIELDS

Sandra Graham Education
Nancy Henley Psychology and Women's Studies
University of California
Los Angeles, CA 90024

Psychology at UCLA, probably like many other departments, was both a wonderful and a terrible place to have a faculty seminar on curricular integration. The department, as one of the largest at the university, had already taken steps toward a more integrated curriculum. An earlier project, funded by the Fund for Post-Secondary Education, had focused on bringing diversity to selected general education courses from six different departments. Introductory Psychology was one of the selected courses. Under this project, files of psychological articles on women and gender and issues related to people of color were amassed, and summaries of literature on selected topics were prepared to serve as aids to lecture preparation. In addition, Elizabeth Bjork, with graduate assistance, had revised the lab manual for the Research Methods Course (required for the major and minor in psychology) to incorporate assignments involving gender and ethnicity issues. The Psychology Department had also been successful in attracting administrative funds for active recruitment of graduate students of color.

Besides this wealth of printed resources and existing interest, we had excellent people to turn to at the university, well known for their work on the psychology of different ethnic groups or of women and gender, including some who combined those interests, such as Vickie Mays, Belinda Tucker, and Gail Wyatt, all respected scholars in the area of psychology of African-American women. Locally, some members of the department were part of a grass roots, issue-oriented, and activist group made up of American Psychological Association (APA) members of the divisions on social issues and on women. Informally, a handful of faculty and graduate students interested in gender and women's issues had been meeting once a month, to discuss readings and research presentations.

We had a richly diverse student body, with 47 percent of undergraduate psychology majors and 26 percent of psychology graduate students claiming Asian/Pacific, Latina/o, African American, Native American, or other non-Anglo origin. And finally, psychology as a discipline, especially as evidenced by the APA and its divisions, showed growing interest in ethnic and gender issues and had been developing excellent resource materials on issues concerning women and gender and people of color. Surely, we were ready to get serious about a psychology that includes women of color.

On the other hand, this increasing attention to diversity seemed to have made little impact on the field of psychology, if one looked at the discipline's journals or asked students what they learned about it in their classes. Although we knew some faculty members who were clearly committed to expanding the curriculum, there were other signs pointing to less than enthusiastic interest in enlarging the scope of psychology. No interest was voiced at faculty meetings for revising the curriculum to recognize ethnic and gender issues, and no one (not even the coordinators) knew about the materials collected in the earlier project, as the faculty had never been notified of their existence. Additionally, the Psychology Department, alone among the twenty-one departments involved in the FEW project, refused to give release time for its faculty (other than a co-coordinator) to participate in the course.

Thus, with both enthusiasm and trepidation, the Seminar on Psychology and Cognate Fields (Education, Communication Studies) opened in the fall quarter of 1989, with twelve faculty participants (eight women and four men) and seven graduate students (six women, one man). The areas of psychology represented were social, clinical, developmental, personality, and cognitive.

Organization of the Seminar

The rationale for the organization of the seminar was twofold. First, given the nature of psychology as an academic discipline, it was felt that the course should have a strong empirical focus. That is, we believed that psychologists committed to curricular revision would benefit most from a course that enhanced their general knowledge about how women of color have been studied in psychological research and what, in fact, the data reveal about the psychology of ethnicity and gender. We reasoned further that it was important to have this solid empirical base as a background for tackling some of the larger theoretical issues about the role of gender, race, and ethnicity in psychological theory and research.

Given, then, an empirical focus, the seminar was next organized around the study of women in four ethnic groups: African American, Latina, Native American, and Asian/Pacific. At least one seminar meeting was devoted to each ethnic group, and scholars in these fields were recruited to lead individual sessions. All of the scholars, members of the ethnic group under study, were female psychologists, each with her own active research program. Each was charged with the task of providing an overview of her field as well as informing participants about her particular research activities. We preferred to focus on specific ethnic groups rather than, for example, a topic-focused approach, given the great disparity in the amount and quality of the research on some of these groups.

Half of the group meetings were devoted to research on women of color, as outlined above. The remaining sessions were designed to facilitate discussion of general issues regarding race, ethnicity, and gender in psychological research, pedagogical concerns, and curricular resources available throughout the UCLA campus. We allocated the last two seminar meetings for presentations by participants of their specific plans for either revising existing courses or developing new courses that incorporate knowledge and research on women of color.

Strengths and Limitations of the Seminar

The focus in the Psychology Seminar on empirical research about specific ethnic groups had both strengths and weaknesses. On the positive side participants developed greater sensitivity to the complexities underlying the study of women of color, including the need to employ less traditional research methodologies and more critical thinking about issues of difference and deficit. As participants, we also became acutely aware of some of the barriers encountered by women of color scholars in their efforts to forge inroads into mainstream psychology against a backdrop of growing marginalization and exclusion from the production of psychological knowledge.

On the other hand, focusing on the acquisition of knowledge about specific ethnic groups in some respects diverted our attention away from discussion of basic issues about gender and ethnicity in psychology. Within the constraints of an eleven-week seminar we had insufficient time, for example, to consider more general feminist and ethnic critiques of traditional theories and methods in psychology or to evaluate how the study of gender and ethnicity can shed light on some of the recurrent themes in psychology, such as the biological versus environmental determinants of human behavior ("nature vs. nurture") or the existence of so-called universal principles of behavior. As organized here, the seminar could easily be extended by two or three weeks to allow time to take up these issues in greater depth.

Looking Back–Looking Forward

The FEW seminar had many beneficial effects, including some not anticipated. Faculty participants have incorporated the planned changes into their courses, and at least one new course proposal developed in the seminar is under formal review.

Not only did we prepare and distribute information about the collection of diversity files to all faculty and graduate students, but we arranged to present the information briefly to the annual teaching assistant (TA) orientation session; some weeks later the FEW project director was invited to make a longer presentation in the TA training course to talk about the FEW resources, such as the bibliographic database, available to them. In the year following the seminar a Curricular and Research Diversity (CARD) study group formed and continued meeting monthly through the next summer. At the beginning of the second year following the seminar an initial mailing about the CARD group received interested responses from thirty-six faculty, postdoctoral scholars and graduate students. Eleven turned out, on somewhat short notice, for the first meeting of the year.

The seminar has influenced the department in more subtle ways, all of which cannot yet be known. As individuals serving on campuswide and departmental committees, we have found the seminar readings and discussions coming up from memory to inform our interaction and debate on diversity issues; we have found both our teaching and our research influenced by our participation in the seminar. We have supplied copies of the syllabus, bibliography, and individual readings to people around the country. We know that other seminar participants are doing similar things on an individual level: one, for example, used the seminar to broaden her knowledge of gender and ethnicity issues as a way to prepare for revising her introductory psychology text. Some of the graduate students in the seminar are nearing completion of their studies and are preparing to take academic jobs in which they too will expand the curriculum beyond their previous limits.

So, with all this activity, is the discipline, or the university, more genuinely diverse, less straitjacketed in its thinking, than before? Not this soon. It is discouraging to find little discernible effect outside a small circle and rising (and often subtle) resistance to diversification, despite our best efforts.

Syllabus

Week 1: Issues, Perspectives, Practices Involved in Transforming the Curriculum

Albert, R. D. (1988). The place of culture in teaching modern psychology. In P. Bronstein & K. Quina (Eds.), *Teaching a psychology of people: Resources for gender and sociocultural awareness* (pp. 12–18). Washington, DC: American Psychological Association.

Andersen, M. (1988). Moving our minds: Studying women of color and reconstructing sociology. *Teaching Sociology, 16,* 123–32.

Bronstein, P., & Quina, K. (1988). Perspectives on gender balance and cultural diversity in the teaching of psychology. In P. Bronstein & K. Quina (Eds.), *Teaching a psychology of people: Resources for gender and sociocultural awareness* (pp. 3–11). Washington, DC: American Psychological Association.

Crawford, M., & Marecek, J. (1989). Psychology reconstructs the female. *Psychology of Women Quarterly, 13,* 147–65.

Expression of ideas. *Publication manual of the American Psychological Association* (3d ed., pp. 43–49). Washington, DC: American Psychological Association.

Rothenberg, P. (1985). Teaching about racism and sexism: A case history. *Journal of Thought, 20,* 122–36.

Rothenberg, P. (1987). Integrating the study of race, gender and class: Some preliminary observations. *Feminist Teacher, 3,* 37–42.

Azuma, H. (1986). Why study child development in Japan? In H. Stevenson, H. Azuma, & K. Hakuta (Eds.), *Child development and education in Japan* (pp. 3–12). New York: W. H. Freeman.

Baumeister, R. F. (1988). Should we stop studying sex differences altogether? *American Psychologist, 43,* 1092–95.

Befu, H. (1986). The social and cultural background of child development in Japan and the United States. In H. Stevenson, H. Azuma, & K. Hakuta (Eds.), *Child development and education in Japan* (pp. 13–27). New York: W. H. Freeman.

Brabeck, M. M. (1989). Comment on Scarr. *American Psychologist, 44,* 847.

Dyal, J. (1984). Cross-cultural research with the locus of control construct. In H. Lefcourt (Ed.), *Research with the locus of control construct* (Vol. 3, pp. 209–306). Orlando, FL: Academic Press.

Eagly, A. H. (1987). Reporting sex differences. *American Psychologist, 42,* 756–57.

Gergen, M. (1989). Fair questions and honest answers: The futile search. *American Psychologist, 44,* 848–49.

Greenfield, P., & Childs, C. P. (1991). Developmental continuity in bio-cultural context. In R. Cohen & A. Siegel (Eds.), *Context and development* (pp. 135–60). Hillsdale, NJ: Erlbaum.

Ibrahim, F. A. (1989), Response to "psychology in the public forum" on socially sensitive research. *American Psychologist, 44,* 847–48.

McHugh, M. C., Koeske, R. D., & Frieze, I. H. (1986). Issues to consider in conducting non-sexist psychological research: A guide for researchers *American Psychologist, 41,* 879–90.

Plomin, R. (1989). Environment and genes: Determinants of behavior. *American Psychologist, 44,* 105–11.

Rothblum, E. D. (1988). More on reporting sex differences. *American Psychologist, 43,* 1095.

Rotheram, M. J., & Phinney, J. S., eds. (1987). Introduction: Definitions and perspectives in the study of children's ethnic socialization. In M. J. Rotheram & J. S. Phinney (Eds.), *Children's ethnic socialization: Pluralism and development* (pp. 10–28). Newbury Park, CA: Sage Press.

Scarr, S. (1988). Race and gender as psychological variables: Social and ethical issues. *American Psychologist, 43,* 56–59.

Scarr, S. (1989). Constructivism and socially sensitive research. *American Psychologist, 44,* 849.

Young, T. W., & Shorr, D. (1986). Factors affecting locus of control in school children. *Genetic, Social and General Psychology Monographs, 112,* 407–17.

Week 3: African-American Women

Guest Lecturer: Elsie Moore, Department of Psychology and Education, Arizona State University

Collins, P. H. (1980). A comparison of two works on black family life. *Signs: Journal of Women in Culture and Society, 14,* 875–84.

Grant, L. (1984). Black females' "place" in desegregated classrooms. *Sociology of Education, 57,* 98–111.

Hall, C.C.I., Evans, B. J., & Selice, S. (1989). Annotated references to journal articles on black females in the United States. In C.C.I. Hall, B. J. Evans, & S. Selice (Eds.), *Black females in the United States: A bibliography from 1967 to 1987* (pp. 1–84). Washington, DC: American Psychological Association.

Ladner, J. A., & Gourdine, R. M. (1984). Intergenerational teenage motherhood. *Sage: A Scholarly Journal on Black Women, 1,* 22–24.

Mays, V. M. (1985). The black American and psychotherapy: The dilemma. *Psychotherapy, 22,* 379–88.

Moore, E.G.J. (1987). CED/WST 591: The development of black women. Course taught in the fall of 1987 at Arizona State University.

Moore, E.G.J., & Hambright, J. E. (1989, Mar. 29). Sexual activity versus abstinence among adolescent girls: The significance of career aspirations and academic achievement. Presented at the American Educational Research Association meeting, San Francisco, CA.

Moore, E.G.J., & Maez, B. (1988). The development of black and Mexican American women: Counseling implications (pp. 3–11). Invited address, Arizona Counseling Association, Tempe, AZ.

Smith, E. (1982). The black female adolescent: A review of the educational, career, and psychological literature. *Psychology of Women Quarterly, 6,* 261–88.

Week 4: African-American Women

Guest Lecturers: M. Belinda Tucker, Acting Director, Center for Afro-American Studies, UCLA; and Gail E. Wyatt, Psychiatry and Biobehavioral Sciences, UCLA

Adams, K. A. (1983). Aspects of social context as determinants of black women's resistance to challenges. *Journal of Social Issues, 39,* 69–78.

Davis, K., & van den Oever, P. (1982). Demographic foundations of new sex roles. *Population and Development Review, 8,* 495–511.

Greene, B. A. (1986). When the therapist is white and the patient is black: Considerations for psychotherapy in the feminist heterosexual and lesbian communities. *Dynamics of Feminist Therapy, 5,* 41–65.

Lykes, M. B. (1983). Discrimination and coping in the lives of black women: Analyses of oral history data. *Journal of Social Issues, 39,* 79–100.

Mays, V. M., & Comas-Diaz, L. (1988). Feminist therapy with ethnic minority populations: A closer look at blacks and Hispanics. In M. A. Dutton-Douglas & L.E.A. Walker (Eds.), *Feminist psychotherapies: Integration of therapeutic and feminist systems* (pp. 228–51). Norwood, NJ: Ablex.

Murray, S. R. (1987). Psychological research methods: Women in the African diaspora. In R. Terborg-Penn, S. Harley, & A. Benton-Rushing (Eds.), *Women in Africa and the African diaspora* (pp. 79–95). Washington, DC: Howard University Press.

Smith, A., & Stewart, A. J. (1983). Approaches to studying racism and sexism in black women's lives. *Journal of Social Issues, 39,* 1–15.

Tucker, M. B., & Mitchell-Kernan, C. (1989). Psychological well-being and perceived marital opportunity. Presented at the American Psychological Association meeting, New Orleans, LA.

Tucker, M. B., & Taylor, R. J. (1989). Demographic correlates of relationship status among black Americans. *Journal of Marriage and the Family, 51,* 655–65.

Wyatt, G. E., & Peters, S. D. (1986a). Issues in the definition of child sexual abuse. *Child Abuse and Neglect: The International Journal, 10,* 231–40.

Wyatt, G. E., & Peters, S. D. (1986b). Methodological considerations in research on the prevalence of child sexual abuse. *Child Abuse and Neglect: The International Journal, 10,* 241–51.

Wyatt, G. E., Peters, S. D., & Guthrie, D. (1988). Kinsey revisited, part II: Comparisons of the sexual socialization and sexual behavior of black women over thirty-three years. *Archives of Sexual Behavior, 17,* 289–332.

Week 5: Resource Session: UCLA Resources on Women of Color Relevant for Psychology Courses and Research

Guest Lecturers: Marjorie Lee, Asian American Studies Reading Room Librarian; Angelina Veyna, Chicano Studies Research Center Librarian; Rita Tamayo, Chicano Studies Research Center Library Assistant; Joan Kaplowitz, Education and Psychology Librarian; and Camille Loya, Women's Studies Librarian

Brown, A., Goodwin, B. J., Hall, B.A., & Jackson-Lowe, H. A. (1985). A review of psychology of women textbooks: Focus on the Afro-American woman. *Psychology of Women Quarterly, 9,* 29–38.

Chabran, R. (Feb. 1986). Selected reference sources in Chicana studies. Presentation at Women: Culture, Conflict, and Consensus Conference, UCLA.

Christensen, L., Shult, L., & Wagner, C. (1987). Asian women in America, a bibliography. Madison: University of Wisconsin System Women's Studies Librarian's Office.

Friedman, M., Fujino, D., Hoisch, M. L., Wang, G., & Williams, C. (1989).

Packet of resources from the FIPSE Curriculum Integration Project and a practical guide for use. Available in the Psychology Department, UCLA.

Goral, M., & Sims, O. (1984). Afro-Americana: Selected resources available in the University Research Library, UCLA.

Henley, N. (1989). Some psychological resources on women of color. Prepared for the seminar in Psychology, UCLA Ford Ethnic Women's Curriculum Transformation Project.

Hirschfelder, A. B., Byler, M. G., & Dorris, M. A. (1983). Sample excerpt. Guide to research on North American Indians (pp. 222–26). Chicago: American Library Association.

McKenna, T., & Ortiz, F. I. (1988). Select bibliography on Hispanic women and education. In T. McKenna & F. I. Ortiz (Eds.), *The broken web: The educational experience of Hispanic American women* (pp. 221–54). Berkeley and Encino, CA: Tomás Rivera Center and Floricanto Press.

Russo, N. F., & Malovich, N. J. (1982). Assessing the introductory psychology course. In J. M. Gappa & J. Pearce (Eds.), *Sex and gender in the social sciences: Reassessing the introductory course* (pp. viii–xii, 1–83). Washington, DC: American Psychological Association.

Salabiye, V. (n.d.). Listing of publications available from the American Indian Studies Center, UCLA.

Schmitz, B. (1988–89). New curricular guides for women's studies. *NWSA Journal, 1,* 302–7.

Veyna, A. F. (1989). Mexican/Chicana/Latina women and psychology, a selected bibliography. Chicano Studies Research Center, UCLA.

Week 6: Native American Women

Guest Lecturer: Teresa LaFromboise, Education Department, Stanford University

Blackwood, E. (1984). Sexuality and gender in certain Native American tribes: The case of cross-gender females. *Signs: Journal of Women in Culture and Society, 10,* 27–42.

LaFromboise, T. D., Heyele, A. M., & Ozer, E. J. (1990). Changing and diverse roles of women in American Indian culture. *Sex Roles, 22,* 455–76.

Witt, S. H. (1976). Native women today: Sexism and the Indian women. In S. Cox (Ed.), *Female psychology: The emerging self* (pp. 249–59). New York: St. Martin's Press.

Week 7: Asian-Pacific-American Women

Guest Lecturer: Maria Root, Psychology Department, University of Hawaii

Chan, C. S. (1987a). Asian-American women: Psychological responses to sexual exploitation and cultural stereotypes. *Asian-American Psychological Association Journal, 12,* 11–15.

Chan, C. S. (1987b). Asian lesbians: Psychological issues in the 'coming-out' process. *Asian-American Psychological Association Journal, 12,* 16–18.

Chow, E. (1989). The feminist movement: Where are all the Asian American women? In Asian Women United of California (Eds.), *Making waves: An anthology of writings by and about Asian American women* (pp. 362–77). Boston: Beacon Press.

Gue, S. (1985). A cross-cultural study of the relation between degree of American acculturation and androgyny. *Asian-American Psychological Association Journal, 10,* 40–51.

Ho, C. (1990). An analysis of domestic violence in Asian American communities: A multi-cultural approach to counseling. In L. Bower & M. Root (Eds.), *Diversity and complexity in feminist therapy* [Special issue]. *Women and Therapy, 9,* 129–50.

Johnson, R. C., & Nagoshi, C. T. (1986). The adjustment of offspring of within-group and interracial/intercultural marriages: A comparison of personality factor scores. *Journal of Marriage and the Family, 48,* 279–84.

Luu, V. (1989). The hardships of escape for Vietnamese women. In Asian Women United of California (Eds.), *Making waves: An anthology of writings by and about Asian American women* (pp. 60–72). Boston: Beacon Press.

Mason, S. (1982). Family structure and acculturation in the Chinese community in Minnesota. In Nobuya Tsuchida (Ed.), *Asian and Pacific American experience: A women's perspective* (pp. 160–71). Minneapolis: Asian/Pacific American Learning Resource Center and General College, University of Minnesota.

Mollica, R. (1988). The trauma story: Psychiatric care of refugee survivors of violence and torture. In F. M. Ochberg (Ed.), *Post-traumatic therapy and victims of violence* (pp. 295–314). New York: Brunner/Mazel.

Root, M. (1985). Guidelines for facilitating therapy with Asian American clients. *Psychotherapy, 22,* 349–56.

Root, M. (1989a). Asian and Pacific American Women seminar syllabus. Prepared for the Ford Ethnic Women's Curriculum Transformation Project Seminar on Psychology and Cognate Fields, UCLA.

Root, M. (1989b). Asian and Pacific American women's bibliography. Prepared for the Ford Ethnic Women's Curriculum Transformation Project Seminar in Psychology and Cognate Fields, UCLA.

Root, M. (1989c). Integrating and representing Asian and Pacific American women into mainstream reading, research, and teaching of psychology. Prepared for the Ford Ethnic Women's Curriculum Transformation Project Seminar in Psychology and Cognate Fields, UCLA.

Suzuki, B. (1977). Education and the socialization of Asian-Americans: A revisionist analysis of the "model minority" thesis. *Amerasia, 4:2,* 23–51.

Tajima, R. (1989). Lotus blossoms don't bleed: Images of Asian women. In Asian Women United of California (Eds.), *Making waves: An anthology of writings by and about Asian American women* (pp. 308–17). Boston: Beacon Press.

True, H. R. (1981). The profile of Asian American women. In S. Cox (Ed.), *Female psychology: The emerging self* (pp. 124–35). New York: St. Martin's Press.

True, H. R. (1987). Therapeutic issues with Asian American women. *Asian-American Psychological Association Journal, 12*, 52–62.

True, H. R. (1990). Psychotherapeutic issues with Asian American women. *Sex Roles, 22*, 477–86.

Villapando, V. (1989). The business of selling mail-order brides. In Asian Women United of California (Eds.), *Making waves: An anthology of writings by and about Asian American women* (pp. 318–26). Boston: Beacon Press.

Woo, D. (1989). The gap between striving and achieving: The case of Asian American women. In Asian Women United of California (Eds.), *Making waves: An anthology of writings by and about Asian American women* (pp. 185–94). Boston: Beacon Press.

Week 8: Chicana/Latina/Hispanic Women

Guest Lecturer: Aida Hurtado, Psychology Department, University of California–Santa Cruz

Amaro, H., & Russo, N. (1987). Hispanic women and mental health: An overview of contemporary issues in research and practice. *Psychology of Women Quarterly, 11*, 393–407.

Amaro, H., Russo, N., & Pares-Avila, J. A. (1987). Contemporary research on Hispanic women: A selected bibliography of the social science literature. *Psychology of Women Quarterly, 11*, 523–32.

de la Cancela, Victor. (1989). Psychotherapy with a chronically mentally ill Puerto Rican male: An emergent perspective. Presented at the American Psychological Association meeting, New Orleans, LA.

Espin, O. M. (1987). Issues of identity in the psychology of Latina lesbians. In Boston Lesbian Psychologies Collective (Eds.), *Lesbian psychologies: Explorations and challenges* (pp. 35–55). Urbana: University of Illinois Press.

Hurtado, A. (1989a). Relating to privilege: Seduction and rejection in the subordination of white women and women of color. *Signs: Journal of Women in Culture and Society, 14*, 833–55.

Hurtado, A. (1989b). Sample bibliographies. Prepared for the Ford Ethnic Women's Curriculum Transformation Project Seminar in Psychology and Cognate Fields, UCLA.

Vasquez, M. (1984). Power and status of the Chicana: A social-psychological perspective. In J. Martínez, Jr., & R. H. Mendoza (Eds.), *Chicano psychology* (pp. 269–87). Orlando, FL: Academic Press.

Vasquez, M., & Gonzales, A. M. (1981). Sex roles among Chicanos: Stereotypes, challenges, and changes. In A. Barton, Jr. (Ed.), *Explorations in Chicano psychology* (pp. 50–70). New York: Praeger.

Vázquez-Nuttall, E., Romero-García, I., & De Leon, B. (1987). Sex roles and perceptions of femininity and masculinity of Hispanic women: A review of the literature. *Psychology of Women Quarterly, 11*, 409–25.

Week 9: Pedagogy

Guest Lecturer: Steven López, Psychology Department, UCLA

Allen, P. G. (1986). Selected bibliography from *The sacred hoop: Recovering the feminine in American Indian traditions* (pp. 287–93). Boston: Beacon Press.

Cheung, K-K. (1989). Asian American literature bibliography: A recommended short list. UCLA.

López, S. R. (1989a). Patient variable biases in clinical judgment: Conceptual overview and methodological considerations. *Psychological Bulletin, 106*, 184–203.

López, S. R. (1989b). Psychology 680: Minority mental health. Taught at the University of Southern California, Spring 1988.

McIntosh, P. (1987). Understanding correspondences between white privilege and male privilege through women's studies work. Presented at the National Women's Studies Association meeting, Spelman College, Atlanta, GA.

McKenna, T. (1990). Chicano literature. In A.L.B. Ruoff & J. W. Ward, Jr. (Eds.), *Redefining American Literary History* (363–72). New York: MLA.

Makarah, O. F., Rice, N. W., & Rowe, K. E. (1989). *Films and videos by and about American ethnic women.* Los Angeles: Center for the Study of Women and the Ford Ethnic Women's Curriculum Transformation Project.

Thorne, B. (1989). Rethinking the ways we teach. In C. Pearson, D. Shavlik, & J. Touchton (Eds.), *Educating the majority: Women challenge tradition in higher education* (pp. 311–25). New York: Macmillan.

Yarborough, R. (1989a). Landmarks in Afro-American literature. Unpublished bibliography. UCLA.

Yarborough, R. (1989b). Recommended books from or about the Harlem Renaissance and a chronology of the Harlem Renaissance. Unpublished bibliography. UCLA.

Yarborough, R. (1989c). Selected works of Afro-American fiction. Unpublished bibliography. UCLA.

Week 10: Presentations

HISTORY SEMINAR

Ruth Bloch History and Women's Studies
Valerie Matsumoto History and Asian American Studies
George Sánchez History and Chicano Studies
University of California
Los Angeles, CA 90024

In the winter quarter of 1990 thirteen faculty members of the UCLA History Department, along with five graduate students and the FEW project staff, engaged in an eleven-week seminar, that produced substantive changes in the history curriculum offered to both undergraduate and graduate student populations at UCLA. Despite the fact that this department emphasizes the quality of its teaching in general, and specifically its attention to issues of women and people of color, the faculty involved in the project saw this as a rare opportunity to discuss the area of teaching itself. In addition, this group benefited tremendously from knowledge generated from previous seminars regarding faculty expectations of the seminar setting and the particular dynamics involved in introducing new material.

The three coordinators of the seminar—Ruth Bloch, Valerie Matsumoto, and George Sánchez—decided to shift the seminar format from a group-centered approach (with specific weeks assigned to African-American women, Latinas, etc.) to one that was topical and linked to the individual interests of specific faculty members enrolled in the seminar. Each faculty participant was asked to organize a session by coming up with at least one or two possible articles to be included. The FEW staff and the seminar coordinators then worked with the faculty member to come up with additional readings for that session. The individual was also asked to lead the discussion during that week.

The first reason for doing this was that over half of the faculty participants regularly taught courses in either women's history or ethnic history, therefore bringing an unusual range of expertise to the intellectual content of the seminar. Despite this expertise, many faculty members who taught in these areas were still searching for methods to introduce materials by and about women of color to their respective courses. Second, the coordinators believed that making faculty participants at least partially responsible for organizing a week's readings and discussion would produce members more committed to the overall goals of the seminar itself. Finally, this structure moved away from a strict reliance on "experts" (usually untenured women of color) to organize each week's sessions, who would then be put in a position of convincing senior colleagues of the worthiness of the scholarship. Rather, agreement on the need for inclusion was taken as a given, and faculty members were each asked to think about how best to integrate materials on women of color into their presentations and, eventually, their courses.

Although all eighty members of the UCLA History Department were invited to apply, the group chosen was heavily weighted toward those faculty members who specifically taught U.S. history. Two faculty members in the seminar who taught outside the American field had specific teaching and research interests that coincided with materials focused on women of color. Seven of the eleven Americanists taught either women's history or some form of ethnic history, along with their other teaching duties. The remaining four faculty members were white males with specific interests in integrating materials on women of color into their courses in urban history, labor history, and twentieth-century U.S. history.

The first two weeks of the seminar were spent exploring the challenge that ethnic women's history poses for established perspectives in women's history courses and courses in ethnic history. These weeks served to introduce the issues that individuals teaching in these areas see as central concerns of inclusion. In the third week we moved to a focus on colonial American history in order to address issues of encounter, conquest, and colonialism—east and west. Historian Deena González of Pomona College helped us look at the expanding material on Native American and Mexican women which opens new perspectives and strategies for teaching a more inclusive colonial history course.

The next four sessions were organized by specific faculty members who regularly taught courses in topical areas stretching from the colonial period to the present. These courses in labor, family, immigration, and urban history mirror some of the most important scholarship produced to date by and about women of color. For example, invited guest speaker Brenda Stevenson, from the University of Texas–Austin (who would join the UCLA faculty the following fall), both reviewed the recent research debates on sex roles and gender conventions in the African American family and presented her own study of families living on small plantations as a counterexample to frequent misassumptions about the disintegrating black family as a result of slavery. Although each session tended to begin by focusing on work dealing with a specific ethnic group—such as Asian American women's labor, women's position and status in Mexican immigrant families, or debates about urban crime in relationship to African American families, unemployment, and poverty—an attempt was made to move the discussion in comparative directions.

The following three sessions were even more closely intertwined with specific faculty interests. Two faculty members led a session on women's leadership in history to focus on both their individual research dilemmas in writing biography and on integrating this sort of material in broader historical courses. In our return to teaching the general survey—this time in twentieth-century American history—we focused on how to integrate the substantial literature by women of color classified as historical fiction into our courses. Finally, our last content-based session combined the expertise of our faculty with our guest, Mills College art historian Moira Roth, to explore the portrayal of ethnic women in popular imagery and art, with particular attention to southwestern Chicana/o artists.

Our last meeting focused on reviewing the individual syllabi and bibliographies produced by faculty and graduate student participants. There was much fruitful and exciting exchange of ideas, which was a result of the ten weeks spent together in a generally mutually supportive environment of intellectual dialogue. In addition, we discussed new campuswide initiatives that may impact our efforts, such as a possible ethnic studies and gender studies requirement, along with curricular developments within our department, including the strengthening of the women's history offerings for graduate students.

The most significant discipline-based discussion during the course of the seminar focused on the importance of abandoning a strict chronological framework in one's courses if this inhibits the introduction of materials that are more topical in nature, as with much of the material produced by and about women of color. A course on the history of the family, for example, could be organized by topics, such as work, childhood, or kinship networks, rather than attempting to develop a chronological narrative that moves over time. This allows for multiple variants of the family to be introduced without relying on one "normal" family model for one's main narrative structure and without introducing materials on ethnic families as deviant or alternative models.

In conclusion, the seminar gave participants the opportunity to read materials well outside of their own specific fields, to talk about teaching in an environment that seldom allows for such discussion, and to get feedback on approaches to integrating new material and broadening existing courses. Most faculty participants used this opportunity to revise existing syllabi and to develop new lectures and readings for courses they teach regularly. For faculty members who teach in areas most closely related to those addressed in the seminar, the seminar provided the chance to consider comparative approaches and to explore the possibility of team teaching in the future. Although participants entered the history seminar with varying levels of expertise in working with materials by and about women of color, every member benefited from the seminar to some degree. While some simply added a new book or lecture to their existing course, others reorganized courses in their entirety or began plans for creating totally new courses for the history curriculum. For facilitators Valerie Matsumoto and George Sánchez the seminar set the stage and provided hands-on experience that enabled them to launch similar faculty development seminars in Asian American Studies on the Japanese internment and in Chicano/Chicana Studies, which undertook a full program reconceptualization. The seminar experience affirmed for both participating faculty and the department at large the importance of rethinking and restructuring more creatively inclusive courses.

Syllabus

Week 1: Women's History

Faculty: Valerie Matsumoto, Ruth Bloch, Ellen DuBois, and Regina Morantz-Sánchez, History, UCLA

Focus: How does the perspective of ethnic women's history challenge our view of women's history?

Andersen, Margaret L. "Moving Our Minds: Studying Women of Color and Reconstructing Sociology." *Teaching Sociology* 16 (April 1988): 123–32.

Gates, Henry Louis, Jr. "Whose Canon Is It, Anyway?" *New York Times Book Review*, 26 February 1989, 1.

Hall, Jacquelyn Dowd. "Partial Truths." *Signs: Journal of Women in Culture and Society* 14 (Summer 1989): 901–11.

Hewitt, Nancy. "Beyond the Search for Sisterhood: American Women's History in the 1980s." *History* 10 (October 1985): 299–321.

Rodríguez, Clara E. "On the Declining Interest in Race." *Women's Studies Quarterly*, nos. 3–4 (1988): 18–32.

Week 2: Ethnic History

Faculty: George Sánchez, Valerie Matsumoto, Robert Hill, and Melissa Meyer, History, UCLA

Focus: How does the perspective of ethnic women's history challenge our view of ethnic history?

Acuña, Rodolfo. "Dialog: Response to Cynthia Orozco." *La Red* 79 (April 1984): 13–15.

Almaguer, Tomas, and Alberto Camarillo. "Urban Chicano Workers in Historical Perspective: A Review of Recent Literature." *The State of Chicano Research on Family, Labor, and Migration*, 3–32. Stanford: Stanford Center for Chicano Research. 1983.

Brown, Elsa Barkley. "African-American Women's Quilting: A Framework for Conceptualizing and Teaching African-American Women's History." *Signs: Journal of Women in Culture and Society* 14 (Summer 1989): 921–29.

Collins, Patricia Hill. "The Social Construction of Black Feminist Thought." *Signs: Journal of Women in Culture and Society* 14 (Summer 1989): 745–73.

Orozco, Cynthia. "Chicana Labor History: A Critique of Male Consciousness in Historical Writing." *La Gente* 16 (November–December 1983): 11–12.

Handouts:
Mujeres Activas en Letras y Cambio Social (MALCS). "Chicanas, Mexicanas: A Selected Bibliography." *MALCS Newsletter* (Summer 1988): 7. The newsletter is published triyearly by the Center for the Research on Women at Memphis State University, Memphis, TN 38152.

Week 3: Colonial Society East and West

Faculty: Ruth Bloch and Melissa Meyer, History, UCLA

Focus: Colonialism through the eyes of Native American and Mexican women

Guest Speaker: Deena González, Assistant Professor, History Department, Pomona College

Etienne, Mona, and Eleanor Leacock. "Introduction." In *Women and Colonization: Anthropological Perspectives,* ed. Mona Etienne and Eleanor Leacock, 1–24. New York: Praeger, 1980.

Gutierrez, Ramón A. "Honor, Ideology, Marriage Negotiation, and Class-Gender Domination in New Mexico, 1690–1846." *Latin American Perspectives* 12 (Winter 1985): 81–104.

Larvin, Asunción. "Female, Feminine, and Feminist: Key Concepts in Understanding Women's History in Twentieth Century Latin America." Lecture delivered, 10 November 1988, to the Hispanic, Portuguese and Latin American Studies Department, University of Bristol. Photocopy.

Paz, Octavio. "The Sons of La Malinche." *The Labyrinth of Solitude: Life and Thought in Mexico,* 65–88. New York: Grove Press, 1961.

Rothenberg, Diane. "The Mothers of the Nation: Seneca Resistance to Quaker Intervention." In *Women and Colonization: Anthropological Perspectives,* ed. Mona Etienne and Eleanor Leacock, 63–87. New York: Praeger, 1980.

Van Kirk, Sylvia. "The Role of Native Women in the Creation of Fur Trade Society in Western Canada, 1670–1830." In *The Women's West,* ed. Susan Armitage and Elizabeth Jameson, 53–62. Norman: University of Oklahoma Press, 1987.

Welch, Deborah. "American Indian Women: Reaching beyond the Myth." In *New Directions in American Indian History,* ed. Colin G. Calloway, 31–48. Norman: University of Oklahoma Press, 1988.

Week 4: Labor

Faculty: Ellen DuBois, History, UCLA

Focus: Asian-American women's labor

Cheng, Lucie. "Free, Indentured, Enslaved: Chinese Prostitutes in Nineteenth-Century America." In *Labor Immigration under Capitalism: Asian Workers in the United States before World War II*, ed. Lucie Cheng and Edna Bonacich, 402–34. Berkeley: University of California Press, 1984.

Clark-Lewis, Elizabeth. " 'This Work Had an End': African American Domestic Workers in Washington, D.C., 1910–1940." In *"To Toil the Livelong Day": America's Women at Work, 1780–1980*, ed. Carol Groneman and Mary Beth Norton, 196–212. Ithaca: Cornell University Press, 1987.

Glenn, Evelyn Nakano. "The Dialectics of Wage Work: Japanese American Women and Domestic Service, 1905–1940." *Feminist Studies* 6 (Fall 1980): 432–71.

Kessler-Harris, Alice. "The Just Price, the Free Market, and the Value of Women." *Feminist Studies* 14 (Summer 1988): 235–50.

Mann, Susan A. "Slavery, Sharecropping, and Sexual Inequality." *Signs: Journal of Women in Culture and Society* 14 (Summer 1989): 744–98.

Zavella, Patricia. " 'Abnormal Intimacy': The Varying Work Networks of Chicana Cannery Workers." *Feminist Studies* 11 (Fall 1985): 541–57.

Handouts:

Root, Maria. "Asian and Pacific Women's Bibliography." 1–22. Prepared for the Ford Ethnic Women's Curriculum Transformation Project seminar in Psychology and Cognate Fields, UCLA, 1989.

————. Maps of the Pacific Islands. 1–4. Prepared for the Ford Ethnic Women's Curriculum Transformation Project seminar in Psychology and Cognate Fields, UCLA, 1989.

Week 5: Family

Faculty: Regina Morantz-Sánchez, History, UCLA

Focus: The debate of the black family: a feminist perspective

Guest Speaker: Brenda Stevenson, History, University of Texas–Austin

Baca Zinn, Maxine. "Family, Race and Poverty in the Eighties." *Signs: Journal of Women in Culture and Society* 14 (Summer 1989): 856–74.

Collins, Patricia Hill. "A Comparison of Two Works on Black Family Life." *Signs: Journal of Women in Culture and Society* 14 (Summer 1989): 875–84.

Fox-Genovese, Elizabeth. "Gender Conventions." *Black and White Women of the Old South: Within the Plantation Household*, 192–241. Chapel Hill: University of North Carolina Press, 1988.

Horton, James Oliver. "Gender Conventions among Antebellum Free Blacks." *Feminist Studies* 12 (Spring 1986): 51–76.

White, Deborah G. "Female Slaves: Sex Roles and Status in the Antebellum Plantation South." *Journal of Family History* 8 (Fall 1983): 248–61.

Handouts:
Brooks-Higginbotham, Evelyn. "History 610: Race, Gender, and Class in American Society." University of Maryland, College Park, MD, Fall 1988.
Harley, Sharon. "Afro-American Studies 428F: Women and Work Syllabus." University of Maryland, College Park, MD, Spring 1989.
Stevenson, Brenda. "Southern Women and the Family, 1650–1865." University of Texas–Austin. MS.

Week 6: Immigration/Culture/Law

Faculty: John Laslett and George Sánchez, History, UCLA

Focus: Patterns of ethnic immigration and relationship to gender, culture, and law

Chato, Genevieve, and Christine Conte. "The Legal Rights of American Indian Women." In *Western Women: Their Land, Their Lives,* ed. Lillian Schlissel, Vicki L. Ruiz, and Janice Monk, 229–46. Albuquerque: University of New Mexico Press, 1988.
di Leonardo, Micaela. "Women's Work, Work Culture, and Consciousness." *Feminist Studies* 11 (Fall 1985): 491–95.
Erickson, Charlotte. "The Safety Valve: Immigrants in Agriculture—Social Adjustment." *Invisible Immigrants: The Adaptation of English and Scottish Immigrants in Nineteenth Century America,* 64–78. Coral Gables, Fla: University of Miami Press, 1972.
———. "Tramping Artisans: Immigrants in Industry—Social Adjustment." *Invisible Immigrants: The Adaptation of English and Scottish Immigrants in Nineteenth Century America,* 225–62. Coral Gables, Fla: University of Miami Press, 1972.
González, Rosalinda M. "Chicanas and Mexican Immigrant Families, 1920–1940: Women's Subordination and Family Exploitation." In *Decades of Discontent: The Women's Movement, 1920–1940,* ed. Lois Scharf and Joan M. Jensen, 59–84. Westport, Conn.: Greenwood Press, 1983.
Mazumdar, Sucheta. "General Introduction: A Woman-Centered Perspective on Asian-American History." In *Making Waves: An Anthology of Writings by and about Asian American Women.* ed. Asian Women United of California, 1–22. Boston: Beacon Press, 1989.
Osumi, Megumi Dick. "Asians and California's Anti-Miscegenation Laws." In *Asian and Pacific American Experiences: Women's Perspectives,* ed. Nobuya Tsuchida, 1–37. Minneapolis: Asian/Pacific American Learning Resource Center and General College, University of Minnestota, 1982.

Sánchez, George. "Go After the Women: Americanization and the Mexican Immigrant Woman, 1915–1929." Working Paper Series no. 6. Stanford: Standford Center for Chicano Research, 1984.

Handouts:
Le May, Michael C. *From Open Door to Dutch Door: An Analysis of U.S. Immigration Policy since 1820.* New York: Praeger, 1987. Excerpts: Table 1.2: "Summary of U.S. Immigration Policy, 1783–1986," 17–18; Table 2.1: "The Origins of U.S. Immigration by Region, 1821–1880," 22; Table 3.1: "The Origins of U.S. Immigration by Region, 1820–1920," 40; Figure 1.2: "Trends in Immigration by Phases, 1920–1980," 8.

Week 7: Urban History

Faculty: Eric Monkkonen, History, UCLA

Focus: Class, poverty, and crime

Abelson, Elaine S. "The Invention of Kleptomania." *Signs: Journal of Women in Culture and Society* 15 (Autumn 1990): 123–43.

Blackwelder, Julia Kirk. "Crime: The Role of Women." *Women of the Depression: Caste and Culture in San Antonio, 1929–1939,* 152–67. College Station: Texas A & M University Press, 1984.

Gordon, Linda. "Family Violence, Feminism, and Social Control." *Feminist Studies* 12 (Fall 1986): 452–78.

Harley, Sharon. "For the Good of Family and Race: Gender, Work, and Domestic Roles in the Black Community, 1880–1930." *Signs: Journal of Women in Culture and Society* 15 (Winter 1990): 336–49.

Hinc, Darlene Clark. "Rape and the Inner Lives of Black Women in the Middle West: Preliminary Thoughts on the Culture of Dissemblance." *Signs: Journal of Women in Culture and Society* 14 (Summer 1989): 912–20.

Jones, Ann. "An Introduction: Women's Rights and Wrongs." *Women Who Kill,* 1–14. New York: Holt, Rinehart and Winston, 1980.

Lane, Roger. "The Price of Crime." *Roots of Violence in Black Philadelphia, 1860–1900,* 134–43. Cambridge: Harvard University Press, 1986.

———. "The Wages of Sin." *Roots of Violence in Black Philadelphia, 1860–1900,* 128–33. Cambridge: Harvard University Press, 1986.

Neckerman, Kathryn M., Robert Aponte, and William Julius Wilson. "Family Structure, Black Unemployment and Social Policy." In *The Politics of Social Policy in the United States,* ed. Margaret Weir, Ann S. Orloff, and Theda Skocpol, 391–419. Princeton: Princeton University Press, 1988.

Week 8: Ideology

Faculty: Robert Hill and Steven Zipperstein, History, UCLA

Focus: Women's leadership and the uses of biography

Carby, Hazel V. " 'Woman's Era': Rethinking Black Feminist Theory." *Reconstructing Womanhood: The Emergence of the Afro-American Woman Novelist,* 3–19. New York: Oxford University Press, 1987.

"A Conversation with Orlando Patterson." Interview in the *Harvard Gazette,* 5 January 1990, 5.

Denzer, LaRay. "The Influence of Pan-Africanism in the Career of Constance A. Cummings-John." In *Pan-African Biography,* ed. Robert A. Hill, 137–60. Los Angeles: African Studies Center, UCLA and Crossroads Press/ African Studies Association, 1987.

Drew, Allison. "Andrée Blouin and Pan-African Nationalism in Guinea and the Congo." In *Pan-African Biography,* ed. Robert A. Hill, 209–17. Los Angeles: African Studies Center, UCLA and Crossroads Press/African Studies Association, 1987.

Giddings, Paula. " 'To Sell My Life as Dearly as Possible': Ida B. Wells and the First Antilynching Campaign." *When and Where I Enter: The Impact of Black Women on Race and Sex in America.* 17–31. New York: Bantam Books, 1984.

Gornick, Vivian. *Fierce Attachments: A Memoir,* 3–27. New York: Simon and Schuster, 1987.

Hall, Jacquelyn Dowd. " 'The Mind That Burns in Each Body': Women, Rape, and Racial Violence." In *Powers of Desire: The Politics of Sexuality,* ed. Ann Snitow, Christine Stansell, and Sharon Thompson, 328–49. New York: Monthly Review Press, 1983.

Harley, Sharon, Rosalyn Terborg-Penn, and Andrea Benton Rushing, ed. *Women in Africa and the African Diaspora.* Washington, D.C.: Howard University Press, 1987.

Hill, Robert A. Foreword to *Pan-African Biography,* ed. Robert A. Hill, ix–x. Los Angeles: African Studies Center, UCLA and Crossroads Press/African Studies Association, 1987.

Hyman, Paula E. "Culture and Gender: Women in the Immigrant Jewish Community." In *The Legacy of Jewish Migration: 1881 and Its Impact,* ed. David Berger, 157–68. Brooklyn College Studies on Society in Change no. 24. New York: Brooklyn College Press, 1983.

Shepperson, George A. Introduction to *Pan-African Biography,* ed. Robert A. Hill, xi–xv. Los Angeles: African Studies Center, UCLA and Crossroads Press/African Studies Association, 1987.

Week 9: Twentieth-Century History

Faculty: Richard Weiss and Bruce Schulman, History, UCLA

Focus: How can we integrate writings by women of color into the general survey course?

Gillenkirk, Jeff. "Crossing Over." Review of *Migrant Souls* by Arturo Islas. *Nation,* 5 March 1990, 313–14.

Reed, Ishmael, Shawn Wong, Bob Callahan, and Andrew Hope. "Is Ethnicity Obsolete?" In *The Invention of Ethnicity,* ed. Werner Sollors, 226–35. New York: Oxford University Press, 1989.

Rodríguez, Richard. "An American Writer." In *The Invention of Ethnicity,* ed. Werner Sollors, 3–13. New York: Oxford University Press, 1989.

Rosaldo, Renato. "Others of Invention: Ethnicity and Its Discontents." Review of *Machines as the Measure of Men* by Michael Adas, *The Invention of Africa* by V. Y. Mudimbe, and *The Invention of Ethnicity* by Werner Sollors. *Voice Literary Supplement* (February 1990): 27–29.

Sollors, Werner. Introduction to *The Invention of Ethnicity,* ix–xx. New York: Oxford University Press, 1989.

Srole, Carole. *Intersections and Differences: Integration of Women into the United States Survey Course, Part 1.* Los Angeles: California State University, 1989: Photocopy.

Thorne, Barrie. "Rethinking the Ways We Teach." In *Educating the Majority: Women Challenge Tradition in Higher Education,* ed. Carol S. Pearson, Judith G. Touchton, and Donna L. Shavlik, 311–25. New York: Macmillan, 1989.

Choose one for discussion:

Jeanne Wakatsuki Houston and James Houston, *Farewell to Manzanar: A True Story of Japanese American Experience during and after the WWII Internment* (1973).

Beverly Hungry Wolf, *The Ways of My Grandmothers* (1980).

Maxine Hong Kingston, *The Woman Warrior: Memoirs of a Girlhood among Ghosts* (1975).

Toni Morrison, *Beloved* (1987).

Suggested Other Titles

Maya Angelou, *I Know Why the Caged Bird Sings* (1969).
  Gather Together in My Name (1974).
  All God's Children Need Traveling Shoes (1987).
  Singin', Swingin', and Gettin' Merry Like Christmas (1976).
  The Heart of a Woman (1981).
Louis Chu, *Eat a Bowl of Tea* (1961).

Michael Dorris, *A Yellow Raft in Blue Water* (1987).

Roberta Durán, Judith Ortiz Cofer, and Gustavo Pérez Firmat, *Triple Crown: Chicano, Puerto Rican and Cuban American Poetry* (1987).

Louise Erdrich, *Love Medicine* (1985).

    The Beet Queen (1986).

    Tracks (1988).

Janet C. Hale, *The Jailing of Cecelia Capture* (1985).

Le Ly Hayslip, *When Heaven and Earth Changed Places: A Vietnamese Woman's Journey from War to Peace* (1989).

Cynthia Kadohata, *The Floating World* (1989).

Nella Larsen, *Passing* (1929).

Mountain Wolf Woman, *Mountain Wolf Woman: Sister of Crashing Thunder; Autobiography of a Winnebago Indian* (1961).

Paule Marshall, *Praisesong for the Widow* (1983).

    Brown Girl, Brownstones (1959).

Terry McMillan, *Mama* (1986).

Louise Meriweather, *Daddy Was a Number Runner* (1986).

Valerie Miner, *All Good Women* (1987).

    Trespassing and Other Stories (1989).

Anne Moody, *Coming of Age in Mississippi* (1968).

Toni Morrison, *Sula* (1973).

    Beloved (1987).

    Song of Solomon (1977).

    Tar Baby (1981).

Bharati Mukherjee, *The Middle Man and Other Stories* (1988).

    Darkness (1985).

    The Tiger's Daughter (1987).

    Wife (1987).

    Jasmine (1989).

Gloria Naylor, *The Women of Brewster Place* (1982).

    Linden Hills (1985).

    Mama Day (1988).

Anne Petry, *The Street* (1946).

Etsu Inagaki Sugimoto, *A Daughter of the Samurai* (1932).

Sui Sin Far [Edith Maud Eaton], *Mrs. Spring Fragrance* (1912).

Amy Tan, *The Joy Luck Club* (1989).

Yoshiko Uchida, *Picture Bride: A Novel* (1987).

Lynda Van Devanter with Christopher Morgan. *Home before Morning: The Story of an Army Nurse in Vietnam* (1983).

Anzia Yezierska, *Bread Givers: A Struggle between a Father of the Old World and a Daughter of the New* (1925).

Alice Walker, *Meridian* (1976).

Sherley Anne Williams, *Dessa Rose* (1986).

Week 10: Arts and Imagery

Faculty: Deborah Silverman, History, UCLA

Focus: How have women of color been portrayed in American popular imagery?

Guest Speaker: Moira Roth, Trefethen Professor of Art History, Mills College

Mainardi, Patricia. "Quilts: The Great American Art." In *Feminism and Art History: Questioning the Litany*, ed. Norma Broude and Mary D. Garrard, 331–46. New York: Harper and Row, 1982.

Minh-ha, Trinh T. *Woman, Native, Other: Writing Postcoloniality and Feminism.* Bloomington: Indiana University Press, 1989.

Nochlin, Linda. "Why Have There Been No Great Women Artists?" In *Art and Sexual Politics: Women's Liberation, Women Artists, and Art History*, ed. Thomas B. Hess and Elizabeth C. Baker, 1–43. New York: Art News Series, Macmillan, 1973.

Roth, Moira. "Shifting the Mainstream: A Panel Discussion Addressing Multi-Cultural Identity in the Visual Arts." *Artweek* 20 (1989): 25.

———. "Teaching Modern Art History from a Feminist Perspective: Challenging Conventions, My Own and Others." *Women's Studies Quarterly* 15 (Spring–Summer 1987): 21–24.

Silverman, Debora. "China at Bloomingdale's and the Met: 1980–1981." *Selling Culture: Bloomingdale's, Diana Vreeland, and the New Aristocracy of Taste in Reagan's America,* 21–53. New York: Pantheon Books, 1986.

Handouts:
Roth, Moira. "Art History 192: Seminar on Sources and Connections: Contemporary Women Artists." Mills College, Spring 1989.

———. "Art History 192:001: Seminar on the New Woman in American Life and the Arts, 1893–1920s." Mills College, Fall 1989.

———. "Art History 137: Art of the Twentieth Century: Lecture Outline." Mills College, Fall 1989.

Week 11: Faculty Presentation of Revised and New Courses

INTERDISCIPLINARY SEMINAR

Charlotte Heth Ethnomusicology and American Indian Studies
Richard Yarborough English and Afro-American Studies
University of California
Los Angeles, CA 90024

Selected from two dozen applicants to reflect a balance of disciplines, ethnic groups, genders, ages, and ranks, the faculty members chosen to participate in this interdisciplinary seminar brought a wide range of scholarly perspectives and interests. As was the case in the other UCLA Ford Ethnic Women's Curriculum Transformation Project (FEW) seminars, each faculty member received either release time from teaching or a stipend to attend the meetings; the seven graduate students earned course credit. In addition each faculty member was required to produce a syllabus either for an existing course that she or he had redesigned or for an entirely new offering or, in the case of the graduate students, to develop a course or annotated bibliography.

Because this interdisciplinary seminar took place in spring 1990 after four others that were more narrowly discipline based, the facilitators were able to benefit considerably from the experience gained by project director Karen Rowe (English and Women's Studies) and the FEW project staff in setting up and conducting the course. The presence of the project director as a participant also insured a degree of continuity. In addition, the resources available from the FEW database provided bibliographic materials that aided significantly in the selection and development of readings, although the intent was to venture into new areas—including ethnomusicology, the history of science, and anthropology—in which interdisciplinary scholarship flourished and which had not been included in prior groups. Furthermore, a few of the faculty participants had also been members of the discipline-based seminars and thus were familiar and comfortable with the format. Repeat members came from the fields of comparative literature, women's studies, history, and psychology. All members were selected with an emphasis on their familiarity with and desire to extend interdisciplinary studies, so that each individual might bring to the seminar some fundamental understanding of common challenges facing scholars who seek to integrate ethnic and gender materials. across disciplinary boundaries.

Because of the interdisciplinary nature of the seminar, finding and selecting readings assumed paramount importance. In the two quarters preceding the seminar the facilitators, project director, student assistants, and staff met on a regular basis to review materials. In terms of actual workload, despite our rigorous searches and review process, each seminar member had a weekly reading assignment of approximately two hundred pages. Quite early we realized that we could not represent every ethnic group in every discipline, especially if we tried to incorporate a consistent focus on women at the same time. The literature just did not exist in all relevant areas, with, for instance, the history of science materials skewed noticeably toward recent feminist scholarship, while ethnomusicology had already developed methodologies that addressed issues of culture but often with only a newly emerging emphasis on women. Consequently, we varied our coverage. For example, in some weeks we focused on only two ethnic groups, incorporating information on women in each case. In week 9, which studied biculturalism in Asian American and Chicana literary texts, guest speaker Helena María Viramontes spoke eloquently about the dilemmas of assimilation and co-optation for the Chicana writer whose public acceptance generates soul-searching questions about language, voice, and audience.

The seminar met weekly for three hours with a final, longer gathering (combined with a potluck dinner) at which participants presented their revised and newly created syllabi. After the opening sessions, which focused on general background and pedagogical issues, the class meetings were organized according to discipline, sometimes pairing two fields (sociology and history or psychology and the history of science) in a single seminar, but focused on themes that fully engaged both. We also assigned responsibility for supervising individual sessions to appropriate members of the group, who were then free to contribute readings, bring guest speakers and films, or make their own presentations. The latter served primarily as points of departure for discussion of the readings and of the larger issues raised over the course of the seminar. The discipline-based readings were sometimes quite demanding; consequently, as occurs in virtually any teaching situation, not everyone completed the readings, and not everyone attended all of the meetings.

Aside from attention given to representing fairly the diversity of fields, however, the planners and facilitators designed a progression of topics which began with theoretical issues (displaced to week 3 because of travel conflicts) before launching into three topics grounded broadly in the disciplines of history, sociology, and geography. The intent was to establish the social constructs of cultures and, in particular, to examine how ethnicity and gender are integral to understanding immigration and colonization, particularly in early Spanish and Indian Los Angeles; the internal migrations and urbanization of America, here with an attendant focus on African American labor and family life; and, finally, women's work, with an inclusion of Asian American, Mexican, and African American case studies. The crux in the seminar became how to link issues that seemed defined by the quantitative methods used in the social sciences with the literary and broadly cultural-studies approaches that characterize the humanities. Hence, at the midpoint of the quarter the seminar focused on "ways of knowing," ranging from feminist theories rooted in philosophy to more concrete studies of gendered verbal and nonverbal communications that raised the issue of "difference," as defined in linguistic and epistomological terms.

In the final weeks of the seminar attention turned to the expressive arts, with topics ranging from oral tradition, talk stories, and ceremonial ritual in Native American tribes to the rise of gospel music in Los Angeles and Chicana and Asian American women's fiction and poetry. A return at the end to selected readings in pedagogy as well as theory, including Spelman's "Gender and Race: The Ampersand Problem in Feminist Thought," repositioned us back at the starting point, but with a more finely developed sense of the complexity of the lives of women of color.

The rather unique composition of this seminar presented us with a number of diverse challenges. On the one hand, each member of the group was forced to fill the roles of both "expert" and "novice" depending upon her or his familiarity with the particular set of disciplinary paradigms raised in any given week. It was especially useful that both those not schooled in a particular discipline had to learn new scholarly vocabularies and new sets of methodological assumptions and that the "experts" (a group that, at one point or another, included every member of the seminar) were required to demystify their disciplines for their classmates in order to share their knowledge and experience effectively. The challenge of learning the language of another discipline prompted some of the most intense self-scrutiny among scholars, who often felt themselves "de-authorized" and repositioned as students who must learn to cope with new realms of inquiry.

That pedagogy of dislocation also involved a secondary dislocation, since in many of the fields, including sociology and psychology, the study of ethnicity or gender (not to mention ethnic women) constituted a marginalized branch of research, still struggling to find a place in the methods and theories of the disciplinary mainstream. Furthermore, because teachers from different fields in many ways speak different "languages," communication was sometimes difficult. In particular, tension arose occasionally over the extent to which individual members of the seminar privileged either quantitative and qualitative approaches and over the priority participants gave to either gender or ethnicity as the more salient category of analysis. We attempted to address and resolve these tensions by discussing the conflicts directly as we worked toward a consensus on the validity granted various types of knowledge—and different ways of knowing.

The learning experience in this seminar also involved confronting the gaps and ruptures within disciplines, where the imbalances and imperfections in the state-of-the-art scholarship became all too apparent—yet all the more determinative of future research agendas that might draw more usefully on interdisciplinary models. In sociology and geography, for instance, we learned that women and ethnic groups were not, in every case, purposely neglected but, rather, that they often represented small and statistically unusable samples. The obvious conclusion was that sampling techniques needed to be revised to incorporate them in more significant numbers. In the history of science we learned that what is generally considered intellectual history encompasses primarily European and Asian thought, with little acknowledgment of the contributions of indigenous cultures from Africa and the Americas, partially because of the scarcity of written documents. At another point in the course we discussed how musical form can be taught using songs of American Indians, African Americans, and Europeans. In a similar fashion throughout the quarter information flowed from the seminar presenters to the group, conveying a clearer sense of methodological limitations and at the same time opening the doorway for more imaginative questions and new and different categories and approaches.

Some of the positive results of the seminar were direct, others indirect. First, the intellectual stimulation, the heightened sensitivity on the part of the participants to the crucial issues and approaches in interdisciplinary studies of race and gender, and the inevitable bonding among members of the group were all positive outcomes. A few of the new and revised course syllabi are being taught regularly with enthusiastic student response, and some participants have taken new approaches to their research as a result of the seminar. In addition, colleagues of the seminar members have solicited and used materials from this course in conducting courses of their own on gender and ethnicity. For example, one nonparticipating colleague taught the theory seminar in ethnomusicology on gender issues and incorporated many of our readings into his course. Another faculty member in this same department discovered, as a direct result of being invited to present a guest lecture to this seminar, that she could be focusing more directly on African American women in her own work. Subsequently, she convinced the editors of a reference guide to black music to add more entries on women.

These examples suggest two indirect but potent results of the FEW seminar. That is, not only has it already begun to affect how faculty participants teach their undergraduate courses in their particular disciplines, but it also informs both their own scholarship and also their graduate seminars. The long-term impact of this latter development cannot be overemphasized, for the current generation of graduate students will be playing key roles over the next decade in the ongoing effort to bring about the thorough revision of pedagogical practice with regard to the treatment of gender and ethnicity which this project has begun.

Syllabus

Week 1: General Background and Pedagogical Issues

Faculty: Charlotte Heth, Ethnomusicology and American Indian Studies; Richard Yarborough, English and Afro-American Studies; and Karen Rowe, English and Women's Studies, UCLA

Andersen, Margaret L. "Moving Our Minds: Studying Women of Color and Reconstructing Sociology." *Teaching Sociology* 16 (1988): 123–32.

Butler, Johnnella E. "Transforming the Curriculum: Teaching about Women of Color." In *Multicultural Education: Issues and Perceptions*, ed. James A. Banks and Cherry A. McGee Banks, 145–63. Boston: Allyn, 1989.

Chan, Sucheng. "On the Ethnic Studies Requirement, Part I: Pedagogical Implications." *Amerasia Journal* 15, no. 1 (1989): 267–80.

Mitchell, Jacqueline. "Transforming Community Practices into Pedagogical Strategies: Building a Classroom Community." Paper presented at the American Anthropological Association annual meeting, Washington, D.C., 1989.

Rothenberg, Paula. "Integrating the Study of Race, Gender, and Class: Some Preliminary Observations." *Feminist Teacher* 3, no. 3 (1987): 37–42.

Ruiz, Vicki L. "Teaching Chicano/American History: Goals and Methods." *History Teacher* 20 (1987): 167–77.

Week 2: Immigration and Colonization—The Los Angeles Experience: Asian and Chicano Women

Faculty: George Sánchez, History and Chicano Studies, UCLA

Lipsitz, George. "Cruising around the Historical Bloc: Postmodernism and Popular Music in East Los Angeles." *Time Passages: Collective Memory and American Pop Culture*, 133–60. Minneapolis: University of Minnesota Press, 1990.

Matsumoto, Valerie. "Nisei Women and Resettlement during World War II." In *Making Waves: An Anthology of Writings by and about Asian American Women*, ed. Asian Women United of California, 115–26. Boston: Beacon Press, 1989.

Mazumdar, Sucheta. "General Introduction: A Woman-Centered Perspective on Asian American History." In *Making Waves: An Anthology of Writings by and about Asian American Women*, ed. Asian Women United of California, 1–22. Boston: Beacon Press, 1989.

Reed, Ishmael, Shawn Wong, Bob Callahan, and Andrew Hope. "Is Ethnicity Obsolete?" In *The Invention of Ethnicity*, ed. Werner Sollors, 226–35. New York: Oxford University Press, 1989.

Rodríguez, Richard. "An American Writer." In *The Invention of Ethnicity*, ed. Werner Sollors, 3–13. New York: Oxford University Press, 1989.

Rosaldo, Renato. "Others of Invention: Ethnicity and Its Discontents." Review of *Machines as the Measure of Men* by Michael Adas, *The Invention of Africa* by V. Y. Mudimbe, and *The Invention of Ethnicity* by Werner Sollors. *Voice Literary Supplement* (1990): 27+.

Sánchez, George. " 'Go After the Women': Americanization and the Mexican

Immigrant Woman, 1915–1929." Working Paper Series no. 6. Stanford: Stanford Center for Chicano Research, 1984.

Soja, Edward W. "It All Comes Together in Los Angeles." *Postmodern Geographies: The Reassertion of Space in Critical Social Theory*, 190–221. London: Verso, 1989.

———. "Taking Los Angeles Apart: Towards a Postmodern Geography." *Postmodern Geographies: The Reassertion of Space in Critical Social Theory*, 222–48. London: Verso, 1989.

Sollors, Werner, ed. "Introduction: The Invention of Ethnicity." *The Invention of Ethnicity*, ix–xx. New York: Oxford University Press, 1989.

"Ramona." *Video Presentation*. Los Angeles History Project, KCET, 1989.

Handouts:

Iwata, Edward. "The West—A Literary State." *Los Angeles Times*, 1 April 1990, E1+.

Rich, Alan. "After Sixty-three Years, 'Ramona' Still Packs a Heady Emotional Punch." *Los Angeles Daily News*, 1 May 1990, 20.

Sánchez, George. "The Arts and Material Culture: Four Test Cases of Representation."

Wortham, Thomas. "English 254: California Bibliography."

Week 3: Theoretical Issues

Faculty: Richard Yarborough, English and Afro-American Studies, UCLA

Focus: The debates over curriculum diversity and pluralism

Hook, Sidney. "Culture Vultures: Civilization and Its Malcontents." *National Review*, 13 October 1989, 30–33.

Krupat, Arnold. "The Concept of the Canon." *The Voice in the Margin: Native American Literature and the Canon*, 22–56. Berkeley: University of California Press, 1989.

Radhakrishnan, R. "Culture as Common Ground: Ethnicity and Beyond." *MELUS* 14 (1987): 5–20.

Sacks, Karen B. "Toward a Unified Theory of Class, Race, and Gender." *American Ethnologist* 16 (1989): 534–50.

Short, Thomas. " 'Diversity' and 'Breaking the Disciplines': Two New Assaults on the Curriculum." *Academic Questions* 1 (1988): 6–29.

Sollors, Werner. "A Critique of Pure Pluralism." In *Reconstructing American Literary History*, ed. Sacvan Bercovitch, 250–79. Harvard English Studies no. 13. Cambridge: Harvard University Press, 1986.

Wald, Alan. "Theorizing Cultural Difference: A Critique of the 'Ethnicity School.' " *MELUS* 14 (1987): 21–33.

Yarborough, Richard. "Breaking the 'Codes of Americanness.' " Review of

The Invention of Ethnicity by Werner Sollors. *American Quarterly* 38 (1986): 860–65.

Week 4: Migration and Urbanization

Faculty: Kenneth Bailey, Sociology, and Kathryn Norberg, History and Women's Studies, UCLA

Collins, Patricia Hill. "A Comparison of Two Works on Black Family Life." *Signs: Journal of Women in Culture and Society* 14 (1989): 875–84.

Gresham, Jewell Handy. "White Patriarchal Supremacy: The Politics of Family in America." *Scapegoating the Black Family: Black Women Speak.* Special issue of the *Nation* 24–31 July 1989, 116–22.

Gresham, Jewell Handy, and Margaret B. Wilkerson. "Introduction: The Burden of History." *Scapegoating the Black Family: Black Women Speak.* Special issue of the *Nation* 24–31 July 1989, 115–16.

Harley, Sharon. "For the Good of Family and Race: Gender, Work, and Domestic Roles in the Black Community, 1880–1930." *Signs: Journal of Women in Culture and Society* 5 (1990): 336–49.

Jackson, Jacquelyne J. "Demographic Aspects of Minority Aging." *Minorities and Aging,* 16–43. Belmont: Wadsworth, 1980.

Jones, Jacqueline. "Between the Cotton Field and the Ghetto: The Urban South, 1880–1915." *Labor of Love, Labor of Sorrow: Black Women, Work, and the Family from Slavery to the Present,* 110–51. New York: Vintage, 1985.

———. " 'To Get Out of This Land of Sufrin': Black Women Migrants to the North, 1900–1930." *Labor of Love, Labor of Sorrow: Black Women, Work, and the Family from Slavery to the Present,* 152–95. New York: Vintage, 1985.

Perdue, Theda. "Cherokee Women and the Trail of Tears." *Journal of Women's History* 1 (1989): 14–30.

Terborg-Penn, Rosalyn. "Survival Strategies among African American Women Workers: A Continuing Process." In *Women, Work and Protest: A Century of U.S. Women's Labor History,* ed. Ruth Milkman, 139–55. Boston: Routledge and Kegan, 1985.

Welch, Deborah. "American Indian Women: Reaching beyond the Myth." In *New Directions in American Indian History,* ed. Colin G. Calloway, 31–48. Norman: University of Oklahoma Press, 1988.

Wilkerson, Margaret B., and Jewell Handy Gresham. "Sexual Politics of Welfare: The Racialization of Poverty." *Scapegoating the Black Family: Black Women Speak.* Special issue of the *Nation* 24–31 July 1989, 126–32.

Video Presentation: Bill Moyers. "*The Vanishing Family: Crisis in Black America.* Columbia Broadcasting System (CBS) Special Report, 1986. (Selections from video documentary.)

Week 5: Women's Work

Faculty: C. Cindy Fan, Geography, UCLA

History:

Clark-Lewis, Elizabeth. " 'This Work Had an End': African American Domestic Workers in Washington, D.C., 1910–1940." In *"To Toil the Livelong Day": America's Women at Work, 1780–1980*, ed. Carol Groneman and Mary Beth Norton, 196–212. Ithaca: Cornell University Press, 1987.

Pascoe, Peggy, *Relations of Rescue: The Search for Female Moral Authority in the American West, 1874–1939*. New York: Oxford University Press, 1990.

Ruiz, Vicki L. " 'And Miles to Go . . .': Mexican Women and Work, 1930–1985." In *Western Women, Their Land, Their Lives*, ed. Lillian Schlissel, Vicki Ruiz, and Janice Monk, 117–36. Albuquerque: University of New Mexico Press, 1989.

Geography:

Darden, Joe T. "Asians in Metropolitan Areas of Michigan: A Retest of the Social and Spatial Distance Hypothesis." *Amerasia* 12, no. 2 (1985–86): 67–77.

McHugh, Kevin E. "Hispanic Migration and Population Redistribution in the United States." *Professional Geographer* 41 (1989): 429–39.

McKee, Jesse O. "Humanity on the Move." In *Ethnicity in Contemporary America: A Geographical Appraisal*, ed. Jesse O. McKee, 1–30. Dubuque: Kendall/Hunt, 1985.

Mazey, Mary Ellen, and David R. Lee. "Bibliography." *Her Space, Her Place: A Geography of Women*, 75–83. Washington, D.C.: Association of American Geographers, 1983.

Noble, Allen G. "Rural Ethnic Islands." In *Ethnicity in Contemporary America: A Geographical Appraisal*, ed. Jesse O. McKee, 241–57. Dubuque: Kendall/Hunt, 1985.

Walker, Robert, and Michael Hannan. "Dynamic Settlement Processes: The Case of U.S. Immigration." *Professional Geographer* 41 (1989): 172–83.

Women and Geography Study Group of the IBG. "Bibliography." *Geography and Gender: An Introduction to Feminist Geography*, 147–55. London: Hutchinson and Explorations in Feminist Collective, 1984.

Zeigler, Donald J., and Stanley D. Brunn. "Urban Ethnic Islands." In *Ethnicity in Contemporary America: A Geographical Appraisal*, ed. Jesse O. McKee, 259–83. Dubuque: Kendall/Hunt, 1985.

Handout:

Fixcco, Donald L. "Bibliography." *History of Urban Indians*. MS., University of Wisconsin–Milwaukee.

Week 6: Ways of Knowing: Verbal and Nonverbal Communication

Faculty: Nancy Henley, Psychology and Women's Studies, and Norton Wise, History of Science, UCLA

Collins, Patricia Hill. "The Social Construction of Black Feminist Thought." *Signs: Journal of Women in Culture and Society* 14 (1989): 745–73.

Grant, Linda. "Black Females' 'Place' in Desegregated Classrooms." *Sociology of Education* 57 (1984): 98–111.

Haraway, Donna J. "In the Beginning Was the Word: The Genesis of Biological Theory." *Signs: Journal of Women in Culture and Society* 6 (1981): 469–81.

Hawkesworth, Mary E. "Knowers, Knowing, Known: Feminist Theory and Claims of Truth." *Signs: Journal of Women in Culture and Society* 14 (1989): 533–57.

———. "Reply to Hekman." *Signs: Journal of Women in Culture and Society* 15 (1990): 420–23.

———. "Reply to Shogan." *Signs: Journal of Women in Culture and Society* 15 (1990): 426–28.

Hekman, Susan. "Comment on Hawkeworth's 'Knowers, Knowing, Known: Feminist Theory and Claims of Truth.'" *Signs: Journal of Women in Culture and Society* 15 (1990): 417–19.

Henley, Nancy, and Cheris Kramarae. "Gender, Power and Miscommunication." In *"Miscommunication" and Problematic Talk*, ed. Nikolas Coupland, John Wiemann, and Howard Giles, 18–43. Newberry Park, Calif.: Sage, 1991.

Kochmann, Thomas. "Male and Female Interaction: The First Phase." *Black and Whites Styles in Conflict*, 74–88. Chicago: University of Chicago Press, 1981.

Medicine, Bea. "The Role of American Indian Women in Cultural Continuity and Transition." In *Woman and Language in Transition*, ed. Joyce Penfield, 159–66. Albany: SUNY Press, 1987.

Minh-ha, Trinh T. "Difference: 'A Special Third World Women Issue.'" *Woman, Native, Other: Writing Postcoloniality and Feminism*, 79–116. Bloomington: Indiana University Press, 1989.

Shogan, Debra. "Comment on Hawkesworth's 'Knowers, Knowing, Known: Feminist Theory and Claims of Trust.'" *Signs: Journal of Women in Culture and Society* 15 (1990): 424–25.

Stanback, Marsha Houston. "Language and Black Woman's Place: Evidence from the Black Middle Class." In *For Alma Mater*, ed. P. A. Treichler, C. Kramarae, and B. Stafford, 177–93. Urbana: University of Illinois Press, 1986.

Wetzel, Patricia J. "Are 'Powerless' Communication Strategies the Japanese Norm?" *Language in Society* 17 (1988): 555–64.

Zentella, Ana Celia. "Language and Female Identity in the Puerto Rican Community." In *Woman and Language in Transition*, ed. Joyce Penfield, 167–79. Albany: SUNY Press, 1987.

Week 7: Oral Tradition, Talk Stories

Faculty: Paul Kroskrity, Anthropology and American Indian Studies, UCLA

Allen, Paula Gunn. "Grandmother of the Sun: Ritual Gynocracy in Native America." *The Sacred Hoop: Recovering the Feminine in American Indian Traditions*, 13–29. Boston: Beacon Press, 1986.

————. "Introduction." *The Sacred Hoop: Recovering the Feminine in American Indian Traditions*, 1–7. Boston: Beacon Press, 1986.

————. "Kochinnenako in Academe: Three Approaches to Interpreting a Keres Indian Tale." *The Sacred Hoop: Recovering the Feminine in American Indian Traditions*, 222–44. Boston: Beacon Press, 1986.

————. "The Sacred Hoop: A Contemporary Perspective." In *Studies in American Literature: Critical Essays and Course Design*, ed. Paula Gunn Allen, 3–22. New York: MLA, 1983.

————. "Teaching American Indian Women's Literature." In *Studies in American Literature: Critical Essays and Course Design*, ed. Paula Gunn Allen, 134–44. New York: MLA, 1983.

Basso, Keith H. " 'Stalking with Stories': Names, Places and Moral Narratives among the Western Apache." *Test, Play and Story: The Construction and Reconstruction of Self and Society*, ed. Edward M. Bruner and Stuart Plattner, 19–55. Washington, D.C.: American Ethnological Society, 1984.

Bataille, Gretchen. "Transformation of Tradition: Autobiographical Works by American Indian Women." In *Studies in American Literature: Critical Essays and Course Design*, ed. Paula Gunn Allen, 85–99. New York: MLA, 1983.

Devens, Carol. "Separate Confrontations: Gender as a Factor in Indian Adaptation to European Colonization in New France." *American Quarterly* 38 (1986): 461–80.

Hymes, Dell. "The 'Wife' Who 'Goes Out' like a Man: Reinterpretation of a Clackamas Chinook Myth." *"In vain I tried to tell you": Essays in Native American Ethnopoetics*, 274–308. Philadelphia: University of Pennsylvania Press, 1981.

Mascia-Lees, Frances E., Patricia Sharpe, and Colleen B. Cohen. "The Postmodernist Turn in Anthropology: Cautions from a Feminist Perspective." *Signs: Journal of Women in Culture and Society* 15 (1990): 7–33.

Minh-ha, Trinh T. "Grandma's Story." *Woman, Native, Other: Writing Postcoloniality and Feminism*, 119–51. Bloomington: Indiana University Press, 1989.

Silko, Leslie Marmon. "Language and Literature from a Pueblo Indian Perspective." In *English Literature: Opening up the Canon,* ed. Leslie A. Fiedler and Houston A. Baker, Jr., 54–72. Selected Papers from the English Institute, n.s. 4. Baltimore: Johns Hopkins University Press, 1981.

Wong, Hertha D. "Pictographs as Autobiography: Plains Indian Sketchbooks of the Late Nineteenth and Early Twentieth Centuries." *American Literary History* 1 (1989): 295–316.

Week 8: Music and Expressive Arts

Faculty: Charlotte Heth, Ethnomusicology and American Indian Studies, and Jacqueline Dje Dje, Ethnomusicology and Afro-American Studies, UCLA

Cavanagh, Beverley D. "Music and Gender in the Sub-Arctic Algonkian Area." In *Women in North American Indian Music: Six Essays,* ed. Richard Keeling, 55–66. Special Series no. 6. Urbana: Society for Ethnomusicology, 1989.

Farrer, Claire R. "Singing for Life: The Mescalero Apache Girls' Puberty Ceremony." In *Southwestern Indian Ritual Drama,* ed. Charlotte J. Frisbie, 125–59. Albuquerque: University of New Mexico Press, 1980.

Frisbie, Charlotte J. "Gender and Navajo Music: Unanswered Questions." In *Women in North American Indian Music: Six Essays,* ed. Richard Keeling, 22–38. Special Series no. 6. Urbana: Society for Ethnomusicology, 1989.

Koskoff, Ellen, ed. "An Introduction to Women, Music, and Culture." *Women and Music in Cross-Cultural Perspective,* 1–23. Westport, Conn.: Greenwood Press, 1987.

Stewart, James B. "Relationships between Black Males and Females in Rhythm and Blues Music of the 1960s and 1970s." *Western Journal of Black Studies* 3 (1979): 186–96.

Turnbull, Colin M. "Sex and Gender: The Role of Subjectivity in Field Research." In *Self, Sex, and Gender in Cross-Cultural Fieldwork,* ed. Tony L. Whitehead and Mary E. Conway, 17–27. Urbana: University of Illinois Press, 1986.

Vander, Judith. "From the Musical Experience of Five Shoshone Women." In *Women in North American Indian Music: Six Essays,* ed. Richard Keeling, 5–12. Special Series no. 6. Urbana: Society for Ethnomusicology, 1989.

Whitehead, Tony L., and Mary E. Conway. "Introduction." In *Self, Sex, and Gender in Cross-Cultural Fieldwork,* ed. Tony L. Whitehead and Mary E. Conway, 1–14. Urbana: University of Illinois Press, 1986.

Handout:

Dje Dje, Jacqueline, and Charlotte Heth. "Ethnomusicology: African American and American Indian Women." Bibliography prepared for the Interdisciplinary Seminar, Ford Ethnic Women's Curriculum Transformation Project, UCLA, 1990.

Week 9: Asian American and Chicana Literature; Biculturalism

Faculty: Katherine King, Comparative Literature and Women's Studies, UCLA

Guest Speaker: Helena María Viramontes

Alarcón, Norma. "Making 'Familia' from Scratch: Split Subjectivities in the Work of Helena María Viramontes and Cherríe Moraga." In *Chicana Poetry and Criticism: Charting New Frontiers in American Literature,* ed. María Herrera-Sobek and Helena María Viramontes, 147–59. Houston: Arte Público, 1988.

————. "Chicana's Feminist Literature: A Re-Vision through Malintzin; or Malintzin: Putting Flesh Back on the Object." In *This Bridge Called My Back: Writings by Radical Women of Color,* ed. Cherríe Moraga and Gloria Anzaldúa, 182–90. Watertown, Mass.: Persephone Press, 1981.

Cheung, King-Kok. " 'Don't Tell': Imposed Silences in *The Color Purple* and *The Woman Warrior." PMLA* 103 (1988): 162–74. Reprinted in *Emerging Voices,* ed. Janet Madden-Simpson and Sara Blake, 400–422. Fort Worth: Holt, Rinehart and Winston, 1990.

————. "The Woman Warrior vs. The Chinamen Pacific: Must a Chinese American Critic Choose between Feminism and Heroism?" In *Conflicts in Feminism,* ed. Marian Hirsch and Evelyn Fox Keller, 234–51. New York: Routledge, 1990.

King, Katherine. "Gina Valdés' *Puentes a Fontera:* A Feminist Chicana Version of the Legend of La Llorona." *Contemporary* Latin American Poetry Wor(l)ds of Change Conference, Bangor, Maine, 1990.

Kingston, Maxine Hong. "White Tigers." *The Woman Warrior: Memoirs of a Girlhood among Ghosts,* 23–63. New York: Vintage, 1977.

Límon, José E. "La Llorona, The Third Legend of Greater Mexico: Cultural Symbols, Women, and the Political Unconscious." In *Between Borders: Essays on Mexicana/Chicana History,* ed. Adelaida R. Del Castillo, 399–432. Encino, Calif.: Floricanto Press, 1990.

Miyake, Lynne K. "Woman's Voice in Japanese Literature: Expanding the Feminine." *Women's Studies* 17 (1989): 87–100. Reprinted in *Across Cultures: The Spectrum of Women's Lives,* ed. Emily K. Abel and Marjorie L. Pearson, 87–100. Studies in Gender and Culture, vol 4. New York: Gordon and Breach, 1989.

Root, Maria P. P. "Asian and Pacific American Women's Bibliography," 1–20. Prepared for the Ford Foundation Ethnic Women's Curriculum Transformation Project, UCLA, 1989.

Sánchez, Marta E. "Setting the Context: Gender, Ethnicity and Silence in Contemporary Chicana Poetry." *Contemporary Chicana Poetry: A Critical*

Approach to an Emerging Literature, 1–23. Berkeley: University of California Press, 1985.

Valdés, Gina. *Puentes y Fronteras: Coplas Chicanas.* Los Angeles: Castle Lithograph, 1982. Trans. Katherine King. Contemporary Latin American Poetry Wor(l)d of Change Conference, Bangor, Maine, 1990.

Viramontes, Helena María. "The Cariboo Cafe." *The Moths and Other Stories,* 61–75. Houston: Arte Público, 1985.

———. "Tears on My Pillow." In *New Chicana/Chicano Writing,* ed. Charles M. Tatum, 110–15. Tucson: University of Arizona Press, 1992.

Handouts:

"Ballad of Mulan." *Chinese Poems.* Ed. Arthur Waley, 113–18. London: George Allen, 1976.

Maps of Asia and the Pacific illustrating the geographical and cultural diversity among Asians.

Week 10: Presentation of Pedagogical Issues

Faculty: Charlotte Heth, Ethnomusicology and American Indian Studies; Karen Rowe, English and Women's Studies; and Richard Yarborough, English and Afro-American Studies, UCLA

Busia, Abena. "Towards a Global Herstory of Women's Images in Myth and Literature." In *Global Interdependence and New Jersey Education: Part I Case Studies for the Humanities,* ed. Patricia F. Morrissey, 147–72. Princeton: Woodrow Wilson National Fellowship Foundation, 1985.

Castellano, Olivia. "Canto, locura y poesía: The Teacher as Agent-Provocateur." *Women's Review of Books* 7, no. 5 (1990): 18–19.

Crenshaw, Kimberle. "Demarginalizing the Intersection of Race and Sex: A Black Feminist Critique of Antidiscrimination Doctrine, Feminist Theory, and Antiracist Politics." *Feminism in the Law: Theory, Practice and Criticism,* 139–67. Chicago: University of Chicago Legal Forum, 1989.

Harding, Sandra. "Women's Studies: The Permanent Revolution." *Women's Review of Books* 7, no. 5 (1990): 17.

———. "Taking Responsibility for Our Own Gender, Race, Class: Transforming Science and the Social Studies of Science." *Rethinking Marxism: A Journal of Economics, Culture, and Society* 2 (1989): 8–19.

Heisch, Allison. "Ruling Women Out: The Curious History of Women's Basketball." *Women's Review of Books* 7, no. 5 (1990): 23.

hooks, bell. "From Skepticism to Feminism: Talking with Black Students." *Women's Review of Books* 7, no. 5 (1990): 29.

"An Interview with Estelle Freedman: Fear of Feminism: C-R in the Classroom." *Women's Review of Books* 7, no. 5 (1990): 25–26.

"An Interview with Ruby Sales: In Our Own Words: Teaching Adult Literacy." *Women's Review of Books* 7, no. 5 (1990): 24–25.

Jhirad, Susan. "Gender Gaps: Classroom Dynamics in a Community College." *Women's Review of Books* 7, no. 5 (1990): 30.

Moses, Yolanda. " '. . . but some of us are (still) brave': From a Report on Black Women in Academia." *Women's Review of Books* 7, no. 5 (1990): 31–32.

Pascoe, Peggy. "At the Crossroads of Culture: De-Centering History." *Women's Review of Books* 7, no. 5 (1990): 22–23.

Spelman, Elizabeth V. "Gender and Race: The Ampersand Problem in Feminist Thought." *Inessential Woman: Problems of Exclusion in Feminist Thought*, 114–32. Boston: Beacon Press, 1988.

———. "Now You See Her, Now You Don't." *Inessential Woman: Problems of Exclusion in Feminist Thought*, 160–87. Boston: Beacon Press, 1988.

Thorne, Barrie. "Rethinking the Ways We Teach." In *Educating the Majority: Women Challenge Tradition in Higher Education*, ed. Carol Pearson, Donna L. Shavlik, and Judith G. Touchton, 311–25. New York: Macmillan, 1989.

Week 11: Presentation of Revised Syllabi

AMERICAN ETHNIC STUDIES SEMINAR

Paula Gunn Allen English and American Indian Studies
Eric Sundquist English and American Studies
University of California
Los Angeles, CA 90024

The challenge for the UCLA Ford Ethnic Women's Curriculum Transformation Project (FEW) faculty development seminar on American Ethnic Studies (fall 1990), which constituted the sixth in UCLA's series, was to draw together a rapidly expanding group of Americanists, both tenured and recently hired in the English department, and to create a forum in which to think seriously about how inclusively to embrace ethnic women's voices and stories within an American literature canon and curriculum. The seminar provided the first opportunity for faculty to engage one another in discussions of teaching and in debating the often contentious theoretical issues surrounding the field of American literary study and, more specifically, the new cultural, ethnic, and gender studies.

Participants included two facilitators, twelve faculty members (four assistant professors, eight tenured, two of whom were auditors), and seven graduate students, two serving as project research assistants and participants. Evenly divided between men and women (plus two female auditors), the faculty brought richly varied and cross-cutting backgrounds, including two literary theorists; an art historian and American Studies scholar who is also a gallery director; an African folklorist studying women's diaspora narratives; a colonialist; and nineteenth-century Americanists with interests in race, frontier, and western literature, popular images of women, and the Lacanian gaze and female desire. All of the women had a working familiarity with feminist scholarship, though not as extensively with recent ethnic women's criticism and writing, while generally the men had more limited exposure to ethnic women's literature and theory, though frequently with deeper commitments to postmodern psychoanalytic and philosophical theories. There were four faculty members with specialized expertise in Asian American, Chicana/o, and American Indian literature, and we invited our colleague Richard Yarborough to conduct a special session on the work of Paule Marshall. Ethnic women faculty included two assistant professors and one professor, while there were three African American graduate students and one graduate student from India, the latter working on postcolonial literatures. Despite the wealth of potential contributors and expertise, none of the faculty felt comfortable in a spectrum that fully embraced all of the ethnic women's literatures, new cultural theories of discourse, and postcolonial studies nor in their ability as identifiable members of one culture to know how, within a course and classroom, to claim the teaching of other voices, other cultures. Even given highly developed skills as literary critics and theorists, most participants felt ill equipped to deal with conflict either in the seminar or in ethnically diverse classrooms.

Borrowing from models for the earlier American and Related Literatures and History seminars, the FEW director and seminar facilitators designed the framework of the syllabus to achieve three goals: first, to provide coverage of various new ethnic women writers, likely to be adopted for teaching in American literature courses; second, to introduce relevant critical, gender, and ethnic studies approaches; and third, to engage faculty and graduate student participants themselves as "expert" contributors cum seminar leaders as part of the process of taking ownership. We consciously sought to highlight ethnic women's writing, but also to create dialogues across ethnic groups around particular themes and commonalities. The frame-setting weeks with the facilitators as discussion leaders featured their own selections of readings or ones collaboratively agreed upon, while subsequent readings were selected in consultation with faculty participants, who led a weekly session, usually focusing on specific texts, criticism, and/or ways in which they taught the materials in their own courses.

The syllabus was designed to address head-on the hotly contested theoretical and critical debates, in week one about canonicity in American literature and in week two on "culturality" and "ethnicity" as concepts and experiences. In retrospect, the structure of these two weeks may have replicated what is the privileged status of "male" theorists engaged in "inventions" of ethnicity or academic debates about "who belongs" and "what constitutes a canon" and thereby implicitly remarginalized ethnic women speakers and writers to the position of "cultural Other," whose voice speaks from a gendered and ethnically specific experience deemed to be atheoretical or lacking in literary quality. These first weeks set in relief debates over whether ethnic women's writing is "really good literature," or what "we'" as a community of scholars and teachers use as criteria for assessing literature, whether "assessment of value or inclusion in a canon" is a relevant point of departure, and how to develop a countervailing critical methodology that focuses first on expressed experience, story, voice, genre, and form and only then (if at all) works inductively to construct theoretical models. Some participants clung to "theory" both as a defense and a definition of what constitutes intellectual work, while others challenged the limited perspective of theories that neither hear nor see nor know women of color. The reenactment testifies to the still fraught battleground within literary studies, in which the need for women of color to be heard as colleagues among equals still constitutes a seeming powerful threat from the subversive other to a discipline that invokes canons, quality, and theory to protect its traditions and privilege.

Although these issues resurfaced, the remaining nine weeks were focused intensively on ethnic women's voices, their writings, and the teaching of new texts. Writings included works by major new-generation authors, including

Paula Gunn Allen, Anna Lee Walters, Gloria Anzaldúa, Cherríe Moraga, Helena Viramontes, Toni Morrison, Harriet Jacobs, Paule Marshall, Maxine Hong Kingston, Bharati Mukherjee, Hisaye Yamamoto, and Ronyoung Kim. Accompanying ethnic and/or feminist criticism represented new approaches from the tribal feminism of Gunn Allen to the geopolitical theories of borderlands to black feminist criticism, from the emerging Asian American textual criticism of silence and invisibility to a lesbian aesthetic to works of feminist theory and pedagogy. In order to create continuities among tests we focused during the first half on issues of landscape and space, while the second half focused on the theme of spirituality, the latter sparked by the frequency with which invisible presences, voices, ghosts, and rituals, including *vodoun*, ancestors, and matriarchal spirits guide the writing, the "talk-stories," and the heroine's self-discovery in many recent fictions by ethnic women, most notably *Beloved, Ceremony, Ghost Singer, The Woman Warrior, Praisesong for the Widow,* and *Borderlands / La Frontera.* Not simply the registering of common themes linked texts or discussions, but just as often the perceived differences among ethnic women's perspectives, ones that were mirrored in different analytic approaches or cultural traditions among the participants themselves. A week midway devoted to pedagogy generated reflections on the position of the Euro-American teacher in the ethnically diverse classroom, as did the final two weeks in which faculty generously shared with one another recommendations for improving and strengthening syllabi.

The experiential learning often came during intense, even painfully emotional miscommunications, in which misused terms, misunderstood statements, and the dynamics of conflicts became the basis for examining what too often goes unnoted or unexamined in our own classrooms. "Ruptures" and confrontations revealed far more explicitly than the materials under study the inherent power structures within academic departments, the too easily assumed "authority" of knowledge without the "authority" of experience, the retreat into intellectual rationalism as a vehicle for addressing conflict in values and among cultures, and the contested terrain within which ethnic women's literature and criticism struggles to be heard and acknowledged within a Euro-American Western tradition of scholarship. But by stretching ourselves to hear different voices, to know better our own unstated assumptions, to interrogate our authority, and to consider what each individual's tolerance and comfort may be for working within productively conflicted classrooms, we all learned to heed rather than ignore the multivocal, multilingual "wild" tongues, which Gloria Anzaldúa claims.

Facilitators Eric Sundquist and Paula Gunn Allen reflect below two different visions that capture vividly issues raised here from the perspective of the FEW project director. In this trinity of responses we have tried consciously to represent the diversity within any faculty development seminar. Not all participants, nor all facilitators, nor any individual, will evaluate the experience through the same lens of perception and reaction. Constituting curriculum transformation seminars is an imperfect art, particularly when ethnicity and gender so centrally challenge the values and traditions of the discipline and society itself and when the seminar mirrors the inherent divisions within academic groups, disciplines, and communities. But we all agree that, despite or perhaps because of the process itself, the American Ethnic Studies seminar yielded surprisingly strong, often radically revisionary syllabi that continue to shape and reshape a new American literature curriculum eloquently resonant with the voices of ethnic women.

Karen E. Rowe

What Do You Want on Your Tombstone?

The FEW seminar participants were mostly literary specialists and brought particular course outlines they wished to revise with a greater inclusion of female non-Western writers. Conceptually, the seminar seemed potentially of great value; the area of focus, literature by women of color, is an exciting field within the overall body of American literature and one whose many texts and critical offerings provide a profuse commentary on a neglected area of American experience. The best feature of the seminar was the wide knowledge and openness of the participants, a number of whom also offered lectures to the assembled. The most productive of the sessions were the final two, which offered the actual course outlines, rationales, and bibliographies for discussion.

On the whole, however, the seminar suffered from a format and list of readings that were widely at odds with the stated goals of the seminar, and intersocial conflicts often turned what should have been a lively inquiry into a killing field. The problems seemed to stem from two organizational weaknesses. First, too many of the critical readings assigned were works that seemed to have only marginal pertinence to the literature of women of color. This deficiency created an underlying tension between the professed focus of our study and our actual discussions. What ensued led to barely contained debates, serious distress, and exchanges that essentially impeded the development of creative growth and intellectual competence. Second, and unfortunately, the community of scholars in the United States is in the throes of cultural readjustment, and far too many interracial and intergender tensions from the academic community and the larger society around us impinged on our attempts to discuss a truly fascinating and powerful body of literature and criticism.

As a new faculty member at UCLA, here for my first quarter, the experience was traumatic. As an American Indian woman, writer, and critic, I found it alienating. I had hoped to explore and discuss work that is central to my professional and artistic life. Alas, the battle between the blacks and the whites created painful interchanges. Though the course outlines turned out very well, their strength and thoughtfulness was more a consequence of their authors' dedication to good teaching and good literature than to the critical readings or the acrimonious discussions. Were I to facilitate a similar enterprise in the future, I think I would carefully define the parameters of the discussions, keep the readings to the actual subject under consideration, and focus on the syllabi being revised as the centerpiece of the discussions.

Paula Gunn Allen

Reflections on the American Ethnic Studies Seminar

I would dissent in some particulars from the assessment of my colleague and cofacilitator, Paula Gunn Allen. But I share her view that the seminar meetings characteristically balanced innovation and creative dialogue against tension and moments of near recrimination. Perhaps this was unavoidable. Our syllabus makes evident what the seminar aimed to and did largely accomplish, and I would call particular attention to the fact that we sought both to spend significant time on the variety of ethnic cultural experiences and to carry certain themes and problems through the entire course of readings. Of necessity we tried to be all things to all people, with the perhaps unavoidable consequence that some explorations of a given topic became haphazardly exploratory, even as they were deep and enlightening. There was a rich array of texts and issues under discussion each week, and the diverse group of participants energized our conversations. I would agree with Paula, moreover, that the participants' contributions at the conclusion, in the form of syllabi and bibliographies, were in some respects the best part of the seminar and should have been incorporated over the course of the term.

Leaving aside the question of whether all racial and ethnic groups could be adequately studied in such a format as this seminar, other structural issues might be addressed. I attribute some problems in the seminar not to the racial mix of the syllabus or the group itself, but, rather, to three factors, which I would invite others who plan such seminars to contemplate. First, the preparation and range of reading brought to the seminar varied widely, such that experts, novices, and those in between were mixed into one discussion. Sometimes useful pedagogy was the result, but there were a number of occasions when such heterogeneity was a roadblock. The meetings uncomfortably fused a true seminar with rudimentary instruction of the uninformed. It may be that this is a problem inherent in the very enterprise, but in any event it is one to be reckoned with. Second, and in the same vein, the mix of senior faculty, junior faculty, and graduate students was sometimes a decided problem. On the one hand, such a mix allowed new and more traditional perspectives to meet in conversation, and no one doubted that the younger scholars had fresh points of view that were revelatory to their senior colleagues and their teachers. On the other hand, the students, and to a lesser extent the junior faculty, said that they felt inhibited from speaking freely on controversial matters, or ones on which they felt unprepared, for fear of censure. (This was exacerbated by the fact that a few senior faculty not actually participating in the seminar sat in as auditors, with the result that they at times appeared to be some sort of observing witnesses.) For their part senior faculty in particular felt that they could not always speak freely about pedagogy, affirmative action, and other such matters that may have involved sensitive interests of the junior faculty and students.

Both of the preceding issues created a third: namely, that there was, in my view, a reluctance on the part of almost all to speak openly and debate the very premises of the seminar and its readings. For good reason, people took exceptional care not to offend others, but the result was that a number of important questions were simply set aside when controversy began to appear. My view here might conflict with Paula's, but I think in retrospect that we might have better integrated counterperspectives (white, male, conservative, whatever the case may be) throughout the seminar. Such a strategy, however, raises a yet larger question: Is a "separatist" curricular focus—in this case a focus on the work of women of color—the proper way institutionally to contemplate problems of canon and pedagogy? I would say that, for all the reasons already cited, this issue was not given enough honest attention.

Both in its intentions and its problems, however, the seminar therefore posed very useful questions to us all. Is literary study now a "discipline" at all, or do the very notions of the multicultural and the interdisciplinary, which we rightly treat with certain but often opaque reverence, contradict the factual knowledge and intellectual rigor necessary to do significant work in any given field(s)? Is the most worthwhile scholarly work even possible when the specter of "politicization" is always on the horizon—or in the foreground? The difficulties that confront literary studies today make strong interdisciplinary work more likely even as they place it under stronger pressures of self-scrutiny and self-justification. At a moment when few scholars—certainly few recently trained in American graduate programs or few conversant with the wealth of currently available theory—would claim *not* to be engaged in some version of cultural studies, new historicism, gender theory, and the like, there is a significant challenge to remind ourselves and our students that neither a command of the relevant methodologies nor an ability to recognize and create new knowledge comes easily.

The movement for curricular change of the sort promoted by the Ford Foundation program ought also to carry consequent responsibilities: to understand the changing vernacular of professional life generated by multiculturalism; to educate students and the public about the legitimate rewards of work that breaks with, while building knowledgeably upon, established disciplinary traditions; and to pursue interdisciplinary work with dedication to high standards. Most of all, it ought to aim toward inclusion, not exclusion—toward free speech and academic freedom. The seminar in which I participated as a facilitator attempted to meet all of these demands, and sometimes we got it right.

Eric Sundquist

Syllabus

Week 1: Introduction: Canonicity

Faculty: Eric Sundquist, English and American Studies, UCLA

Andersen, Margaret L. "Moving Our Minds: Studying Women of Color and Reconstructing Sociology." *Teaching Sociology* 16 (1988): 123–32.

Gates, Henry Louis, Jr. "Whose Canon Is It, Anyway?" *New York Times Book Review,* 26 February 1989, 1+.

Gunn, Giles. "Beyond Transcendence or beyond Ideology: The New Problematics of Cultural Criticism in America." *American Literary History* 2 (1990): 1–18.

Krupat, Arnold. "The Concept of the Canon." *The Voice in the Margin: Native American Literature and the Canon,* 22–56. Berkeley: University of California Press, 1989.

Minh-ha, Trinh T. "Difference: 'A Special Third Women Issue.' " *Woman, Native, Other: Writing Postcoloniality and Feminism,* 78–116. Bloomington: Indiana University Press, 1989.

Morrison, Toni. "Unspeakable Things Unspoken: The Afro-American Presence in American Literature." *Michigan Quarterly Review* 28 (1989): 1–34.

Saldívar, Ramón. "Conclusion: The Reconstruction of American Literary History." *Chicano Narrative: The Dialectics of Difference,* 204–18. Madison: University of Wisconsin Press, 1990.

Yarborough, Richard. "Breaking the 'Codes of Americanness.' " Review of *Beyond Ethnicity: Consent and Descent in American Culture* by Werner Sollors. *American Quarterly* 38 (1986): 860–65.

Week 2: Culturality: Changing Our Own Words

Faculty: Paula Gunn Allen, English and American Indian Studies, UCLA

Braxton, Joanne M. "Afra-American Culture and the Contemporary Literary Renaissance." In *Wild Women in the Whirlwind: Afra-American Culture and the Contemporary Literary Renaissance,* ed. Joanne M. Braxton and Andrée N. McLaughlin, xxi–xxx. New Brunswick, N.J.: Rutgers University Press, 1990.

Henderson, Mae G. "Speaking in Tongues: Dialogics, Dialectics, and the Black Woman Writer's Literary Tradition." In *Changing Our Own Words:*

Essays on Criticism, Theory, and Writing by Black Women, ed. Cheryl A.
Wall, 16–37. New Brunswick, N.J.: Rutgers University Press, 1989.

Kondo, Dorinne K. "The Eye/I." *Crafting Selves: Power, Gender, and Discourses of Identity in a Japanese Workplace*, 3–48. Chicago: University of Chicago Press, 1990.

McLaughlin, Andrée N. "A Renaissance of Spirit: Black Women Remaking the University." In *Wild Women in the Whirlwind: Afra-American Culture and the Contemporary Literary Renaissance*, ed. Joanne M. Braxton and Andree N. McLaughlin, xxxi–xlix. New Brunswick, N.J.: Rutgers University Press, 1990.

Minh-ha, Trinh T. "Grandma's Story." *Women, Native, Other: Writing Postcoloniality and Feminism*, 118–51. Bloomington: Indiana University Press, 1989.

Radhakrishnan, R. "Culture as Common Ground: Ethnicity and Beyond." *MELUS* 14 (1987): 5–20.

Reed, Ishmael, Shawn Wong, Bob Callahan, and Andrew Hope. "Is Ethnicity Obsolete?" In *The Invention of Ethnicity*, ed. Werner Sollors, 226–35. New York: Oxford University Press, 1989.

Rodríguez, Richard. "An America Writer." In *The Invention of Ethnicity*, ed. Werner Sollors, 3–13. New York: Oxford University Press, 1989.

Rosaldo, Renato. "Others of Invention: Ethnicity and Its Discontents." Review of *Machines as the Measure of Men* by Michael Adas, *The Invention of Africa* by V. Y. Mudimbe, and *The Invention of Ethnicity* by Werner Sollors. *Voice Literary Supplement*, February 1990, 27–29.

Smith, Barbara. "The Truth That Never Hurts: Black Lesbians in Fiction in the 1980s." In *Wild Women in the Whirlwind: Afra-American Culture and the Contemporary Literary Renaissance*, ed. Joanne M. Braxton and Andrée N. McLaughlin, 213–45. New Brunswick, N.J.: Rutgers University Press, 1990.

Sollors, Werner. "Introduction: The Invention of Ethnicity." *The Invention of Ethnicity*, ix–xx. New York: Oxford University Press, 1989.

Week 3: Landscape and Space: American Indian

Faculty: Paula Gunn Allen and Kenneth Lincoln, English and American Indian Studies, UCLA

Allen, Paula Gunn. "Evil Kachina Steals Yellow Woman," 182–86; "Introduction," 1–25; "Sun Steals Yellow Woman," 186–87; "Whirlwind Man Steals Yellow Woman," 187–88—all in *Spider Woman's Granddaughters: Traditional Tales and Contemporary Writing by Native American Women*, ed. Paula Gunn Allen. Boston: Beacon Press, 1989.

———. *The Woman Who Owned the Shadows*. San Francisco: Spinsters, Ink, 1983.

Basso, Keith H. " 'Stalking with Stories': Names, Places and Moral Narratives among the Western Apache." In *Text, Play, and Story: The Construction and Reconstruction of Self and Society*, ed. Edward Bruner and Stuart Plattner, 19–55. Washington, D.C.: American Ethnological Society, 1984.

Lincoln, Kenneth. "Ancestral Voices in Oral Traditions." *Native American Renaissance*, 41–59. Berkeley: University of California Press, 1983.

Momaday, N. Scott. "Man Made of Words." *Indian Voices: The First Convocation of American Indian Scholars*. 1970. Reprinted in *Literature of the American Indians: Views and Interpretations*, ed. Abraham Chapman, 96–110. New York: New American Library, 1975.

Silko, Leslie. "Yellow Woman." In *Spider Woman's Granddaughters: Traditional Tales and Contemporary Writing by Native American Women*, ed. Paula Gunn Allen, 189–97. Boston: Beacon Press, 1989.

Smith, Patricia Clark, and Paula Gunn Allen. "Earthly Relations, Carnal Knowledge: Southwestern American Indian Women Writers and Landscape." In *The Desert Is No Lady*, ed. Janice Monk and Vera Norwood, 174–96. New Haven: Yale University Press, 1987.

Handouts:

Allen, Paula Gunn. "Selected Bibliography." *The Sacred Hoop: Recovering the Feminine in American Indian Traditions*, 287–93. Boston: Beacon Press, 1986.

Adnan, Etel. "The Indian Never Had a Horse." *The Indian Never Had a Horse and Other Poems*, 1–35. Sausalito, Calif.: Post-Apollo, 1985.

Lorde, Audre. "What Is at Stake in Lesbian and Gay Publishing Today?" *Lambda Book Report*, 11. Washington, D.C.: Lambda Rising Bookstore, 1990.

Sánchez, Carol Lee. "The Last Days of the Monarchs." *Conversations from the Nightmare: Poems by Carol Lee Sánchez*. San Francisco: Casa Editorial Publications, 1975.

Week 4: Urban Landscapes, Arts, and Culture
Chicano Arts: Resistance and Affirmation (CARA)

Faculty: Edith Tonnelli, Director, Frederick S. Wight Art Galley, UCLA

Acosta-Colón, María. "Chicano Art: Time for a New Aesthetic. . . ." *Los Angeles Times*, 24 September 1990, F:3

Berger, Maurice. "Speaking Out: Some Distance to Go . . .—'An Interview with Johnnetta B. Cole.' " *Art in America* 78 (September 1990): 84–85.

Clifford, James. "Histories of the Tribal and the Modern." *The Predicament of Culture: Twentieth-Century Ethnography, Literature, and Art*, 189–214. Cambridge: Harvard University Press, 1988.

———. "On Collecting Art and Culture." *The Predicament of Culture:*

Twentieth-Century Ethnography, Literature, and Art, 215–51. Cambridge: Harvard University Press, 1988.

Garfias, Robert. "Cultural Diversity and the Arts in America." A report prepared for the Special Task Force on Performance, sponsored by the National Endowment for the Arts and the Rockefeller Foundation, 1–19. September 1989. Typescript.

González, Alicia, and Edith Tonelli. "Compañeros and Partners: The CARA Project." In *Museums and Communities: The Politics of Public Culture*, ed. Ivan Karp, Christine Mullen Kreamer, and Steven D. Levine, 262–84. Washington, D.C.: Smithsonian Institution Press, 1992.

hooks, bell. "Critical Interrogation: Talking Race, Resisting Racism." *Art Forum* (May 1989): 18–20; reprinted in *Inscriptions*, no. 5 (1989): 159–64.

Images from *CARA*, the *Chicano Art: Resistance and Affirmation, 1965–1985* Exhibit. Los Angeles: Wight Art Gallery, UCLA, 1991; and *The Decade Show: Frameworks of Identity in the 1980s*. New York: The Museum of Contemporary Hispanic Art, the New Museum of Contemporary Art, and the Studio Museum of Harlem, 1990.

Mesa-Bains, Amalia. "El Mundo Femenina: Chicana Artists of the Movement—A Commentary on Development and Production." In *Chicano Art: Resistance and Affirmation, 1965–1985*, ed. Richard Griswold del Castillo, Teresa McKenna, and Yvonne Yarbro-Bejarno, 131–40. Los Angeles: Wight Art Gallery, UCLA, 1991.

Monk, Janice, and Vera Norwood, eds. "Conclusion." *The Desert Is No Lady*, 223–34. New Haven: Yale University Press, 1987.

―――. "Introduction: Perspectives on Gender and Landscape." *The Desert Is No Lady*, 1–9. New Haven: Yale University Press, 1987.

Nochlin, Linda. "Women, Art, and Power." *Women Art, and Power and Other Essays*, 1–36. New York: Harper, 1989.

Pohl, Frances K. "The World Wall: A Vision of the Future without Fear: An Interview with Judith F. Baca." *Frontiers* 11 (1990): 33–43.

Pollock, Griselda. "Feminist Interventions in the Histories of Art: An Introduction." *Vision and Difference: Femininity, Feminism, and Histories of Art*, 1–17. London: Routledge, 1988.

Rebolledo, Tey Diana. "Tradition and Mythology: Signatures of Landscape in Chicana Literature." In *The Desert Is No Lady*, ed. Janice Monk and Vera Norwood, 96–124. New Haven: Yale University Press, 1987.

Santos, John Phillip. "In 1940, All Things Mexican Were All the Rage." *Los Angeles Times*, 30 September 1990, Calendar, 80.

―――. "3000 Years of Mexican Art." *Los Angeles Times*, 30 September 1990, Calendar, 3+.

Wilson, William. "Chicano Show Mixes Advocacy, Aesthetics." *Los Angeles Time*, 12 September 1990, F1+.

Ybarra-Frausto, Tómas. "Rasquachismo: A Chicano Sensibility." In *Chicano Art: Resistance and Affirmation, 1965–1985*, ed. Richard Griswold del

Castillo, Teresa McKenna, and Yvonne Yarbro-Bejarno, 155–62. Los Angeles: Wight Art Gallery, UCLA, 1991.

Week 5: Literary Representations of Space / Body in Chicana Literature

Faculty: Sonia Saldívar-Hull, English and Chicano/Chicana Studies, UCLA

Anzaldúa, Gloria. *Borderlands / La Frontera: The New Mestiza.* San Francisco: Spinsters / Aunt Lute, 1987.

Fernández, Roberta. " 'The Cariboo Cafe': Helena María Viramontes Discourses with Her Social and Cultural Context." In *Across Cultures: The Spectrum of Women's Lives,* ed. Emily K. Abel and Marjorie L. Pearson, 71–85. New York: Gordon and Breach, 1989

Moraga, Cherríe. *Loving in the War Years: Lo que nunca pasó por sus labios.* Boston: South End Press, 1983.

Saldívar, Ramón. "The Dialectics of Subjectivity: Gender and Difference in Isabella Ríos, Sandra Cisernos, and Cherríe Moraga." *Chicano Narrative: The Dialectics of Difference,* 171–99. Madison: University of Wisconsin Press, 1990.

Saldívar-Hull, Sonia. "Feminism on the Border: From Gender Politics to Geopolitics." In *Criticism in the Borderlands: Studies in Chicano Literature,* ed. Hector Calderon and Jose David Saldívar, 203–20. Durham, N.C.: Duke University Press, 1991.

Viramontes, Helena Maria. "The Cariboo Cafe." *The Moths and Other Stories,* 61–75. Houston: Arte Público, 1985.

Zavella, Patricia. "The Problematic Relationship of Feminism and Chicana Studies." In *Across Cultures: The Spectrum of Women's Lives,* ed. Emily K. Abel and Marjorie L. Pearson, 25–36. New York: Gordon and Breach, 1989.

Handouts:

Castillo-Speed, Lillian. "Chicana Studies: A Selected List of Materials since 1980." *Frontiers* 11 (1990): 66–84.

Eysturoy, Annie O., and José A. Gurpegui. "Chicano Literature: Introduction and Bibliography." *American Studies International* 28 (April 1990): 48–82.

McKenna, Teresa. "Chicano Literature." In *Redefining American Literary History,* ed. A. LaVonne Brown Ruoff and Jerry W. Ward, 363–72. New York: MLA, 1990.

"Table of Contents." *Frontiers: A Journal of Women Studies* 11 (1990). Special issues on Chicanas and Chicana studies.

Week 6: Pedagogy

Faculty: Paula Gunn Allen, English and American Indian Studies, and Eric Sundquist, English and American Studies, UCLA

Allen, Paula Gunn. "Kochinnenako in Academe: Three Approaches to Interpreting a Keres Indian Tale." *The Sacred Hoop: Recovering the Feminine in American Indian Traditions,* 224–44. Boston: Beacon Press, 1986.
————. "Teaching American Indian Women's Literature." *Studies in American Indian Literature: Critical Essays and Course Designs,* 134–44. New York: MLA, 1983.
Butler, Johnnella E. "Transforming the Curriculum: Teaching about Women of Color." In *Multicultural Education: Issues and Perceptions,* ed. James A. Banks and Cherry A. McGee Banks, 145–63. Boston: Allyn and Bacon, 1989.
Chan, Sucheng. "On the Ethnic Studies Requirement, Part I: Pedagogical Implications." *Amerasia* 15 (1989): 267–80.
Mitchell, Jacquelyn. "Transforming Community Practices into Pedagogical Strategies: Building a Classroom Community." Paper presented at the American Anthropological Association annual meeting, Washington, D.C., November 1989.
Ruiz, Vicki L. "Teaching Chicano/American History: Goals and Methods." *History Teacher* 20 (1987): 167–77.

Handouts:
Hale, Sondra. "Fifteen Pedagogical Strategies." From *Pedagogy and Diversity: Some Problematics in Feminist Teaching at the University.* Paper presented at the SC/WCA Annual Conference, October 1990.
"The Heath Travesty of American Literature." *New Criterion* (October 1990): 3–5.

Week 7: African American Spirits

Faculty: Eric Sundquist and Deborah Garfield, English and American Studies, UCLA

Andrews, William L. "The Novelization of Voice in Early African American Narrative." *PMLA* 5 (January 1990): 23–34.
Christian, Barbara. " 'Somebody Forgot to Tell Somebody Something': African American Women's Historical Novels." In *Wild Women in the Whirlwind: Afra-American Culture and the Contemporary Literary Renaissance.* ed. Joanne M. Braxton and Andrée N. McLaughlin, 326–41. New Brunswick, N.J.: Rutgers University Press, 1990.

Crouch, Stanley. "Aunt Medea." *Notes of a Hanging Judge: Essays and Reviews, 1979–89,* 202–9. New York: Oxford University Press, 1990.

Jacobs, Harriet A. [Linda Brent]. *Incidents in the Life of a Slave Girl: Written by Herself.* Ed. Jean Fagan Yellin. Cambridge: Harvard University Press, 1987.

McDowell, Deborah E. "Reading Family Matters." In *Changing Our Own Words: Essays on Criticism, Theory, and Writing by Black Women,* ed. Cheryl A. Wall, 75–97. New Brunswick, N.J.: Rutgers University Press, 1989.

Morrison, Toni. *Beloved.* New York: Knopf, 1987.

Omolade, Barbara. "The Silence and the Song: Toward a Black Woman's History through a Language of Her Own." In *Wild Women in the Whirlwind: Afra-American Culture and the Contemporary Literary Renaissance,* ed. Joanne M. Braxton and Andrée N. McLaughlin, 282–95. New Brunswick, N.J.: Rutgers University Press, 1990.

Smith, Valerie. "Black Feminist Theory and the Representation of the 'Other.' " In *Changing Our Own Words: Essays on Criticism, Theory, and Writing by Black Women,* ed. Cheryl A. Wall, 38–57. New Brunswick, N.J.: Rutgers University Press, 1989.

Handout:
Stewart, María W. *Religion and the Pure Principles of Morality, the Sure Foundation on Which We Must Build.* Pamphlets on Slavery, no. 18. Boston: Garrison and Knapp, 1831.

Week 8: Ancestors and Spirituality

Faculty: Donald Cosentino, English, and Folklore and Mythology, and Richard Yarborough, English and Afro-American Studies, UCLA

Allen, Paula Gunn. "The Sacred Hoop: A Contemporary Perspective." *The Sacred Hoop: Recovering the Feminine in American Indian Traditions,* 54–75. Boston: Beacon Press, 1986.

Busia, Abena. "What Is Your Nation?: Reconnecting Africa and Her Diaspora through Paule Marshall's *Praisesong for the Widow.*" In *Changing Our Own Words: Essays on Criticism, Theory, and Writing by Black Women,* ed. Cheryl A. Wall, 196–211. New Brunswick, N.J.: Rutgers University Press, 1989.

Cosentino, Donald. "Deconstructing Legba." In *Yoruba Vibrations in the New World,* ed. Robin Poyner, Gainesville: University of Florida Press, forthcoming.

Fischer, Michael M. J. "Ethnicity and the Post-Modern Arts of Memory." In *Writing Culture: The Poetics and Politics of Ethnography,* ed. James

Clifford and George E. Marcus, 194–233. Berkeley: University of California Press, 1986.

Marshall, Paule, *Praisesong for the Widow.* 1983. Reprint. New York: Dutton, 1984.

Teish, Luisah. "Nature Worship." *Jambalaya: The Natural Woman's Book of Personal Charms and Practical Rituals,* 53–66. San Francisco: Harper and Row, 1985.

Walters, Anna Lee. *Ghost Singer.* Flagstaff, Ariz.: Northland, 1988.

Handouts:

Rowe, Karen E. "Biography and Bibliography for Paule Marshall." UCLA, 1990.

Yarborough, Richard. "Landmarks in Afro-American Literature." UCLA, 1989.

————. "Selected Works of Afro-American Fiction." UCLA, 1989.

Week 9: Asian American: Whispered Legacies

Faculty: King-Kok Cheung, English and Asian American Studies, UCLA

Cheung, King-Kok. " 'Don't Tell': Imposed Silences in *The Color Purple* and *The Woman Warrior.*" *PMLA* 103 (March 1988): 162–74. Reprinted in *Emerging Voices,* ed. Janet Madden-Simpson and Sara Blake, 400–422. Ft. Worth, Tex.: Holt, 1990.

————. "Double-Telling: Intertextual Silence in Hisaye Yamamoto's Fiction." *American Literary History.* #3 (1991): 96–113.

————. "Introduction." *Seventeen Syllables and Other Stories* by Hisaye Yamamoto, xi–xxv. New York: Kitchen Table / Women of Color Press, 1988.

————. "The Woman Warrior versus the Chinaman Pacific: Must a Chinese American Critic Choose between Feminism and Heroism?" In *Conflicts in Feminism,* ed. Maríanne Hirsch and Evelyn Fox Keller, 234–51. New York: Routledge, 1990.

Kim, Ronyoung. "Faye." *Clay Walls,* 185–301. 1986. Reprint. Seattle: University of Washington Press, 1990.

Kingston, Maxine Hong. "The Song of the Barbarian Reed Pipe." *The Woman Warrior: Memoirs of a Girlhood among Ghosts.* New York: Vintage Press, 1977.

Mukherjee, Bharati. "The Management of Grief." *The Middleman and Other Stories,* 179–97. New York: Grove, 1988.

Yamada, Mitsuye. "Invisibility Is an Unnatural Disaster: Reflections of an Asian American Woman." In *This Bridge Called My Back: Writings by Radical Women of Color,* ed. Cherríe Moraga and Gloria Anzaldúa, 35–40. New York: Kitchen Table / Women of Color Press, 1981.

Yamamoto, Hisaye. "The Legend of Miss Sasagawara," 20–33; "Seventeen

Syllables," 8–19; "Yoneko's Earthquake," 46–59. *Seventeen Syllables and Other Stories.* New York: Kitchen Table / Women of Color Press, 1988.

Handouts:
"The Ballad of Mulan." *Chinese Poems.* Ed. Arthur Waley, 113–18. London: George Allen, 1976.
Rowe, Karen. "Biography and Bibliography for Maxine Hong Kingston." UCLA, 1990.

Week 10: History and Change
Participants' Presentations

Faculty: Eric Sundquist, English and American Studies, UCLA

Busia, Abena. "Towards a Global Herstory of Woman's Images in Myth and Literature." In *Global Interdependence and New Jersey Education: Part I Case Studies for the Humanities,* ed. Patricia F. Morrissey, 147–72. Princeton: Woodrow Wilson National Fellowship Foundation, 1985.
Cheung, King-Kok. "Reflections on Teaching Literature by American Women of Color." *Pacific Coast Philology* 25 (November 1990): 19–23.
Lauter, Paul. "Notes on Teaching a Reconstructed American Literature." *Heath Anthology of American Literature Newsletter* 4 (Fall 1990): 1–6.
de Lauretis, Teresa. "Feminism and Its Differences." *Pacific Coast Philology* 25 (November 1990): 24–30.
McKenna, Teresa. "Intersections of Race, Class, and Gender: The Feminist Pedagogical Challenge." *Pacific Coast Philology* 25 (November 1990): 31–38.
Spelman, Elizabeth V. "Gender and Race: The Ampersand Problem in Feminist Thought." *Inessential Woman: Problems of Exclusion in Feminist Thought,* 114–32. Boston: Beacon Press, 1988.

Week 11: Participants' Presentations

Faculty: Eric Sundquist, English and American Studies, and Paula Gunn Allen, English and American Indian Studies, UCLA

Novels, Stories, Poetry
Allen, Paula Gunn. *The Woman Who Owned the Shadows.* San Francisco: Spinsters, Ink, 1983.
Anzaldúa, Gloria. *Borderlands / La Frontera: The New Mestiza.* San Francisco: Spinsters/Aunt Lute, 1987.
Kingston, Maxine Hong. *The Woman Warrior: Memoirs of a Girlhood among Ghosts.* New York: Vintage, 1977.

Jacobs, Harriet A. *Incidents in the Life of a Slave Girl: Written by Herself.* Ed. Jean Fagan Yellin. Cambridge: Harvard University Press, 1987.

Kim, Ronyoung. *Clay Walls.* 1986. Reprint. Seattle: University of Washington Press, 1990.

Marshall, Paule. *Praisesong for the Widow.* 1983. Reprint. New York: Dutton, 1984.

Moraga, Cherríe. *Loving in the War Years: Lo que nunca pasó por sus labios.* Boston: South End Press, 1983.

Morrison, Toni. *Beloved.* New York: Knopf, 1987.

Viramontes, Helena Maria. *The Moths and Other Stories.* Houston: Arte Publico, 1985.

Walters, Anna Lee. *Ghost Singer.* Flagstaff, Ariz.: Northland, 1988.

Yamamoto, Hisaye. *Seventeen Syllables and Other Stories.* New York: Kitchen Table / Woman of Color Press, 1988.

Films

Bowman, Arlene. *Navajo Talking Picture.* (1986; 40 mins.) Documentary of Ms. Bowman's struggle to overcome her grandmother's refusal to participate in the film. Excellent treatment of the generation and cultural gaps that separate the non–Navajo-speaking granddaughter from her non–English-speaking grandmother.

Makarah, O.Funmilayo. *Define.* (1988; 5 mins.) This is an experimental dramatic video that weaves color, voice, and image to investigate the question of who has the right to define how women of color will exist. The video draws on the life experiences of three women—one black, one Japanese American, and one Chicana—as they explore this question.

Tanaka, Janice. *Department of Amnesia.* Creative multimedia documentary of the life of one Japanese-American woman (1930–70) through photographs and memories of her children.

Rachmuhl, Sophie. *On the Other Side: Portraits of Two L.A. Poets.* (1988; 10 mins.) Marisela Norte, a Chicana poet from East L.A. who is well known for her involvement in the Los Angeles Chicano art scene, discusses her Spanish-infused poetry and some of the experiences that have influenced her work. Wanda Coleman, a Guggenheim recipient, describes how her politics and experiences as an African American blend in her poetry.

Creisler, Derek and Nancy Johnston. *Princess of the Pow-Wow.* (1987; 23 mins.) A video tribute to Ella Aquino, the eighty-five-year-old Lummi Yakima Native American, whose volunteer work helped to establish the American Indian Women's Service League and many of the social services for Seattle's "urban tribe."

THE AMERICAS: CROSSING BORDERS, CROSSING CULTURES

Michael R. Curry Geography
C. Cindy Fan Geography
University of California
Los Angeles, CA 90024

"The Americas: Crossing Borders, Crossing Cultures," conducted in spring 1991, was the last seminar in the multiyear Ford Ethnic Women's Curriculum Transformation Project (FEW) at UCLA. Earlier seminars had focused on a variety of disciplines, sometimes individually, sometimes together; this seminar was directed at the transformation of coursework in geography, planning, and architecture. Participants were about equally divided between those in geography and those in planning and architecture. About two thirds were faculty members and about one third graduate students.

Although geography at UCLA is in the College of Letters and Science, and planning and architecture in the separate Graduate School of Architecture and Urban Planning (GSAUP), there appeared in this instance to be several good reasons for combining the two groups. One was simply fortuitous: there are a number of geographers in GSAUP, and there is already substantial interaction among the two groups. The second was conceptual: geographers study the nature of places, the spatial organization of phenomena on the Earth's surface, and the impact of humans on the natural world; architects and planners are among the most prominent of professions engaged in each of those areas—in designing places and spatial systems and in effecting changes on the face of the Earth.

The course was organized around those themes. After an initial discussion of the nature of curriculum transformation we moved to the geography/ planning/architecture portion of the course. We first discussed issues that surround the creation of places and the establishment of systems of symbolic order, particularly with respect to the encounter of European with Native American cultures, both historically and today. We then turned to the roles of gender and ethnicity in migration and mobility research, and the effects on women and members of ethnic groups in particular.

In the next two weeks we considered the establishment of communities. In the first week the topic was agricultural communities and the nature of gender relationships within them. In the second the topic was the creation of symbolic centers by ethnic groups. Two visitors, Dolores Hayden and Deanna Matsumoto, presented results of their research. Hayden presented several parts of a collaborative project, entitled "The Power of Place," which commemorates ethnic women's history through new public art; most prominent was a public installation commemorating Biddy Mason, an African

American midwife in Los Angeles in the late nineteenth century. Matsumoto presented her award-winning student paper on the creation of a sense of place and home in World War II Japanese internment camps. Although the presentations concerned historical cases, in both instances the focus was on the possibilities for using such cases as means for drawing attention to the contributions of ethnic women.

In the next three weeks the subject matter was decidedly more contemporary and the approach rather more theoretical and political, less cultural and historical. In each week we discussed issues surrounding the status of women and ethnic groups in contemporary U.S. urban society. In one week the focus was changing employment opportunities and, more specifically, the mechanisms by which recent female immigrants have come to be incorporated into a revivified system of sweatshops. In the second the focus was on the nature of urban poverty; a visitor, James Johnson, discussed his and others' current research and theorizing on the nature of the urban underclass. In the third week we considered proposed solutions, through housing design to enable and encourage home work to the problems discussed in the first two weeks. In each of the three weeks the issue was the possibility of establishing forms of urban order which would better enable women to gain economic power outside of the traditional, and low-paying, service and industrial sectors of the economy.

Finally, we turned to issues related to the professions. In one week the topic was the gendering of the health care system and its effects on women's health; in the second the topic was the status of women in the profession of architecture, the ways in which they have remained invisible in official histories, and the features of the educational process which discourage their participation.

The seminar closed with two weeks of presentations by the participants. Faculty presentations were divided about equally in half, with one half involving the reorientation of courses in order to include more material about ethnic women and the other half involving the development of entirely new courses, specifically about women, and including substantial portions on ethnicity.

Although the participants ranged widely—from designers and historians to students of cultural phenomena, students of Third World agriculture to social scientists whose work is decidedly quantitative—the seminar almost immediately moved to a central set of questions: Can the social and economic status of ethnic women be understood purely as a result of the action of market processes on people of little power? Can economics account for the persistence of these effects? And on the other hand, in attempting to account for the unequal status of women, and especially ethnic women, is it possible to frame alternatives to an economic explanation without appealing to a simply biological notion of gender? This set of themes recurred throughout the course, with the elegance of economic explanations almost inevitably countered with the brute fact of the persistence of inequality across wide ranges of cultures and economies.

Syllabus

Week 1   Curriculum Transformation Background

Facilitators: C. Cindy Fan and Michael R. Curry, Geography, UCLA

Issues: Multiculturalism, concepts of culture, theoretical issues, how gender and ethnicity impact disciplines together, what role ethnicity plays in looking at gender differences

Barth, Fredrik, ed. Introduction to *Ethnic Groups and Boundaries: The Social Organization of Culture Differences,* 9–38. Boston: Little, Brown, 1969.

Bowlby, Sophie, Jane Lewis, Linda McDowell, and Jo Foord. "The Geography of Gender." In *New Models in Geography: The Political-Economy Perspective,* ed. Richard Peet and Nigel Thrift, 157–75. London: Unwin Hyman, 1989.

Butler, Johnnella E. "Transforming the Curriculum: Teaching about Women of Color." In *Multicultural Education: Issues and Perceptions,* ed. James A. Banks and Cherry M. Banks, 145–63. Boston: Allyn and Bacon, 1989.

Monk, Janice. "Integrating Women into the Geography Curriculum." *Journal of Geography* 82 (1983): 271–73.

Reed, Ishmael, Shawn Wong, Bob Callahan, and Andrew Hope. In *The Invention of Ethnicity,* ed. Werner Sollors, 226–35. New York: Oxford University Press, 1989.

Rodríguez, Richard. "An American Writer." In *The Invention of Ethnicity,* ed. Werner Sollors, 3–13. New York: Oxford University Press, 1989.

Rosaldo, Renato. "Others of Invention: Ethnicity and Its Discontents." Review of *Machines as the Measure of Men* by Michael Adas, *The Invention of Africa* by V. Y. Mudimbe, and *The Invention of Ethnicity* by Werner Sollors. *Voice Literary Supplement,* February 1990, 27–29.

Sandercock, Leonie, and Ann Forsyth. *Gender: A New Agenda for Planning Theory.* Working Paper Series. Berkeley: Institute of Urban and Regional Development, University of California–Berkeley, 1990.

Sollors, Werner, ed. "Introduction: The Invention of Ethnicity." In *The Invention of Ethnicity,* ix–xx. New York: Oxford University Press, 1989.

Week 2   The Nature of Landscapes: Investing Place with Meaning

Facilitator: Michael R. Curry, Geography, UCLA

Issues: Place and meaning, origins, Native American perspectives, cosmology, relation of Native American culture to European culture

Allen, Paula Gunn, "Kochinnenako in Academe: Three Approaches to Interpreting a Keres Indian Tale." *The Sacred Hoop: Recovering the Fem-*

inine in American Indian Traditions, 222–44. Boston: Beacon Press, 1986.

Basso, Keith H. " 'Stalking with Stories': Names, Places, and Moral Narratives among the Western Apache." In *Text, Play, and Story: The Construction and Reconstruction of Self and Society*, ed. Edward Bruner and Stuart Plattner, 19–55. Washington, D.C.: American Ethnological Society, 1984.

Berkhofer, Robert F. "The Idea of the Indian: Invention and Perpetuation." *The White Man's Indian: Images of the American Indian from Columbus to the Present*, 3–31. New York: Knopf, 1978.

Chato, Genevieve, and Christine Conte. "The Legal Rights of American Indian Women." In *Western Women: Their Land, Their Lives*, ed. Lillian Schlissel, Vicki Ruiz, and Janice Monk, 229–46. Albuquerque: University of New Mexico Press, 1988.

Paz, Octavio. "The Sons of La Malinche." *Labyrinth of Solitude: Life and Thought in Mexico*, 65–88. New York: Grove Press, 1961.

Rothenberg, Diane. "The Mothers of the Nation: Seneca Resistance to Quaker Intervention." In *Woman and Colonization*, ed. Mona Etienne and Eleanor Leacock, 63–87. New York: Praeger, 1980.

Smith, Sherry L. "Beyond the Princess and Squaw: Army Officers' Perceptions of Women." In *The Women's West*, ed. Susan Armitage and Elizabeth Jameson, 63–75. Norman: University of Oklahoma Press, 1987.

Week 3   Moving Around: Migration and Migrants

Facilitator: C. Cindy Fan, Geography, UCLA

Gender and Ethnicity in Migration Research

Issues: Differentials in likelihood to move between men and women; the role of marital status in decision to move; the function of migration in reducing earnings differentials by race and gender

Krieg, Randall G. "Does Migration Function to Reduce Earnings Differentials by Race and Gender?" *Annals of Regional Science* 24 (1990): 211–21.

Maxwell, Nan L. "Economic Returns to Migration: Marital Status and Gender Differences." *Social Science Quarterly* 69 (1988): 108–21.

Stapleton, Clare M. "Sex Differentials in Recent U.S. Migration Rates." *Urban Geography* 3 (1982): 142–65.

Wekerle, Gerda R., and Brent Rutherford. "The Mobility of Capital and the Immobility of Female Labor: Responses to Economic Restructuring." In *The Power of Geography: How Territory Shapes Social Life*, ed. Jennifer Wolch and Michael Dear, 139–72. Boston: Unwin Hyman, 1989.

Chai, Alice Y. "Coping with the Oppressions of Gender, Class and Race." *Engage/Social Action* 92 (April 1983): 56–62.

Guendelman, Sylvia. "The Incorporation of Mexican Women in Seasonal Migration: A Study of Gender Differences." *Hispanic Journal of Behavioral Sciences* 9 (1987): 245–64.

Ong, Paul M. "Immigrant Wives' Labor Force Participation." *Industrial Relations* 26 (1987): 296–303.

Weiner, Elizabeth, and Hardy Green. "A Stitch in Our Time: New York's Hispanic Garment Workers in the 1980s." In *A Needle, a Bobbin, a Strike: Women Needleworkers in America*, ed. Joan M. Jensen and Sue Davidson, 278–96. Philadelphia: Temple University Press, 1984.

Wilkinson, Clive. "Women, Migration and Work in Lesotho." In *Geography of Gender in the Third World*, ed. Janet H. Momsen and Janet G. Townsend, 225–39. London: SUNY Press and Hutchinson, 1987.

Week 4   Settling In: Agricultural Land and Livelihood

Facilitators: Judith Carney, Geography, and Susanna Hecht, Graduate School of Architecture and Urban Planning, UCLA

Resource Rights and Tenure Systems

Issues: Contrasts between Western and non-Western property rights regimes and tenure systems, with emphasis on access to and control over resources.

Feeny, David, Fikret Berkes, Bonnie J. McCay, and James M. Acheson. "The Tragedy of the Commons: Twenty-Two Years Later." *Human Ecology* 18 (1990): 1–19.

Fortmann, Louise. "The Tree Tenure Factor in Agroforestry with Particular Reference to Africa." *Agroforestry Systems* 2 (1985): 229–51.

Friedmann, Harriet, "Patriarchy and Property: A Reply to Goodman and Redclift." *Sociologia Ruralis* 26 (1986): 186–93.

Guha, Ramachandra. "The Mountains and Their People," 9–34; "Peasants and 'History,' " 185–96; and "A Sociology of Domination and Resistance," 1–8—all in *The Unquiet Woods: Ecological Change and Peasant Resistance in the Himalaya*. Berkeley: University of California Press, 1989.

Keller, Robert H. "America's Native Sweet: Chippewa Treaties and the Right to Harvest Maple Sugar." *American Indian Quarterly* 13 (1989): 117–35.

Okoth-Ogendo, H.W.O. "Some Issues of Theory in the Study of Tenure Relations in African Agriculture." *Africa* 59 (1989): 6–17.

Gender and Ethnicity in Agroforestry Systems

Issues: Historical and contemporary perspectives on social relations, with particular emphasis on the gender division of labor and ethnicity

Carney, Judith, and Michael Watts. "Disciplining Women? Rice, Mechanization, and the Evolution of Mandinka Gender Relations in Senegambia." *Signs: Journal of Women in Culture and Society* 16 (1991): 651–81.

Deere, Carmen Diana, and Magdalena León de Leal. "Peasant Production, Proletarianization, and the Sexual Division of Labor in the Andes." In *Women and Development,* ed. Lourdes Beneria, 65–93. New York: Praeger, 1982.

Haraway, Donna. "Teddy Bear Patriarchy: Taxidermy in the Garden of Eden, New York City, 1908–1936." *Primate Visions,* 26–58. New York: Routledge, 1989.

————. "Women's Place Is in the Jungle." *Primate Visions,* 279–303. New York: Routledge, 1989.

Hecht, Susanna B., Anthony B. Anderson, and P. May. "The Subsidy from Nature: Shifting Cultivation, Successional Palm Forest, and Rural Development." *Human Organization* 47 (1988): 25–35.

Young, Kate. "Modes of Appropriation and the Sexual Division of Labour: A Case Study from Oaxaca, Mexico." In *Feminism and Materialism: Women and Modes of Production,* ed. Annette Kuhn and Ann Marie Wolpe, 124–54. London: Routledge and Kegan Paul, 1978.

Week 5   Ethnic Women, Family, Community, and the Built Environment

Facilitator: Dolores Hayden, Graduate School of Architecture and Urban Planning, UCLA

Guest: Deanna Matsumoto, Student, Graduate School of Architecture and Urban Planning

Issues: Family patterns, community perspectives, uses of domestic space and domestic art by different cultures

Hayden, Dolores. "Biddy Mason's Los Angeles, 1856–1891." *California History* (Fall 1989): 86–99.

Mason, Sarah R. "Family Structure and Acculturation in the Chinese Community in Minnesota." In *Asian and Pacific American Experiences: Women's Perspectives,* ed. Nobuya Tsuchida, 160–71. Minneapolis: Asian/Pacific Learning Resource Center and the General College University of Minnesota, 1982.

Matsumoto, Deanna. 1990. "The Built Environment of America's Concentration Camps, 1942–1945." Photocopy.

Oldershaw, Barbara. "Blackfeet American Indian Women: Builders of the Tribe." *Places* 4 (1987): 38–47.

Week 6 Civic Organization: Industrialization, Urbanization, and the Role of Cities

Facilitator: Allen J. Scott, Geography, UCLA

Issues: Contemporary, shift from industrial to service economies, patterns of occupational segregation

Amott, Teresa L., and Julie A. Matthaei. "Race, Class, Gender, and Women's Work: A Conceptual Framework," 11–30; "The Transformation of Women's Wage Work," 315–48—both in *Race, Gender and Work: A Multicultural Economic History of Women in the United States.* Boston: South End Press, 1991.

Clark-Lewis, Elizabeth. " 'This Work Had an End': African American Domestic Workers in Washington, D.C., 1910–1940." In *"To Toil the Livelong Day": American Women at Work, 1780–1980,* ed. Carol Groneman and Mary Beth Norton, 196–212. Ithaca: Cornell University Press, 1987.

Hanson, Susan, and Geraldine Pratt. "Geographic Perspectives on the Occupational Segregation of Women." *National Geographic Research* 6 (1990): 376–99.

Keller, John F. "The Division of Labor in Electronics." In *Women, Men, and the International Division of Labor,* ed. June Nash and María Patricia Fernández-Kelly, 346–73. Albany: SUNY Press, 1983.

Kondo, Dorinne K. "The Eye/I." *Crafting Selves: Power, Gender and Discourses of Identity in a Japanese Workplace.* 3–48. Chicago: University of Chicago Press, 1990.

Nelson, Kristin. "Labor Demand, Labor Supply, and the Suburbanization of Low-Wage Office Work." In *Production, Work, Territory: The Geographical Anatomy of Industrial Capitalism,* ed. Allen J. Scott and Michael Storper, 149–71. Boston: Allen and Unwin, 1986.

Week 7 Humanizing the Urban Environment I: Dealing with Urban Poverty

Facilitator: Dean Toji, Graduate Student, Geography, UCLA

Guest: James Johnson, Geography, UCLA

Issues: Systemic conditions of poverty, gender and ethnic differences, relationship between urban poverty, ethnic women, and family

Baca Zinn, Maxine. "Family, Race and Poverty in the Eighties." *Signs: Journal of Women in Culture and Society* 14 (1989): 856–74.

Bane, Mary Jo. "Household Composition and Poverty." In *Fighting Poverty: What Works and What Doesn't,* ed. Sheldon H. Danziger and Daniel H. Weinberg, 209–31. Cambridge: Harvard University Press, 1986.

Johnson, James H., Jr., and Oliver, Melvin L. "Economic Restructuring and

Black Male Joblessness in U.S. Metropolitan Areas." *Urban Geography* 12 (1991): 542–62.

————. "Modeling Urban Underclass Behavior: Theoretical Considerations." Unpublished manuscript.

McLanahan, Sara S., Annemette Sorensen, and Dorothy Watson. "Sex Differences in Poverty, 1950–1980." *Signs: Journal of Women in Culture and Society* 15 (1989): 102–22.

Wilson, William Julius, and Kathryn M. Neckerman. "Poverty and Family Structure: The Widening Gap between Evidence and Public Policy Issues." In *Fighting Poverty: What Works and What Doesn't*, ed. Sheldon H. Danziger and Daniel H. Weinberg, 232–59. Cambridge: Harvard University Press, 1986.

Week 8 Humanizing the Urban Environment II: Health, Housing, and Homework Issues

Facilitators: Jacqueline Leavitt, Graduate School of Architecture and Urban Planning, and Steven Matthews, Geography, UCLA

Housing and Home work

Issues: Public housing, home work, alternative design, child care

Ahrentzen, Sherry Boland. "Home as a Workplace in the Lives of Women." In *Place Attachment*, ed. Irwin Altman and Setha Lowe, 113–38. Human Behavior and Environment no. 12. New York: Plenum Press, 1992.

Boris, Eileen. "Black Women and Paid Labor in the Home: Industrial Homework in Chicago in the 1920s." In *Homework: Historical and Contemporary Perspectives on Paid Labor at Home*, ed. Eileen Boris and Cynthia R. Daniels, 33–52. Urbana: University of Illinois Press, 1989.

Daniels, Cynthia R. "Between Home and Factory: Homeworkers and the States." In *Homework: Historical and Contemporary Perspectives on Paid Labor at Home*, ed. Eileen Boris and Cynthia R. Daniels, 13–32. Urbana: University of Illinois Press, 1989.

Fernández-Kelly, M. Patricia, and Anna M. García. "Hispanic Women and Homework: Women in the Informal Economy of Miami and Los Angeles." In *Homework: Historical and Contemporary Perspectives on Paid Labor at Home*, ed. Eileen Boris and Cynthia R. Daniels, 165–79. Urbana: University of Illinois Press, 1989.

Harley, Sharon. "For the Good of Family and Race: Gender, Work, and Domestic Roles in the Black Community, 1880–1930." *Signs: Journal of Women in Culture and Society* 15 (1990): 336–49.

Leidner, Robin. "Home Work: A Study in the Interaction of Work and Family Organization." *Research in the Sociology of Work* 4 (1988): 69–94.

Leavitt, Jacqueline, and Susan Saegert. "Tenant Cooperatives." In *Abandon-*

ment to Hope: Community Households in Harlem, 35–63. New York: Columbia University Press, 1990.

Mangin, William, and John C. Turner. "The Barriada Movement." *Progressive Architecture* (May 1968): 154–62.

Plunz, Richard. "Aesthetics and Realities." *A History of Housing in New York City*, 164–206. New York: Columbia University Press, 1990.

———. "Government Intervention." *A History of Housing in New York City*, 207–46. New York: Columbia University Press, 1990.

Ungerson, Clare. "Why Do Women Care?" In *A Labour of Love: Women, Work and Caring*, ed. Janet Finch and Dulcie Groves, 31–50. London: Routledge and Kegan Paul, 1983.

Health

Issues: Access to health care; women and people of color as caregivers

Doyal, Lesley, with Imogen Pennell. "Women, Medicine and Social Control: The Case of the National Health Service (NHS)." *The Political Economy of Health*, 215–38. London: Pluto Press, 1979.

Duffy, John. "Medical Education, Women, and Minorities." *The Healers: A History of American Medicine*, 260–90. Chicago: University of Illinois Press, 1979.

Kobrin, Frances E. "The American Midwife Controversy: A Crisis of Professionalization." *Bulletin of the History of Medicine* 40 (1966): 350–63. Reprinted in *Sickness and Health in America: Readings in the History of Medicine and Public Health*, ed. Judith Leavitt and Ronald Numbers, 217–25. Madison: University of Wisconsin Press, 1980.

Oakley, Ann. "Doctor Knows Best." In *Women Confined: Towards a Sociology of Childbirth*, 170–75. New York: Schocken Books, 1980.

Saunders, David. "Medicine, Business, and the State." *The Struggle for Health Medicine and Politics of Underdevelopment*, 111–29. New York: Macmillan, 1985.

Turshen, Meredeth. "Women's Health." *The Politics of Public Health*, 91–118. New Brunswick, N.J.: Rutgers University Press, 1989.

Women and Geography Study Group of the Institute of British Geographers (IBG). "Access to Facilities." *Geography and Gender: An Introduction to Feminist Geography*, 89–105. London: Hutchinson Press and the Explorations in Feminism Collective, 1984.

Week 9 Working to Shape the Environment: Women in Architecture and Related Professions

Facilitator: Diane Favro, Graduate School of Architecture and Urban Planning, UCLA

Theory and Historiography

Issues: Women in architecture; power and hierarchy in the design professions

Berkeley, Ellen Perry. "Architecture: Toward a Feminist Critique." In *New Space for Women,* ed. Gerda R. Wekerle, Rebecca Peterson, and David Morley, 205–18. Boulder: Westview Press, 1980.

De Bretteville, Sheila Levrant. "Feminist Design." *SD 90 06:*72–73.

Hankwitz, Molly. "The Right to Rewrite: Feminism and Architectural Theory." *Inland Architect* 35 (1991): 52–55.

Kampen, Natalie, and Elizabeth G. Grossman. "Feminism and Methodology: Dynamics of Change in the History of Art and Architecture." Working Paper no. 122, 1–34. Wellesley, Mass.: Wellesley College Center for Research on Women, 1983.

Kennedy, Margrit. "Seven Hypotheses on Male and Female Principles in Architecture." *Heresies 11,* no. 3 (1981): 12–13.

Kingsley, Karen. "Gender Issues in Teaching Architectural History." *Journal of Architectural Education* 41 (Winter 1988): 21–25.

Scott Brown, Denise. "Room at the Top?—Sexism and the Star System in Architecture." *SD 90 06:*73–75.

Thompson, Jane. "Urbanist without Portfolio: Notes on a Career." *SD 90 06:*73.

Case Studies

Cole, Doris. "Frontier Traditions: Pioneers and Indians." In *From Tipi to Skyscraper: A History of Women in Architecture,* 1–27. Boston: I Press, 1973.

Dozier, Richard K. "The Black Architectural Experience in America." *American Institute of Architecture Journal* 65 (1976): 162–68.

Gilman, Charlotte Perkins. "The Passing of the Home in Great American Cities." *Heresies 11,* no. 3 (1981): 53–55.

Grossman, Elizabeth G., and Lisa B. Reitzes. "Caught in the Crossfire: Women and Architectural Education, 1880–1910." In *Architecture: A Place for Women,* ed. Ellen Perry Berkeley and Matilda McQuaid, 27–39. Washington, D.C.: Smithsonian Institution Press, 1989.

Hayden, Dolores. "The Power of Place: A Proposal for Los Angeles." *Public Historian* 10 (Summer 1988): 5–18.

Hayden, Dolores, and Peter Marris. "The Quiltmaker's Landscape." *Landscape* 25, no. 3 (1981): 39–47.

Hess, Jean E. "Domestic Interiors in Northern New Mexico." *Heresies 11,* no. 3 (1981): 30–33.

Howett, Catherine M. "Careers in Landscape Architecture: Recovering for Women What the 'Ladies' Won and Lost." In *Feminist Visions: Toward a Transformation of the Liberal Arts Curriculum,* ed. Diane L. Fowlkes and Charlotte S. McClure, 139–48. University: University of Alabama Press, 1984.

Lobell, Mimi. "The Buried Treasure: Women's Ancient Architectural Heritage." In *Architecture: A Place for Women*, ed. Ellen Perry Berkeley and Matilda McQuaid, 139–57. Washington, D.C.: Smithsonian Institution Press, 1989.

Pollock, Nancy Lee. "Women on the Inside: Divisions of Space in Imperial China." *Heresies 11*, no. 3 (1981): 34–37

Week 10   Re-Covering Pedagogy I: Devising and Revising Courses/ Participant Presentations

Facilitators: C. Cindy Fan and Michael R. Curry, Geography, UCLA

Bowlby, Sophia, and Linda McDowell. "Teaching Feminist Geography." *Journal of Geography in Higher Education* 7 (1983): 97–108.

Chan, Sucheng. "On the Ethnic Studies Requirement, Part I: Pedagogical Implications." *Amerasia* 15 (1989): 267–80.

Crenshaw, Kimberle Williams. "Foreward: Toward a Race-Conscious Pedagogy in Legal Education." *National Black Law Journal* 11 (Winter 1989): 1–14.

Deutsche, Rosalyn. "Boys Town." *Environment and Planning D: Society and Space* 9 (1991): 5–30.

Leavitt, Jacqueline. "Introducing Gender into Architectural Studios." Graduate School of Architecture and Urban Planning, UCLA, 1991.

Massey, Doreen. "Flexible Sexism." *Environment and Planning D: Society and Space* 9 (1991): 31–57.

Matsuda, Mari. "Affirmative Action and Legal Knowledge: Planting Seeds in Plowed-Up Ground." *Harvard Women's Law Journal* 7 (Spring 1988). 1–17.

"Methods for Gender-Free Teaching in Geography: Report of a One-day Conference Organized by the Women and Geography and Higher Education Learning Study Groups of the IBG at UCL, 10 November 1984." *Area* 17 (1985): 255.

Mitchell, Jacquelyn. "Transforming Community Practices into Pedagogical Strategies: Building a Classroom Community." Paper presented at the American Anthropological Association meeting, Washington, D.C., November 1989.

Peake, Linda. "Teaching Feminist Geography: Another Perspective." *Journal of Geography in Higher Education* 9 (1985): 186–90.

Thorne, Barrie. "Rethinking the Ways We Teach." In *Educating the Majority: Women Challenge Tradition in Higher Education*, ed. Carol Pearson, Donna Shavlik, and Judith Touchton, 311–25. New York: Macmillan, 1989.

Week 11   Re-Covering Pedagogy II: Devising and Revising Courses/ Participant Presentations

MODEL UNDERGRADUATE CURRICULUM

LITMUS TESTS FOR CURRICULUM TRANSFORMATION

Liza Fiol-Matta

Transformation ". . . does not stop at adding and celebrating diversity. It demands that we do something with these experiences, this diversity, in order ultimately to understand the whole. It demands that we add, delete, de-center, re-vision and re-organize in order to transform our curricula to reflect a kind of unity, a wholeness that is all-inclusive in its content, methodology, and pedagogy."[1]

Johnnella E. Butler

It is impossible to succeed at transformation without questioning certain components of our tasks as educators. Curriculum transformation begins with critiquing our disciplines and our assumptions of how knowledge is passed along in our fields. These questions are most effectively asked in collaboration with colleagues in our institutions and disciplines. Then, once questioned, we can move on to effect the change in our classrooms and research. Most faculty participants in the Ford Mainstreaming Minority Women's Studies Program began revision of their courses by attending workshops that asked questions something like these:

1. What are the underlying assumptions, principles, or norms of your discipline? What kind of knowledge is valued?
2. What kind of teaching style is valued by those in your discipline?
3. Who are your students? What do they need to know?
4. How would your discipline have to change to incorporate previously excluded groups?[2]

My concern here is not, however, the initial questioning that we must do before engaging in changing our courses but, rather, the kinds of practical questions we can ask of ourselves and our syllabi if we want to continue the generative change that transforming is about. Designing a new course, or updating a syllabus, may seem initially sufficient, but what can we do to make sure that our courses continue to reflect the diversity and fluidity of race, gender, ethnicity, and class concerns of this world? I have tried to incorporate disciplinary as well as classroom indicators of change in the following list of questions for assessment of change, which is offered as a starting point for self-critique and definition of our goals and pedagogy.

LITMUS TESTS FOR CURRICULUM TRANSFORMATION

1. What previously excluded groups have I included, and where in the course outline do they appear?
2. How often do I talk about these groups instead of letting them speak for themselves? How much of that representation is in new scholarship? How much new knowledge by women of color researchers have I included?
3. How often do I tell students what they will or must find in the materials or the course? How have I provided for letting them find what is there for themselves and sharing their discoveries?
4. How often in the making of this syllabus have I sought conceptual critiquing and discussion of issues or concerns from someone more knowledgeable in the area or with a different outlook than mine? How often was this contact primarily to ask a colleague for a list of names or books to add to a reading list or bibliography?
5. How have I facilitated, or helped facilitate, dialogue with colleagues in ethnic studies or women studies? How have I facilitated other cross-discipline contact?
6. What tangible (obvious) change can I point to in my revised syllabus or course outline that reflects my new thinking? The new scholarship? Is this change woven through the design of the course, or have I segmented, subdivided, tacked on the new? If so, why?
7. What tangible change can I talk about in how I see my discipline? What tangible change has occurred in how I see my role as teacher or researcher?
8. How am I teaching the methodology of my discipline? What am I teaching as research methodology and subjects of legitimate study? How has that changed or had to change from what and how I was taught?
9. How have I integrated that change in disciplinary methodology into my syllabus? What do I expect the impact of this change to be? How will my students be learning differently than those of a semester before? Than five years ago? How am I assessing this?
10. What are the underlying assumptions imbedded in my syllabus or course outline? What learning style or method, if any, am I privileging or fore-

grounding (collaboration, group-/teamwork, individualism, competition, binary thinking, etc.), and why do I want to do so?

11. What have I done, given the restrictions that my course may have (size, departmental final, mandated textbook, etc.), to engage students in critical and creative thinking? What role do students themselves play in shaping the course?

12. What would I call what I have done to my syllabus: mainstreaming, balancing, integrating, transforming? What are the implications of that?

13. What are the race, gender, and class underpinnings of my course or syllabus? Where are these manifested?

14. What examples or materials have I planned to use and how "culture bound" are they? How conscious am I of the language and manner of my teaching? What voice do my students have (and, what voice do my students hear?) in the classroom? What do I do about it?

NOTES

1. Epigraph: "The Difficult Dialogue of Curriculum Transformation: Ethnic Studies and Women's Studies," in Johnnella E. Butler and John C. Walter, *Transforming the Curriculum: Ethnic Studies and Women's Studies*, 1–19. Albany: SUNY, 1991.

2. I am indebted to Betty Schmitz for these questions.

REFLECTIONS ON TEACHING LITERATURE BY AMERICAN WOMEN OF COLOR

King-Kok Cheung

Last year UCLA received a Ford Foundation grant to integrate material by and about women of color into the undergraduate curriculum. As someone who has taught courses on American female writers of color writers and cofacilitated a faculty development seminar funded by the grant, I would like to venture some suggestions on how to decenter long-standing assumptions and approaches.[1] I believe that the greatest challenge in teaching such classes is not introducing new material but, rather, ushering in alternative critical perspectives, especially if instructors seek to go beyond the integration of texts to the transformation of mind-sets. To achieve these goals it may be necessary to cross all kinds of boundaries, not just ethnic but also generic, disciplinary, political, epistemological, and even metaphysical boundaries.

SUSPEND ESTABLISHED LITERARY CRITERIA

Susan Stanford Friedman has demonstrated convincingly that genre is often gender and, one may add, culture specific: "A binary system in particular has shaped the expectations governing the reading and writing of epic and lyric poetry, a dualism that intersects with the cultural opposition of masculine and feminine." She contends that in choosing to use the masculine genre, female poets such as Elizabeth Browning and H.D. "self-consciously reformulated epic conventions to suit their female vision and voice."[2] We can detect analogous innovations among female writers of color who appropriate the conventional forms of autobiography and novel and who frequently dissolve the boundary between the two genres. Works such as Sandra Cisneros's *The House on Mango Street*, Alice Walker's *Meridian*, and Maxine Hong Kingston's *China Men* pulsate with personal experiences, yet they are also imaginative works with strong political implications. Instead of asking whether these authors are capable of maintaining the detachment or artistic distance of novelists, we must question our received notion that the rendition of certain experiences is too personal or too political to be taken seriously as literature. Following the lead of feminist critics who have shown that women often express themselves artistically in journals and letters, we must invent new criteria that do not make light of texts that deviate from established norms. If we hold on to a critical apparatus designed to serve a white male canon, not only will some works by women of color seem to fall short but their cultural specificities and subversive energy will also go unnoticed.

Similar cautions must be exercised against placing these works in a purely Western literary tradition. Both Kingston's *Tripmaster Monkey* and Leslie Silko's *Ceremony* (which, incidentally, also blurs the boundary between prose and poetry) abound with allusions, respectively, to Chinese epics and Native American myths, and both authors draw on oral legacies of storytelling. No less influential are musical forms such as *corridos* and *canciones* on Chicano poetry or spirituals and blues on African American poetry. Such resources ought to be reckoned with as part of the American heritage.

QUESTION GLOBALIZING FEMINIST ASSUMPTIONS

Women of color have repeatedly challenged white feminist theories. Paula Gunn Allen argues that patriarchy, as such, did not exist in many Indian tribes (which had been gynocratic) until they were colonized by whites.[3] Even common notions of masculinity and femininity are by no means universal. Both Tayo in Silko's *Ceremony* and Lipsha in Louise Erdrich's *Love Medicine* are "feminine" figures by white standards. And then there are men of color who have been emasculated in America. The opening myth in Kingston's *China Men*, in which a Chinese man is transformed by force into a woman, underlines the parallels between the racist treatment of Chinese-American men and the sexist subjugation of women. Even the misogyny of Cholly Breedlove in Toni Morrison's *The Bluest Eye* or of Grange Copeland in Alice Walker's *The Third Life of Grange Copeland* must be viewed within the context of racial inequality. Theories that at once polarize the sexes and equalize men and women tend to drown the particular pathos dramatized in these texts.

DECENTER WESTERN IDEALS AND DOMINANT MODES OF SEEING

While ideals such as rationalism and competitive individualism may be shared by people of color, women of color frequently present competing sets of beliefs. Instead of seeing and judging diverse cultures from Eurocentric perspectives, these perspectives must themselves be interrogated, and oppositional viewpoints be entertained. For instance, when we encounter ghosts and spirits in works such as Paule Marshall's *Praisesong for the Widow*, Toni Morrison's *Beloved*, Silko's *Ceremony*, and Ana Castillo's *Mixqiahuala Letters*, we must not jump to the conclusion that the characters are superstitious or hallucinatory or, what is equally problematic, assume that those beliefs are shared by all members of the ethnic group under discussion.[4] Unless we refrain from relegating works of literature by people of color to the realms of the benighted or the exotic, they can never become sites for possible transformative thinking.

Harking back to my first point, the resurgence of alternative cultural ethos may well be one reason why works by women of color so often depart from conventional aesthetic structures. For instance, while a single hero is the norm in traditional novels, fiction by women of color (e.g., Gloria Naylor's *The Women of Brewster Place*, Erdrich's *Love Medicine*, Amy Tan's *The Joy Luck Club*) is often family or community centered; it contains multiple protagonists and points of view rather than a single hero(ine) or narrator. Granted that these writers may be influenced by modernist techniques, their worldviews tend toward connection rather than fragmentation.

CONTEXTUALIZE WITHOUT CONFLATING TEXT WITH CONTEXT

Historically and socially anchored criticism is indispensable. For instance, knowledge of Japanese-Canadian internment is crucial in studying Joy Kogawa's *Obasan*, and information about the Korean independence movement will enhance our understanding of Theresa Cha's *Dictee* or Kim Ronyoung's *Clay Walls*.

At the same time, we must avoid seeing creative work by one writer as testimony for the entire race. The controversies surrounding *The Color Purple* and *The Woman Warrior* amply reflect these assumptions. Both Walker and Kingston are accused of reinforcing stereotypes of sexism in the African American and the Chinese American cultures, respectively. Such insistence on representativeness, in precluding the possibility of a private vision, denies subjectivity to the author. It is, furthermore, a burden borne exclusively by ethnic—especially ethnic women—writers. (Norman Mailer is seldom taken to be representative of the entire white race.)

CONFRONT THE ISSUES OF MARKETABILITY AND AUDIENCE

bell hooks argues that creative work by African Americans "is shaped by a market that reflects white supremacist values and concerns": "In this social context . . . novels highlighting black male oppression of black females while downplaying white racist oppression of black people would be more marketable than the reverse."[5] Students can read more critically if they are made aware of this interface of literature and politics.

A distinction should be made, however, between an author's accomplishment and responsibility and the forces of cultural production such as publishers' decisions, marketing strategies, readers' predilections, and misappropriation. Just because a work is a national best-seller does not necessarily mean that the author is a "sellout," as some critics have insinuated.

In addition, an author's ethnicity frequently skews a reader's response. A work that is perceived to be progressive and funny when written by a Mark Twain may be judged as militant or bitter (if not self-interested) when written by an Alice Walker. Texts, pace the New Critics and Roland Barthes, are seldom read independently of the authors.

AVOID TOKENISM OR GHETTOIZATION

On the one hand, it is important to show that race and gender do not merely affect the literary production of women and ethnic minorities but that they shape the work of canonized authors as well. (How anxiety about white ideology informs Melville's *Moby Dick* has been brilliantly illustrated by Toni Morrison.)[6]

On the other hand, we must overcome the prevailing assumption that works by women or people of color are studied largely because of their gender and ethnic quotient. In many Survey of American Literature courses, and even in courses on female writers, it is not uncommon to see these works assigned only in the one week thematically devoted to "Gender and Race." Instructors may want to consider distributing these works throughout the syllabus and unlocking them from preconceived categories. Writers of whatever gender and color go for style, poetic or narrative strategies, and "universals."

STRETCH THE BOUNDS OF GENDER AND CULTURAL IDENTITIES

Gender and cultural stereotyping is not peculiar to "outsiders." The pervasive belief within one school of Asian American critics that there is a "fake" and a "real" Asian American sensibility and the reluctance among some black scholars to address feminist and gay issues (dismissed as "white") suggest that there are certain essentialist prescriptions for being Asian American and African American. (Yet no one says, "White men don't do this.") In place of paradigms that further exclude the marginal we need feminist and cultural theories that allow for fluid identities—identities that are neither color-blind nor color bound, that are defined neither by nor merely in binary opposition to white male constructions. Julia Kristeva, for one, has advocated a new *"signifying space, a both corporeal and desiring mental space"* beyond gender dichotomies out of which emerge exclusion and violence.[7] Perhaps a similar space is needed which can go beyond racial opposition and which can accommodate multiplicity of identifications.

These points, I must stress, are more reflections than considered or proved pedagogies, and certainly not the final word. In fact, a bonus of the Ford seminar, in which everyone was challenged at one time or another, was the displacement of authority. Where lively exchange, passionate confrontation, and critical dissent can take place, however painful at times, there is still hope for radical transformation.

NOTES

This essay was originally presented at the 1989 PAPC Convention in the session on "Feminism and Ethnicity in the Professions: Theory and Pedagogy."

1. I owe many of my ideas to my students and to the participants of the Ford seminar. I would like to thank in particular Karen Rowe, the principal investigator of the Ford project, and Brenda Marie Osbey, my cofacilitator.

2. "Gender and Genre Anxiety: Elizabeth Browning and H.D. as Epic Poets," *Tulsa Studies in Women's Literature* 5, no. 2 (1986): 203–4.

3. Paula Gunn Allen, guest lecture in the Ford seminar. See also Gunn Allen, *The Sacred Hoop: Recovering the Feminine in American Indian Traditions* (Boston: Beacon Press, 1986), 30–42.

4. Such condescending attitudes not only interfere with appreciation of the texts but also provoke hostility in the classroom. According to Johnnella Butler, one of the forces polarizing the classroom into black versus white is that "white students insist on reducing all experience to the same—theirs" ("Toward a Pedagogy of Everywoman's Studies," in *Gendered Subjects: The Dynamics of Feminist Teaching,* ed. Margo Culley and Catherine Portuges [Boston: Routledge and Kegan Paul, 1985], 232). An example occurred within the Ford seminar itself, when a black colleague was asked to explain what she meant by "spiritual encounter." She said she knew she was visited by the spirits when she felt a sudden surge of energy while jogging. She was understandably chagrined and offended when another colleague rephrased her experience as a "second wind."

5. "The Politics of Radical Black Subjectivity," *Zeta Magazine* (April 1989): 53–54.

6. "Unspeakable Things Unspoken: the Afro-American Presence in American Literature," *Michigan Quarterly Review* 28, no. 1 (Winter 1989): 14ff.

7. "Women's Time," *Signs* 7, no. 1 (1981): 33. See also Barbara Frey Waxman's "Canonicity and Black American Literature: A Feminist View," *MELUS* 14, no. 2 (1987): 87–92; Waxman discusses how Kristeva's idea may be used to expand the borders of the black American literary canon (88).

HUMANITIES

INTRODUCTION TO TWENTIETH-CENTURY AMERICAN CULTURE

Howard Gillette American Studies Program
Phyllis Palmer American Studies Program
George Washington University
Washington, DC 20052

Course Objectives

The purpose of this course is to introduce students to various cultural works and communicative formats (e.g., film, television, music) which have expressed values of people in the United States during the twentieth century. Students will gain skills in "reading" various cultural forms: autobiographies, novels, movies, museum exhibits, and music. The primary theme of the course is the movement from a white, Euro-American, middle-class, Protestant cultural dominance at the start of the century to a multiracial, multiethnic, multireligious, universalist culture by 1990. We stress how gender is constructed within these cultural shifts.

Required Texts

Jane Addams, *Twenty Years at Hull House*
Maya Angelou, *I Know Why the Caged Bird Sings*
Saul Bellow, *Seize the Day*
John Dos Passos, *The Big Money*

Janet Campbell Hale, *The Jailing of Cecelia Capture*
LeRoi Jones, *Blues People*

Films and Television Programs

Wild Women Don't Get the Blues
42nd Street
The City
Life and Times of Rosie the Riveter
Episodes of "I Love Lucy" and "Dragnet"
Eyes on the Prize, part 2
El Norte

Syllabus

Class 1	*On the Eve of "America's Century."*
	Addams, *Twenty Years at Hull House*, 1–132
Class 2	*Jane Addams, Women's Culture, and Progressivism.*
	Discussion sessions on Jane Addams
Class 3	*Immigration and Leisure Culture in the City.*
	Addams, *Twenty Years*, 133–256.
	Discussion sessions on feminine, Protestant, midwestern culture versus eastern and southern European immigrant cultures
Class 4	*Dos Passos, World War I, and the Lost Generation.*
	Dos Passos, *The Big Money*, 1–124
Class 5	*"The Invisible Hand": New Technology, Science, and Corporate Power.*
Class 6	*Advertising and Modern Consumerism.*
	Dos Passos, *Big Money*, 124–300.
	Discussion sessions on masculine technological culture and human worth
Class 7	*The Automobile and American Culture.*
	Dos Passos, *Big Money*, 301 to end
Class 8	*"Wild Women Don't Get the Blues."*
	Discussion sessions on technocratic versus artistic cultural values
Class 9	*Blues and African-American Culture.*
	Jones, *The Blues People*, 1–174
Class 10	*Depression and 1930s America.*
	42nd Street.
	Discussion sessions on race and class differences and the

pressures and problems of cultural assimilation and negotiation

Class 11   *Documentary Tradition: The City.*
Class 12   *The 1939 World's Fair and Ideas of Progress.*
Class 13   *Midterm Examination.*
Class 14   *Great Migrations: Blacks, Okies, Gays.*
            Angelou, *I Know Why the Caged Bird Sings*
Class 15   *Gender Change and Cultural Reversion.*
            Life and Times of Rosie the Riveter.
            Discussion sessions on challenges and accommodations
            to values of racial, ethnic, gender, class, and culture hierarchy
Class 16   *Post–World War II Transitions.*
Class 17   *Suburban Dream, Urban Nightmare.*
            Saul Bellow, *Seize the Day.*
            Discussion sessions on gender roles and family norms
Class 18   *Television and American Culture.*
            "I Love Lucy" and "Dragnet"
Class 19   *Eyes on the Prize," part 2.*
            Discussion sessions on values purveyed by television and
            television's power as a documentary medium
Class 20   *The 1960s and the Emergence of the Counterculture.*
            Hale, *The Jailing of Cecilia Capture*
Class 21   *Vietnam, Protest, and Cultural Politics.*
            Discussion sessions on images of America and rewriting
            U.S. history
Class 22   *The Women's Movement and American Pluralism.*
Class 23   *Contemporary Popular Culture.*
            Jones, *The Blues People,* 175 to end
            Discussion sessions on cultural pluralism and power
Class 24   *America in the World at the End of the Twentieth Century.*
            El Norte
Class 25   *Ronald Reagan, the Pursuit of Happiness, and American
            Exceptionalism.*
Class 26   *Summary.*

RENAISSANCE ART OUT OF THE CANON: ART, GENDER, AND CULTURAL DIVERSITY, 1500–1600

Claire Farago Department of Fine Arts
University of Colorado
Boulder, CO 80309

Course Description

This course examines European Renaissance art in a global context, incorporating culturally diverse material. The course is organized thematically and provides an introduction to recent scholarship addressed to the history of race, ethnicity, gender, and class concerns through the examination of visual evidence and primary period documents as they intersect with the visual arts. Critical thinking is incorporated into the course through group discussion, collaborative projects, oral reports, and short papers. The course is focused upon two historical problems: (1) the new, theoretical status granted to painting, sculpture, and architecture in Italy during the fifteenth and sixteenth centuries; and (2) the ways in which non-Western art was perceived by Europeans during this period.

Course Requirements

The emphasis of this course is on lecture material and class discussion, with readings supplementing both. There is no text to replace lectures. Students are expected to complete all of the readings and be prepared to raise questions and issues for discussion. The requirements include five individual position papers leading to collaborative presentations, three slide quizzes, and a ten-page final paper on a topic pertinent to the course.

Syllabus

Part 1

Class 1   *The European Concept of Renaissance.*
                   Erwin Panofsky, chapter 2 of "Renaissance and Renascences," in part 1, *Renaissance and Renascences* (1960; reprint, New York, 1972), 42–54.

Class 2	*Recent Feminist Revisionist Art History.*
	Christian Klapisch-Zuber, "Holy Dolls: Play and Piety in Florence in the Quattrocento," in *Women, Family, and Ritual in Renaissance Italy*, trans. L. Cochrane (Chicago and London, 1985).
Class 3	*Renaissance Views of Women.*
	Ian MacLean, "Theology, Mystical and Occult Writings," in *The Renaissance Notion of Woman: A Study in the Fortunes of Scholasticism and Medical Science in European Intellectual Life* (Cambridge, 1980), 6–27.
Class 4	*Renaissance Images of Women.*
	Elizabeth Cropper, "The Beauty of Woman: Problems in the Rhetoric of Renaissance Portraiture," in *Rewriting the Renaissance: The Discourses of Sexual Difference in Early Modern Europe*, ed. Margaret Ferguson et al. (Chicago, 1986), 175–90.
Class 5	*European Views of Non-European Peoples before the Accidental Discovery of the American Continent.*
	Richard Bernheimer, "The Natural History of the Wild Man," in *Wild Men in the Middle Ages: A Study in Art, Sentiment, and Demonology* (Cambridge, Mass., 1952), 1–20.

Part 2

Class 6	*Colonialization/Invasion of the Americas.*
	J. H. Elliot, "The Uncertain Impact," in *The Old World and the New, 1492–1650* (Cambridge, 1970), 1–27.
Class 7	*The First Images of the Inhabitants of the "New World."*
	William C. Sturtevant, "First Visual Images of Native America," in *First Images of America: The Impact of the New World on the Old*, ed. Fredi Chiappelli et al., 2 vols. (Berkeley, 1976), 1:415–55.
Class 8	*The Literary Background.*
	Lewis Hanke, "America as Fantasy," in *Aristotle and the American Indians: A Study in Race Prejudice in the Modern World* (London, 1959), 1–11.
Class 9	*The Politics of Conflict.*
	Juan Marichal, "The New World from Within: The Inca Garcilaso," in Chiapelli et al., *First Images*, 1:57–63.
Class 10	*Imperialism and the Catholic Reformation.*
	John W. O'Malley, "The Discovery of America and Re-

	form Thought at the Papal Court in the Early Cinque-cento," in Chiapelli et al., *First Images*, 1:185–200.
Class 11	*Reformation Art in America: Current State of the Issues.* Jorge Alberto Manrique, "The Progress of Art in New Spain"; and Johanna Hecht, "Mexican Architecture and Sculpture in Renaissance Modes," in *Mexico: Splendors of Thirty Centuries* (exhibit catalog), by Octavio Paz et al., Metropolitan Museum of Art, New York, 1990, 237–42, 280–85.
Class 12	*European Collectors of New World Art: Attitudes and Artifacts.* Laura Laurencich-Minelli, "Museography and Ethnographical Collections in Bologna during the Sixteenth and Seventeenth Centuries," in *The Origins of Museums: The Cabinet of Curiosities in Sixteenth- and Seventeenth-Century Europe*, ed. Oliver Impay and Arthur MacGregor (Oxford, 1985), 17–23.

Part 3

Class 13	*Collaborative Art.* Elizabeth Hill Boone with Eloise Quiñones Keber, "Painted Manuscripts," in Paz et al., *Mexico*, 268–79.
Class 14	*African Art for European Collectors.* Peter Mark, "European Perceptions of Black Africans in the Renaissance," in *Africa and the Renaissance: Art in Ivory*, by Ezio Bassani and William B. Fagg, ed. Susan Vogel et al. (exhibit catalog) (New York and Houston, 1988), 21–32.
Class 15	*Depictions by the Dispossessed.* Rolena Adorno, "The Depiction of Self and Other in Colonial Peru," in *Art Journal* 49, no. 2 (Summer 1990): 110–18.
Class 16	*The Graphic Arts I: Exemplars in Mexican Devotional Art.* Detlet Heikamp and Ferdinand Anders, in *Mexico and the Medici* (Florence, 1972).
Class 17	*The Graphic Arts II: European Theories of Imagination.* David Summers, "Michelangelo on Architecture," in *Art Bulletin* 54 (1972): 146–72.
Class 18	*Development of Mexican Themes in European Art.* Benjamin Keen, in *The Aztec Image in Western Thought* (New Brunswick, N.J., 1971), 173ff.

Class 19	*The First Academy of Art.*
	Karen Edis-Barzman, "Liberal Academicians and the New Social Elite in Grand Ducal Florence," in *World Art: Themes of Unity in Diversity*, Acts of the 25th International Congress of the History of Art, 3 vols., ed. Irving Lavin, 1:459–64.
Class 20	*Renaissance Art Criticism in the Americas and in Europe.*
	George Kubler, "The Aesthetic Recognition of Ancient American Art (1492–1842)," in Lavin, *World Art*, 1:27–48.
Class 21	*Revising History: Doubling the Categories of Race and Gender.*
	Marianna Torgovnick, "Taking Tarzan Seriously," in *Gone Primitive: Savage Intellects, Modern Lives* (Chicago, 1990), 42–72.
Class 22	*Field Trip to the Taylor Museum, Colorado Springs.*
	William Wroth, *Christian Images in Hispanic New Mexico: The Taylor Museum Collection of Santos* (Colorado Springs, 1982).
Class 23	*Revisioning History: On Black Athena and Other European Categories.*
	Reports from field trip
Class 24	*Field Trip to the Frank Mayor Collection of Mexican Colonial Art, Denver Art Museum.*

Part 4

Class 25	*The "Shrinking Globe": A Cultural Parallel with Japan.*
	Edward Said, "Orientalism Reconsidered," in *Europe and Its Others*, Proceedings of the Essex Conference on the Sociology of Literature, July 1984, ed. Francis Barker (Essex, 1985), 14–27.
Class 26	*Patronage: Collection Preferences in Japan during the Muromachi Era.*
	David Pollack, "The Informing Image: 'China' in *The Tale of Genji*," in *The Fracture of Meaning: Japan's Synthesis of China from the Eighth through the Eighteenth Centuries"* (Princeton, 1986), 55–76.
Class 27	*The Image of Asia in Europe.*
	Leonardo Olschki, "Asiatic Exoticism in Italian Art of the Early Renaissance," in *Art Bulletin*, 26 (1944): 95–106.

Part 5

Class 28   *Future Interpretations of the "Renaissance."*
                Benita Parry, "Problems in Current Theories of Colonial
                Discourse," in *Oxford Literary Review* 9 (1988): 27–58.
Class 29   *On Categories of "Art" and "Ethnography."*
                John Howland Rowe, "Ethnography and Ethnology in
                the Sixteenth Century," in *Kroeber Anthropological Soci-
                ety Papers*, no. 30 (Spring 1964): 1–14.
Class 30   *Toward a Revisionist History of Renaissance Art.*
                Lucy Lippard, "Mapping," in *Mixed Blessings: New Art
                in a Multicultural America* (New York, 1990), 3–18.

HISTORY OF ART II

Virginia Jenkins Department of Visual Arts
University of Northern Colorado
Greeley, CO 80639

Course Description and Objectives

History of Art II is a survey course designed to introduce students to the
Western art tradition from the Proto-Renaissance (1250–1400) to the Postmodern period (1990s). The course is a requirement for visual arts majors
and is also offered for credit in the general education curriculum. Most students will have taken History of Art I, but for some this course will be their
first exposure to a survey of the visual arts.

The goal of the course is to provide a general view of the work of artists
who shaped the western tradition and an exposure to the cultural forces that
influenced the development of the styles and schools that will be examined.

The format of the course is slide lecture, video presentations, and discussions.
Exams closely follow the material in the texts and in the lectures.

Artists studied include many of the major artists representing the traditional periods and styles and those whose work presents variations on mainstream styles. Most of the artists in the Gardner text are male Caucasians; a
few are Caucasian women. Most of the artists in the *Artists of Color / Women
Artists* supplement are of other ethnic origins. These include Caucasian
women, and men and women of African-American, Asian-American, Native
American, and Chicana/Chicano ancestry. In examining their work, the student will be exposed to the influences of many cultures and ideas. Gender,
ethnicity, and the cultural and historical contexts in which the work was pro-

duced are all examined as possible sources of influence on the artist. Exposure to the work of these artists and the forces that influenced the creation of their work will provide the student with a better understanding of the pluralistic, global society in which we live and help them comprehend the crucial role and function the visual arts have in our society.

Required Texts

H. Gardner, *Art Through the Ages*, 8th ed.
Virginia Jenkins, *Artists of Color / Women Artists*
New York Graphic Society, *Pocket Edition of Art Terms*, 2d rev. ed.
Henry M. Sayre, *Writing about Art*

Syllabus

Week 1	*Discuss Class Objectives.*
	Read Gardner, 3–19
Week 2	*Introduce Art Historical Concepts and Terminology.* Proto-Renaissance.
	Read Gardner, 521–47. Includes the Pisanos, Duccio, Giotto, Lorenzetti
Week 3	*Italian Renaissance.*
	Read Gardner, 550–75; Jenkins (17th and 18th c.). Includes Brunelleschi, Ghiberti, Donatello, Masaccio, Botticelli
Week 4	*High Renaissance.*
	Read Gardner, 575–630. First paper due. Includes Leonardo, Michelangelo, Raphael, Anguissola, Correggio
Week 5	*Mannerism and the Venetian Renaissance.*
	Read Gardner, 631–53. Includes Parmigiano, Bronzino, Cellini, Palladio, Titian, Bellini
Week 6	*Northern Renaissance.*
	Read Gardner, 656–707. Exam. Includes the Limbourg brothers, van Eyck, van der Weyden, Durer, Brueghel, El Greco
Week 7	*Baroque Art.*
	Read Gardner, 710–67. Includes Bernini, Caravaggio, Gentileschi, Leyster, Velazquez, Rubens, Rembrandt, van Ruisdael, Poussin, Le Brun, Sirani
Week 8	*Rococo Art.*
	Read Gardner, 770–84. Second paper due. Includes Juvara, Watteau, Fragonard, Chardin, Hogarth

Week 9	*Romanticism and Neoclassicism in Art.* Read Gardner, 785–835; Jenkins (early 19th c.). Includes Jefferson, Houdon, Gainsborough, Vigee-Lebrun, Kauffman, David, Blake, Canova, Goya, Gericault, Delacroix, Bannister, Duncanson, Native American Art, Cole
Week 10	*Realism and Impressionism in Art.* Read Gardner, 836–62; Jenkins (later 19th c.). Exam. Includes Millet, Daumier, Eakins, Powers, Homer, Tanner, Monet, Degas, Cassatt, Manet. Mary Cassatt video
Week 11	*Postimpressionism and Symbolism in Art.* Read Gardner, 863–80; Jenkins (early 20th c.). Includes Moreau, Beardsley, Van Gogh, Cezanne, Rousseau, Seurat, Gauguin, Toulouse-Lautrec
Week 12	*Cubism, Fauvism, Surrealism, Expressionism, Dada.* Read Gardner, 881–926; Jenkins (later 20th c.). Third paper due. Includes Munch, Lewis, Sullivan, Kollwitz, Picasso, Kahlo, Varo Dali, Klee, Duchamp, Douglas, Motley, Pippin, Stacey, Woodruff. Frida Kahlo video
Week 13	*Architecture Pre–World War II, Expressionism, Realism, Abstract Formalism, Pop Art.* Read Gardner, 927–56. Includes O'Keeffe, Kokoschka, Kandinsky, Shahn, Hopper, Jones, Lawrence, Lehmbruck, Catlett, Burke, Frankenthaler. Georgia O'Keeffe video
Week 14	*Pop Art, Postmodernism, Post-World War II Architecture.* Read Gardner, 957–75. Includes Corbusier, van der Rohe, Bacon, Pollock, Rothko, Newman, Nevelson, Johns, Rauschenberg, Marisol, Estes, Hessing, Abakanowicz, Asawa, Hunt, Kisto. Louise Nevelson video
Week 15	*Architecture, Earth Works, Other.* Exam. Includes Smithson, Tinguely, Ringgold, Saar, Christo, Golub, Mendieta, Kusama, Stout, Wright, Lin, Baca, Woods. Christo video
Week 16	*Final Exam*

Museum/gallery papers: Visit a minimum of three museums or gallery exhibitions. Compile critical reports of each exhibit into a typewritten paper, double spaced. Each paper should be a minimum of three pages in length. One of these papers must be from the Denver Art Museum on work from the Renaissance on. One must use examples of art that has been directly influenced by technology. One of the papers must be about the work of artists of color and/or female artists. Denver-area galleries are suggested for the last two topic papers.

INTRODUCTION TO THE HISTORY OF ARCHITECTURE

Diane Favro Architecture and Urban Planning
University of California
Los Angeles, CA 90024

Course Description and Objective

This course provides a threshold, allowing students from throughout the university to explore the complexities of architecture. Due to time restrictions, the class focuses on diverse approaches to historical inquiry rather than seeking full-breadth coverage. Histories of architecture have long focused on great buildings by great men, with a geographic emphasis on the Western world. To provide a more pluralistic view, the course broadens the discourse to include non-Western and vernacular examples and deals with gender and race as determinants in architectural production and use.

Speaking to an assembly of architecture students, Philip Johnson once noted, "You cannot not know history." The study of the past enriches the architects' understanding of the field. Among many benefits architectural history provides ways of exploring architectural problems, professional, gender, and racial issues, theories of form and technology, contextual issues, and stylistic and typological traditions.

This course introduces students to the riches of historical knowledge. The course is spread over an academic year: the first two quarters examine architectural developments from prehistory to the present; the third quarter studies the evolution of urban design. The course examines diverse architectural issues, methods for historical analysis, and successive developments in architectural form. Proceeding chronologically, each lecture centers on a single issue. This is not to imply that other issues were less important for any one era; rather, the organization allows the class to consider many different approaches and examples in a single academic quarter.

The assignments expand upon the thematic approach. The written assignment for the first quarter is a focused research paper. That for the second quarter explores the evolution of a particular issue through time. At the completion of the course students will have a general understanding of historical process, the framework and skills to conduct their own examinations of historical architecture, and an overview of Western architecture.

Required Text

Kostof, Spiro. *A History of Architecture: Settings and Rituals.* New York: Oxford University Press, 1985.

Recommended Text

Doris Cole. *From Tipi to Skyscraper: A History of Women in Architecture.* Boston, 1973.
Kostof, Spiro, ed., *The Architect.* New York, 1977.
Sylvan Barnet. *A Short Guide to Writing about Art.* Boston, 1985.
For students unfamiliar with architectural terms a specialized dictionary is useful. Many paperback versions exist, including the recommended text: Cyril Harris, ed., *Illustrated Dictionary of Historic Architecture.* New York, 1977.

Course Requirements

Focused Research Paper
First quarter

Goal: The purpose of this assignment is to give experience in writing and in conducting research and analysis focusing on a single issue and a specific example.

Parameters: Examine an issue/topic in relation to a single, focused example not discussed in class or in any other assignment. Your subject of analysis may be a building, urban complex, or an individual.

Samples:

• Gynecomorphic symbolism in prehistoric architecture
• Technological determinism in the development of Greek classicism
• The impact of ritual in the design of Roman bath buildings
• Gender determinants in the layout of the Roman house
• Social factors in the design of Romanesque monasteries

Second Quarter

Goal: To examine a single issue and its ramifications in several different historical periods.

Parameters: Select an issue (e.g., technological determinism) and examine its impact on architectural design in two or three different periods covered by this course. Choose your examples with care to support a particular point of view.

Samples:

• Light as a design factor in religious architecture (Boromini's San Carlino, LeCorbusier's Ronchamp)
• Gender implications in residential design (Renaissance palazzo, Baroque manor, 19th-c. applied theories)
• Technology as a determinant of architectural form (Brunelleschi's Dome, Florence and Soufflot's Dome, Pantheon, Paris)
• Architecture as self-promotion (Alberti's Treatise and the writings of Louis Sullivan)

Proposal: On one page identify the topic/issue, period, and example to be analyzed. Briefly justify your selection, (i.e., why the example is appropriate to the topic). On a separate page give a preliminary bibliography following standard presentation formats (see reference works listed above). Take advantage of available library systems (Orion, Melvyl, indices, etc.) to do in-depth research. The bibliography must be annotated, with a few words describing the focus and relevance of each source selected. The proposal must be typed. Submit along with your brief identification of assignment 2.

Research Paper: The research paper should be a maximum of fifteen pages (typed, double-spaced); with footnotes, bibliography, and illustrations, if appropriate. An organizing outline is strongly recommended. The short format requires careful consideration. Remember Cicero's caveat: "If I had had more time I would have written less." Take the time to write less.

Syllabus

This syllabus is for the first two quarters of a three-quarter course.

First Semester

Class 1	*Marking the Land: Prehistory and Mesopotamia.* Kostof, 3–41, 50–65. [Matriarchal influences in architectural form. Supplementary reading: Mimi Lobell, "The Buried Treasure: Women's Ancient Architectural Heritage," in *Architecture: A Place for Women,* ed. E. P. Berkeley and M. McQuaid]
Class 2	*Eternal Ritual: Egypt.* Kostof, 67–89 [Black female aesthetic. Supplementary reading: Nancy Luomala, "Matrilineal Reinterpretation of Some Egyptian Sacred Cows," in *Feminism and Art History: Questioning the Litany,* ed. N. Broude and M. D. Garrard]

Class 3	Anthropomorphism: Greece.
	Kostof, 115–35, 146–59. Proposal due. [Female proportional systems. Supplementary reading: P. Allen, *The Concept of a Woman: The Aristotelian Revolution*]
Class 4	Cosmopolitan Worldview: Hellenistic Sanctuaries.
	Kostof, 161–79
Class 5	Architecture as Politics: Romanization.
	Kostof, 194–215
Class 6	Form Follows Injunction: Roman Law.
	Kostof, 194–217. [Female property rights. Supplementary reading: J. Balsdon, *Roman Women*]
Class 7	City and the Garden: The Far East.
	Kostof, 225–241. Paper due.
Class 8	Seeking the Center: Pantheon, Minerva Medica, Haghia Sophia.
	Kostof, 217–41, 250–57
Class 9	City Masters: The Middle Ages.
	Kostof, 269–314. [Female cloistering. Supplementary reading: Christine de Pisan, *The Book of the City of Ladies*]
Class 10	Final Examination

Second Quarter

Class 1	Individualism: Architect and Client in the Early Renaissance.
	Kostof, 371–86. [Women clients and architectural form. Supplementary reading: C. Jordan, *Renaissance Feminism*]
Class 2	Ideas and Architecture: Renaissance Treatises.
	Kostof, 403–10
Class 3	The Zeitgeist: Architectural Responses to the Reformation.
	Kostof, 412–24, 500–509. Proposal due. [Household reassessments. Supplementary reading: A. Clark, *The Working Life of Women in the Seventeenth Century*]
Class 4	Intangibles: Music and Light in Baroque Architecture.
	Kostof, 511–26
Class 5	Rationalist Tradition: Laugier to Guadet.
	Kostof, 457, 569. [The noble savage. Supplementary reading: E. Weatherford, "Women's Traditional Architecture," *Heresies* (May 1977)]
Class 6	New Technologies / New Needs: Typological Responses to the Industrial Revolution.
	Kostof, 577–602, 640–47. [Women and the working envi-

	ronment. Supplementary reading: D. Thomas, *Women at Work: The Transformation of Work and Community in Lowell, Massachusetts*]
Class 7	*Social Aspects of the Profession: Nineteenth-Century America.* Kostof, *The Architect*, chaps. 9–11. Paper due. [Supplementary reading: E. Birch, "Women-Made America," in D. A. Krueckeberg ed., *The American Planner*]
Class 8	*The Genius Architect: Frank Lloyd Wright.* Kostof, 646–66, 681–85. [Women and the star system. Supplementary reading: D. Scott Brown, "Room at the Top?—Sexism and the Star System in Architecture," in *Architecture: A Place for Women*, ed. E. P. Berkeley and M. McQuaid]
Class 9	*Modernity: Modernism and the New Moderns.* Kostof, 685–754. [Gender and race in contemporary architecture. Supplementary reading: R. Dozier, "The Black Architectural Experience in America," *AIA Journal* (July 1976)]
Class 10	*Final Examination.*

NOTE

Text in [ ] indicates the gender/racial content of each lecture and the supplementary readings assigned.

WOMEN IN LITERATURE AND CULTURE: ROLES, POWER, AND THE VIEW FROM THE MARGIN

Celia Deutsch Department of Religion
Barnard College
New York, NY 10027

Course Description

Women in Literature and Culture is part of the First-Year Seminar Program at Barnard College. First-year seminars provide an opportunity for entering students to develop writing skills and engage in interdisciplinary discussion.

The Women in Literature and Culture seminars, which form part of that program, set out to "investigate the ways in which women's experience has been imagined in literature and constructed in culture." Two thirds of the curriculum for these seminars is composed of theoretical literature by feminist scholars as well as a selection of major Western and non-Western literary works. The professor then constructs the remainder of the syllabus as she or he sees fit.

I used work by Rosaldo, Lamphere, and Gilligan to provide a theoretical framework for an ongoing discussion of power and authority vis-à-vis gender roles in the literary works. *Antigone* exemplified a male author's articulation of his society's expectations regarding women's roles, ways in which those might be challenged, and the cost for doing so.

I decided to include biblical texts for several reasons. Biblical studies is my field. The Bible forms part of not only the Western literary canon but, for many, the basis of a religious canon as well. I believe it is important to reread these texts from the perspective of women's experience.

As You Like It and *Anna Karenina*, two works from very different periods, authors, and cultures, completed the section on major literary works. *As You Like It*, with the motif of cross-dressing, was a rather lighthearted example of one author's fantasy of a world in which gender roles and possession of power and authority are turned topsy-turvy. *Anna Karenina* was a rich source of discussion of gender roles and their relationship to economic and social status.

I chose the works in the section "Minority and Immigrant Women" because they represent minority and immigrant experiences from a variety of cultural and ethnic viewpoints. In this section we explored ways in which the fact of belonging to an immigrant or minority group heightened the experience of marginality and influenced perspectives on power and authority.

All of us enjoyed the seminar. We came from a variety of ethnic and minority backgrounds, and so the reading and discussion had a certain personal significance. Moreover, students learned from one another; for example, all appreciated a Chinese American's reflection on her experience in response to *The Woman Warrior.*

Students found the stream-of-consciousness quality and the use of fantasy in Morrison, Kingston, and Silko quite difficult, even disturbing. Nonetheless, discussion was very lively and sensitive, and I will probably retain those works for the syllabus in the coming year.

Statement of Purpose

In this seminar we will explore ideal roles prescribed for women and the relationship of those roles to issues of power and authority. Our investigation will include classics from the Western literary tradition as well as a cross-cultural selection of American minority and immigrant women's literature. Theoretical studies will help us to frame our questions and listen to women's voices as they speak through these texts.

Required Texts

R. Anaya, *Bless Me, Ultima*
Bible
Carol Gilligan, *In a Different Voice*
Maxine Hong Kingston, *The Woman Warrior*
Toni Morrison, *Beloved*
Michelle Z. Rosaldo and Louise Lamphere, *Woman, Culture and Society*
William Shakespeare, *As You Like It*
Leslie Marmon Silko, *Ceremony*
Sophocles, *Antigone*
Leo Tolstoy, *Anna Karenina*
Anzia Yezierska, *Bread Givers*

Class 1	Introduction

Theory

Class 2	Rosaldo and Lamphere, "Woman, Culture and Society: A Theoretical Overview," in Rosaldo and Lamphere, 17–42; Chodorow, "Family Structure and Feminine Personality," in Rosaldo and Lamphere, 43–66
Class 3	Gilligan, 1–23, 151–74

| Class 4 | Ortner, "Is Female to Male as Nature Is to Culture?" in Rosaldo and Lamphere, 67–88. Discussion comparing Rosaldo and Lamphere, Chodorow, Gilligan, and Ortner |

Classical Texts

Class 5	*Antigone.* Writing assignment: a three-page essay discussing *Antigone* in light of the theoretical material
Class 6	Discuss essays
Class 7	Biblical Women. Gen 1:1–3:35; Jg 4–5; 2 K 22:1–20; 1 Sm 1–2
Class 8	Matriarchs and Patriarchs. Gen 12:1–35:29. N. Steinberg, "Gender Roles in the Rebekah Cycle," *USQR* 39 (1984): 175–88
Class 9	*As You Like It.* Writing assignment: rewrite as a five-page essay the class 5 assignment, incorporating suggestions, corrections, and new ideas; or write a five-page critical essay on Steinberg's analysis of Gen 12:1–35:29
Class 10	Discuss essays
Classes 11, 12, 13, 14	*Anna Karenina*

Minority and Immigrant Women

Class 15	*Bread Givers.* Writing assignment: a five-page essay on views of women's and men's roles in *Anna Karenina*
Class 16	Discuss essays
Classes 17, 18	*Beloved*
Classes 19, 20	*Ceremony*
Classes 21, 22	*Bless Me, Ultima.* Writing assignment: a ten-page critical and comparative essay discussing the portrayal of women in classical texts and immigrant and minority literature in light of the theoretical essays. Due Class 22
Class 23	Discuss essays
Classes 24, 25	*Woman Warrior*
Class 26	Evaluation

Study Questions

General

1. Who is the "other"?
2. Who makes the rules? Who defines gender roles? Who gets what?
3. Under what conditions do women break out of assigned gender roles?
4. How are men's roles described? Who assigns them?
5. Do men break out of assigned gender roles? Under what circumstances?

Theory

I. Rosaldo and Lamphere, *Woman, Culture and Society*
   A. Identify one idea presented by the authors which was new to you.
   B. On p. 19 we read: "male, as opposed to female, activities are always recognized as predominantly important, and cultural systems give authority and value to the roles and activities of men." Do you agree? Disagree? Give reasons.
   C. How do you understand the distinctions between power and authority as articulated in this article?
   D. Rosaldo notes that two ways of enhancing women's status are women entering the public world or men entering the home. Do you agree with her analysis?
II. Chodorow
   A. Discuss notions of dependence, independence, and "mature dependence," as described by Chodorow. Do these concepts help/not help you to articulate your ideas of gender roles?
   B. Chodorow speaks of the effect of women's "universal mothering" role on personality development of children of both sexes. Discuss the different ways in which that role operates in various cultures. Is her description helpful to you? If so, in what way?
III. Gilligan, *In a Different Voice*
   A. How would you summarize Gilligan's analysis of moral development in women and men?
   B. How does Gilligan distinguish patterns of emotional development in men and women?
   C. Research samples (e.g., educational, sociological, medical) are often taken from an all-male population. What are the implications of this?
   D. In what ways does Gilligan expand on Rosaldo and Lamphere? on Chodorow? Do you find any of Gilligan's ideas to be incompatible with those of Rosaldo and Lamphere? of Chodorow?
IV. Ortner
   A. On p. 70 Ortner observes that some cultures give women powers and

rights that place them "in fairly high positions" and yet hold them inferior to men. Give examples.
  B. The awarding of such powers and rights can actually serve to *keep* women in subordinate status. Do you agree or disagree? Give examples.
  C. Do you find Ortner's categories of "nature" and "culture" helpful in understanding the status of women?
  D. Ortner speaks of "woman's nearly universal unquestioning acceptance of her own devaluation." Do women actually accept, or do they protest, their own devaluation?
  E. What have you found most helpful / least helpful in the readings of the past three classes?
  F. Identify one new idea that has occurred to you as a result of the readings from the past three classes.

Classical Texts

V. *Antigone*
  A. What does the nonburial of Polyneices represent? Why is it so significant that he is not buried? What does his nonburial represent to Antigone? To Creon?
  B. Describe Antigone's relationships with Polyneices, Ismene, and Creon.
  C. Explain Creon's reactions to Antigone's defiance.
VI. *Biblical Women*
  A. Regarding Gen 1–3: What kinds of questions are the authors asking? What views of women and men emerge from an attentive reading of the text?
  B. What do you expect to find in biblical stories about women?
  C. What did you actually find in these stories? Were there any surprises?
  D. If there were, how do you account for them?
  E. Why do you think these accounts were recorded? What purpose might they have served in a patriarchal society?
VII. *The Matriarchs*
  A. How do the women in these stories relate to the men? To one another?
  B. What does the male child represent to the men? To the women?
  C. Do the stories surprise you in any way?
VIII. *As You Like It*
  A. What kinds of relationships between men and women are depicted? Between men and men? Women and women?
  B. What views of love, relationship, and marriage are expressed?
  C. What does cross-dressing signify in the play?
IX. *Anna Karenina*

A. Describe relationships between men and men, women and women, women and men. Give specific examples.
B. In what ways does Anna's and Vronsky's relationship seem to change or stay the same? If there are changes, to what do you attribute them?
C. What does the relationship between Anna and Vronsky represent?
D. What kinds of social changes are reflected in the novel?

Minority and Immigrant Women

X. *Bread Givers*
   A. Describe the relationship between Sara and her father. Describe the relationship between Hugo Seelig and Sara.
   B. How is status achieved? displayed?
   C. How does Yezierska describe the conflict of cultures? What does she consider essential to the "Old World"? to the "New World"?
   D. How does Yezierska describe Old World roles for women and men? What does she imply about gender roles in the New World?
   E. How do the characters in *Bread Givers* experience American-born people and society?
XI. *Beloved*
   A. What is the sense, the meaning, of time for the characters?
   B. What does the relationship between Paul D and Sethe do for each of them?
   C. Who are white people—the dominant culture—for the characters? What is their experience of the dominant group? How does that experience shape the ways in which they understand themselves?
   D. What does *Beloved* teach you about African-American experience? About women's experience?
   E. What happens to Sethe and Paul D because of their relationship?
   F. How does Denver fit into the book?
XII. *Ceremony*
   A. Why does Silko set her novel in the period following World War II, rather than the Korean War or the Vietnam War?
   B. How do you explain Tayo's illness?
   C. How do Native Americans and whites see each other in this book? How do they interact with one another?
   D. Describe the women in *Ceremony*. What roles do they fulfill? In what ways do they reflect various ways in which Native Americans understand themselves and white society?
   E. Why does Silko write a novel about a person who is *half*–Native American? What is Tayo's position vis-à-vis Native American society? white society?
XIII. *Bless Me, Ultima*
   A. Describe the women in *Bless Me, Ultima* and their roles.

B. What is Ultima's relationship with her community?

C. Does she possess power, authority, or both?

D. How do the characters in *Bless Me, Ultima* understand themselves and the dominant Anglo society? Do those understandings influence women's status and roles?

XIV. *The Woman Warrior*

A. What is the meaning of the title? Who are the ghosts?

B. Regarding the time overlap, why does Kingston present past, present, and future in an undifferentiated fashion?

C. What kind of relationship does Kingston have with her mother? How does she present it?

D. What is the significance of speech and silence?

E. Where do you find traces of the conflict over Chinese and American values?

Suggested topics for the final paper:

1. Describe ways in which women are positioned at the center and/or margin of society.

2. Does the experience of being a woman differ among women of color and/or immigrant women from women of the dominant culture? In what way(s)?

3. Compare/contrast Antigone and Sara.

4. Compare/contrast the relationships between Kitty and Levin, on the one hand, and Sara and Hugo, on the other hand.

5. Analyze father-daughter relationships in *As You Like It, Anna Karenina,* and *Bread Givers.*

HISTORY, TRUTH, AND FICTION

Temma Kaplan Barnard Center for Research on Women
Barnard College
New York, NY 10027

Course Description

Fiction, history, sociology, memoirs, and oral histories are all written from particular perspectives, with an eye toward posterity. Frequently, even history is really a set of arguments about what is presently happening in the writers' society. Through close consideration of one mystery story, several sociological studies, and an assortment of novels, histories, works of literary criticism, and oral testimonies that highlight African-American women and family relations, the class will consider how the search for truth is undertaken and how evidence is assessed by different disciplines. This will entail close, critical readings of a variety of texts and sharply analytical papers discussing how race, gender, and historical experiences influence the views people hold.

Course Requirements

Six typed short papers and rewrites. Close and considerate reading of classmates' work as assigned by the instructor and careful revision of one's own work.

As part of the requirement of the course, you must keep an intellectual journal, which will be collected but not graded. You can take any intellectual issue raised in class and explain how it comes up in another class, in your job, in your extracurricular activities, or in your discussions with friends. The journal entries can vary from a few sentences to a paragraph to a page long, and there must be five or more a week.

Required Reading

Barbara Christian, *Black Feminist Criticism: Perspectives on Black Women Writers*, selections

Barbara Christian, "Somebody Forgot to Tell Somebody Something: African American Women's Historical Novels," *Barnard Occasional Papers on Women's Issues* 3, no. 2: 29–54 (on reserve)

Paul D. Escott, *Slavery Remembered: A Record of Twentieth-Century Slave Narratives*, selections

Herbert G. Gutman, *The Black Family in Slavery and Freedom, 1750–1925*

Harriet A. Jacobs, *Incidents in the Life of a Slave Girl Written by Herself*, ed. Jean Fagan Yellin

Harriette Pipes McAdoo, "A Portrait of African American Families in the United States," in *The American Woman, 1990–91: A Status Report*, ed. Sara E. Rix, for the Women's Research and Education Institute (on reserve)

Toni Morrison, *Beloved*

Daniel Patrick Moynihan, *The Negro Family: The Case for National Action*, The Moynihan Report (on reserve)

Rayna R. Rapp, *Toward an Anthropology of Women*, selection (on reserve)

George P. Rawick, ed., *The American Slave: A Composite Autobiography*, selections

Josephine Tey, *The Daughter of Time*

Sherley Ann Williams, *Dessa Rose*

Syllabus

Class 1	Introduction and distribution of study questions.
Class 2	Tey, *The Daughter of Time* (first half). Begin the discussion of preconceptions and what structures them. How did the detective's view about Richard III change, and why? How did he assess the arguments of different chroniclers? Was his reasoning good? *Recommended:* Carlo Ginsburg, "Morelli, Freud, and Sherlock Holmes," *History Workshop Journal*
Class 3	Finish *The Daughter of Time.* Consider Tey's views about order, human nature, popular movements, and powers of deduction. Or, since the detective and Richard III are both male, assess why the title is *The Daughter of Time.*
Class 4	One-page paper due, discussing one of the questions raised in class. Members of the class will exchange papers and say what impressed them in the paper they read.
Class 5	Read Daniel Patrick Moynihan, *The Negro Family: The Case for National Action,* 51–91. Discuss his arguments about black matriarchy and his views about "the Tangle of Pathology." Be especially attentive to the analogies he makes between women and disease. (His article may make you angry.)
Class 6	Read chapters 1 and 2 of Gutman, *The Black Family in Slavery and Freedom, 1750–1925,* 3–100.
Class 7	A two-page analysis is due in class showing what views Moynihan and Gutman share about the importance of the nuclear family and the different roles fathers and mothers play in the African-American family. To what extent did either author consider slave mothers and their positive contributions to group identity and survival in slave communities? There will be a discussion in which students will exchange ideas they have developed in their papers.
Class 8	Williams's *Dessa Rose* (first half) and Barbara Christian, "Somebody Forgot to Tell Somebody Something," *Barnard Occasional Papers.* If writing history is really an exercise in writing about the present, what are some reasons for writing historical novels? What do you learn about patriarchy and relations between women in *Dessa Rose?*
Class 9	Finish *Dessa Rose.* What questions would you raise about motherhood, individual women, black-white relationships, and community identity? Papers on Gutman

	and Moynihan will be returned, and you will consider the arguments you and your classmates made in light of your reading; then you will rewrite your papers.
Class 10	*Incidents in the Life of a Slave Girl Written by Herself* (first half). What would lead you to believe that an abolitionist rather than a former slave woman wrote the memoir? How would you refute such an argument?
Class 11	Finish *Incidents* and consider the memoir and the letters with Gutman's *The Slave Family* in mind.
Class 12	Submit a two-page essay comparing Jacobs's, Gutman's, and Williams's views about the resourcefulness of slave women, about how choices are made and what enables certain women to act on their own behalf, about the contradictory images of women as victims and as historical actors, or about patriarchy as a system of domination. We will discuss your views in class and exchange papers.
Class 13	Read Barbara Christian, "Images of Black Women in Afro-American Literature," *Black Feminist Criticism*; and Gutman, chap. 7, "To See His Grand Son Samuel Die." In what ways does the enhancement of the image of black men tend to be at the expense of black women? Or was family and community so strong under slavery that it is impossible to consider such contrasts?
Class 14	Read the first fifty pages of Toni Morrison's *Beloved*. From preliminary reading would you agree with the South African writer Nadine Gordimer that if you really want the truth you must read fiction? How does the style of *Beloved*, especially its use of flashbacks, contribute or detract from your understanding of the effect of slavery and its aftermath on African-American women?
Class 15	Read the next seventy-five pages of *Beloved* (50–124). Consider what Harriet Jacobs might have done in place of Beloved's mother. How might the story you have read be written in the form of a memoir? In the form of a history? How would the story be told by one of the male characters in the novel?
Class 16	Read the next forty pages of *Beloved* (125–65); and Barbara Christian, "Community and Nature: The Novels of Toni Morrison," *Black Feminist Criticism*. Consider the notions of "motherlove" and "hard love" and the role of religion in the lives of African-American women. What does Morrison imply about the importance of the mother-child bond versus the ties of lovers?

Class 17	Finish *Beloved;* and read Barbara Christian, "The Concept of Class in the Novels of Toni Morrison," *Black Feminist Criticism.* Discuss notions of community and notions of women's individual rights.
Class 18	Three- to five-page paper due, analyzing *Beloved* in terms of the ideas of Moynihan, Gutman, Christian, Jacobs, or Williams. Be sure to consider only one issue, whether of style, use of evidence, presentation of motherhood or matriarchy, individual choice, class and racial injuries, or views of history. It might be especially interesting to examine the differences in Williams's and Morrison's use of the historical novel.
Class 19	Read Barbara Christian, "Images of Afro-American Literature," and "Community and Nature: The Novels of Toni Morrison," *Black Feminist Criticism.* Review her article, "Images of Black Women in Afro-American Fiction." Outline one of the three articles in a page or less, paying attention to the themes Christian is trying to develop. If you prefer, take a concept such as class, community, nature, or tradition that Christian develops and modify it according to some idea you have already developed in one of your earlier papers.
Class 20	Read Paul D. Escott, Introduction to *Slavery Remembered: A Record of Twentieth-Century Slave Narratives;* and one half of the selections from *The American Slave,* edited by George Rawick. Discuss the value of reminiscences of aged, former slave women. To what extent do you suspect that their views have a lot to do with what happened to them between liberation and the Great Depression, when the narratives were gathered?
Class 21	Finish the slave narrative selections. Consider the differences in what men and women remembered, especially about motherhood, fatherhood, and the role of children in the slave community.
Class 22	Four- to six-page paper due on one of the following assignments. Either imagine Sethe or Harriet Jacobs as a woman in her nineties in the 1930s as she reminisces about her life under or after slavery to a Works Progress Administration interviewer; or compare two or three of the interviewers you have read in the real slave narratives, explaining what you have figured out about their prejudices and preoccupations.
Class 23	Read Harriette Pipes McAdoo, "A Portrait of African-American Families in the United States." On the basis of

all you have read in the course and what you have read in this article, what would you say about the legacy of slavery on the lives of African-American women?

Class 24   Read Susan E. Brown, "Love Unites Them and Hunger Separates Them: Poor Women in the Dominican Republic," in Rapp. Consider the role of economic conditions in shaping cultural expectations among women in the Dominican Republic on the basis of what you have learned about the relationship between culture and economics among African Americans in the United States.

Class 25   Read Anna Rubbo, "The Spread of Capitalism in Rural Colombia: Effects on Poor Women," in Rapp. A four- to six-page paper is due in class contrasting the cultural importance of poverty in the Dominican Republic, Colombia, and the United States with regard to the articles and books read in class this semester.

Class 26   Read Susan Harding, "Women and Words in a Spanish Village," in Rapp.

Class 27   Last day of class. In-class party. Submit a five- to eight-page reconsideration of issues raised in earlier papers or a dialogue, history, short story, or effort at literary criticism dealing with one of the topics. For example, you can consider Jacobs's memoir or the slave narratives as literary texts, or you can write a history of African-American women using *Beloved* and *Dessa Rose*. Or you can model your paper on *The Daughter of Time* and cast yourself as the detective.

WOMEN AND THE FANTASTIC IN LITERATURE

Catharine Nepomnyashchy Russian Department
Barnard College
New York, NY 10027

Course Description

This course seeks to explore the boundaries of the fantastic (as opposed to the simply "fictional") in literature specifically in relation to women's experience. The first part of the course focuses on connections between the fantastic and gender-bound metaphors for the act of writing, raising issues regarding the portrayal of female characters in myth and in texts by male authors. The second part of the course concentrates on the use of the fantastic in works by female authors, with particular attention to the ways in which gender, ethnicity, and cultural context enter into the experience of storytelling and with emphasis on the exploitation of oral tradition, myth, and legend to explore concepts of identity and human relationships.

Course Requirements

Four three- to five-page typed, double-spaced papers. The topics of the first two papers will be assigned by the instructor. Students will select their own topics for the last two papers in consultation with the instructor. The first two papers will be revised and rewritten after individual discussion of original drafts with the instructor. Periodic unannounced in-class writing assignments on topics assigned by the instructor. These essays will not be graded.

Required Texts

Louise Erdrich, *Tracks*
Zora Neale Hurston, *Mules and Men*
Maxine Hong Kingston, *The Woman Warrior*
Toni Morrison, *Beloved*
Plato, *The Symposium*
Mary Shelley, *Frankenstein*
Tatyana Tolstaya, *On the Golden Porch* (selected stories)

Course Packet

Bruno Bettelheim, *The Uses of Enchantment* (selections)
Sigmund Freud, "The Uncanny"
Sandra M. Gilbert and Susan Gubar, *The Madwoman in the Attic* (selection)
E.T.A. Hoffman, "The Sandman"
"Snow White"

Syllabus

Class 1   Introduction.
                     Discussion of syllabus and goals of course. In-class essay: pick an episode from your past reading which you believe exemplifies the fantastic in literature and explain why it is fantastic.

Class 2	Genesis 1–3 and Native American creation myths. Begin by discussing problems of defining the boundaries of the fantastic in literature, by drawing on examples taken from the in-class essays from the preceding class. Use the reading assignment for the day to raise the issue of the status of myth in relation to the fantastic. What is the function of creation myths in different cultures? Do we see significant differences between the roles assigned to women in Genesis and in Native American creation myths?
Class 3	Plato, *The Symposium* (first half). Discuss Platonic myth versus Platonic dialogue as distinct modes of discourse. How and why does Plato use myth?
Class 4	Finish *The Symposium.* Discuss Plato's vision of the relationship between love and creativity. Does Plato's use of giving birth as a metaphor for creativity seem to exclude women from the creative process? What is the function of Diotima in the narrative and philosophical structure of *The Symposium?*
Class 5	Handouts on writing strategy, including short text for students to edit and critique. In preparation for the first writing assignment, discuss what constitutes an *explication de texte,* focusing on a sample text. How can a discussion of a brief passage of a literary text be effectively organized, and why is it interesting to point out?
Class 6	Write a three- to five-page *explication de texte* of a passage from *The Symposium* assigned by the instructor. Read excerpts from *The Uses of Enchantment.* How, according to Bettelheim, do fairy tales work? How does he define the differences between fairy tales and myths? Do either myths or fairy tales belong in the realm of the fantastic in literature? What is "externalization," and how might we relate this concept to fantastic literature?
Class 7	Read "Snow White" and Bettelheim's discussion of "Snow White" (*Uses of Enchantment,* 194–215). In-class writing assignment: describe briefly an experience with a fairy tale that you remember from your childhood. Discuss Bettelheim's analysis of "Snow White." All students must sign up for appointments to see instructor in the course of the following week to go over *explications de texte.*
Class 8	Read "The Queen's Looking Glass: Female Creativity,

	Male Images of Women, and the Metaphor of Literary Paternity" (3–44), in *The Madwoman in the Attic*. Discuss Gilbert and Gubar's analysis of literary metaphors that link literary creativity with male sexuality and paternity. Compare Gilbert and Gubar's analysis of "Snow White" with Bettelheim's.
Class 9	Read Hoffman's "The Sandman." Discuss the portrayal of male and female characters and of the relationships between them in "The Sandman." Is this story "fantastic" in a different sense than are fairy tales and myths?
Class 10	Read Freud's "The Uncanny." Finish rewrite of *explication de texte*. Discuss Freud's analysis of "The Sandman" and how his definition of the "uncanny" relates to the fantastic in literature. Does Freud's discussion exhibit a gender bias?
Class 11	Read Shelley, *Frankenstein* (first third). In-class writing assignment: Have you ever felt as if you were a monster? If so, describe the experience. Discuss the circumstances surrounding Shelley's writing of *Frankenstein* and how they may be related specifically to the fantastic nature of the work. Discuss the narrative structure of the novel in terms of gender (male narrators vs. female reader).
Class 12	Read *Frankenstein* (second third). Discuss the creation and education of the monster in *Frankenstein*. What is the significance of the fact that the monster's narrative stands at the center of the novel? What patterns do we see in the portrayal of women in the novel?
Class 13	Finish reading *Frankenstein*. Discuss *Frankenstein* as a woman's narrative in relation to the myths of Prometheus and the Fall. How can a female writer locate herself in relation to a patriarchal myth structure, and what role does the fantastic play in this process?
Class 14	Read two essays distributed in class and analyze in what ways they are successful or unsuccessful in writing and structure. Discuss the assigned essays, encouraging students to apply what they have learned in looking at other people's writing to their own writing.
Class 15	Write a three- to five-page paper on the topic: The role

of the Female Monster in Mary Shelley's *Frankenstein*.
Read Hurston, *Mules and Men* (first half).

Discuss the problems an anthropologist confronts in attempting to "straddle" different cultures, specifically in relation to Hurston and to gender. Does this work suggest any patterns relating storytelling to gender? How can we classify this text in relation to the fantastic and fictionality? All students must make appointments to see instructor next week for conferences on paper rewrites.

Class 16   Finish reading *Mules and Men*.

Discuss the problem of defining the fantastic in relation to cultural context. To what extent does defining the fantastic in literature depend on "nonliterary" beliefs that change from culture to culture?

Class 17   Read and think about handout of quotations on the fantastic by writers and literary theorists.

Use the handout to focus an open discussion of the issues raised thus far in the course.

Class 18   Finish rewrite of second paper. Read Kingston's *The Woman Warrior* (first half).

Begin discussion by comparing *The Woman Warrior* with *Mules and Men*. In what ways are both their structures and the issues they raise similar? Focus on the role of the mother as storyteller and on the daughter's attempts to come to terms with the heritage of narratives her mother imposes on her.

Class 19   Finish reading *The Woman Warrior*.

In-class essay: Have you ever felt as if you were invisible? Describe the experience. Focus on the daughter as storyteller. How is "finding one's voice" developed, in *The Woman Warrior*, as a metaphor for writing? How does fantasy or the fantastic help the narrator find her voice?

Class 20   Read Erdrich, *Tracks* (first half).

Compare the two narrators, one male and one female, of *Tracks*. How do they differ in attitudes toward characters and events and in beliefs? How are their differences reflected in the stories they tell, specifically as this relates to the fantastic? Can we draw a line between what happens in the narrators' minds and what happens in "reality" in this text? How does that affect our perception of fantastic events?

Class 21   Finish reading *Tracks*.

Discuss how the inclusion (or exclusion) of fantastic

events in this narrative reflects cultural difference. Does the fantastic disappear from this text, and, if so, what does this disappearance mean? To whom is this story being told? What is the significance of the title?

Class 22 Write a three- to five-page paper on *Mules and Men, The Woman Warrior,* or *Tracks* on a topic of your choice (which must be discussed beforehand with the instructor). Read Morrison, *Beloved* (3–105).

Discuss the role of storytelling in *Beloved.* Which characters tell stories to whom, and when? How does the characters' storytelling help create the novel's dual plot structure? How does this narrative process relate to the central issue of being haunted by "rememories"?

Class 23 Read *Beloved* (106–65).

Discuss Sethe as the murderer of her own child, comparing her with Medea. How does Morrison refocus the traditional myth of the mother who murders her own child by placing it within the context of slavery and telling it from the woman's point of view?

Class 24 Finish reading *Beloved.*

Focus discussion on the question: Who is Beloved? How do we find out, and when do the characters find out? What clues are there earlier in the narrative? How does Morrison exploit the fantastic in her narrative? Does the disappearance of Beloved at the end of the novel have anything in common with the disappearance of the fantastic at the end of *Tracks?*

Class 25 Read "On the Golden Porch" and "Date with a Bird," in Tolstaya's *On the Golden Porch.*

Discuss the role played by fantasy and the fantastic in Tolstaya's stories. What relationship is there in these stories between the fantastic and childhood?

Class 26 Write a three- to five-page paper on *Beloved* on a topic of your own choice (which must be approved by the instructor). Read "Fire and Dust" and "Fakir," in Tolstaya's *On the Golden Porch.*

Discuss the role of the fantastic and fantasy specifically as it relates to the portrayal of women in these Tolstaya stories. When does fantasy become delusion? How does the fantastic shape women's relationships with "reality" in these works?

Class 27 Concluding discussion of major issues raised in course.

ILLNESS AND SOCIETY

Theresa Rogers Department of Sociology
Barnard College
New York, NY 10027

Course Description

In this seminar we will explore and analyze explanations of illness, the meanings it has for the individual, family, friends, and the wider society, and the social and moral values that may surround it. We will see how one comes to be labeled "well" or "ill" and the stigma that may accompany illness when it departs from society's standards of what is normal. At various times during the semester the responses to illness presented in a text will be compared with those that prevail today in the United States. The latter will include responses by the medical profession, by self-help organizations, and by those considered outside orthodox Western medicine (e.g., holistic medicine, herbal, nutritional, and Eastern therapies).

The texts span a wide range. They include a moving English poem that is a translation of *The Book of Job*, masterpieces of nineteenth- and twentieth-century fiction, an autobiographical essay, a short story by a contemporary Chinese writer on the life and values of a physician in her country, a biography of a black physician written by her daughter, and the oral history of a black midwife who practiced in rural Alabama throughout much of this century. All the texts have been chosen for their insights into the social meanings assigned to health and illness and the roles performed by various providers of care, ranging from the physician to a family member or friend. Consideration will be given to the values and interests of those who are not part of the dominant groups in American society, particularly, people of color and new minorities.

Attention to people of color and new minorities represents a reconceptualization of health and illness as it is examined in this seminar. We will read texts by such authors, explicate passages from them, and discuss the health concerns and issues that these texts raise and how they may suggest in what ways race, culture, and social class differentially affect majority and minority constituencies in this society today.

Required Texts

The Book of Job, translated by Stephen Mitchell
Albert Camus, *The Plague*
Frederick Crews and Sandra Schor, *The Borzoi Handbook for Writers*, 2d ed.

Joan Didion, "Why I Write," in *The Writer on Her Work*, edited by Janet Sternburg
Charlotte Perkins Gilman, *The Yellow Wallpaper*
Ken Kesey, *One Flew over the Cuckoo's Nest*
S. L. Lightfoot, *Balm in Gilead*
Onnie Lee Logan, *Motherwit: An Alabama Midwife's Story*
Nancy Mairs, "On Being a Cripple," in *Plain Text*
Chen Rong, "At Middle Age," in *Roses and Thorns*, edited by Perry Link
Leo Tolstoy, *The Death of Ivan Ilyich*
William Carlos Williams, "The Use of Force," in *The Norton Anthology of Short Fiction*, edited by R. V. Cassill

Syllabus

At various points in the course calendar questions are raised about the text assigned. These questions are to stimulate your thinking. In class we'll be interested in these questions and those you raise.

Class 1	Goals of the course; definitions of health and illness; students' interests in the subject matter
Class 2	Gilman, *The Yellow Wallpaper*. Bring to class two or three paragraphs that you have written on anything in *The Yellow Wallpaper* which fascinated you. Tell me what it is (use a short quote, if you like) and why it fascinated you. If nothing about this work fascinated you, tell me in two or three paragraphs why this was so.
Class 3	Handout: writing the draft of paper 1
Class 4	Mairs, "On Being a Cripple." What makes this essay a strong statement of a patient's response to a chronic health problem? Identify the author's sources of emotional support and consider how they may or may not be the lot of other patients whose economic circumstances are less fortunate.
Class 5	Continued discussion of Mairs's essay; plus read the sections in *The Borzoi Handbook for Writers* on sexist language.
Class 6	Williams, "The Use of Force" and Didion, "Why I Write." Come to class prepared to write on the board one sentence about each of these essays which tells us the most important thing you take away from them. Hand in the draft of paper 1. Individual conferences with instructor on the draft of paper 1. Come prepared to talk

	about what was easy about writing this draft and what was not so easy.
Class 7	Tolstoy, *The Death of Ivan Ilyich*. Tolstoy begins chapter 2 of this story with the following sentence: "Ivan Ilyich's life had been most simple and commonplace—and most horrifying." In no more than two paragraphs be prepared to write in class why you think Tolstoy made this harsh judgment of Ivan's life. I'll collect the paragraphs, and then we will begin our discussion of this book with the sentence quoted above.
Class 8	Hand in the revision of paper 1.
Class 9	Hand in a journal entry, about a half-page in length, which records how an experience during the past week elicited thoughts about our seminar—for example, an idea from a text, an attitude expressed by one of us, an implication that you drew from a section of a reading, a lesson about life you think important.
Class 10	*The Book of Job*. Read through "The First Round"; complete the reading of *Job*. What do you make of Job's trials? How does he defend himself? What do you make of his friends?
Class 11	Continued discussion of *Job*. Job exercises the right to stand up to authority. In what ways does this poem suggest the relationship of the weak to the powerful in the arena of health care? In what ways does *Job* suggest stereotypes that may be in evidence at this time?
	Bring two copies of the first draft of paper 2 to class.
Class 12	Writing workshop in class
Class 13	Lightfoot, *Balm in Gilead*. What stands out about Dr. Margaret Lawrence? How does she come to achieve such distinction, and how do you account for her victories in face of the racial and gender discrimination she experienced? What forms did the discrimination take? What mechanisms did she use to deal with them?
Class 14	Hand in: (1) the original draft of paper 2; (2) two copies of your revised draft; (3) the one-page response sheets your readers completed; and (4) the one-page self-evaluation sheet.
Class 15	Open discussion of readings to date. During the last fifteen minutes of class you are to write about: (1) one idea from a reading that has stayed with you (what it is and how it has stayed with you); and (2) one idea about writing which you find especially helpful (what it is and how it has been helpful).

Class 16	Camus, *The Plague*. Bring to class one or two paragraphs that you have written which tell us either: (1) what you find especially compelling about the book thus far; or (2) something about it which is puzzling. Excerpt the text to make your point, whether you choose 1 or 2.
Class 17	Continued discussion of *The Plague*. What does this book suggest about responses to AIDS? Bring copies of your draft of paper 3 to give to members of your writing group; arrange a convenient time within the next two days to receive your reader's completed response sheets and marked copies of your draft so that you will have read these pages before you come to the next class.
Class 18	Writing workshop in class
Class 19	Rong, "At Middle Age." How do the values of Dr. Lu Wenting's society differ from those of mainstream America? This novella has been described as empowering. In terms of the goals of this seminar, how would you interpret that statement?
Class 20	Hand in: (1) the original draft of paper 3; (2) two copies of your revised draft; (3) the one-page response sheets your readers completed; and (4) the one-page self-evaluation sheet.
Classes 21, 22	Logan, *Motherwit*. What makes this book so alive? In what ways does it matter that the heroine is black? In what ways does it not matter?
Class 23	Kesey, *One Flew over the Cuckoo's Nest*. This book admits to many interpretations. What is yours? What do you make of the stigma of mental illness? of the stereotypes of race and gender the author seems to glory in? Draft of paper 4 due. Individual conferences with instructor on the draft of paper 4
Class 24	Revision of paper 4 due Film, *One Flew over the Cuckoo's Nest*
Class 25	Last class

ELITES IN SOCIETY

Judith Russell Department of Political Science
Barnard College
New York, NY 10027

Elites in Society is an introductory seminar that aims to introduce students to a variety of themes—and scholarly literature—on elite theory in political sociology.

Because gender, race, and ethnicity bring important dimensions to the classic views on elitism, and are a particular interest of mine, they are central to the course. Understanding the dynamics of racism and male authority, in particular, is essential to understanding the intractability of elite structures everywhere and, thus, to challenging them.

Literature has been selected with the aim of introducing students to some of the classic literature in the field, engaging them intellectually, and tapping their intuitive—but perhaps unconscious—critical sensibilities regarding issues of sexism and racism. Although sections dealing with gender and race are formally designated, in fact these are running themes from day one.

In the course we study the idea of the inevitability of elites in every type of society, and we challenge this notion. We wonder how—or if—the imperatives of elite control would be different were societies free from the biases of race and gender.

We consider classic views on how elites have maintained themselves and the relevance of these views for today, which is considerable. We explore ideology in this context. We address the contradiction of elitism under democracy and socialism and, in this way, introduce the notion of class.

We look at cross-cutting dimensions of authority and control in which gender, race, and class intersect, and we examine the consequences of this.

The seminar is a study of elite behavior and adaptation to social change. We will examine elite theorists who have had an important effect on modern social philosophy. We will also study the thinking of other theorists on the formation of elites. In doing this, certain questions will organize the class. Students will write a series of short papers over the semester to develop critical thinking and analysis.

Our seminar will come together three or four times over the semester with Professor Elizabeth Swain's First-Year Seminar, Rebellious Women, for films and discussion related to the themes of our joint classes.

Required Texts

Natalie Harris Bluestone, *Women and the Ideal Society*
Angela Davis, "Reflections on the Black Woman's Role in the Community of Slaves"
Carol Gilligan, *In a Different Voice*
Jacqueline Jones, *Labor of Love, Labor of Sorrow*
Gerda Lerner, *The Creation of Patriarchy*
Niccolo Machiavelli, *The Prince and the Discourses*
James Madison et al., *The Federalist Papers*
Karl Marx, *The German Ideology* (International Publishers)
Gaetano Mosca, *The Ruling Class*
Carole Pateman, *Participation and Democratic Theory*
Plato, *The Republic*
Joseph Schumpeter, *Capitalism, Socialism and Democracy*
Ronald Takaki, *Strangers from a Different Shore: A History of Asian-Americans*
Virginia Woolf, *Three Guineas*

Syllabus

Class 1   Introduction

I. Are elites inevitable?

Does every society have elites? Has this always been the case? What are some explanations for why we have elites? What are some challenges to these views?

Classes 2, 3   Plato, *The Republic*, books 5, 6, and 7
Class 4   Natalie Harris Bluestone, "The Prevalence of Anti-Female Bias in Plato Scholarship, 1870–1970: Seven Types of Hostility," in Bluestone, *Women and the Ideal Society*
Class 5   First paper due
                    Film: Sophocles' *Antigone*

II. How have elites retained power?

Classes 6, 7   Niccolo Machiavelli, *The Prince and the Discourses*, chapters 1, 2, 3, 5, 9, 10, 11, 14, 15, 17, 18, 25, and 26
Classes 8, 9   Gaetano Mosca, *The Ruling Class*, introduction, chapters 2, 3, 4, 6, 12, and 15

III. Elite response to the challenge of democracy

Class 10	Second paper due
	James Madison et al., *The Federalist Papers*, nos. 10, 47, 49, 51, and 58
Class 11	Joseph Schumpeter, *Capitalism, Socialism and Democracy*, chapters 21, 22, and 33
Class 12	Carole Pateman, *Participation and Democracy*, chapters 1, 2, and 6
Class 13	Karl Marx, *The German Ideology*, part 1: Fuerbach, 64–95

IV. Gender and elitism

Classes 14, 15	Third paper due Class 15
	Gerda Lerner, *The Creation of Patriarchy*, introduction, chapters 2–7, and 11
Class 16	Carol Gilligan, *In a Different Voice*
Class 17	Virginia Woolf, *Three Guineas*
Class 18	Film: Virginia Woolf's *A Room of One's Own*

V. Race, ethnicity, and elitism

Classes 19, 20	Fourth paper due Class 20
	Jacqueline Jones, *Labor of Love, Labor of Sorrow*, chapters 7 and 8
Class 21	Angela Davis, "Reflections on the Black Woman's Role in the Community of Slaves," in *Black Scholar* 3, no. 4 (December 1971)
Class 22	Film: Ntozake Shange's *For Colored Girls Who Have Considered Suicide When the Rainbow Is Enuf*
Classes 23, 24	Ronald Takaki, *Strangers from a Different Shore: A History of Asian-Americans*

VI. Discussion: Are elites inevitable?

Classes 25, 26	Fifth paper due

HISTORY OF THE UNITED STATES

Matthew Dennis Department of History
University of Oregon
Eugene, OR 97403

Course Description

This course examines the creation of America as a society, culture, and polity
in the colonial and early national periods (to about 1830). It is the first term
in a three-quarter introductory survey of U.S. history. Each term may be
taken separately and is group satisfying; the entire sequence fulfills a social
science cluster requirement.

Using chronology as a framework (not as a goal in itself), this course will
emphasize the social and material context and the changing structure of early
American life. Attention will focus on the experience of various Americans—
native, African, European; women, men, and children; slave and free; poor
and rich—their interactions with one another and their "New World," and
their roles in determining the course of American development.

Course Format and Readings

This class will meet for lectures three times weekly. In addition, each student
will have enrolled in a discussion group that meets for one hour every week.
Although lectures, readings, and discussion are carefully coordinated, each
will introduce material not available elsewhere. Therefore, attendance at lectures and discussion sessions, and careful reading of all assignments, is crucial to success in the course. Attendance will be taken at weekly discussion
sessions. These sessions are particularly important: they provide an opportunity to clarify and respond to issues raised in lectures and readings; they are
the setting for lively discussion and debate impossible in the larger lecture
context; they are the place to overcome anonymity and personally engage the
subject; and they are your source of information and guidance on practical
matters, such as paper assignments, tests, and so forth.

Required Texts

Robert A. Gross, *The Minutemen and Their World* (New York: Hill and Wang,
1976).

Mary Beth Norton et al., *A People and a Nation: A History of the United States, Brief Edition*, 3d ed. (Boston: Houghton Mifflin, 1991). (Referred to as "Text" below.)

Neal Salisbury, *Manitou and Providence: Indians, Europeans, and the Making of New England, 1500–1643* (New York: Oxford University Press, 1982).

Peter H. Wood, *Black Majority: Negroes in Colonial South Carolina from 1670 through the Stono Rebellion* (New York: Norton, 1975).

A packet of photocopied documents (referred to as "Documents" below).

Lecture and Reading Schedule

Week 1   *Before Columbus and in His Wake*
                Introduction
                Aboriginal America
                Discovery and "Invention" of America
                Reading: Text, chapter 1; Salisbury, 3–84; Documents:
                Columbus's Landfall, van der Donck's *Description of
                New Netherlands*

Week 2   *Settlement and Unsettlement*
                Columbian Exchange
                Anglo-American Beachheads: Roanoke and Beyond
                Chesapeake: Freedom, Servitude, Life and Death
                Reading: Wood, xiii–xix, 3–91; Salisbury, 85–109; Docu-
                ments: Jesuit Relation, "Lawes Divine, Morall and
                Martiall," "Tragical Relation," Sentence of John Punch
                and Petition of Philip Corven

Week 3   *Settlement and Unsettlement in the American Northeast*
                "Bible Commonwealth"
                New England Communities
                Middle Colonies
                Reading: Text, chapter 2; Salisbury, 110–235; Documents:
                Sermon on Calling, Winthrop on "Liberty," Underhill's
                Account of Pequot War, Salem Witchcraft Trial Records,
                Novum Belgium (present-day New York)
                Paper Due

Week 4   *Settlement and Unsettlement: Columbian Legacy and the
                Bonds of Slavery*
                Columbus Day: Myth, History, Symbol, and Ritual,
                1492–1991
                Slave Trade and Middle Passage
                Slavery and African-American Culture
                Reading: Text, chapter 3; Wood, 96–130, 167–91; Docu-
                ments: Life on Board a Slave Ship, Slave Folktales

Week 5	*The Bonds of Womanhood: Women's Experience* African- and Native American Women Euro-American Women
	America at Mid-Century: Intellectual Shifts Awakening and Enlightenment *Reading:* Wood, 195–268, 271–307; Documents: Runaway Slave Advertisements, Iroquois Gynecocracy, Reports on Whitefield and Religious Excesses, Franklin's "Way to Wealth"
Week 6	*America at Mid-Century: Order and Ferment* Imperial Relations to 1763 Politics of Upheaval: Class, Race, and Region *Reading:* Text, chapter 4; Gross, 3–108 Mid-term Examination.
Week 7	*Revolution* Crisis and Mobilization Military Conflict as Revolution "Contagions of Liberty" and Social Revolution? Reading: Text, chapter 5, and read through the Declaration of Independence, Appendix A-5 to A-6; Gross, 109–70; Documents: Patrick Henry's Speech, Boston Massacre Accounts, Runaway Slave Notice, Phillis Wheatley's Poem, Black Petitioners on Taxation without Representation, Washington's Position on Slavery
Week 8	*Revolutionary Settlement* Confederation and Constitution Evolving Constitution and Framers' Legacy Challenges to National Unity Reading: Text, chapter 6, and read through the Constitution, Appendix, A-6 to A-10; Gross, 171–91; Documents: Madison's *Federalist No. 10*, Benjamin Rush on Republican Education, Letters from Eliza Southgate
Week 9	*Slavery and Freedom, Opportunity and Exploitation in Early National America* "A Covenant with Death": Slavery as a National Political Issue Empire of Liberty: The New Nation and the West Empire of Death: America and Native America Reading: Text, chapters 7 and 8, chapter 11 (209–13); Documents: Jefferson's *Notes on the State of Virginia*, Linda Brent, *Life of a Slave Girl*, Davy Crockett Autobiography, Andrew Jackson's Second Inaugural Message, and Memorial and Protest of the Cherokee Nation Paper due.

Week 10	*Reform: Remaking America and Its History*

Week 10   *Reform: Remaking America and Its History*
Strains of Revival and Reform
History and Ethnogastronomy of Thanksgiving
Reading: Text, chapter 12 (217–25); Documents: Sarah
Grimke Letters, Constitution of Brook Farm Association

Week 11   *Democracy in America*
Economic Expansion and the Market Economy
Work and Experience in Industrializing America
America at 1830; Conclusion and Review
Reading: Text, chapters 9 and 10, chapter 11 (195–209);
Documents: Nathan Appleton on Manufacturing and
Morals, Lucy Larcom's Factory Experience, Frances Trollope's *Domestic Manners*

Final Examination

SELECTED BIBLIOGRAPHY: "WOMEN OF COLOR" IN EARLY AMERICA

Matthew Dennis, Department of History
University of Oregon
Eugene, OR 97403

In an effort to incorporate consideration of neglected groups in the study of early American history (i.e., America roughly through the revolutionary period), I have compiled the brief, selective bibliography below, targeting articles and books that examine the experience, meaning, and impact of non-European women in the American colonial world. "Women of color," a preferred label in current discourse, can be problematic of course; for early America it is particularly imprecise and anachronistic, not simply because the term had no contemporary currency but also because the category does not correspond well to its current composition in recent America. "Women of color" as an artificial class might also tend to suggest—erroneously—that those placed under such an umbrella by scholars shared a single, common experience, interest, or consciousness. The bibliography focuses on Native American and African-American women and emphasizes recent works, in large part because it is only recently that scholars have initiated such investigations.

Native American Women

Books

"The Autobiography of a Fox Woman," ed. and trans. Truman Michelson. U.S. Bureau of American Ethnology *Annual Report,* no. 40. Washington, D.C., 1925.

Frankly told life story of Fox [Masquakie] woman, born in late nineteenth century who lived in various midwestern communities. Though the narrative comes from a later chronological period, through the judicious use of ethnohistorical approach of "upstreaming" one can gather great in-sights into Native American women's lives in the face of ongoing coloni-alism. Critical reading is necessary to compensate for the mediation of the white, male anthropologist-collector. Good antidote to romanticized im-ages of Native American women's experience.

Axtell, James, ed. *The Indian Peoples of Eastern America: A Documentary History of the Sexes.* New York: Oxford University Press, 1981.

Collection of primary source materials, organized in terms of Native American life cycles and experiences (e.g., birth, coming of age, love and marriage, work, war and peace). Descriptions of women's experience by European observers and by native women as well. Primarily concerned with colonial period, but some nineteenth-century material as well. Excel-lent introductions, notes, and bibliography.

Brown, Jennifer S. H. *Strangers in Blood: Fur Trade and Company Families in Indian Country.* Vancouver: University of British Columbia Press, 1980.

Recognizes importance of women on the "frontier"—especially Native American women who crossed the cultural divide and helped mediate cross-cultural relations. Undercuts whatever tendency there might be to develop an Anglo- or Franco-American "La Malinche" model of women as cultural or racial "traitors."

Campisi, Jack, and Lawrence Hauptman, eds. *The Oneida Indian Experience: Two Perspectives.* Syracuse: Syracuse University Press, 1988.

Perspectives on Oneida history from scholars and native people, includ-ing a few short biographies of notable Oneida women, native reminis-cences, and miscellaneous tidbits. Good material for a case study of one tribe, which has been consistently "loyal" to the United States, paid a great price for that loyalty, and yet survived, in large part through the ef-forts of women.

Clifton, James A., ed. *Being and Becoming Indian: Biographical Studies of North American Frontiers*. Chicago: Dorsey Press, 1989.

Explores the acculturation process among Native Americans through historical biographical studies. Four chapters on Native American women, and some treatment of women in other biographical chapters. No material particularly on native women in the colonial period, however. Designed for classroom use.

Devens, Carol. *Countering Colonization: Native American Women and Great Lakes Missions, 1630–1900*. Berkeley: University of California Press, 1992.

Explores the colonial encounter as if women mattered. Analyzes the active role of Native American women in accommodating and resisting colonization.

Landes, Ruth. *The Ojibwa Woman*. New York: Columbia University Press, 1938.

Classic account of Ojibwa women, based on 1930s fieldwork by Landes in western Ontario. Useful in reconstructing the historical-cultural experience of Native American women in an earlier period, if careful use of ethnohistorical approach employed.

Lurie, Nancy Oestreich, ed. *Mountain Wolf Woman, Sister of Crashing Thunder: The Autobiography of a Winnebago Indian*. Ann Arbor: University of Michigan Press, 1961.

Classic in ethnography and American Indian women's autobiography—an old woman tells her life to her adopted niece (Lurie, the anthropologist), who provides notes, background. Like previous citation, valuable if used with care in reconstructing earlier experience of Native American women.

Powers, Marla N. *Oglala Women: Myth, Ritual, and Reality*. Chicago: University of Chicago Press, 1986.

One of the best, recent ethnographic treatments of women within an often misunderstood and stereotyped Native American group. Makes an interesting contrast with "matriarchal" groups, such as the Iroquois.

Spindler, Louise S. *Menomini Women and Culture Change*. American Anthropological Society, Memoir 91. Menasha, Wis., 1962.

Argues many Menomini women, regardless of acculturation level (even Christians) covertly retained many older concepts of female identity.

Wallace, Anthony F. C. *The Death and Rebirth of the Seneca*. 1970. Reprint. New York: Vintage Books, 1972.

Traces Senecas from eighteenth-century heyday to postrevolutionary decline, to rebirth to revitalization movement of prophet Handsome Lake. Though not his primary purpose, Wallace provides good portrait of the Iroquois "Matriarchate" through this tumultuous era.

Willis, Jane. *Geniesh: An Indian Girlhood.* Toronto: New Press, 1973.
Autobiography of James Bay Cree woman (b. 1940) and experiences in government and church schools for Indians. Though compiled in a much later period, narrative is suggestive of new ways to read older historical sources.

Articles

Becker, Marshall J. "Hannah Freeman: An Eighteenth-Century Lenape Living and Working among Colonial Farmers," *Pennsylvania Magazine of History and Biography* 114, no. 2 (April 1990): 249–69.
Creative reconstruction of the life of a marginal Indian woman in eighteenth-century Pennsylvania, based on a fragmentary "autobiography." Represents a very rare example of Native American women's biography for the colonial period and illuminates the process of colonization and accommodation. Works well in course packet.

Bonvillain, Nancy. "Gender Relations in Native North America," *American Indian Culture and Research Journal* 13, no. 2 (1989): 1–28.
Useful, brief synthesis by an anthropologist of historical gender relations among Native Americans, with specific sections treating the following: Montagnais-Naskapi, Navajo, Eskimo, Iroquois, Plains cultures.

Brown, Judith. "Iroquois Women: An Ethnohistorical Note," in *Toward an Anthropology of Women,* ed. Rayna B. Reiter. New York: Monthly Review Press, 1975.
Historical and anthropological case made for understanding high status of Iroquois women in terms of control over work and its products. Cf. Jensen's piece on Seneca women and agriculture.

Devens, Carol. "Separate Confrontations: Gender as a Factor in Indian Adaptation to European Colonization in New France," *American Quarterly* 38, 3 (1986): 461–80.
Important article with much broader implications for other historical periods and regions of North America. A model for ethnohistory that takes gender seriously.

Green, Rayna. "The Pocahontas Perplex: The Image of Indian Women in American Culture," *Massachusetts Review* 16 (1975); reprinted and in various anthologies, including *Unequal Sisters: A Multi-Cultural Reader in*

U.S. Women's History, ed. Ellen Carol DuBois and Vicki L. Ruiz, 15–21. New York: Routledge, 1990.

Provocative suggestions about image of Indian women in American culture; of course, little on actual nature of Native American women's lives but useful as beginning point in challenging offensive and inaccurate images and stereotypes.

Hampton, Carol M. "Why Write History? A Caddo Grandmother's Perspective," *Creative Woman* 8, no. 3 (1987): 13–14.

Part of special tenth anniversary issue on American Indian women; guest editor, Clara Sue Kidwell.

Jensen, Joan M. "Native American Women and Agriculture: A Seneca Case Study," *Sex Roles* 3, no. 5 (1977): 432–41. Reprinted in various anthologies.

Somewhat simplistic but roughly accurate portrait of eighteenth-century Seneca women, arguing that their high status in their community was a function of their economic role.

Leacock, Eleanor. "Montagnais Women and the Jesuit Program for Colonization," in *Women and Colonization: Anthropological Perspectives*, ed. Mona Etienne and Eleanor Leacock. New York: Praeger, 1980.

Volume contains other articles of interest concerning women of color in America.

———. "Women's Status in Egalitarian Society: Implications for Social Evolution," *Current Anthropology* 19 (1978): 247–75.

Leacock pursues her anthropological concerns by studying the historical experience of Native American women of the North American subarctic.

McCartney, Martha W. "Cockacoeske, Queen of the Pamunkey: Diplomat and Suzeraine," in *Powhatan's Mantle: Indians in the Colonial Southeast*, ed. Peter H. Wood et al., 173–95, Lincoln: University of Nebraska Press, 1989.

A rare biographical treatment, or "life story," of a Native American woman, which provides important insight into native experience in the face of English colonial invasion as well as the course of the larger colonial history of Virginia and Maryland.

Perdue, Theda. " 'Domesticating the Natives: Southern Indians and the Cult of True Womanhood," in *Women, Families, and Communities: Readings in American History*, ed. Nancy A. Hewitt, 1:159–70. Glenview, Ill.: Scott, Foresman, 1990. Originally in *The Web of Southern Social Relations: Women, Family, and Education*, ed. Walter J. Fraser, Jr., et al. Athens: University of Georgia Press, 1985.

Excellent, brief discussion of the different impact of forced assimilation on women and men in Cherokee society; demonstrates that attention to gender is central to understanding of colonization, assimilationist campaign, and the era of Removal.

Peterson, David. "Celiast Smith, ca. 1804–1891: Pioneer Woman, Indian Woman" (unpublished paper written originally in history department seminar, University of Oregon, June 3, 1991).

Fascinating and insightful life story of a remarkable Indian woman of early Oregon, which provides a brilliant case study of accommodation, survival, even triumph in the face of American colonialism in the Northwest. Its publication will make this important paper more widely available.

Tooker, Elisabeth. "Women in Iroquois Society," in *Extending the Rafters: Interdisciplinary Approaches to Iroquoian Studies*, ed. Michael K. Foster, Jack Campisi, and Marianne Mithun, 109–23. Albany: State University of New York Press, 1984.

A recent, authoritative appraisal of the Iroquois "matriarchate" by a prominent anthropologist of the Iroquois.

Trask, Haunani-Kay. "From a Native Daughter," in *The American Indian and the Problem of History*, ed. Calvin Martin, 171–79. New York: Oxford University Press, 1987.

Thoughts about history, culture, and colonialism by a native Hawaiian woman who teaches American studies at the University of Hawaii. Suggests that colonialism in America needs to be considered more broadly, chronologically and geographically.

Whiteman, Henrietta. "White Buffalo Woman," in *The American Indian and the Problem of History*, ed. Calvin Martin, 162–70. New York: Oxford University Press, 1987.

Cheyenne view of history through eyes of White Buffalo Woman (b. 1852), presented by her great-granddaughter. Evocative of struggle to live in two worlds and to conflate two very different histories.

African-American Women

Books

Bush, Barbara. *Slave Women in Caribbean Society, 1650–1838*. Bloomington: Indiana University Press, 1990.

Though beyond the present bounds of the United States, the Caribbean was an important part of the colonial Anglo-American world, and Bush's description and analysis of female slavery there informs our understanding of the British colonial mainland experience of African-American slave women as well. Nothing comparable exists treating women and slavery in mainland North America in the early American period.

See also Peterson, " 'I Will Never in My Life Go Back to You': Violence Against Native American Women," ch. 2 in "Eden Defiled: A History of Violence against Wives in Oregon," Ph.D. diss., University of Oregon, 1993.

Fox-Genovese, Elizabeth. *Within the Plantation Household: Black and White Women of the Old South.* Chapel Hill: University of North Carolina Press, 1988.

Focuses especially on the complex, intimate, violent web of connections between white and black women, particularly in the antebellum period, but beginning in an earlier time. Unlike many previous works, it accounts for the impact of gender as well as race and class on the southern slave society. A vast, important book that defies easy summary.

Gutman, Herbert G. *The Black Family in Slavery and Freedom, 1750–1925.* New York: Pantheon, 1976.

Though emphasis on later period, important revision of earlier treatment of black family. Unfortunately, underemphasis of role of black women within family.

Hoffman, Ronald, and Peter J. Albert, eds. *Women in the Age of the American Revolution.* Charlottesville: University Press of Virginia, 1989. Part 3: Dreams and Limitations: The World of Black Women, 293–444.

Part 3 includes important, state-of-the-art articles (ca. 1989) on the status of slave women, on the meaning of the revolution for blacks in general and women in particular, and on early American racism as seen through a biographical case study of Phillis Wheatley, an African-American woman and one of revolutionary America's most important poets.

Jones, Jacqueline. *Labor of Love, Labor of Sorrow: Black Women, Work, and the Family from Slavery to the Present.* New York: Basic Books, 1985.

Though emphasis on nineteenth century, provides detailed analysis of black slave women's experience, much of which can inform our understanding of an earlier, poorly documented time; wealth of information useful for lectures.

Kulikoff, Allan. *Tobacco and Slaves: The Development of Southern Cultures in the Chesapeake, 1680–1800.* Chapel Hill: University of North Carolina Press, 1986.

Culmination of much important work on slavery in the Chesapeake which Kulikoff has published. Less cultural than materialist social history here, but some excellent material on the African origins of black slaves and on the formation of the African-American family; not particularly sensitive to gender analysis but, instead, an emphasis on class and race.

Lebsock, Suzanne. *The Free Women of Petersburg: Status and Culture in a Southern Town, 1784–1860.* New York: W. W. Norton, 1984.

With Jones's book, one of the more important, intimate treatments of black women in the early national and antebellum period, with important implications for the colonial era, when slave society emerged.

Sobel, Mechal. *The World They Made Together: Black and White Values in Eighteenth-Century Virginia.* Princeton: Princeton University Press, 1987.

Cultural historical analysis of the intimate connections between whites and blacks and the hybrid cultural world that they constructed; fascinating material on African and African-American sense of time, space, relationships, and the mental and physical world. Suggests importance of black women as intercultural mediators.

White, Deborah Gray, *Arn't I a Woman? Female Slaves in the Plantation South.* New York: W. W. Norton, 1985.

Like many other works cited here, focuses on a later period, but there is much in the book that suggests the nature of black women's experience in the earlier years of slavery; wonderfully evocative and filled with material useful for lectures.

Articles

Grimsted, David. "Anglo-American Racism and Phillis Wheatley's 'Sable Veil,' 'Length'ned Chain,' and 'Knitted Heart,'" in Hoffman and Albert (eds.), *Women in the Age of the American Revolution,* 338–444.

Examination of the exceptional black female poet as case study in American racism of the revolutionary era. Provides important information about Wheatley's life and achievement and makes the case, implicitly, that the revolutionary era, and much of subsequent history, cannot be understood apart from examination of issues of race and gender.

Gunderson, Joan Rezner. "The Double Bonds of Race and Sex: Black and White Women in a Colonial Virginia Parish," *Journal of Southern History,* 52 (August 1986): 351–97. Reprinted in Dinnerstein and Jackson, *American Vistas, 1607–1877,* 6th ed., 1:79–97. New York: Oxford University Press, 1991.

Rare treatment of black women specifically in colonial America and, with comparative focus, provides good material for lectures.

Hine, Darlene Clark. "Lifting the Veil, Shattering the Silence: Black Women's History in Slavery and Freedom," in *The State of Afro-American History: Past, Present, and Future,* ed. Darlene Clark Hine, 223–49. Baton Rouge: Louisiana State University Press, 1986.

Recent historiographical piece of general interest and with important implications for the study of early America. Like other recent writing, it emphasizes complex interrelationship of gender, race, and class.

Jones, Jacqueline. "Race, Sex, and Self-Evident Truths: The Status of Slave Women during the Era of the American Revolution," in Hoffman and Albert (eds.), *Women in the Age of the American Revolution,* 293–337.

Important recent attempt to synthesize literature of meaning of American Revolution for blacks in general and black women in particular. Argues black people and white women appropriated ideas of 1776, but their causes never joined in any meaningful way, notwithstanding later inspiration of abolitionism for female activists in nineteenth century or foundation for modern civil rights and women's movement in 1950s and 1960s.

Lebsock, Suzanne. " 'No Obey': Indian, European, and African Women in Seventeenth-Century Virginia," originally in *A Share of Honour: Virginia Women, 1600–1945.* Virginia Women's Cultural History Project, 1984. Reprinted in *Women, Families, and Communities: Readings in American History,* ed., Nancy A. Hewitt, 1:6–20. Glenview, Ill.: Scott, Foresman, 1990.

Focusing on the seventeenth century, the article very generally lays out a sort of "prehistory" for the later colonial and antebellum periods. Though a period of fluidity and possibility, seeds of later oppression clearly visible, especially in treatment of Native Americans.

Menard, Russell R. "The Maryland Slave Population, 1659 to 1730: A Demographic Profile of Blacks in Four Counties," *William and Mary Quarterly,* 3d ser., 32 (1975): 29–54. Reprinted in *Colonial America: Essays in Politics and Social Development,* ed. Stanley N. Katz and John M. Murrin, 3d ed., 290–313. New York: Knopf, 1983.

Provides important demographic and social information of slave population of colonial Maryland. Maryland's slaves in this period were overwhelmingly immigrants (rather than native born) and males (a sex ratio as high as 6:1), facts of enormous importance for understanding both women's experience and the larger society they lived in.

Soderland, Jean R. "Black Women in Colonial Pennsylvania," in *Our American Sisters: Women in American Life and Thought,* ed. Jean E. Friedman et al., 55–75. Lexington, Mass.: D. C. Heath, 1987. Originally published in *Pennsylvania Magazine of History and Biography.*

Provides important analysis on the different sort of slavery that played a critical role in the early history of the Middle Colonies. Particularly good in its illumination of the contours of women's slavery in the colonial period as well as in anticipating the nature of life for black women and men after the abolition of slavery in Pennsylvania later in the eighteenth century.

U.S. HISTORY TO 1877

Barbara Winslow Department of History
Hunter College, City University of New York
New York, NY 10021

Course Description

This is an introductory course to U.S. history. For too long U.S. history has been taught from the vantage point of presidents and other "important" people, their politics, their wars, their lives and values. This course will not only look at this nation's elite but also, and equally important, the lives, experiences, and contributions of ordinary people. Indians, slaves, indentured servants, free blacks, craft workers, small farmers, factory workers, and the myriad groups of immigrant workers are a central focus of the course. Class, race, gender, and national origins will also be a major area of study. Outside readings, films, and videos will be used to supplement the course.

Required Texts

Who Built America? vol. 1, American Social History Project. New York: Pantheon, 1989.
    Paul F. Boller and Ronald Story, *A More Perfect Union: Documents in U.S. History*, vol. 1: to 1877, 2d ed. Boston: Houghton Mifflin, 1987.

Syllabus

Week 1   *Introduction.* What is U.S. history? Discussion of class format, requirements, and historical concepts.
            Read chapter 1 in *Who Built America*, Rayna Green, "The Pocahontas Perplex: The Image of Indian Women in American Culture," reprinted in *Unequal Sisters: A MultiCultural Reader in U.S. Women's History*, edited by Ellen Dubois and Vicki Ruiz.

Week 2	Lecture and discussion of the readings. Points to think about: What were the differences in cultures between the New World natives and the European explorers? Why did Eureopeans come to the New World? Why and how did slavery develop? Is there a relationship between capitalism and colonization?
Week 3	Read chapter 2 in *Who Built America*, "Slavery and the Growth of the Southern Colonies"; readings on Virginia slave legislation in Boller and Story.
	Lecture and discussion of the readings. Points to think about: What is meant by "free" labor and "unfree" labor? Who were slaves and why? Who were indentured servants and why? Was there a difference in the treatment and relationships between female slaves? indentured servants? What were the characteristics of the planter class? How did slave legislation determine future patterns and development of racism? What was the importance of the House of Burgesses?
Week 4	Read chapter 3 in *Who Built America*, "Free Labor and the Growth of the Northern Colonies"; readings in Boller, "The Mayflower Compact," "The Bloody Tenet of Persecution," "A Model of Christian Charity."
	Lecture and discussion of the readings. Points to think about: How did the northern colonies differ from those in the South in terms of economic development, religion, forms of political organization, treatment of the Indians, position of women? What are mercantilism and imperialism?
Week 5	First quiz based upon all the readings and discussions up through chapter 3 in *Who Built America*. Read chapter 4, "The Greatness of This Revolution"; watch film: *Tea Party Etiquette*.
	Points to think about: What was the structure of life in colonial society? What was the role of ordinary colonists in "crowd" actions such as the Boston Tea Party in pushing the colonies toward revolution?
Week 6	Continue reading chapter 4; also read The Declaration of Independence and the U.S. Constitution, in Boller and handout.
	Lecture and discussion of the readings. Points to think about: What did Jefferson mean when he wrote, ". . . all men are created equal"? How did the American Revolution affect the status and consciousness of free blacks and slaves? What did the Republican ideal offer women?

What is the meaning and importance of the Bill of Rights? Why did political parties emerge, and what did they stand for?

Week 7   Read chapter 5 in *Who Built America*, "The Growth of the Slave South"; Deborah Gray White, "Female Slaves: Sex Roles and Status in Antebellum Plantation South," in *Unequal Sisters*; watch film: *Doing as They Can: Slave Life in the American South*.

Points to think about: What was the slave's view of slavery, and how do we know about it? How did the invention of the cotton gin and the subsequent change in the price of cotton affect slaves' lives? Why did most white non–slave owners accept slavery? Was there a difference in the tasks assigned to male and female slaves? How did the spread of slavery to the West affect slave families?

Week 8   Read chapter 6 in *Who Built America*, "The Free Labor North."

Lecture and discussion of readings; film: *Daughters of Free Men*. Points to think about for the film: How did the cotton economy affect the lives of textile workers like Lucy Hall? How did the daily life of Lucy Hall compare and contrast with that of the daily lives of female slaves? What are the different meanings of "independence" and "equality" for George Hewes, Harriet Jacobs, and Lucy Hall? Points to think about from chapter 6: How did the "new" immigrants of 1840–60 (Irish and German) differ from the older, settled people from Europe? What was Jacksonian democracy? Explain the role of the Democratic party during the period 1824–50.

Week 9   Read chapter 7 in *Who Built America*, "Changing Patterns of Social Life."

Lecture and discussion of the readings. Points to think about: What were the economic and technological changes taking place in U.S. society from 1820 to 1860? What was the middle-class ideal? What was the reality for slaves, free blacks, small farmers, artisans, and laborers? How did northern and southern families differ? How did leisure differ for the middle class, the working class, the slaves? How did religion play a central role in the lives of Americans?

Midterm examination: the midterm will be based upon all the readings from the first quiz to the present.

Week 10   Read chapter 8 in *Who Built America*, "The Fight for Free Labor in the North."

Lecture and discussion of the readings. Points to think about: What were the different ways in which skilled, unskilled, and female workers organized to fight for "free" labor? How did the fluctuation in the U.S. economy affect the lives of working people? What were the cooperative and communal experiments, and what did they have to offer to women? free blacks? slaves? working people? Watch film: *Five Points: New York's Irish Working Class in the 1850s.*

Points to think about: How did the work life of Mary Mulvahill compare with Lucy Hall's work life in the Lowell mills? How would her workload compare with a slave woman in the south? How did the ideal of "separate spheres" affect the family structure of Yankee farm families, slave families, and Irish immigrant families?

Week 11   Read chapter 9 in *Who Built America*, "The Struggle over Slave Labor"; readings in Boller, "David Walker's *Appeal, Declaration of Sentiments, The Seneca Falls Resolutions,* 1848.

Lecture and discussion of the readings. Points to think about: What were the different ways in which slaves resisted and adapted to slavery? What did the abolitionists stand for? Were there differences among the abolitionists about issues of politics, the use of violence, religion, the role of women, gradualism, African-American leadership? What was the reaction by the white South to the abolition movement? What was the reaction by northern workers? What was the relationship between the women's rights movement and the abolitionist movement? What did the *Declaration of Sentiments* have to say about slave women? What is the relationship of the *Declaration of Sentiments* to the Declaration of Independence?

Week 12   Continue the readings.

Lecture and discussion of the readings. Points to think about: What were the goals and motivations of westward expansion? How did Manifest Destiny first become a powerful nationalizing force then a powerful sectional force? What was the importance of John Brown's raid? What did the Republican party stand for? What did the Democratic party stand for?

Week 13   Read chapter 10 in *Who Built America*, "The Civil War: America's Second Revolution." Paper due.

Lecture and discussion of the readings. Points to think about: What were the differing opinions within the North and within the South regarding secession and war? How did the slaves and free blacks press the issue of emancipation? How did the Civil War transform the North? the South? What was the role of women in the war effort in both the North and the South? Why did the North win the Civil War?

Week 14   Watch film: *Glory*.

Week 15   Discussion of the film *Glory*. Points to think about: Did the movie give an accurate historical picture of the Civil War? of the lives of soldiers? What does the movie say about the Civil War? about wars in general? Do you think the black soldiers were assigned to lead the assault on Fort Wagner because white officers wanted blacks to suffer such high casualty rates?

Week 16   Read chapter 11 of *Who Built America*, "Emancipation and Reconstruction"; know the Thirteenth, Fourteenth, and Fifteenth Amendments to the U.S. Constitution.

Lecture and discussion of the readings. Points to consider: How did emancipation change the lives of African Americans (former slaves and free blacks)? How did the Reconstruction amendments change our ideals of independence, liberty, and equality? Think about the idea of competing and limited rights in the debates over the Fourteenth and Fifteenth Amendments. What were the origins of terrorist organizations such as the Ku Klux Klan, and what was their role in bringing reconstruction to an end? What were the accomplishments of Reconstruction? Why did Reconstruction come to an end? What has been the permanent legacy of the end of Reconstruction in terms of race relations in the United States in the twentieth century?

Final take-home examination due.

HISTORY OF THE UNITED STATES (THE TWENTIETH CENTURY)

Howard Brick Department of History
University of Oregon
Eugene, OR 97403

Course Description

The conclusion of a three-term sequence, this course offers an introductory survey of U.S. history from the tumultuous 1890s to the years of the Reagan presidency. Over this period the country has become knit together more tightly by economic ties and new forms of transportation and communications, while attempts to fashion a common American culture for the country's people have been only partially successful. This course asks: What makes an "American" nation out of the heterogeneous people who have lived in the United States and the varied social experiences they have had? While all inhabitants are affected by common experiences (e.g., wars, depressions, and national governments), they are also differentiated by their ethnicity or racial designation, by their social class, by sex and gender, and by generation—and by all the ways these categories overlap to mark the differences between, for example, a Chicana housekeeper of New Mexico in 1913, an Anglo businessman in Boston 1935, and a young Italian-American autoworker in 1973. What have they shared, and what haven't they, as Americans? Being an "American," this course will show, has meant different things for different social groups, and their ideas about "America" have been shaped in part by the relationships of power, inequality, conflict, and compromise among them.

Required Texts

Bell, Thomas, *Out of This Furnace* (Pittsburgh: University of Pittsburgh Press, 1976), is a novel, originally published in 1940, describing an East European immigrant family whose life is bound up with the steel mills of western Pennsylvania.

Norton, Mary Beth, et al., *A People and a Nation* (3d brief ed., Boston: Houghton Mifflin, 1991), is the textbook for the course, providing an overview of the development of life in the United States during the time we are discussing. It provides the basic information on which the lectures and the more specialized readings will build.

Robinson, Jo Ann G., *The Montgomery Bus Boycott and the Women Who Started It* (Knoxville: University of Tennessee Press, 1987), describes first-

hand one of the first major actions against racial segregation laws in the
Deep South.

Silko, Leslie Marmon, *Ceremony* (New York: Viking Penguin, 1990), is a cel-
ebrated novel about a Pueblo veteran of World War II, who turns toward
traditional Pueblo practices in his search for a place in the postwar world.

Takaki, Ronald, *Strangers from a Different Shore: A History of Asian Americans* (New York: Viking Penguin, 1990), is a general history of Asian Americans, those immigrants to the United States who crossed the
Pacific—from China, Japan, Korea, the Philippines, and the East Indies.

Reserved Readings

(selections indicated on class schedule)

Jane Addams, *Twenty Years at Hull House*

James A. Clifton, ed., *Being and Becoming Indian: Biographical Studies of
North American Frontiers*

Mike Davis and Michael Sprinker, eds., *Reshaping the U.S. Left*

Sarah Deutsch, *No Separate Refuge: Culture, Class and Gender on an Anglo-
Hispanic Frontier in the American Southwest, 1880–1940*

Ellen Carol DuBois and Vicki L. Ruiz, eds., *Unequal Sisters: A Multicultural
Reader in U.S. Women's History*

Mamie Garvin Fields, with Karen Fields, *Lemon Swamp and Other Places*

Paula Giddings, *When and Where I Enter: The Impact of Black Women on
Race and Sex in America*

Jacqueline Jones, *Labor of Love, Labor of Sorrow: Black Women, Work and
the Family, from Slavery to the Present*

Margot Liberty, *American Indian Intellectuals*

Robert S. McElvaine, *Down and Out in the Great Depression: Letters from
the "Forgotten Man"*

Robin Morgan, *Sisterhood Is Powerful: An Anthology of Writings from the
Women's Liberation Movement*

Dorothy Sterling, ed., *We Are Your Sisters: Black Women in the Nineteenth
Century*

Syllabus

Week 1   *On the Eve of a New Century.*
                  Introduction: The Meanings of Americanism. The Tumul-
                  tuous 1890s.
                  Optional evening film: *The Ballad of Gregorio Cortez.*
                  Required Reading: Norton et al., chaps. 19 and 21, pp.
                  345–58, 376–91; Bell, *Out of This Furnace,* part 1, pp.

	3–117. Recommended Reading: Selections from the diary
	of Ida B. Wells, 479–95, in Sterling, *We are Your Sisters*.
Week 2	*Conflict and Consensus in the "Progressive Era."*

Work and Family in the Early Twentieth Century. Movements for Social Change: Labor, Big Business, Suffragists, and Settlement House Workers. Progressives as Leaders and Lawmakers

Optional evening film: *Ethnic Notions*. Required Reading: Norton et al., chap. 20, pp. 359–75; Bell, *Out of This Furnace*, parts 2 and 3, pp. 119–258; Takaki, *Strangers from a Different Shore*, chap. 5, pp. 179–229. Recommended Reading: "Between the Cotton Field and the Ghetto," 110–51, in Jones, *Labor of Love, Labor of Sorrow;* "To Be a Woman Sublime," 95–117, in Giddings, *When and Where I Enter;* "The Subjective Necessity for Social Settlements," in Addams, *Twenty Years at Hull House*

Week 3   *The Coming of World War I.*

Race and Racism in the Progressive Era. Woodrow Wilson and U.S. Participation in World War I. The Success of Women's Suffrage Optional evening film: *The Birth of a Nation*. Required Reading: Norton et al., chap. 22, pp. 392–410; Bell, *Out of This Furnace*, part 4, pp. 259–413. Recommended Reading: George J. Sánchez, " 'Go After the Women': Americanization and the Mexican Immigrant Woman, 1915–1929," 250–63, in DuBois and Ruiz, *Unequal Sisters*

Week 4   *Culture and Politics in the 1920s.*

The United States in the World. Conflict of Modern and Traditional Culture. Mass Media and the Arts (Movies, Jazz, Expatriates, and the Harlem Renaissance)

Optional evening film: *The Jazz Singer*. Required Reading: Norton et al., chaps. 23 and 25, pp. 411–28, 451–57; Takaki, *Strangers from a Different Shore*, chaps. 6–8, pp. 230–314. Recommended Reading: "On the Margins: Chicano Community Building in Northern Colorado, the 1920s," 127–61, in Deutsch, *No Separate Refuge;* "Moving North" and "Coming Home," 159–203, in Fields and Fields, *Lemon Swamp and Other Places*

Week 5   *The Depression and Social Change.*

The Origins and Impact of the Depression. The Appeal of Communism. What Made the New Deal New

Optional evening film: *Union Maids*. Required Reading: Norton et al., chaps. 24 and 25, pp. 429–50, 457–66;

Takaki, *Strangers from a Different Shore,* chaps. 9–10, pp. 315–405. Recommended Reading: Selected letters, 35–94, in McElvaine, *Down and Out in the Great Depression;* "Enter Mary McLeod Bethune," 199–203, in Giddings, *When and Where I Enter;* "Flora Zuni," 217–25, in Liberty, *American Indian Intellectuals;* "Maud Claremont," 249–75, in Clifton, *Being and Becoming Indian*

Week 6   *War and the American Century.*

From Neutrality to War. The Conduct of the War and World Politics. Americanism in World War II and Its Aftermath

Take-home midterm due

Optional evening film: *Life and Times of Rosie the Riveter.* Required Reading: Norton et al., chap. 26, pp. 467–84; Silko, *Ceremony*

Week 7   *The Cold War and Anticommunism.*

From Hot War to Cold War. Hollywood and Communism: Ronald Reagan's Beginnings. The Kennedy Mystique and the Cold War.

Optional evening film: *The Salt of the Earth.* Required Reading: Norton et al., chaps. 27–28, pp. 485–520; Robinson, *The Montgomery Bus Boycott*

Week 8   *The Matter of "Race" in Postwar America.*

Civil Rights and the New Protest. Building a Great Society in the 1960s. The Vietnam War I: The Vietnamese

Short paper due

Optional evening film: *The War at Home.* Required Reading: Norton et al., chaps. 29 and 31, pp. 521–33, 554–69

Week 9   *Vietnam's Aftermath.*

The Vietnam War II: The Americans. Forms of Cultural Nationalism. The Rise of Women's Liberation and the Antifeminist Backlash

Optional evening film: *The Willmar Eight.* Required Reading: Norton et al., chaps. 30 and 32, pp. 534–53, 570–86; Takaki, *Strangers from a Different Shore,* chaps. 11–12, pp. 406–91. Recommended Reading: Robin Morgan, "The Women's Revolution"; Frances Beal, "Double Jeopardy"; Enriqueta Longauex y Vasquez, "The Mexican-American Woman," xv–xlvi, 382–96, 426–32, in Morgan, *Sisterhood Is Powerful;* Alma M. García, "The Development of Chicana Feminist Discourse, 1970–1980," 418–31, in DuBois and Ruiz, *Unequal Sisters.*

Week 10   *What Was the "Reagan Revolution"?*
Conservative Revival and the Reagan Administration. National Unity and Conflict in the Contemporary United States
Required Reading: Norton et al., chap. 33, pp. 587–607.
Recommended Reading: Frank Bardacke, "Watsonville: A Mexican Community on Strike," in Davis and Sprinker, *Reshaping the U.S. Left*

HISTORY OF WOMEN IN THE UNITED STATES: 1890 TO THE PRESENT

Lee Chambers-Schiller Department of History
University of Colorado
Boulder, CO 80309

Course Objectives

The purpose of this class is threefold:

1. to offer an overview of women's experience in U.S. society with a view to continuities and discontinuities within and between the experiences of various groups of American women over the twentieth century
2. to develop a sense of the similarities and differences among American women by emphasizing how women of different racial, ethnic, class, religious, and regional backgrounds experience work (domestic, agricultural, industrial, and white collar), family (marriage, childbearing and child rearing, ideological constructions of the role of the family in the community, and the woman in the family), sexuality (cultural constructions of female sexuality and the female construction of sexuality in oppressive environments and different times), politics (the women's movement and movements for liberation or civil rights), and cross-race or cross-class relations between women (within the women's movement and in other social or political contexts such as social welfare programs or antivice campaigns)
3. to develop skills in careful reading, historical analysis, critical thinking, and historical writing. To this end different kinds of primary source material will serve as the basis for class discussions of epistemological and methodological issues.

It is my hope that students will leave this class with a sense of the richness and diversity of women's lives and historical experience, some open questions about what we know of these lives and how we know it, and a yearning to learn more about and contribute to this knowledge.

Required Reading

Text

Nancy Hewitt, ed., *Women, Families, and Communities. Reading in American History*, vol. 2: *From 1865.*

Primary Sources

Victoria Byerly, *Hard Times Cotton Mill Girls*. Oral histories of black and white industrial workers in southern mill towns across the century.

Sara Davidson, *Loose Change*. An autobiographical novel about the experience of four white women during the social and political turmoil of the mid-1960s.

Mamie Garvin Fields, with Karen Fields, *Lemon Swamp and Other Places: A Carolina Memoir*. A southern, black grandmother's memoir of her life, work, family, and community activism from Reconstruction through the 1940s, based on oral interviews with her northern granddaughter.

Elia Peattie, *The Precipice*. A 1911 novel about white college and professional women in the urban Midwest, their attitudes toward work, marriage, and feminism.

Dorothy Richardson, *The Long Day*. A white, investigative reporter's view of female industrial workers and their lives in New York City early in the century.

Yoshiko Uchida, *Picture Bride*. A novel about a Japanese woman immigrant, her views of love and marriage, her work in her husband's store and a white woman's home, her relationship with her acculturated daughter, and her displacement to a relocation camp during World War II.

Course Packet

Selected letter of mothers to the Woman's Bureau, from Molly Ladd-Taylor's *Raising a Baby the Government Way*.

Kathy Peiss, " 'Charity Girls' and City Pleasures: Historical Notes on Working-Class Sexuality, 1880–1920."

Jessie Rodrique, "The Black Community and the Birth-Control Movement."

Evelyn Glenn, "The Dialectics of Wage Work: Japanese American Women and Domestic Service, 1905–1940."

Salt of the Earth (and edited version of the film script).

"The Gang's All Here," chapter 4 of Allan Bérubé's, *Coming Out under Fire: The History of Gay Men and Women in World War II.*

Madeline Davis and Elizabeth Kennedy, "Oral History and the Study of Sexuality in the Lesbian Community: Buffalo, New York, 1940–1960."

Course Requirements

Study questions and paper topics will be handed out for the three papers required for the course: these will be on *Lemon Swamp, Hard Times Cotton Mill Girls,* and *Loose Change.* Study questions will also be handed out for *The Precipice, The Long Day, Picture Bride,* and "Salt of the Earth." These will be the focus of classroom discussion.

Note that the study questions for all texts are introduced by a brief discussion of the critical problems raised by these texts. Think about these issues as they, too, will be discussed in class.

Paper Topics

Lemon Swamp

1. Karen Fields tells us that this is the story of "proud men freeing their wives from 'work out.'" What does she mean by this? What does this memoir tell us about the nature of gender roles among Charleston blacks of Mamie's generation? Are the issues the same for men and women of Karen's?

2. With reference to the life and works of Mamie Garvin Fields, think about the words of Mary Church Terrell: "We have our own lives to lead. We are daughters, sisters, mothers, and wives. We must care for ourselves and rear our families, like all women. But we have more to do than other women. Those of us fortunate enough to have education must share it with the less fortunate of our race. We must go into our communities and improve them; we must go out into the nation and change it. Above all, we must organize ourselves as Negro women and work together." What does this memoir tell us about black women's views of race, community, and social welfare? Do black and white women of this time share a common perception of their roles and responsibilities as women?

3. In a famous essay historian C. Vann Woodward has said: "The ironic thing about these two great hyphenated minorities, Southern-Americans and Afro-Americans, confronting each other on their native soil for three and a half centuries, is the degree to which they have shaped each other's destiny, determined each other's isolation, shared and molded a common culture. It is, in fact, impossible to imagine the one without the other and quite futile to try." Do you agree or disagree with Woodward's analysis?

Discuss it as viewed through the lens of Mamie Garvin Fields's life and experience.

4. This book is the product of a dialogue across the generations. Karen Fields acknowledges tension between her view and her grandmother's view of American society and the possibilities and routes toward change. She acknowledges differences between them over the structure of the book and the meaning of the story. Discuss these generational tensions and their impact on this memoir. What, ultimately, does Karen learn as the "lessons of her heritage"?

Hard Times Cotton Mill Girls

1. What is the role of women's work outside the home in these families? Is the role the same across race? Is it the same across time? Is the work the same across race and time?

2. Discuss the views of sex, marriage, and motherhood among these women. What common patterns do you see in their personal histories? What is the impact of their personal history on their work history, and vice versa? What do you make of this?

3. Mill towns are close-knit communities of individuals and families, management and labor. What changes in the relationship of management and labor do you see across the time span covered by these interviews? What factors influence these changes? How do these changes affect the mill women specifically?

4. This is a well-edited and well-written work of oral history. Without the question-answer format of the interviews, however, it is difficult for the reader to enter into the process of historical interpretation. Byerly had done that in her editorial process. Analyze this book from Byerly's perspective. What does it say about her concerns and her values? How do you see these at work in the interviews themselves and in the selection and ordering of the book? What is the moral of the story that she has constructed?

Loose Change

1. The "new politics" consisted of many things but included a new mode of political organization, "participatory democracy," and a new process, the "consciousness-raising" group. Did these terms have the same meaning for men and women in the New Left? Were women empowered? Discuss the role of this process in the novel and its implications for political activism and social change at the time.

2. A new theoretical framework also emerged from the "new politics." Simply stated, it was that "the personal is political." Discuss the meaning of

this statement. Describe the gradual realization of its meaning for Susie and its transformation of her work, marriage, and sense of self.
3. This book is about power relations between men and women. Describe the structure of these relations and discuss how and why they changed over time. What is familiar about this structuring of gender relationships, and what has changed for your generation?
4. There was a certain conformity at work in this age of "do your own thing"—a conformity of dress, of language, and of behavior which separated the "cool" from the "square." What was the prevailing view in this subculture of female and male nature, of female and male roles, of femininity and masculinity, of female and male sexuality? Were these views so different from those of their parents' generation? from your own?

Syllabus

Week 1	*Introduction to Course, Its Theoretical Underpinnings, and Themes.*
Week 2	*Women's Public Activism, 1870–1890 (Chicago, New York, New Orleans, San Francisco).* Municipal Housekeeping and Social Feminism
	Read in text: Jacqueline Jones, "Freed Women? The Civil War and Reconstruction"; Rosalind Moss, "The Girls from Syracuse: Kansas Women in Politics, 1887–1890"; Kathryn Sklar, "Hull House in the 1890s: A Community of Women Reformers"
Week 3	*Woman's Suffrage Movement and New Feminism.* Discussion: *The Precipice*
Week 4	*Antilynching Campaign.* Black-White Conflict in Political Movements
	Read in text: Julie Jeffrey, "Farmers' Wives and the New South: Women in the Southern Farmers' Alliance"; Jacquelyn Dowd Hall: "A Common Bond of Womanhood? Building an Interracial Community in the Jim Crow South"
	Read in packet: Selected letters from Molly Ladd-Taylor, *Raising a Baby the Government Way*
Week 5	*Scientific Motherhood and Eugenics.* Discussion and paper due: *Lemon Swamp*
Week 6	*Modernism and Leisure: Class, Race, and Sexuality.* Birth Control Movement and State Regulation of Sex and Reproduction
	Read in text: Ruth Cowan, "Two Washes in the Morning and a Bridge Party at Night: Consumer Culture and the

American Housewife between the Wars"; Joanne Meyerowitz, "The Roaring Teens and Twenties Reexamined: Sexuality in the Furnished Room Districts of Chicago"

Read in packet: Kathy Peiss, " 'Charity Girls' and City Pleasures: Historical Notes on Working Class Sexuality, 1880–1920"; Jessie Rodrique, "The Black Community and the Birth-Control Movement"

Industrial Work and Labor Organization. Discussion: *The Long Day*

Week 7   *Agricultural Work and Southern Industrialization. Domestic Service and Minority Women's Work.*

Read in text: Susan Levine, "The Transformation of a Laboring Community: Mechanization and the Mobilization of Women Weavers"; Paula Hyman, "Immigrant Women, Community Networks, and Consumer Protest: The New York City Kosher Meat Boycott of 1902"; Sara Deutsch, "Transforming Hispanic Communities: World War I and Americanization in the Southwest"

Read in packet: Evelyn Glenn, "The Dialectics of Wage Work: Japanese American Women and Domestic Service, 1905–1940"

Week 8   *Depression: Rural and Urban.*

Discussion and paper due: *Hard Times Cotton Mill Girls*

Week 9   *Immigration: Comparative Patterns. World War II: Changing Home and Work.*

Read in text: Julia Blackwelder, "Women of the Depression: Anglo, Black, and Hispanic Families in San Antonio"; Alan Clive, "The Home Front and the Household: Women, Work and Family in Detroit"

Read in packet: Allan Bérubé, "The Gang's All Here"; "Gay Life and Vice Control"

Week 10   Discussion: *The Picture Bride.* Postwar Containment and Family Ideology

Week 11   *Sexual Containment: Race, Class and Deviance.*

Discussion: *Salt of the Earth*

Read in text: James Davidson and Mark Lytle, "From Rosie to Lucy: The Mass Media and Changing Images of Women and Family"

Week 12   *Second Wave: Roots in Civil Rights and the New Left. Sexual Revolution and Politics: Lesbian Rights.*

Read in text: David Garrow, "The Origins of the Montgomery Bus Boycott"

Read in packet: Madeline Davis and Elizabeth Kennedy,

	"Oral History and the Study of Sexuality in the Lesbian Community: Buffalo, New York, 1940–1960"
Week 13	*Transformation of Private Life: Family and Sex, 1970–80.* Discussion and paper due: *Loose Change*
Week 14	*Transformation of Public Life: Work in 1970s–80s. Transformation of Politics: The Politics of Difference and the "Gender Gap".*

Read in text: Jane Mansbridge, "Embattled Women: The Defeat of the Equal Rights Amendment in Illinois"; Ruth Milkman, "A Statistical Portrait"

HISTORY OF THE FAMILY IN THE UNITED STATES, 1870–1990

Regina Morantz-Sánchez Department of History
University of California
Los Angeles, CA 90024

Parents first embody love and power, and each of their actions conveys to the child, quite independently of their overt intentions, the injunctions and constraints by means of which society attempts to organize experience. If reproducing culture were simply a matter of formal instruction and discipline, it could be left to the schools. But it also requires that culture be embedded in personality. Socialization makes the individual want to do what he has to do; and the family is the agency to which society entrusts this complex and delicate task.

—Christopher Lasch, *Haven in a Heartless World*

Course Objectives

This course aims to give a perspective on the contemporary family by studying the development of this important institution in the American past. Particular emphasis will be placed on changing attitudes and experiences of sex roles, sexuality, child rearing, work patterns, and relationships between men, women, children. We will explore race, ethnicity, and class as well as shifting conceptions of the role of the state and how these factors have affected family life in America. We will want to ask ourselves how much the family has changed over time and try to project, on the basis of historical evidence, whither the family is going.

Course Requirements

Course work will consist of readings, lectures, and discussion. There will be a ten-page historical paper required of all students on some aspect of the history of your own family. The object is to use the historical perspective gained in this course to evaluate and analyze historical changes in your family over time. Two essay exams will be given, a take-home midterm and an in-class final.

Required Texts

Elizabeth Ewen, *Immigrant Women in the Land of Dollars*
N. Ray Hiner and Joseph Hawes, *Growing Up in America: Historical Essays*
Sue Miller, *The Good Mother;* or Gloria Naylor, *The Women of Brewster Place;* or Amy Tan, *The Joy Luck Club* (pick one)
Alejandro Morales, *The Brick People*
Ruth Sicelk, *Women and Children Last*

Assignments

Types of Families: Variations on a Theme

Questions:	How does class, race, and ethnicity affect family structure, sex roles, and childhood experience? How does historical context, environment, and economic and social organization shape family life? Does family organization shape the environment and economic and social structure?
Classes 1, 2, 3	Sylvia Van Kirk, "The Role of Women in the Creation of Fur Trade Society in Western Canada, 1670–1830," in Armitage and Jameson, *The Women's West.* Theda Purdue, "Cherokee Women and the Trail of Tears," *Journal of Women's History* (1989). Sondra Herman, "Loving Courtship or the Marriage Market? The Ideal and Its Critics, 1871–1911," *American Quarterly* (May 1973). Christine Stansell, "Women, Children and the Uses of the Streets: Class and Gender Conflict in New York City, 1850–1860," *Feminist Studies* (September 1982). Gwendolyn Wright, "Victorian Suburbs and the Cult of Domesticity"; and "Americanization and Ethnicity in Urban Tenements," *Building the Dream.* Peggy Pascoe, "Gender Systems in Conflict: The Marriages of Mission-

	Educated Chinese American Women, 1847–1939," in DuBois and Ruiz, *Unequal Sisters.* Highly recommended: Paula Baker, "The Domestication of Politics: Women and American Political Society, 1780–1920," *American Historical Review* 89 (June 1984): 620–47.
Class 4	Jacqueline Jones, "A Bridge of 'Bent Backs and Labouring Muscles': The Rural South, 1880–1915," in *Labor of Love, Labor of Sorrow.* James Oliver Horton, "Gender Conventions among Antebellum Free Blacks," *Feminist Studies* (Spring 1986). Carol Stack, "Child-Keeping: 'Gimme a Little Sugar,' " in Graff, *Growing Up in America.*
Class 5	The film *A Singing Stream* (1988; 57 mins.) will be shown.

Ethnic and Working-Class Families

Questions:	How does ethnic acculturation occur? How does it shape families and sex roles? How do cultural assumptions about family and sex roles shape ethnic acculturation? Do ethnic cultures differ and, if so, in what ways? How do these differences affect the way immigrant families adjust to the American environment? What do we mean when we speak of the "American" environment, and what role do native Anglo-Americans play in immigrant adjustment? What is the difference between class, race, and ethnicity?
Classes 6, 7	Elizabeth Ewen, *Immigrant Women in the Land of Dollars.* Lucy Cheng, "Free, Indentured, Enslaved: Chinese Prostitutes in Nineteenth-Century America," *Signs* (1979): 2–29. George Sánchez, " 'Go After the Women': Americanization and the Mexican Immigrant Woman, 1915–1929," in DuBois and Ruiz, *Unequal Sisters.* Evelyn Nakano Glenn, "The Dialectic of Wage Work: Japanese-American Women and Domestic Serrvants, 1905–1940," *Feminist Studies* (Fall 1980). Highly recommended: Rosalinda Gonzalez, "Chicanas and Mexican Immigrant Families, 1920–1940: Women's Subordination and Family Exploitation," in Scharf and Jensen, *Decades of Discontent.*
Class 8	The film *Hester Street* (1974; 89 mins.) will be shown.

Work

Questions:

Do men define themselves by their work? Do women? Does society define men and women by their work? How, historically, has women's work been distinguished from men's? How has the idea that "a woman's place is in the home" affected family life in different classes, ethnic groups, and races? Has this idea been shared by all families? Is women's unwaged work in the family really "work?" Is it recognized as work by economists and social theorists? In what ways are women disadvantaged in the workplace? What does their disadvantaged position have to do with their relationship with their family roles? Do they view themselves as disadvantaged? What is the "double day"? Do all women experience the double day? How do different kinds of families view the work of their members? How do differing cultural attitudes toward men's and women's work affect marriage and family relationships?

Classes 9, 10

Alejandro Morales, *The Brick People.* Elizabeth Clark-Lewis, " 'This Work Had an End': Afro-American Domestic Workers in Washington, D.C., 1910–40," in Groneman and Norton, *To Toil the Livelong Day.* Martha May, "The Historical Problem of the Family Wage," *Feminist Studies* (Summer 1982). Margery Davies, "Woman's Place Is at the Typewriter," *Radical America* 8 (July–August 1974). Regina Morantz-Sánchez, "The Compassionate Professional: Historical Notes on the Woman Physician's Dilemma," in Brehm, *Seeing Female.* "Men are Queer That Way," *Scribner's Magazine* (1933). Ruth Schwarz Cowan, "The Industrial Revolution in the Home," in Kerber and Mathews, *Women's America.* Highly recommended: Herbert Gutman, "Work, Culture and Society in Industrializing America," *American Historical Review* #78 (June 1973). Heidi Hartmann, "The Family as a Locus of Gender, Class, and Power: The Case of Housework," *Signs* 6 (Spring 1981). Review Purdue, "Cherokee Woman"; Glenn, "Dialectic of Wage Work"; and González, "Chicanas."

Class 11

The film *"Life and Times of Rosie the Riveter"* (60 mins.) will be shown. Midterm examination handed out

Class 12

The film *Salt of the Earth* (1954; 94 mins.) will be shown.

Class 13

Midterm examination due

Sexuality, Leisure, and Consumerism

Questions: Do different classes and ethnic groups have different at-
                  titudes toward sex, leisure, and consumerism? What is
                  the relationship of capitalism, industrialization, and con-
                  sumerism to sexual attitudes and sexual behavior? How
                  do ideas about sexuality help to construct ideas about
                  proper masculine and feminine behavior? about class and
                  race? Do feminists support "sexual liberation"?

Classes 14, 15   Linda Gordon and Ellen Dubois, "Seeking Ecstacy on
                  the Battlefield: Danger and Pleasure in Nineteenth Cen-
                  tury Feminist Sexual Thought," *Feminist Studies* (Spring
                  1983): 7–25. Anthony Rotundo, "Body and Soul: Chang-
                  ing Ideals of American Middle-Class Manhood,
                  1770–1920," *Journal of Social History* 16 (September
                  1983): 23–38. Regina Morantz, "The Scientist as Sex Cru-
                  sader: Alfred Kinsey and American Culture," *American
                  Quarterly* (Winter 1977). Kathy Peiss, "Charity Girls and
                  City Pleasures," in Snitow, Stansell, and Thompson, *Pow-
                  ers of Desire*. Christina Simmons, "Companionate Mar-
                  riage and the Lesbian Threat," *Frontiers* (Fall 1979). John
                  D'Emilio, "Capitalism and Gay Identity," in Snitow,
                  Stansell, and Thompson, *Powers of Desire*. Jacquelyn
                  Dowd, " 'The Mind That Burns in Each Body': Women,
                  Woman Rape, and Racial Violence," in Snitow, Stansell,
                  and Thompson, *Powers of Desire*. Hazel Carby, " 'It Jus
                  Be's Dat Way Sometime': The Sexual Politics of Women's
                  Blues," in DuBois and Ruiz, *Unequal Sisters*. Highly rec-
                  ommended: Ellen Kay Trimberger, "Feminism, Men, and
                  Modern Love," in Snitow, Stansell, and Thompson, *Pow-
                  ers of Desire*.

Childhood, Youth, Adolescence

Questions: Do children from different classes and races experience
                  childhood differently? How intrusive has the state been
                  in determining the experience of childhood for different
                  racial and ethnic groups? How much control do parents
                  have over the lives of their children in different classes
                  and ethnic groups? Do all children in our society have
                  equal opportunity? What has been the role of the state in
                  children's lives, and what should it be?

Class 16	Read articles by Daniel Rodgers, D'Ann Campbell, Margaret Szasz, Melvin D. Williams, Barbara Finkelstein, and Nancy Pottishman Weiss, in *Growing Up in America*. Steven Schlossman, "The Crime of Precocious Sexuality: Female Juvenile Delinquency in the Progressive Era," *Harvard Educational Review* 48 (February 1978): 65–94. Jeffrey P. Hantover, "The Boy Scouts and the Validation of Masculinity," in Pleck and Pleck, *The American Man*. Highly recommended: Nancy Chodorow, "Family Structure and Feminine Personality," in Rosaldo and Lamphere, *Women, Culture and Society*. Linda Gordon, "Be Careful about Father: Incest," *Heroes of Their Own Lives*, 204–49.
Class 17	The film *Sixteen in Webster Grove* (1967; 60 mins.) will be shown.

The Family in Contemporary Society, 1950–90

Questions:	Has our definition of what constitutes a family changed over time? How? Why? What kinds of problems are families facing today? How does the cultural definition of family square with the reality of family life today? Is family life at risk? How do cultural, class, and racial differences play out in contemporary family organization? How many of the historical questions we have been dealing with in this course are still relevant?
Classes 18, 19, 20	Ruth Sidel, *Women and Children Last*. Jane de Hart, "The New Feminism and the Dynamics of Social Change," in Kerber and Mathews, *Women's America*. Robert A. Fein, "Men and Young Children," in Pleck and Sawyer, *Men and Masculinity* (1974). Betty Rollin, "Motherhood: Who Needs It?" reprinted from *Look* magazine, March 16, 1971. Maxine Baca Zinn, "Family, Race, and Poverty in the Eighties," *Signs* (September 1989). Sue Miller, *The Good Mother*; or Gloria Naylor, *The Women of Brewster Place*; or Cynthia Kadohata, *The Floating World*.
Class 21	Final examination

Lectures

Class 1	What Is a Family?
Class 2	Native American Families. Early Euro-American Families. Legacies Tape #6 (Trail of Tears)
Class 3	Legacies Tape #2 (A Little Commonwealth). Emergence of the Domestic Family?
Class 4	Legacies Tape #10 or 11
Class 5	*A Singing Stream*
Class 6	Immigration
Class 7	Immigration. Begin *Hester Street*
Class 8	*Hester Street*
Class 9	Men and Work. Slide Tape: "To Be a Man"
Class 10	Women and Work
Class 11	Women and Work. *Rosie the Riveter*
Class 12	*Salt of the Earth*
Class 13	*Salt of the Earth*
Class 14	Sexuality
Class 15	Sexuality
Class 16	Childhood, Youth, Adolescence
Class 17	*Sixteen in Webster Groves*
Class 18	The 1950s Family
Class 19	The 1960s Family
Class 20	Summary
Class 21	Final Examination

SURVEY OF AMERICAN LITERATURE
(Two-Semester Course)

Robert Combs Department of English
George Washington University
Washington, DC 20052

Course Development and Description

With the help of a grant from the Ford Foundation, twenty-six faculty members at George Washington University took part in a process of transforming the undergraduate liberal arts curriculum to include more material about women of color. The attached syllabi represent my first steps in this process, an effort to revise Survey of American Literature, a course that has traditionally focused almost exclusively on works by white male authors. The transformation of this course is far from complete, and far from completely successful, but the effort to open the course to real cultural diversity has engaged the students, by their own admission, and has completely *revived* the course, in my judgment.

The first half of this course must begin, it seems to me, with an apology and an admission of shame for the holocaust of the American Indians and for the institution of slavery. At the first class meeting I begin by reading a commencement speech given at George Washington University in 1989 by Senator Daniel Inouye, in which he describes atrocities committed through the government "removal policy" and urges the audience to become conscious of Native Americans' history, sufferings, and needs. The D. C. Heath selections under "Native American Tradition" are also useful in introducing students to a non-Cartesian sense of reality, a respect for the sacredness of the earth, and a type of religious fable, that of the trickster Raven—all parts of a culture they are not used to regarding as "American." Then selections from a discovery narrative by Cabeza de Vaca and a captivity narrative by Mary Rowlandson are used to view Indian culture suddenly from the "outside." Students begin to understand the process by which people and cultures become invisible to one another or, worse, become invested with attributes of evil, as the selections from Cotton Mather's descriptions of the Salem witch trials demonstrate.

Olaudah Equiano, Phillis Wheatley, Frederick Douglass, Harriet Jacobs, Sojourner Truth, Harriet Wilson—all these black writers articulate black experience, including memories of slavery, from the inside. All are important, but Frederick Douglass should be required reading for Americans. The dehumanizing effects of slavery on "masters" and "slaves" alike are emphasized throughout his autobiography to such an extent that a social definition of evil—as absolute power over others—clearly emerges. He also defines the origin of jazz and blues when he describes the slaves' music as "the most pathetic sentiment in the most rapturous tone, and the most rapturous sentiment in the most pathetic tone." Finally, Douglass's narrative is a confession of the evolution of a new attitude or style of consciousness normative for black people, one based on radical distrust as a way of life: "The motto which I adopted when I started from slavery was this—Trust no man!" It is also important for students to understand that good intentions and literacy are no proof against racism, whether naively internalized in these lines by Phillis Wheatley—

> Some view our sable race with scornful eye,
> "Their colour is a diabolic die."
> Remember *Christians*, *Negros*, black as *Cain*
> May be refined, and join the angelic train.

—or less innocently passed along by James Fenimore Cooper in *The Pioneers*, when he describes a character shooting pigeons, "as if he was shooting nothing but Mingo warriors." Sojourner Truth is one of my personal favorites among the additions to this course, showing that confrontation can be loving, and vice versa.

An early feminist theorist such as Margaret Fuller is of great help in clarifying the dynamics of oppression through prejudice wherever it is found and in suggesting an alternative. "Knowing that there exists in the minds of men a tone of feeling towards women as toward slaves," students see the mutually supportive roles played by stereotypes of gender and race. And when Fuller urges women to "retire within themselves," rather than trusting men to do the work of equality, she is expressing the hope that a mature feminism may be able to address injustice, which crosses over boundaries of race and class. When Harriet Beecher Stowe's heroine Eliza struggles across the frozen river to freedom, "while blood marked every step," she anticipates a whole tradition of soldierly feminism and the values of matriarchy in black familial and religious life.

There are strong feminist elements throughout the works of American Romantics, especially Nathaniel Hawthorne's *Scarlet Letter* and "Rappaccini's Daughter," which allegorically recasts the Garden of Eden story, in which evil comes into the world with the help of woman. Henry David Thoreau and Walt Whitman also challenge patriarchal assumptions by expressing the values of Being over Doing, in the sense of achieving, and the values of Being in the Body, that is, valuing oneness with the body's life moment by moment. The leaning toward Eastern philosophy we find in Romanticism, and toward a prota-Catholicism, also implies, I believe, a discovery of sources of feminine life and hope far from the too serious and decidedly cruel male rationalism of the Puritans. Dickinson, representing the "Royal Minority" of herself, is perhaps the first fully successful self-reliant voice in American literature.

My additions to the second half of this course are so numerous that I can only mention them. I have increased the number of African-American male writers, and African-American, Native American, Chicana, and Asian-American women as well as women of mixed heritage. This is a perfectly natural thing to do and does no violence to the tendencies of modern literature, which are much more heterogeneous than in earlier periods. In fact, the alienation and angst of great modern masters make a new kind of sense when we look at the whole picture of the human family. Existential despair may well reflect an unbearable isolation that the white world has brought upon itself as it has denied equal reality to others. I have added Ghost Dance songs and African-American folktales and works by Pauline Hopkins, Charles Eastman, Standing Bear, Abraham Cahan, Mary Antin, Gertrude Bonnin [Zitkala-Sa], Edith Maud Eaton, Booker T. Washington, W.E.B. Du Bois, Alain Locke, Langston Hughes, Zora Neale Hurston, and Audre Lorde. Richard Wright, Ralph Ellison, and James Baldwin were already included. Last year I was able also to include Black Elk, Leslie Marmon Silko, Denise Chávez, Louise Erdrich, Simon J. Ortiz, Lorna Dee Cervantes, and Cathy Song, and will again. But the riches of the Heath anthology, and a need I feel constantly to vary the material for my own sake, requires a certain amount of revising the selections year by year.

In the first half of the course I ask students to write an American "self-portrait" that includes one major nineteenth-century Romantic, one black writer, and one Native American. In the second half I ask for an original essay on *Song of Solomon*, by Toni Morrison, or *House Made of Dawn*, by N. Scott Momaday. Students do not fail to notice that large parts of modern and postmodern literary masterpieces by white males are concerned with despair. And while the works of so-called minorities may be about struggle and suffering, they are not about despair. Surely this is a fact worth celebrating.

Required Texts

Heath Anthology of American Literature, vols. 1 and 2
Toni Morrison, *Song of Solomon*

Syllabus—First Semester

Class 1	*Introduction.* "Prelude—Descent into Hell," *The Tales of Jacob,* by Thomas Mann. Transcribed text of the commencement address to the 1989 graduating class of George Washington University by Senator Daniel K. Inouye.
Class 2	"Colonial Period: To 1700," "Talk Concerning the First Beginning," "Raven Makes a Girl Sick and Then Cures Her"; Cabeza de Vaca, "Relation of . . ."; Rowlandson, "A Narrative of Captivity."
Class 3	Bradford, *Of Plymouth Plantation;* Bradstreet, "Meditations Divine and Moral," "To My Dear and Loving Husband," "Before the Birth of One of Her Children"; Wigglesworth, "God's Controversy with New-England"; selections from *The Bay Psalm Book* and *The New England Primer;* Taylor, "Huswifery."
Class 4	Mather, "The Wonders of the Invisible World," *Magnalia Christi Americana,* "The Conclusion; or, Eliot Expiring"; Edwards, *Resolutions, Personal Narrative,* "Sinners in the Hands of an Angry God."
Class 5	Woolman, *Journal,* "Some Considerations on the Keeping of Negroes"; "Colonial Period: 1700–1800."
Class 6	Franklin, *Autobiography,* parts 1 and 2.
Class 7	Franklin, "The Way to Wealth"; Olaudah Equiano, *The Interesting Narrative of . . . The African;* Paine, *Common Sense, The Age of Reason;* Wheatley, selected poems, letters.
Class 8	Crèvecoeur, *Letters from an American Farmer;* Cooper, *The Pioneers,* chapters 1 and 12 ("The Pigeon Shoot").
Class 9	Tyler, *The Contrast;* Irving, "The Legend of Sleepy Hollow."
Class 10	Brown, "Somnanbulism, a Fragment"; Freneau, "The House of Night," "The Wild Honey Suckle," "On Observing a Large Red-streak Apple," "The Indian Burying Ground."
Class 11	Bryant, "Thanatopsis," Emerson, "Nature."
Class 12	Emerson, "Self-Reliance," "The Poet," "The Rhodora," "The Snow-Storm."
Class 13	Emerson, "Circles," "Experience."
Class 14	Thoreau, selections from *Walden;* "Resistance to Civil Government."
Class 15	Whitman, *Song of Myself.*

Class 16	Whitman, "Out of the Cradle Endlessly Rocking," "When Lilacs Last in the Dooryard Bloom'd," "The Sleepers."
Class 17	Whitman, *Democratic Vistas*.
Class 18	Midterm examination.
Class 19	"Early Nineteenth Century"; Chief Seattle, "Speech"; Douglass, *Narrative of the Life of . . . an American Slave*.
Class 20	Jacobs, *Incidents in the Life of a Slave Girl*; Fuller, *Women in the Nineteenth Century*.
Class 21	Sojourner Truth, "Reminiscences . . . ," "Speech . . . ," "Address . . ."; Stowe, *Uncle Tom's Cabin*.
Class 22	Sedgwick, *Hope Leslie*; Kirkland, *A New Home—Who'll Follow?*; Wilson, *Our Nig*.
Class 23	Poe, "The Raven," "Annabel Lee," "Sonnet—To Science," "Israfel," "The City in the Sea," "The Sleeper," "Sonnet—Science," "Eldorado," "Alone," "The Philosophy of Composition."
Class 24	Poe, "Ligeia," "The Tell-Tale Heart," "The Purloined Letter."
Class 25	Hawthorne, "Young Goodman Brown," "The Minister's Black Veil."
Class 26	Hawthorne, "The Birth-mark," "Rappaccini's Daughter."
Class 27	Melville, "Bartleby, the Scrivener."
Class 28	Dickinson, poems 67, 130, 241, 249, 258, 280, 288, 303, 324, 328, 338, 341, 348, 435, 441, 465, 501, 520, 640, 670, 712, 754, 986, 1129, 1400, 1463, 1755, 1760, letters.

Syllabus—Second Semester

Class 1	*Introduction*.
Class 2	Pauline Elizabeth Hopkins, *Contending Forces*, 174–91. Sarah Orne Jewett, "A White Heron," 112–18. Ghost Dance songs, 743–45. Charles Alexander Eastman, "The Ghost Dance War," 747–54. Standing Bear, "What I Am Going to Tell You," 740–42.
Class 3	African-American Folktales: Memories of Slavery, Conjure Stories, John and Old Marster, 204–14. Mark Twain [Samuel Langhorne Clemens], *The Adventures of Huckleberry Finn*, chapters 1–11, pp. 243–81.
Class 4	Henry James, "The Beast in the Jungle," 597–626; "The Art of Fiction."
Class 5	Kate Chopin, "A Respectable Woman," 632–35; "The Story of an Hour," 635–37. Charlotte Perkins Gilman,

	"The Yellow Wallpaper," 761–73; *Herland*, 774–82. Ambrose Bierce, "Chickamauga," 654–58.
Class 6	Stephen Crane, "A Mystery of Heroism," 691–97; "The Open Boat," 697–714; *War Is Kind*, 722–25. Jack London, "To Build a Fire," 727–37.
Class 7	Abraham Cahan, *Yekl*, 878–84. Mary Antin, *The Promised Land*, 925–31. Gertrude Bonnin [Zitkala-Sa], *School Days of an Indian Girl*, 914–21; "Why I Am a Pagan," 921–23. Edith Maud Eaton [Sui-Sin Far], "Leaves from the Mental Portfolio of an Eurasian," 885–95.
Class 8	Booker T. Washington, *Up from Slavery*, 853–77. W.E.B. Du Bois, *Souls of Black Folk*, 785–97; "The Song of the Smoke," 797–98.
Class 9	Edwin Arlington Robinson, poems, 962–70. Edgar Lee Masters, poems, 1035–38. Robinson Jeffers, poems, 1090–98.
Class 10	Robert Frost, poems, 1101–17. Sherwood Anderson, "Death in the Woods," 1119–27.
Class 11	Ezra Pound, poems, "A Retrospect," "A Few Don'ts," 1166–89. H.D. [Hilda Doolittle], poems, 1279–86.
Class 12	Gertrude Stein, all selections, 1191–1204. e. e. cummings, poems, 1288–98.
Class 13	T. S. Eliot, all selections, 1301–33.
Class 14	Midterm examination.
Class 15	William Carlos Williams, poems, 1207–24.
Class 16	Wallace Stevens, poems, 1394–1405. Hart Crane, poems, 1435–44.
Class 17	F. Scott Fitzgerald, "Babylon Revisited," 1335–49. Ernest Hemingway, "Hills like White Elephants," 1390–95.
Class 18	Alain Locke, "The New Negro," 1460–68. Langston Hughes, poems, 1488–92; "Radioactive Red Caps," 1506–8. Zora Neale Hurston, "Sweat," 1537–45.
Class 19	Richard Wright, "The Man Who Was Almost a Man," 1788–96. Ralph Ellison, *Invisible Man*, 1845–54. James Baldwin, "Sonny's Blues," 1913–35.
Class 20	Eudora Welty, "The Wide Net," 1797–1812. Flannery O'Connor, "A Good Man Is Hard to Find," 1937–47.
Class 21	Tennessee Williams, "Portrait of a Madonna," 2192–2201. Edward Albee, "The Zoo Story," 2264–80.
Class 22	Theodore Roethke, poems, 2280–92. Sylvia Plath, poems, 2431–38. Adrienne Rich, poems, 2410–16. James Dickey, poems, 2350–58.
Class 23	Lawrence Ferlinghetti, poems, 2333–39. Allen Ginsberg,

	poems, 2378–87. Grace Paley, "The Loudest Voice," 1883–88.
Class 24	Thomas Pynchon, *The Crying of Lot 49*, 2066–72. Donald Barthelme, "The School," 1980–82.
Class 25	Michael Herr, *Dispatches*, 2087–94. Bobbie Ann Mason, "Shiloh," 2116–26. Audre Lorde, poems, 2456–61.
Class 26	Toni Morrison, *Song of Solomon*

SURVEY OF AMERICAN LITERATURE TO 1865

Mary E. Wood Department of English
University of Oregon
Eugene, OR 97403

Course Development and Description

From 1989 to 1991, as part of the Ford Foundation project to integrate materials by and about women of color into the curriculum at the University of Oregon, I revised my American literature survey course. This course, which fulfills a lower-division English major requirement as well as an Arts and Letters general education requirement, was originally designed to cover American literature from the Puritans to the Civil War. I had already begun to revise the course when the project began, but, as I read more and participated in the seminars, lectures, and discussions, I realized that my whole conception of the course was beginning to change, far beyond the question of which texts I was going to include. I can say that I ended up reconceiving the course on every level, including in ways that are not necessarily represented by the syllabus itself.

In my original revision I decided to move back to before the Puritans to raise questions about first encounters between European "explorers" such as Columbus and Native Americans already living on the continent. From here I moved into the Puritans, including a week on the Puritan writers Anne Bradstreet and Mary Rowlandson. The next two weeks looked at the myth of the self-made man (Edwards and Franklin) and the challenges to that myth presented by, for example, African-American poet Phillis Wheatley, African-American autobiographer Gustavas Vassa, and Native American writer John Ridge. Then we looked at Lydia Maria Child's representation of Puritan and Native American cultures in her novel *Hobomok*. The next three weeks examined three themes—nature, history, and modernization—in canonical works in American literature (Emerson, Thoreau, Hawthorne, Melville). The course ended with a discussion of slavery, as we read Melville's "Benito Cereno" and Douglass's *Life and Times*.

While this syllabus raised issues of racism and cultural domination, it still gave primary emphasis to male writers of European heritage. By reverting to a kind of minicourse on the canon in the middle of the term, the syllabus tended to support students' notions that this was the "real" literature. This idea was reinforced by the fact that I had included very little literature by people of color and had spent only one class day on a female writer of color, Phillis Wheatley. While through Wheatley's poems I tried to convey a positive sense of African-American culture, I think the students came away at the end with the idea that American literature consisted of intense cultural domination with little cultural expression on the part of the dominated. Students themselves complained of this failing in the course and rightly criticized the syllabus for presenting too many texts by Euro-American writers.

I realized through the experience of this course and as the Ford Foundation project progressed that it was not enough to teach about the ways cultural oppression, sexism, and racism worked through literature. Students also needed to learn about the ways that oppressed and marginalized groups could produce culture in the midst of oppression. In other words, I needed to learn more about the American cultures and American literatures that I had not been taught about in undergraduate or graduate school. As I revised the course again, I also had to confront the prejudices of my own education (and of many of my colleagues), the voices that told me that I could not possibly teach a course on early American literature without including Melville *and* Hawthorne *and* Thoreau *and* Emerson *and* Cooper and that whatever revising I did had to work around these important writers. I had to be willing to eliminate certain canonical writers in favor of examining the dialogue between dominant and marginalized cultures. I also decided along the way that most students had had some exposure to the writers of the dominant culture and would emerge better educated from my course if they learned about important writers who they may never have heard of before.

So, in revising the course this time, I eliminated my three weeks on the canon and designed the whole course around the notion of encounter among various cultures which makes "American literature" what it is. Crucial to this way of looking at American literature is an understanding of both the cultural dominance of Euro-Americans and the continued resistance and expression of oppressed and marginalized cultures. As part of this project, I shortened the section on the Puritans and expanded the sections on African-American and Native American cultures. I included two books by African-American women, *Our Nig* by Harriet Wilson and *Incidents in the Life of a Slave Girl* by Harriet Jacobs, in order to give students the chance to spend time on the longer writings of two specific authors. Throughout the course I emphasize the ways these various texts speak to one another, whether or not the writers intended them to. We look, for example, at Wilson's challenge to the myth of the self-made man put forth by Franklin.

One of the major issues raised for me by the curriculum integration project was the extent to which the university itself, in everything from its physical structure to its organizational hierarchy to its basic philosophies of education, is a product of dominant Euro-American culture. It became clear to me, for example, in our lectures and discussions on integrating materials on Native American cultures, that, even in the act of bringing those cultures into its curriculum, the institution tends to mold them into its own shape. A course that is arranged historically and chronologically, as most of the courses in the English department are (as well as the English major and graduate program), is called into question by Native American cultures that see time as cyclical and connected to the seasons. In order to highlight this cultural difference, I included some poems by Chrystos, a contemporary Native American poet. I hope this revision in the syllabus will also communicate to students that Native American cultures are present and dynamic in the United States today.

As I continue to revise this course in the future, I anticipate that it will go more in the direction of dialogue between past and present, involving the inclusion of more contemporary texts. As things stand, I think this will be difficult, given that my course is part of a year-long historical sequence taught by several members of the department and conceived of as one component of a historically designed major. In other words, what is needed at this point is a much larger curricular reform geared not only to the individual course but also to majors, departments, and disciplines.

Ultimately, my experience with curricular revision has led me to feel that a course that addresses racism, sexism, and cultural difference (as well as class and other forms of difference) needs to be accompanied by a series of workshops on "unlearning" the "isms" most of us are taught as children. I know that in the American literature survey class I taught last year, in which Native American scholar Inez Talamantez gave a lecture, Euro-American students who had been open and accepting of nineteenth-century texts by people of color became furious when told it might not be respectful for Boy Scouts to dress up as Indians. I think "unlearning -isms" workshops are needed among faculty as well as students, especially at an institution such as the University of Oregon, where the voices of people of color are often not present in discussions of racism and cultural difference. I think faculty are often concerned about teaching students about racial and gender oppression before we have worked through these issues in our own lives and in our own interpersonal and community relations. As I continue to revise my courses, I want to think of ways that intercultural relations among students and faculty themselves can somehow be made part of such an American literature course.

Course Requirements

Requirements for the course are two five-page papers and a final examination. Students may choose to substitute a group presentation for one of the papers. One day per week we will break into discussion groups of eight to ten students. In addition to providing a forum for discussion, each group will be responsible for developing a question for the final examination.

Required Texts

Lydia Maria Child, *Hobomok*
Harriet Jacobs, *Incidents in the Life of a Slave Girl*
Harriet Wilson, *Our Nig; or, Sketches from the Life of a Free Black*
Course packet

Syllabus

Week 1 First Encounters: What Is American Literature?

Class 1	Introduction to course.
Class 2	"from *The Journal of the First Voyage*" and "from *Michele de Cuneo's Letter*," packet; "Meeting the Whites (Hitchiti)," "Meeting the Whites (Alabama)," packet; Richard Comstock, "On Seeing with the Eye of the Native European," packet.
Class 3	Native American Oral Poetry: "The Beginning of Sickness," "They Came from the East"; Captain John Smith, "The Generall Historie of Virginia, New England, and the Summer Isles," "A Description of New England"; Rayna Green, "The Pocahontas Perplex." All in packet.

Week 2 How Did Puritan Men and Women Read and Write America?

Class 4	William Bradford, excerpt from *Of Plymouth Plantation*, packet; John Winthrop, excerpts from "The History of New England," packet.
Class 5	Anne Bradstreet, poems, packet; Mary Rowlandson, excerpt from *A Narrative of the Captivity and Restauration of Mrs. Mary Rowlandson*, packet.
Class 6	Discussion.

Week 3 How Have the Myths of Democracy and the Self-Made Man Shaped American Culture?

Class 7	Jonathan Edwards, "Personal Narrative," packet. Paper due.
Class 8	Benjamin Franklin, excerpt from *The Autobiography*," packet.
Class 9	Discussion.

Week 4 How Have African-American Experience and Literature Challenged the Myth?

Class 10	Phillis Wheatley, poems, packet; June Jordan, "The Difficult Miracle of Black Poetry in America," packet.
Class 11	Gustavus Vassa, excerpt from *The Interesting Narrative of the Life of Oloudah Equiano*, packet.
Class 12	Discussion.

Week 5 How Have Native Americans and American History Been Represented in Anglo-American Literature?

Class 13	Child, *Hobomok*
Class 14	Child, *Hobomok*, continued
Class 15	Discussion.

Week 6 Continuation of Child, Hobomok

Class 16	Child, *Hobomok*, continued
Class 17	Discussion.

Week 7 How Have Native Americans Represented Themselves?

Class 18	John Ridge, "Essay on Cherokee Civilization," packet; Henrietta Whiteman, "White Buffalo Woman," packet.
Class 19	Chrystos, poems from *Not Vanishing*, packet.
Class 20	Discussion.

Week 8 How Have Slavery and Racism Shaped American Literature?

Class 21	Wilson, *Our Nig*. Second paper due.
Class 22	Wilson, *Our Nig*, continued
Class 23	Discussion.

Week 9 More on Slavery and Racism

Class 24	Wilson, *Our Nig*, continued.
Class 25	Discussion.

Week 10

Class 26	Frederick Douglass, excerpt from *The Life and Times of Frederick Douglass*, packet.
Class 27	Jacobs, *Incidents*.
Class 28	Discussion.

Week 11

Class 29	Jacobs, *Incidents*, continued.
Class 30	Jacobs, *Incidents*, continued.
Class 31	Discussion.
Class 32	Final examination.

BRIEF BIBLIOGRAPHY OF NATIVE AMERICAN RESOURCES FOR AMERICAN LITERATURE SURVEY

Paul Dresman Department of English
University of Oregon
Eugene, OR 97403

Angulo, Jaime de. *Indian Tales*. New York: Hill and Wang, 1953. A free agent linguist and ethnographer besides being a physician, de Angulo spent enough years with Native Americans to become a tale teller of their myths and song cycles in a way that is meaningful to European Americans. The best children's bedtime book ever written. If you have time, the students in a university course can experience a version of oral storytelling through this text.

Astrov, Margot, ed. *The Winged Serpent: An Anthology of American Indian Prose and Poetry*. New York: John Day, 1946. A 360-page collection with several examples of women's stories and songs, including the great Papago women's songs rendered by Ruth Underhill and Frances Densmore.

Barnstone, Aliki, and Willis Barnstone. *A Book of Women Poets from Antiquity to Now*. New York: Shocken Books, 1980. The selections by Native American women range from Eskimo to United States (Apache puberty ritual) to South American. Barnstone favors poetically engaged translations over quantity. This is fine except when it is Barnstone (Willis) redoing Frances Densmore or ignoring Rothenberg because of sectarian battles on American poetry turf.

Bataille, Gretchen M., and Kathleen Mullen Sands. *American Indian Women: Telling Their Lives.* Lincoln: University of Nebraska Press, 1984. Thanks to the grant, I learned of this book. It is thoughtful, perhaps groundbreaking—but I am not conversant enough with this area of criticism to say.

Bean, Lowell John, and Katherine Siva Saubel. *Temalpakh: Cahuilla Indian Knowledge and Usage of Plants.* Morongo Indian Reservation: Malki Museum Press, 1972. This book demonstrates the wide cultural context of Native American knowledge and experience that integrates literature, ritual, and plant lore in a way that defies the usual categories. Siva has been an important figure, a Cahuilla woman who organized the museum and the press.

Dearborn, Mary V. *Pocahontas's Daughters: Gender and Ethnicity in American Culture.* New York: Oxford University Press, 1986. Another book I learned of through this grant. Less about the precolonial period than I would like to read, but the questions posed against assumption are of interest.

Dresman, Paul. "Internal Resistances: Edward Dorn on the American Indian." In *Internal Resistances: The Poetry of Edward Dorn,* ed. by Donald Wesling. Berkeley: University of California Press, 1985. In speaking of Dorn's variety of expression about the Native American–White American interaction, I learned about ethnicity in precolonial and colonial culture as well as later. The women who appear (from the Apache warrior woman, Luzon, to the beset modern Eskimo, Ramona) in his work as historical and fictional figures may be of interest.

Hirschfelder, Arlene B. *American Indian and Eskimo Authors.* New York: Association of American Indian Affairs, 1973. This surely has been supplanted, but I have been using it for several years, and I like the annotations.

Kraak, Manfred. *The Forgotten Artist: Indians of the Anza-Borrego and Their Rock Art.* Borrego Springs, Calif.: Anza-Borrego Natural History Association, 1988. It becomes arguable that, in the absence of written texts and due to the time lag when ethnographers began to gather oral tradition, the art of rock painting should be considered as a text—especially because the paintings were often conceived as mnemonic guides to song and myth cycles or, like these paintings of the southern California desert, as initiation ritual designs for adolescent boys and girls. Since I know this area and some of these sites, I can attest to the author's excellent knowledge.

Kroeber, A. L. *Handbook of the Indians of California.* New York: Dover, 1976. An immense compendium originally published as a (BAE) bulletin. There is a wealth of material about Native American women here. It was from this book and other studies by Alfred Kroeber that Theadora Kroeber drew upon for the next entry.

Kroeber, Theadora. *The Inland Whale.* 1959. Reprint. Berkeley: University of California Press, 1971. T. Kroeber approximates de Angulo's technique of retelling Native American tales. She is more conscious of literary resonances (as in the incest tragedy of "Loon Woman"). I used her version of a Mojave cycle, "Tesilya, Sun's Daughter," since Kroeber consciously chose to render this story because of the individualistic female figure. In her afterword Kroeber speaks about the role of women in Mojave culture as independent, and the afterword becomes helpful for students.

Krupat, Arnold. *For Those Who Come After: A Study of Native American Autobiography.* Berkeley: University of California Press, 1985. This may be indebted to Bataille's work. The interest here would be the application of structuralist and poststructuralist theory to Native American autobiography problems.

Niatum, Duane, ed. *Harper's Anthology of Twentieth Century Native American Poetry.* New York: Harper and Row, 1988. While this is not much use for this particular course, it is a quite recent attempt to be comprehensive and does deserve recognition. Half of the poets are women.

Quasha, George, and Jerome Rothenberg, eds. *America: A Prophecy.* New York: Vantage Book, 1974. Still the most interesting collection of American poetry from pre-Columbian times to the present ever assembled. The Native American representations here are superb, (but this is natural, since Rothenberg had already assembled *Shaking the Pumpkin,* an anthology of Native Americans) and I used several for my classes. Why this book remains out of print is a question for the ages. Many women are represented here.

Rexroth, Kenneth. "American Indian Poetry," *Assays.* New York: New Directions, 1961. I used this essay for my supplement to the students because Rexroth explains the collection of Native American materials, the half-century role of Frances Densmore, how she prefigured imagism with her pre-1910 translations from the Chippewa, and why Native American poetry is sacred and Western European poetry is not and because he gives a generous sampling of Densmore's translations from several tribes, many by or about women and all excellent examples of poetry in any language.

THE AMERICAN NOVEL

Sonia Saldívar-Hull Department of English
University of California
Los Angeles, CA 90024

Course Objectives

This course is for non-English major undergraduates and fulfills a general education requirement. The course is an introduction to the central concepts and contexts of novels written in the United States. The readings will emphasize the diversity of the experience of becoming an "American." Identity and subject formation will be analyzed as will constructions of gender, ethnicity, class, and sexual orientation. We will explore the ramifications of identity as well as historicize the literary production of the texts and their canonization or marginalization within academia. We will begin and end the course with novels that were "best-sellers" in their respective periods.

Essay Topics

Choose one of the following for your essay.

1. We have discussed "the cult of domesticity" as an ideological apparatus in which women are urged to find fulfillment in marriage and motherhood. Consider the female characters in *Charlotte Temple, The Blithedale Romance, Their Eyes Were Watching God,* and *The House on Mango Street* and write an essay using one of the novels to discuss how these women conform to this ideology or subvert it.
2. Write an essay comparing Charlotte and LaRue in *Charlotte Temple* and Maruca and Maria Elena in *George Washington Gomez* as "fallen women." Consider their historical specificities in your paper.
3. Discuss Esperanza in *The House on Mango Street* and Gualinto in *George Washington Gomez* as characters whose ideological imperative is to return to their hometowns and somehow "save" or help the ones "who cannot out." Using textual evidence, imagine Esperanza after college. How might she choose George's path or a different one?
4. Both *George Washington Gomez* and *The Rain God* deal with specific codes of acceptable masculine behavior in the Tejanao border communities they portray. What does "manhood" mean to Gualinto and Feliciano? How do Miguel Chico and Felix accept or subvert codes of masculine behavior? Your essay should include a discussion of Paredes's and Islas's attitudes toward these codes. Consider the author's and/or main characters' attitudes toward homosexuality and homophobia/heterosexism.

5. Zora Neale Hurston, Americo Paredes, Leslie Marmon Silko, and Amy Tan all draw upon oral traditions by weaving stories, folktales, and myths into their novels. Discuss the function of these stories as they illuminate important themes or narrative strategies of the novel as a whole. You may choose to focus exclusively on one novel, or you may choose instead a comparison of no more than two novels.

6. In *Charlotte Temple, Their Eyes Were Watching God*, and *The Joy Luck Club* we find some interesting mother-daughter relationships. Choose one or two of the novels and write an essay that focuses on the lessons daughters learn from their mothers; whether or not those lessons are subversive or hegemonic; and how the daughters follow or depart from their mothers' lessons.

7. In what ways do *George Washington Gomez* and *Ceremony* rewrite the history of Manifest Destiny? You should think about how history can serve both hegemonic and subversive ideologies. You may also want to consider why it is important to "write" or "tell" historical "truth."

8. Consider the role of education in one or two of the novels assigned in this course. What do the characters expect from a formal education? Do they get what they expect? What about the education they receive outside of school? Does it conflict with their school education?

9, Investigate the case of Zenobia's drowning. Was her death a suicide, an accident, or a murder? Use textual evidence and include an analysis of Coverdale's role.

10. Consider the disturbing ending of *George Washington Gomez*. What seems to motivate Gualinto's decision to become George G. Gomez? What are the key issues at stake in Gualinto's/George's struggle to form his own identity? Be sure to consider how Maria and Feliciano influence his struggle.

Required Texts

Sandra Cisneros, *The House on Mango Street*
Nathaniel Hawthorne, *The Blithedale Romance*
Zora Neale Hurston, *Their Eyes Were Watching God*
Arturo Islas, *The Rain God*
Americo Paredes, *George Washington Gomez*
Susanna Rowson, *Charlotte Temple*
Leslie Marmon Silko, *Ceremony*
Amy Tan, *The Joy Luck Club*

Syllabus

Week 1   *Introduction.* The making of "American" literature, the canon, and "reading from the margins"

Week 2   Susanna Rowson, *Charlotte Temple.* Patriarchy and the cult of domesticity

Week 3   Nathaniel Hawthorne, *The Blithedale Romance.* Patriarchal narrative strategies, feminist subversions, and female agents of the patriarchy

Week 4   Zora Neale Hurston, *Their Eyes Were Watching God.* The Harlem Renaissance, double consciousness, and the feminist vernacular

Week 5   Americo Paredes, *George Washington Gomez.* Chicano double consciousness (or living on the border, on the margin); Chicano patriarchal strategies of containment

Week 6   Leslie Marmon Silko, *Ceremony.* American Indian tribal feminisms, Native cosmologies and political strategies

Week 7   Arturo Islas, *The Rain God.* Magical realism as aesthetic and political poetics, critique of family, gender constructions, "epistemology of the closet"

Week 8   Sandra Cisneros, *The House on Mango Street.* The domestic site of struggle, form as resistance, women's struggles and women's voices

Week 9   Amy Tan, *The Joy Luck Club.* Oral traditions and literary traditions, formation of the ethnic bourgeois subject, mothers and daughters

Week 10   A revised American literary tradition

AMERICAN NOVEL

Paul Dresman Department of English
University of Oregon
Eugene, OR 97403

Introducing Minority Women's Fiction

When I teach fiction by women of color, as in the course called Development of the American Novel, I approach each novel with background lectures, materials, and films. While the specifics may change from year to year, as I learn more, the general approach remains consistent. Here I describe how the stage is set for the three novels in the accompanying syllabus.

For Toni Morrison's *Song of Solomon* I begin with a review of African-American literature and experience. I include nonfiction writers such as Frederick Douglass and W.E.B. Du Bois. In both instances their life experiences are stressed as well as certain passages from their writing (e.g., chapter 7, "Of the Black Belt," in Du Bois's *The Souls of Black Folk*). Mention can also be made of such works as *Our Nig*, but time limits the discussion, and I like to dwell more on the Harlem Renaissance period when I can discuss, in particular, figures such as Langston Hughes (the section "When the Negro Was in Vogue" from his autobiography, *The Big Sea*) and Zora Neale Hurston. I also distribute an essay by Alice Walker, "In Search of Our Mothers' Gardens," because it helps to familiarize the students with one of the earliest African-American female authors, Phillis Wheatley, and with the general situation of black women who have been denied access to the official and established means of cultural expression. There is also an essay on Phillis Wheatley by June Jordan which might be used here. I find it relevant to mention the 1960s and figures such as Amiri Baraka, since Morrison engages themes from that period such as nationalism, the return to the roots, and extremist revenge for injustices. While I have pointed out the use of African folklore that appeared as an African-American heritage in the novel, this is the weakest part of my introduction: I simply need to learn more about Africa.

With at least some contrast my introduction to Maxine Hong Kingston's *The Woman Warrior* is more thorough about China and Chinese civilization, partly because of a long-standing personal interest, some courses I took, and a year spent teaching in Beijing. I begin by lecturing on China and Chinese civilization as it is particularly relevant to this novel in terms of folklore, the history of relations with the West which led to Chinese immigration, and even the Chinese written character. One thing I have learned to be wary about: students tend to deflect the feminist argument of the book by assigning patriarchal attitudes to China, per se, and neglecting the same critique in relation to the United States (which Kingston does not). A few films are useful to introduce *The Woman Warrior*. *Chan Is Missing* excels in its presentation of the problems of Asian-American immigrants, while *Dim Sum* is excellent as a focus on a parallel mother-daughter relationship. Most of all, the Bill Moyers PBS interview with Kingston presents the author's range of serious concerns and contains important insights about *The Woman Warrior.*

For the novel *Love Medicine* by Louise Erdrich I concentrate on some examples of Native American literature and experience. I have learned that it is important to emphasize the range and diversity of traditional literature and culture. The large number of separate languages in an area such as California can be shown on a drawn map that includes linguistic families, for instance. I also distribute a Mohave myth rendered by Theodora Kroeber in *The Inland Whale*, since it has a female heroine and gives more attention to Native American women than is typical. In a related way I like to discuss the issues of Native American autobiography, specifically *The Autobiography of Delfina Cuero*, a Diegueno woman whose story of the transition period is quite poignant. Because I have researched the area, I also lecture on the Ghost Dance period because it affords commentary on the traditional culture, the conflict with Euro-Americans, early reservation traumas, and the subsequent resistance and its results. Due to our particular region of the Northwest, mention is made of Mourning Dove (Cristal Quintasket), who published *Cogewea*, regarded as (arguably) the first novel by a Native American woman (1927). Complete recognition for this accomplishment is sometimes withheld for a couple of reasons: her white mentor's interpolations and the fact that the author was part white (but this latter reason relates to Erdrich, too). A more contemporary reference can be made to Leslie Marmon Silko: many of the students have read her much anthologized story "Lullaby." The next time I teach *Love Medicine* I plan to use a recent video from Canadian television on the Native American experience at government boarding schools as it provides reasons for the pervasive dislocations of reservation individuals. Amid this introductory material, and with all such approaches to literature by people of color, it is crucial *not* to leave the students with the sense of victimization. Fortunately, the novels themselves answer this potential problem in a far more complete way than any surveyor of cultural and historical background might be able to do.

Course Description and Requirements

In this course we will read a selection of American novels written in this century. I will use the occasion of each novel to speak about other works of prose fiction, literary currents, and cultural issues that are relevant. Mostly, our attention will be given to the works themselves as they exemplify the development of the American novel.

Don DeLillo, *The Names*
Louise Erdrich, *Love Medicine*
F. Scott Fitzgerald, *The Great Gatsby*
Jack Kerouac, *On the Road*
Maxine Hong Kingston, *The Woman Warrior*
Toni Morrison, *Song of Solomon*
John Steinbeck, *The Grapes of Wrath*

In terms of requirements, students will be asked to write typed papers of one to two pages in response to questions I will give about each of the novels. Due to the heavy reading load, this course will require a consistent effort on the part of each student to attend class prepared to discuss the novel. While the amount of reading required for this course is a formidable prospect for the student, allow me to say that it will also be a rewarding pursuit. Due to the extent of possible choices for selections in this course, the job of selection was more difficult for me than you might think. I have tried to choose certain books, especially the first three we read, which stand for particular eras in American writing and historical experience up to the middle of this century. The remaining four novels reflect more recent developments in expression—particularly by writers who represent areas of American experience and culture which were too long neglected. To be able to offer excellent novels by African-American, Asian-American, and Native American female writers in a course such as this one describes how much has changed since I was a student and, perhaps, begins to describe a long overdue fulfillment of American writing not only in this century but in American history altogether.

Syllabus

Class 1	Introduction to course
Class 2	Background lecture on the American novel
Class 3	Developments in early twentieth century American fiction
Class 4	*The Great Gatsby*
Class 5	*The Great Gatsby*
Class 6	The sociopolitical novel. First paper due
Class 7	*The Grapes of Wrath*
Class 8	*The Grapes of Wrath*
Class 9	The aesthetics of improvisation in midcentury America
Class 10	Continuation of above lecture. Second paper due
Class 11	*On the Road*
Class 12	*On the Road*
Class 13	African-American literature
Class 14	*Song of Solomon*
Class 15	*Song of Solomon*. Third paper due
Class 16	*Song of Solomon* concluded and review
Class 17	Midterm examination
Class 18	Asia and America: an overview
Class 19	Postmodernism and the boundaries of writing
Classes 20, 21, 22	*The Woman Warrior*
Class 23	Fiction since the 1950s: entropy and paranoia. Fourth paper due
Classes 24, 25	*The Names*
Class 26	Native American literature. *Love Medicine*
Class 27	*Love Medicine*. Fifth paper due

Class 28   Review
Class 29   Final examination

AMERICAN REALISM

Ann Romines Department of English
George Washington University
Washington, DC 20052

Course Objectives

This annual course had traditionally been an examination of realist impulses in American literature during the period 1865–1905. Over several years I had revised the nearly all-male version of the course I inherited to include an equal number of works by women and men. But all the female writers I was teaching were still white and middle class. Spurred (and shamed!) by the Ford Foundation project, I made changes to facilitate discussion of issues of gender, race, ethnicity, and writing in late-nineteenth-century American culture. Far more than I could have anticipated, these seemingly modest changes transformed the course, pushing me and my students to see this yeasty period in terms of multiple, competing "realisms," each with priorities of race, gender, and class.

I still begin with *Life in the Iron Mills*, emphasizing Davis's double narrative of male artist and female subject/reformer and the narrative voice's difficulties and hesitancies in getting this story *told* without a supporting tradition of American realism. Then we read autobiographical texts by Harriet Jacobs and Mark Twain, considering the narrative strategies available to black woman and white man for telling and inventing tales of coming to age and power in America. These first writers lay out issues that permeate the course in terms of three important careers, all very problematically "realist."

Next we focus on narrative traditions and innovation in a sampling of short stories. I launch this section with Twain's "A True Story" (the very title of which raises a realist red flag), in which a black former slave woman is provoked into telling a story out of her life to a white male listener (possibly Samuel Clemens), whom she suspects is incapable of comprehending the truth of her tale. These issues of form, audience, and point of view continue in problematic stories by black and white men and women, including Chesnutt, Harte, Freeman, Gilman, and Harris, ending with a traditional oral Sioux tale, transcribed by Zitkala-Sa in 1901 for *Atlantic Monthly*. In these classes we concentrate on the conventions and cultural consensus that make the fiction of a "true story" possible. The Sioux tale (in which no character is human) pulls the rug from under our conclusions and underlines how much consensus *does* exist, by contrast, in even the most problematic other fictions we've read. Then Howells's sprawling New York novel, *A Hazard of New Fortunes*, returns us to a complex portrayal of urbanizing America. By now we are simultaneously aware of this novel's relative openness to issues of gender, class, region, and politics and its contrastingly narrow construction of ethnicity.

Next, we turn to several canonical staples of American realism as it begins to take a naturalist turn into the 1890s, and, as we discuss James, Jewett, and Crane, questions about gendered culture and its resources and limits inevitably arise. Moving on to *McTeague*, we consider the heightened stereotypical versions of ethnicity Norris constructs, and we concentrate on his complex, problematic portrait of the South American woman, Maria Macapa, one of the earliest and most troubling versions of a Hispanic woman in American literature. With Maria issues of access and the "true story" of the woman of color arise again. Then Chopin's *Awakening* confronts us with an alternative female version of the Darwinian "romantic fiction" argued by Norris, and, when we insert the more obviously polemical black agenda of Harper's *Iola Leroy* among these other fictions of the 1890s, we encounter a powerfully different female project.

As I have restructured it, this course is framed by autobiographical works that highlight questions about realism and the "true stories" of American lives. Remembering Jacobs and Twain, we end the class with two turn-of-the-century narratives of traditional American childhoods that were followed by the displacements and acceleration of late-nineteenth-century America. Zitkala-Sa's 1900 account of her Yankton Sioux upbringing and her subsequent removal to a Christian Indian school and an eastern college counters the story of privilege and prerogative which underlies Adams's education. Thus, the course ends—appropriately and turbulently!—with stories of education which remind us of the range and the continuing costs of our versions of American realism.

The important thing for me, as I continue teaching this course annually, is that the new version, however successful it has been, is not harden into canonical stone. So I continue to experiment with texts, looking for as wide, representative, and provocative a selection as possible. The range of class and ethnicities in this course still need to be broadened. Since the Ford Foundation project I think of my own more elastic sense of this period's multicultural riches and my increasing skepticism of realist labels as my primary assets in teaching this engrossing undergraduate course.

Essays

In short (4–5 pp.) initial essays students choose an aspect of "realism" which emerges from our initial attempts to describe and define the movement, an aspect that they often consider problematic. Then they explore the nature of this "problem" in one or two of the texts. For a second, longer (8–10 pp.) essay students choose, in individual consultation with me, a topic that allows them to explore an issue that has arisen in our reading and discussion. Many choose issues of gender, race, ethnicity, and representation; this past semester's group produced the best set of student essays in my several years' experience with the course.

Extra-Credit Assignments

Students were encouraged to attend one or more lectures in an on-campus series, "Gender and Ethnicity," sponsored by the Ford Foundation project, to visit an exhibit of slave quilts at nearby Renwick (Smithsonian) Gallery, and to attend several special events (lectures, slide shows, demonstrations) connected with the quilt show. To receive extra credit for attending one of these events, they wrote a 750-word description and critique, briefly relating it to issues of our course. They were also encouraged to propose other local events spotlighting the cultures of women of color which class members might like to attend, and several such events were publicized through the class.

Required Texts

Rebecca Harding Davis, *Life in the Iron Mills*, Feminist
Frances E. W. Harper, *Iola Leroy*, Beacon
William Dean Howells, *A Hazard of New Fortunes*, Signet
Harriet Ann Jacobs, *Incidents in the Life of a Slave Girl*, Harvard
Henry James, *The Portrait of a Lady*, Penguin
Sarah Orne Jewett, *The Country of the Pointed Firs and Other Stories*, Norton
Frank Norris, *McTeague*, Penguin
Norton Anthology of American Literature, vol. 2, 3d ed.
Selected Shorter Works of Mark Twain, Riverside
Zitkala-Sa, *American Indian Stories*, Nebraska

Syllabus

Class 1	Introduction to the course and to Ford Foundation project
Class 2	Davis, *Life in the Iron Mills*

Classes 3, 4	Jacobs, *Incidents in the Life of a Slave Girl*
Class 5	Twain, "The Notorious Jumping Frog," "The Private History of a Campaign That Failed," "The Whittier Birthday Speech"
Class 6	Twain, "Old Times on the Mississippi," "Fenimore Cooper's Literary Offenses"
Class 7	How to Tell a Realist Story: Twain, "A True Story"; Harris, Uncle Remus tales, "Free Joe and the Rest of the World"; Chesnutt, "The Goophered Grapevine"
Class 8	Harte, "The Outcasts of Poker Flat"; Freeman, "A New England Nun"
Class 9	Gilman, "The Yellow Wallpaper"; Zitkala-Sa, "The Warlike Seven" (photocopy)
Classes 10, 11	Howells, *A Hazard of New Fortunes*
Classes 12, 13, 14	James, *The Portrait of a Lady*
Class 15	Jewett, *The Country of the Pointed Firs*. Essay 1 due.
Class 16	Midterm examination
Class 17	Crane, "An Experiment in Misery," "The Blue Hotel"
Class 18	Crane, "The Open Boat," poems
Classes 19, 20	Norris, *McTeague*
Classes 21, 22	Chopin, *The Awakening*
Classes 23, 24	Harper, *Iola Leroy*
Class 25	Adams, selections from *The Education*
Classes 26, 27	Zitkala-Sa, *American Indian Stories*. Essay 2 due.
Class 28	Wrap-up discussion, including discussion and evaluation of Ford Foundation project

Final examination

CONTEMPORARY MOVEMENTS IN MODERN THEOLOGY

Sonya Quitslund Women's Studies Program
George Washington University
Washington, DC 20052

Revising Theology from the Perspective of Women of Color

Mainstreaming minority women's studies in the curriculum, when taken seriously, means much more than adding a lecture or a reading to a preexisting syllabus. In the case of Contemporary Movements in Theology, with its emphasis on liberation theology, the temptation was to do what I had done in the past: tack on some articles by women of color after the subject had been thoroughly defined and the male authorities had been introduced and studied. Suddenly I realized that this approach simply perpetuated woman's, and especially woman of color's, inferior status.

Mainstreaming assumes that the candidate "fits in." In the case of theology it implies that women fit in as theologians and have theological insights as valid as those of men. How does one convey this to students, whose ideas are probably still being formed to begin with? Instead of turning immediately to theological methodology and writers, I selected essays by women of color which dealt with life experiences through which views of God emerged, for theology is first and foremost human reflection on the reality we name God. Because these readings were not by "professionals," they lacked the normal overlay of theological jargon, which made it easier for students to grasp the key points at first glance. The readings, lectures, and discussions of the first weeks left the students reeling as they confronted their comfortable worldviews in light of the shattering reality of the lived experience of more than half of the world's population and the truly deplorable situation of women of color.

Sensitized to the life experience of the real-world majority, and with some initial critical skills for identifying key theological issues, we then looked at feminist liberation theology: essentially white, middle-class, and North American. It did not take the students long to identify a certain shallowness in the analyses of some of the earlier North American feminists. Basically, this shallowness arose from their assumption that the needs and goals they defined apply equally to all women. Placed side by side with the life-and-death issues affecting the world of color, American criticisms of the systemic evils of our societal and religious structures lost some of their force. Antimale authors such as Mary Daly offered little or nothing substantive in solving the crushing poverty of the vast majority of Third World women.

When we reached what originally had been the starting point of the course—Protestant Theology 1900–60—the students expressed a certain disengagement from the content. The theological concerns of European and North American male society did not possess the holistic embrace of reality initially encountered in the world of color which the students had found so challenging. They found the all-male worldview overly engrossed in language games and often somewhat removed from the more basic issues of life and personal relationships. As we moved through the various liberation theologies, the students were generally much more enthusiastic about the female authors. Even when dealing with classical theological themes and treatises such as God, Christology, and the Trinity, the women brought a greater newness and creativity to their reflections than did most of the male theologians. In particular, the students noted the inclusive emphases in the writings of women of color in contrast to the sexist, even racist, viewpoints apt to surface in writings by men of color. Fortunately, this is less evident in more recent African-American writings, undoubtedly because the men have begun to take seriously womanist criticism.

One of the unstated goals of the course was to counter cultural and religious imperialism. Students were expected to come prepared to discuss the assigned readings for the day in terms of the particular historical and cultural situation of the writer(s). Since most were unfamiliar with histories of the writers and their positions, introductory comments helped clarify the context. With all writers the goal was to get inside their minds, to try to identify priorities, theological themes, and concerns as well as general attitudes toward their particular life experiences. While North Americans, both black males and white females, were apt to focus on their experiences as victims and expend much energy railing against the white or white male establishment and an overly male-oriented religious tradition, Third World women tended to take a more positive attitude toward their suffering, strengthening their identification with the suffering Christ. Students were either ambivalent about this or at a total loss about how to deal with the willingness of Third World women and men to die in order to help bring in a new and better world for their children. In the process many students began to grasp the wide chasm between their middle-class values and expectations and the values of Third World people.

The students left the course perhaps lacking in mastery and/or appreciation of the theological tradition that led up to the twentieth century, something most former students had acquired. They certainly expressed an impatience both with certain features of the older tradition and with its patriarchal, paternalistic, or androcentric carryovers into twentieth-century theology and the work of twentieth-century theologians. Not all felt free to view the female authors through equally critical lenses, possibly still trying to come to terms with their own feelings of guilt and complicity in the plight of women of color and overwhelmed with a sense of helplessness before the array of data presented during the semester.

In addition to the stated content and regular doses of gender statistics, the students viewed the work of a Peruvian Indian artist, Jimenez Quispe, and were shocked at the violence he portrayed in depicting First World exploitation. Two guest speakers of color, a Mexican woman knowledgeable in Latin American liberation theology and an African-American male military chaplain with a special interest in women's spirituality, brought additional insights to the students. Class projects focused on the role of women in theology and religion in African-American, African, Chinese, and Native American circles.

The projects were intended to immerse students more deeply into a different culture and to examine the impact of religion on the women in that culture. One group chose Africa and focused on female circumcision and the workday of the average woman. All found the practice of female circumcision abhorrent, but their conclusion came as a surprise: given the profound cultural consequences on the fragile situation of women which could be associated with any Western attempt to stamp it out, the students opted for noninterference. They expressed the sincere hope, however, that, with increased education and awareness of the potentially devastating consequences that might be associated with its continued practice (e.g., in areas where it is most widely practiced the incidence of AIDS seems to be highest), the culture itself would change. In terms of countering cultural imperialism, I could not but applaud the sensitivity of the group in this matter.

Regarding the issues of work, the men in the class were appalled to discover that the workday of the women began long before that of their husbands and ended long after the men had retired for the day. They expressed amazement about all that these women did—collect wood and water for cooking and cleaning, raise food and children, and market food—as well as about the fact that these activities were not really viewed as productive work, while what the men did was seen that way. In retrospect, however, they could see some cultural similarities with "woman's work" in the United States.

Where did religion fit in? Traditional religious values generally supported the continuance of this status quo, and the students appreciated efforts by the female Third World theologians to use religious sources to support a more equitable distribution of responsibility within the family. Two student reactions perhaps best illustrate the impact of the course:

> The oppression that so many of these women face gives their testimonies added weight. I can no longer take for granted my privileged role as a white male in the most wasteful society on earth. The concept of God as a dynamic force in history, working through the poor and women, is one that, until now, I never seriously considered.

I admit I did not appreciate the extent to which Third World women are empowering themselves and thereby transforming society. Women are not waiting for church leaders to give their blessing. They are leading the way to a just and peaceful world.

Required Texts

Virginia Fabella and Mercy Amba Oduyoye, *With Passion and Compassion*
Deane Ferm, *Contemporary American Theologies*, vols. 1 and 2
Elsa Tamez, *Through Her Eyes*

Recommended Texts

Deane Ferm, *Profiles in Liberation*
Chung Kyung, *Struggle to Be the Sun Again*
Anselm Min, *Dialectic of Salvation*
J. J. Mueller, *What Are They Saying about Theological Method?*
Delores Williams, *Sisters in the Wilderness*

Class 1	*Introduction to Ford Foundation/Women's Studies Project of Women of Color: What is theology?*
Class 2	*Theologizing from different perspectives—from women of color.* Readings from *The Sacred Hoop* by Paula Gunn Allen; *Home Girls*, ed. Barbara Smith; *Borderlands* by Gloria Anzaldúa
Class 3	*Feminist theology.* Ferm, vol. 1, chap. 5.
Class 4	Ferm, vol. 2, chap. 4.
Class 5	*Discussion:* identify key values and issues raised, concept of Woman, significance of gender, criticism of traditional theology
Class 6	*Protestant theology, 1900–60.* Ferm, vol. 1, chap. 1
Class 7	*Secularism of the 1960s.* Ferm, vol. 1, chap. 2
Class 8	*Discussion.* Ferm, vol. 2, chap. 1.
Class 9	*Black liberation theology.* Ferm, vol. 1, chap. 3
Class 10	Ferm, vol. 2, chap. 2
Class 11	Fabella and Oduyoye, chaps. 1–6
Class 12	*Selected topics*—for example, "Men: Comrades in Struggle." Discussion
Class 13	*Discussion*
Class 14	*Midterm examination*
Class 15	*Latin American liberation theology.* Ferm, vol. 1, chap. 4
Class 16	Ferm, vol. 2, chap. 3
Class 17	Fabella and Oduyoye, chaps. 12–16

Class 18	*Theological issues as viewed by women of color. Concepts of God, Trinity, Christology. Group discussions.* Tamez, *Through Her Eyes*
Class 19	*Discussion*
Class 20	*Asian women.* Fabella and Oduyoye, chaps. 7–11
Class 21	*Work on group presentations*
Class 22	*Evangelical theology.* Ferm, vol. 1, chap. 6; vol. 2, chap. 5
Class 23	*Catholic theology.* Ferm, vol. 1, chap. 7; vol. 2, chap. 6.
Class 24	*Group presentations begin: African-American traditions*
Class 25	*Asian traditions*
Class 26	*Latin American traditions*
Class 27	*Native American traditions*

In lieu of a final exam, undergraduate students may select either of the following options:

1. A reading project in one of the above traditions or focused on one of the theologians mentioned in the readings—five books or a combination of books and articles. Write a two- to three-page evaluation of each reading, including a brief synopsis of its content and a longer discussion of what you got out of the reading. At the end of the project write a two- to three-page summary paper discussing problems raised by the project and what you got out of it.
2. A term paper—follow traditional format, fifteen to twenty pages in length. Topics must deal with theological concepts, movements, or ideas otherwise relevant to the course.

INTRODUCTION TO CREATIVE WRITING

Maxine Clair Department of English
George Washington University
Washington, DC 20052

Word Up: Oral Tradition in the Pedagogy of Creative Writing

Why use oral literature in a creative writing class? The simple answer that oral tradition resonates in the writings of people of color is a sufficient one. Considering, however, the critical arena of creative writing classes, teachers can use oral literature to illuminate some of the essential issues surrounding the ways students perceive and evaluate written literature.

Students choose this course because they want to create texts—a complex process of distilling experience, discovering content and form, and reshaping ideas to a satisfactory product. Because reading is the best preparation for writing, students tacitly agree to read literary works that model the critical choices successful writers make. As they read, they analyze and interpret literary works, scrutinizing the ways particular writers see the world.

Since most beginning creative writing students are unfamiliar with formal literary criticism, they must rely on their own worldviews as they make evaluations. In workshop, the conventional class format in which student writing is the focal point of instruction, students bring these same assumptions about life to bear on the work of other participants. Together writer-teachers and writer-students attempt to discover events, concepts, common experiences, and feelings being examined in the poems and stories. They consider how the writer's choices serve to illustrate, develop, and give fresh perspective to what they perceive as the issue.

Implicit in this process are standards of excellence, criteria for "good" poems and stories. Seasoned writers and readers generally agree on aesthetic criteria such as language, imagery, sound, originality, and others, but we seldom look closely at how our own beliefs, values, thoughts, and behaviors influence our decisions about the quality of a given work. How often do we ask: What constitutes the skillful use of language? Do I believe an elliptical poem is more original, more "poetic," than a narrative poem? Do I believe that the absence of a copula in a sentence is an example of authentic voice or bad English or both, and how does that affect the value I place on the work?

Race, class, and gender prejudices notwithstanding, too often we are unmindful of subjective biases in our determination of what is aesthetically correct. This happens because we are unaware of or uninformed about the culture from which a given work springs. We fail to consider that basic differences in our ideas about the nature of reality spawn differences in literary constructs.

Excellence and legitimacy are not tokens bestowed upon artists in reparation for past exclusions. It becomes apparent, then, that inclusion of more poems and stories by and about women of color in a creative writing course will not insure a wider, more appreciative audience for these voices. How does one modify perception to embrace an aesthetic that more accurately reflects excellence as a multicultural reality? Short of securing a foundation in literary criticism that includes the traditionally marginal literatures, we challenge our fundamental assumptions about the nature of creative expression.

Transforming the curriculum to reflect the lives and works of women of color implies the primary objective of securing greater understanding and appreciation, but it also implies the critical step of exploring cultural traditions. Orality, the literary tradition of Native Americans and African Americans, is a window through which to view tradition.

In both Native America and Native Africa the Word is sacred. Paula Gunn Allen speaks of it in her *Studies in American Indian Literature:* "Instead of 'preachment of truth,' American Indians consider the *sacred power of utterance* a way to shape, mold, direct, and determine the forces that govern and surround life and the lives of all things." Amadou Hampate Ba, the Malian author of "Tongues That Span the Centuries," says:

> African tradition conceives of speech as a gift from God . . . a fundamental force emanating from the Supreme Being. . . . [It] sets latent forces in motion. Oral tradition is the great school of life. It is at once religion, knowledge, natural science, apprenticeship in a craft, history, entertainment, recreation, since any point can take us all the way back to primordial Unity.

Since in both these cultures the sacred gave rise to speech, the maintenance or rupture of harmony in the world is dependent upon speech. In ritual and ceremony sung words accented with movement and percussion intensified the human embodiment of such a power.

In these cultures "master knowers"—great repositories of oral heritage—are learned in all aspects of life and are the keepers of the secrets of cosmic genesis and sciences of life. Gifted with prodigious memories, they are archivists of all events past and present and can recite all or any part at any time without as much as one mistaken word.

In African culture other personages of prodigious memory, whom the French named *griots*, teach by amusing and by putting themselves within their audiences' reach with stories, lyric poetry, tales, and often history and genealogy as well. The history and progress of a people depended largely on the tradition of memory and transmission.

The legacy of oral tradition resonates through Native American literature, in which the distinction between poetry and prose is not an important one. Where works are derived from ceremonial literature, separation of literary forms becomes antithetical to the interrelatedness of all phenomena of life. Songs, dramatic addresses, prayers, ritual movements—all are components of the whole. Ceremony is chanted. Repetition is an implement to attune the mind.

In African-American literature elements such as virtuoso naming, enumeration, and free rhyming echo the master knower's assignations and the *griot's* genealogy. Hyperbolic imagery, improvisation, signifying, and other tropes are all part of the African-American vernacular that informs African-American literature.

For an African-American teacher-writer in an introductory course in creative writing in which, other than one or two people of color, most of the students in the class are European-American, bringing all of the aforementioned to bear became a challenge. Our emphasis was on integrating the writing of women of color into the curriculum, and I decided on oral tradition as a pedagogical approach to writing in order to foster appreciation for their literatures.

This strategy made a subtle nod in the direction of Gordon Allport's "Formation of In-Groups." For the first two class meetings students heard lectures and listened to audiotapes of oral literature. Then, with little guidance they presented one of their own creations.

The students were asked to examine details of their individual backgrounds and, from a fusion of those details, to create the presentation. They were urged to be as spontaneous as possible, relying on memorization and embellishment, although they were allowed to use notes. They had no "tips"; there was no right or wrong way to do the assignment. They were to explore family rituals—preparing meals, taking meals, preparing for bed, household tasks, and so on. They went in memory and imagination to celebrations, ceremonies—weddings, funerals, parties, and picnics. They recalled places, foods, tales, stories, jokes, songs, languages, and accents of the "old folks" and distant kin; they told of fears, crimes, woundings, and triumphs. Forgotten attitudes arose when they lapsed into old patterns of speech, sang old songs, or viewed old photographs.

The results exceeded my optimistic expectations in originality and scope. The students created imaginative, ingenious compositions. Keeping in mind that a written description of an oral presentation clearly has limitations, I merely refer to them topically here.

Presentations included: a bitter prose-poem in the persona of an observer at Auschwitz. (Within the poem the powerful question was asked, "God, were you there, did you breathe deeply, bravely inhaling the fumes?"); a narrator's thoughts about family and his place in it as he surfs, sometimes buoyant, sometimes overwhelmed by waves; a collage of children's hand-clapping ditties interlaced with two African-American voices—one of love, one of protest. And there were many more similar in power.

The dividends of discovering a personal heritage and rendering it in the oral tradition were useful. Not the least among them were representations of various elements of literature which are sometimes difficult to conceptualize but are intricately involved in aesthetics—elements such as tone, diction, syntax, and style, which coalesce in the concept of voice. Their presentations dramatized the convincing effects of a persona, of imagery and improvisation. These were nuances of culture actively informing aesthetics. Together we created a new "in-group" in which each member had a legitimate place.

As the semester progressed, we read and discussed the merits of various writers, among them many women of color. Later in the semester, however, an incident in workshop became a crucible for our experience of class unity. In response to a class assignment an African-American young woman wrote a poem of admonishment, suggesting that politically apathetic African Americans are blind to the passage of time and opportunity. From the issue being examined in the poem one could infer a call to activism.

Most of the students understood the poem as a threatening or accusatory address to European Americans. Several students made comments from that perspective and persisted in their own versions of what the writer meant, despite the words in the text and despite comments to the contrary. They were angry and conducted themselves inappropriately—slamming books and verbally attacking the writer instead of the poem. I restored order, and, as it was the end of a class period, I dismissed them.

Obviously, the resentment had been mounting over time, and quite possibly it grew out of the emphasis on the works of women of color. Some of that hostility was misdirected at the African-American student. At any rate, during the following class period I acknowledged that the prior class had been a complex and disturbing one. Each student then wrote a personal response to the incident and, on a voluntary basis, read her or his response. All the students spoke with candor and some degree of restraint. Their compositions were of anger, apology, resentment, fear, relief, guilt, and indifference.

Most reflected on some aspect of being in the "out-group," whether it was a European-American young woman who felt falsely accused by virtue of being white in a society in which racism flourishes or a European-American young man who felt indifference because he was male and white and therefore not the "person with the problem." The African-American young woman spoke of many conflicting emotions and assigned responsibility for offense to those who were offended by the poem. She was shaken but undaunted. An African-American young man was relieved that the tension he had sensed all along had finally been released and that no one need continue to wear a mask.

I related my own surprise, disappointment, and sense of inadequacy in handling an angry group of students. I suggested that at least some their anger was reactive to the content of the reading material and that we could continue to work together as a class, allowing for misunderstanding and growing from it.

For the remainder of the semester (about five weeks) there was an integrity and openness that had not been as apparent before. Students seemed less reluctant to protect one another's feelings when giving feedback and were therefore more forthright with their praise and criticism. And, clearly, they respected one another.

In course evaluations students found overall that it had been a desirable and positive class in which they became better readers and writers. Although there was no empirical way to determine the causal links that led to success, I believe that their understanding of written literature was enhanced by the knowledge attained through oral literature. The initial intimacy of sharing details of a separate but equally cherished lineage implied the possibility of a certain level of trust. Trust was then useful in the confrontation and mitigation of anger over racial issues.

The students learned more about the world and their own views of it by participating in the tradition that informs aesthetics in the literature of women of color.

Revision of Course

This course has been revised to accommodate curriculum integration. Curriculum integration refers to an innovation in university curricula occurring at various rates in universities across the country. Specifically it was initiated at George Washington University by the Women's Studies Department under a grant from the Ford Foundation with funds from the university. Our course is designed to reflect on the lives and experiences of people who, because of gender, race, class, affectional preference, age, or global location, have not been involved in the creation of academic disciplines and whose products and experiences are typically marginalized or excluded from those disciplines. Our focus is on the transformation of creative writing to include the lives and works of women of color.

Course Objectives

Through reading and writing poems and stories, we will explore your gifts for creative discovery, expression, and communication. We will study and apply processes by which masterful writers have been successful, and you will give and receive constructive criticism on student work.

Course Description and Requirements

We will use a workshop format and make use of in-class exercises. Attendance and active participation in discussions are vital to the success of the class; therefore, participation and attendance will be considered in arriving at a grade for the course. Reading and/or writing assignments will be due each class meeting and will be accepted no more than one week late. Journals will be kept and turned in for review at various intervals during the semester. All students must attend three readings—poetry and/or fiction—during the semester and comment on those experiences in writing. One short paper on a contemporary writer's work and process is also required.

For each class meeting you are expected to bring an expandable file containing your work, so that you are prepared to read and discuss any individual assignment that has been distributed.

Journals: Ideas, seedling journal, five to ten entries (minimum) per week. Lines, fragments, words, images, dialogue, character sketches, story ideas, observations, whatever impresses you. Keep ideas for creative poems and stories. Make writing your habit.

Final papers: This carries the weight of two assignments. Survey the work of a woman of color—several volumes of poems, several collections of short stories, several novels. What are her focus, subjects, voice, style, themes, etc.? Process. Illuminate. Begin early. All the rules of good expository writing apply for this reaction paper. 8–10 pages.

At the end of the semester you will be required to resubmit the entire portfolio of your written work for review.

Required Texts

The Norton Introduction to Poetry, J. Paul Hunter, 4th ed.
The Norton Introduction to Fiction, Jerome Beaty, 4th ed.
Various handouts throughout the semester

Syllabus

Class 1	*Intro class*
Class 2	Reading Poetry, 3–26; "Persimmons," Li Young Lee. Bring poem by favorite contemporary poet.
Class 3	*Oral beginnings: music, ritual, ceremony*
Class 4	*Oral presentations*
Class 5	*Oral presentations*

Class 6	*Oral presentations*
	Speaker, voice, 52–75
	"Letters in the Family," Adrienne Rich, 56
	"Indian Boarding School: The Runaways," Louise Erdrich
	"The Idea of Ancestry," Etheridge Knight, 425
Class 7	*Childhood memory poem*
	"Growing Up," Nellie Wong
	"The Portrait," Stanley Kunitz
	"Sudden Journey," Tess Gallagher
	"Hanging Fire," Audre Lord
Class 8	Tone, voice, 31–50
	"Woodchucks," Maxine Kumin
	"Burning the Cat," W. S. Merwin
	"Those Winter Sundays," Robert Hayden
Class 9	*Persona poem*
	"Journey of the Magi," T. S. Eliot
	"Waiting for Icarus," Muriel Rukeyser
Class 10	Imagery/structure, 161–71
	"not so gd bein born a girl," Ntozake Shange
	"The Glass," Sharon Olds
	"In a Station of the Metro," Ezra Pound
	"The Red Wheelbarrow," William Carlos Williams
Class 11	*Newspaper titles poem*
Class 12	Figurative language, 131–41, 146 51
	"Poem in Praise of Menstruation," Lucille Clifton
	"The Leap," James Dickey, 148
	"The Death . . . ," Randall Jarrell
Class 13	*Photograph poem*
	"Musée de Beaux Arts," W. H. Auden
	"Fifth Grade Autobiography," Rita Dove
	"Photograph of the Girl," Sharon Olds
Class 14	Sound/rhythm/meter, 189–209
	"Mood Indigo," Bill Matthews
	"What the Motorcycle Said," Mona Van Duyn, 191
	"Dear John, Dear Coltrane," Michael Harper, 209
	"The Dance," William Carlos Williams, 183
Class 15	Meter, 224–40
	"Metrical Feet," Samuel Taylor Coleridge, 197
	"Turnabout," Linda Pastan, 237
	"First Fight, Then Fiddle," Gwendolyn Brooks, 235
	"Do Not Go Gentle into That Good Night," Dylan Thomas 472
Class 16	*Metrical poem*

References

Books

Allen, Paula Gunn. *Studies in American Indian Literature.* New York: MLA, 1983.

Allport, Gordon. "Formation of In-Groups." *The Nature of Prejudice.* Cambridge, Mass.: Addison-Wesley, 1954.

Ba, Amadou Hampate, "Tongues That Span the Centuries."

Baker, Houston A., Jr., ed. *Three American Literatures: Essays in Chicano, Native American, and Asian-American Literature for Teachers of American Literature.* New York: MLA, 1982.

Baraka, Imamu Amiri. *The Music: Reflections on Jazz and Blues.* New York: Morrow, 1987.

Jackson, Blyden. *Black Poetry in America: Two Essays in Historical Interpretation.* Baton Rouge: Louisiana State University Press, 1974.

Wiget, Andrew. *Native American Literature.* Boston: Twayne Publishers, 1985.

Audiotapes

"Gargoyle 34." *Gargoyle Magazine.* Bethesda, Md. Washington, D.C.

Hagedorn, Jessica. "Terra Nova." Watershed Tapes, Watershed Foundation, Washington, D.C.

Harjo, Joy. "Furious Light." Watershed Tapes, Watershed Foundation, Washington, D.C.

Jordan, June. "For Somebody to Start Singing." Watershed Tapes, Watershed Foundation, Washington, D.C.

Lorde, Audre. "Shorelines." Watershed Tapes, Watershed Foundation, Washington, D.C.

Shange, Ntozake. "I Live in Music." Watershed Tapes, Watershed Foundation, Washington, D.C.

Videotapes

Power of the Word, with Bill Moyers. PBS. 1989.

DEVELOPMENTAL WRITING (ESL)

Marilyn Manley Department of Academic Skills (SEEK)
Hunter College, City University of New York
New York, NY 10021

Student Demographics

In order to be eligible for the Search for Education, Elevation, and Knowledge (SEEK) Program, a student must have a high school average of 79 percent or below, must come from a low-income family, and must have attended school in an "educationally disadvantaged" neighborhood. If these criteria may be construed as the proverbial "three strikes," the ESL (English as a Second Language) student enters college with *five* strikes against her, adding to those three difficulty with the English language and tension between the original and the U.S. cultures and value systems. It is not surprising, then, that there is a high attrition rate and a low graduation rate among ESL students in the SEEK Program at Hunter College at the City University of New York (CUNY).

My students are, for the most part, in their late teens and early twenties. Approximately 80 percent are women. There is presently an Asian majority, made up of young people from Hong Kong, the People's Republic of

China, South Korea, Vietnam, and Cambodia; approximately one fourth are Haitian; and about 20 percent are Latina.

Regardless of ethnicity, national origin, or gender, a typical ESL student in the SEEK Program: (1) rarely uses English as a medium of communication outside the classroom; (2) is employed, working an average of twenty hours per week; and (3) travels long distances to come to school. When we add to this picture the fact that many of our students struggle with problems of ill health and domestic difficulties, it is understandable that they tend to be prone to stress, depression, and fatigue.

Statement of Purpose

Our primary goal in the Hunter/SEEK ESL Writing sequence is to help students develop their English language skills to the point at which they are able to pass the infamous CUNY Writing Assessment Test. Along the way, however, the teacher must function as cheerleader, counselor, and friend. Materials and methodology must be carefully selected to match the ability levels and interests of students.

Although I am teaching a skill, I attempt to do so through the medium of content that has intrinsic value to my students' lives. I am grateful for the stimulating and inspiring seminar on "Infusing Women of Color into the Curriculum" for having brought to my attention a multitude of new resources on which I can draw.

Required Readings

Instead of using a textbook that contains both readings and exercise materials, I have assigned a textbook that contains exercise materials only (*The Comp-Lab Exercises: Self-Teaching Exercises for Basic Writing*, Epes, Kirkpatrick, and Southwell, 2d ed. [Prentice-Hall, 1986]), and I'll duplicate and hand out readings of my own selection (many of them culled from our seminar) for students to keep in a loose-leaf notebook, along with discussion questions and writing topics based on the readings. (Note: I'm still searching for reading selections that reflect the Haitian-American and the Korean-American experience in positive ways.)

Unit 1 (4 weeks) Who Am I? Exploring the Intersection of Culture and Personality

Readings: "Back, but Not Home," an essay by Maria L. Muñiz. A Cuban-
   American woman shares her feelings concerning her dual heritage.
Excerpt from *Foreigner,* a novel by Nahid Rachlin. An Iranian woman who

has lived in the United States for fourteen years returns to her homeland.
Excerpt from *The Woman Warrior*, a novel by Maxine Hong Kingston. Growing up female and Chinese American.
"Child of the Americas," a poem by Aurora Levins Morales. On being female
and a "U.S. Puerto Rican Jew."

Film: A Great Wall. A Chinese-American family travels to mainland China to
visit relatives.

Unit 2 (6 weeks) Who Are You? Seeing beyond Stereotypes

Readings: "Mother Pearson of Mother's Love," an autobiographical essay by
Mildred Pearson, published in *The Body Positive* (April 1990). An African-
American woman who lost her son Bruce to AIDS has founded a support
group for other mothers of HIV-infected children.
"Elio Robertson: A Dream Fulfilled at Seventy-nine Years of Age," a translation of an article by Dora Rubiano, published in *El Diario–La Prensa*. Biographical sketch of a Cuban-American elementary school dropout who
resumed his studies after the age of seventy, enrolled in Hunter/SEEK,
and received the bachelor of arts degree in 1989.
"Sure You Can Ask Me a Personal Question," a poem by Diane Buruz. A Native American poet responds to the clichéd questions that people ask regarding her heritage.
"Sr. Eugenia Choi: Interview with a Chinese-American Nun," by Marilyn
Manley.
Excerpts from *The House on Mango Street*, by Sandra Cisneros. Reflections
on a Mexican-American girlhood.

Speakers: Kenshasa Shebaka, psychologist, consultant on stress management, and counselor in the SEEK Program: "Overcoming Negative
Stress."
Phyllis Rubenfeld, counselor in the SEEK Program and an expert on legislation affecting persons with disabilities: "Students with Disabilities."

Unit 3 (4 weeks) Who Are We? Fellow Passengers on an Endangered Planet

Readings: "The Web of Life," excerpt from a letter by Chief Seattle.
"No Man Is an Island," poem by John Donne.
"Threats to Our Planet," four articles I am writing/compiling on:

• Environmental Pollution: Its Causes and Consequences
• The Rape of Earth

- The Roots of War
- The Population Bomb

Field Trip: Visit to the Rainforest and Polar habitats at the Central Park Zoo

Wherever I can tie in contributions of women of color to the environmental movement, I shall do so. I am still researching this area.

SOCIAL SCIENCES

ANTHROPOLOGY

ANTHROPOLOGY: COMPARATIVE VALUE SYSTEMS

Ruth M. Krulfeld Department of Anthropology
George Washington University
Washington, DC 20052

Course Rationale

This course is designed to make the undergraduate students who take it as an elective aware of differences in values cross-culturally and how their own values may be different from those of other Americans from different socioeconomic classes, ethnic groups, and generations. It was initially a course with several topical foci, apart from the theoretical and methodological areas of values studied cross-culturally in order to explore both the range of variation and universals. Formerly, the course explored such issues as values relating to aggression and nonaggression, conformity and individualism, life and death, and aging (in U.S. society as well as in other societies); gender was covered in only two class meetings, while people "of color," whether ethnic minorities in American society or the Third and Fourth World people of other parts of the world, have long been the subjects of anthropological study, gender issues per se have only recently become a major area for study.

The study of how gender concepts are culturally constructed, negotiated, and manipulated in changing contexts has been of great interest to me in my own research on Southeast Asian refugees, who, torn from their own cultures, have had to adjust rapidly to life in new homelands with very different dominant cultures, maintaining some parts of their traditional cultures while changing others. How this is accomplished with regard to gender concepts and roles seemed an exciting area to add to my course. While keeping the early part of the course focused on American values and changes in values through time, in order to facilitate the student's understanding and participation at the outset of the course, I introduced gender as a major part of this study. The next part of the course dealt primarily with Southeast Asian–Americans and refugee women as they coped with their adjustment to the dominant American society.

In order to add to the excitement of this new intellectual area, I decided to include new firsthand experiences for my students. First, I invited several Asians to speak to the class about their research on women or their own life experiences, in one case inviting my own informants, a Laotian-American Buddhist nun (who has had significant impact on women's roles in her own culture in the United States) and a Buddhist monk to talk about gender roles in Lao culture. The monk also invited students to attend a Buddhist celebration at the local Lao temple, offering them an opportunity to experience another culture in U.S. society firsthand. Students reacted enthusiastically to these encounters.

Second, I decided to discuss my own ongoing research on Laotian refugees to United States. I had just organized a panel for the American Anthropological Association annual meetings on "Gender and New Traditions: The Dynamics of the Refugee Experience" and presented a paper on renegotiating and manipulating gender roles by Lao refugees in their new homeland. The students seemed pleased to have the opportunity to ask questions and gain further information, learning more about anthropology, fieldwork, and values than normally would be the result of reading other people's work without having the scholar or the subjects of the study around to respond to their questions. Both of these teaching techniques resulted in greater student interest and participation, and I intend to use them again.

Third, a major innovation in the teaching of this course was the use of workshops, that is, dividing the class into two to three smaller groups for the purpose of enabling greater participation in the less threatening atmosphere of peer groups, four times during the semester. To prepare for these workshops students were presented with a limited choice of readings that clearly made major points to be presented and discussed. To insure the participation of each student, all students reported to their groups on their readings, followed by a discussion of the major value issues involved. Each group appointed a reporter, who recorded and reported back to the entire class the several major points covered in that workshop. A general class discussion followed. These workshops had as their desired purpose participation by all of the students, and the students commented on how useful and stimulating the workshops were.

Fourth, I gave two homework assignments on gender which involved the students using their own experiences. In one students had to write down and explore their own attitudes toward gender and how they learned them; they were asked to interview three of their friends on this, finally comparing their attitudes and values concerning gender roles and behavior with those of their parents and their friends and with those of other societies we had studied. In the second assignment students interviewed someone from a different culture (i.e., from another country or from a different ethnic group or socioeconomic class) about gender and how they feel about American gender values and roles. It was particularly useful that the class, while composed primarily of white middle-class women, had two males as well as the sixteen female students, that two of the women were somewhat older, and that there were an Egyptian, a Japanese, and a Dutch foreign student. The object of this exercise was to make students aware of their own biases with regard to gender, of variation within their own society, and of changes through time as well as of cross-cultural variation. These exercises were preceded by comments about my own life and gender experiences growing up in the U.S. South during the 1940s, about my experiences as a graduate student at Yale University during the late 1950s, and my more current experiences as a mother, wife, professional, and anthropologist conducting research in different cultures. One class was designed to generate a discussion of articles written by women of color expressing their rage over the problems in their lives of "invisibility," disadvantage, and low self-esteem resulting from their treatment by the dominant society.

The first two homework assignments made the students aware of their own values with regard to gender and how these differed from those of their parents and from those of people from other cultures, other ethnic groups, or other classes within their own society. Two students interviewed homeless people and were amazed by the information they obtained. Similarly, the recounting by the three foreign students in the class of their own values related to gender also provided an interesting cross-cultural experience for everyone involved. The class assignment on the anger of women of color, however, did not achieve the purpose for which it was designed. Students were generally reluctant to discuss the assigned readings, except for one on Chinese women (see reading assignments for class 15). As I tried to explore what was creating the difficulty, the discussion that finally did take place turned into a verbal attack by some of the women on the two males in the class.

At least one of the reasons these students did not generate the usual enthusiastic discussion that I had come to expect of them was that they were trying to understand the values expressed by the women of color by attempting some degree of objectivity, in spite of class discussions on whether or not objectivity was even possible. Perhaps as white middle-class students they could not deal with the rage expressed in the writings of these women of color. Perhaps the students felt uncomfortable that these women were responding with anger toward the society that most of these students shared. In any case, they seemed to react by rejecting otherness. Some of the females turned on the males, saying that they wished that the class were entirely female, that they felt more comfortable with other women (perhaps this meant with people most like themselves?). The only article they were willing to discuss was one on how Chinese female social subordination was reflected in naming and terms of address. I believe they felt this article to be emotionally safer since it dealt with customs of another society and its goal was to describe behavior rather than to express feeling. I had tried to explain the reason for the assignment, that is, to bring to their attention the anger that can be generated by problems of invisibility or experiences of rejection because of color or ethnic background and the effect of these experiences on self-esteem. It was only when I began to discuss some of my own experiences that they began to respond with theirs. It is possible that this class had a greater impact on the students than their lack of willing participation indicates.

According to student feedback on evaluations as well as my own observations, the course was highly successful overall. In future courses I intend to retain the use of speakers (both women of color who are anthropologists working on these issues and key informants from the cultures under discussion in the course), workshops breaking the course up into smaller discussion groups, and assignments related to the students' own experiences.

Syllabus

No single text was used for this course. Books, articles, and papers were placed on library reserve.

Class 1 — *Introduction:* what values are and how they relate to world-view and behavior. Ethnocentrism, culture boundness, and culture shock. Cultural differences in values.

Class 2 — *Definitions and examples.* Values, core values, value orientations, value systems; dominant and variant value orientations within the same society; changes through time. Readings: Bohannon, "Shakespeare in the Bush"; and Richard B. Lee, "Eating Christmas in the Kalahari."

Class 3 — *American values and change.* Readings: Robert N. Bellah et al., *Habits of the Heart: Individualism and Commitment in American Life* (1985), 275–96 ("Transforming American Culture").

Class 4 — *The relation of values to class, ethnicity, and gender.* Readings: Elliot Liebow, *Tally's Corner: A Study of Negro Street Corner Men;* James P. Spradley, *You Owe Yourself a Drunk;* Joseph T. Howell, *Hard Living on Clay Street;* Helen Safa, *The Urban Poor of Puerto Rico: A Study in Development and Inequality.* Students will choose *one* of the readings. Class discussion will be based on these readings following lecture.

Class 5	*Some current value issues:* gender, age violence; who shall live and who shall die and who decides; commitment; individualism versus conformity; treatment of the aged. Readings: Bellah et al., *Habits of the Heart,* 85–112 ("Love and Marriage"); 142–63 ("Individualism"); 275–96 ("Transforming American Culture"); also current articles on above topics in newspapers and magazines.
Class 6	Class will view film on Chinese women and gender: *A Small Happiness.*
Class 7	Class workshops on students' own life experiences as well as their readings to date on value issues: conformity and individualism; life and death; violence. The class will be divided into three work groups of six students each for this purpose. For the final twenty minutes the whole class will hear brief reports from one student from each workshop who recounts the major points covered, and there will be a general discussion of these issues.
Class 8	*Anthropological theories and methods in the study of values.* Lecture: overview; conflicting interpretations of values in the same society: Oscar Lewis's and Robert Redfield's studies of Tepotzlan; conflicting conclusions about Pueblo culture.
Classes 9, 10	*The cross-cultural comparison of value systems:* lectures on the Eskimo, the Mae Enga, the Etoro, the Amish, the Sasak.
Class 11	Class workshops on values related to aggression and non-violence cross-culturally. Readings for workshop A: Chagnon, *Yanomamo: The Fierce People;* Turnbull, *The Mountain People.* Readings for workshop B: Denton, *The Semai: The Non-Violent People;* Turnbull, *The Forest People;* Briggs, *Never in Anger.* Workshops meet and discuss issues and readings separately and then rejoin class for discussion. Participants in each workshop choose *one* of the readings for their group.
Class 12	Lecture on professor's own research on the Sasak of Indonesia, Jamaican peasants, and Laotian refugees.
Class 13	*Midterm examination*
Class 14	Lecture: values related to gender; definition of gender, approaches to the study of gender; how gender is culturally constructed, negotiated, and manipulated and how it affects self-esteem, autonomy, and access to power. Read-

ings: Rosaldo and Lamphere, eds., *Women, Culture and Society* (read chapters by Ortner and Chodorow); Krulfeld, "Sasak Attitudes towards Polygyny and the Changing Position of Women in Sasak Peasant Villages," in *Visibility and Power: Essays on Women in Society and Development*, ed. Dube, Ardner, and Leacock; also see Leacock, "Women, Power, and Authority."

Class 15   *Cross-cultural studies of gender:* the Yanomamo, the Eskimo, the Mae Enga, the Sasak; class discussion of the following reading assignment: Watson, "The Names and the Nameless: Gender and Person in Chinese Society," *American Ethnologist* 13, no. 4 (1986): 619–29; Ntozake Shange, "Is not good to be born a girl," in *Racism and Sexism: An Integrated Study*, ed. Rothenberg, 131–32; Wong, "When I Was Growing Up"; Mitsuge Yamada, "Invisibility Is an Unnatural Disaster: Reflections of an Asian-American Woman," in *This Bridge Called My Back*, ed. Moraga and Anzaldúa; Nelson, "Racism, Rudeness, and Revenge: When Whites Treat Blacks as Invisible," *Washington Post*, 2 April 1989.

Class 16   Discussion of gender experiences; reports on gender assignments of (1) what students think are the major characteristics of being male or female (how males and females differ in attitudes and behavior in ways that *immediately* come to mind); (2) *what* they were taught by their parents or guardians as essentially characteristic of being male or female and *how* they were taught this; (3) interviews of three friends on what they considered to be basic female versus male characteristics; (4) an analysis of how 3 fits with 1 and 2 and how 1 and 2 differ.

Class 17   *Discussion of assignment:* students interview someone from a culture different from their own about what characteristics and behavior are valued for females and for males in their society; who taught them gender roles and behavior; what they considered appropriate gender relationships to be; and how the person interviewed felt about American gender values (i.e., what is considered appropriate male or female behavior, attitudes, characteristics, aspirations, and gender relationships). For this assignment the person interviewed could be someone from another country or someone from a different ethnic group or socioeconomic class.

Class 18   *Workshops on gender.* Students each choose a reading to discuss in their workshop. The class is divided into three workshops.

Readings: Babb, "Indigenous Feminism in a Modern Hindu Sect," *Signs* 9 (1984): 399–416; Buckley, "Menstruation and the Power of Yurok Women: Methods in Cultural Reconstruction," *American Ethnologist* 9 (1982): 47–60; DiLeonardo, "The Female World of Cards and Holidays: Women, Families, and the Work of Kinship," *Signs* 12 (1987): 440–53; Draper, "Cultural Pressure on Sex Differences," *American Ethnologist* 2 (1975): 602–16; Early, "Catharsis and Creation: The Everyday Narratives of Baladi Women of Cairo," *Anthropological Quarterly* 58 (1985): 172–81; Eisenhart and Holland, "Learning Gender from Peers: The Role of Peer Groups in the Cultural Transmission of Gender," *Human Organization* 42, no. 4 (1983): 321–32; Fernandez-Kelly, "The Sexual Division of Labor, Development and Women's Status," *Current Anthropology* 22 (1981): 414–19; Gmelch, "Economic and Power Relations among Urban Tinkers: The Role of Women," *Urban Anthropology* 6 (1977): 237–47; Gregory, "The Myth of the Male Ethnographer and the Woman's World," *American Anthropologist* 86 (1984): 316–27; Higgins, "Women in the Islamic Republic of Iran: Legal, Social, and Ideological Changes," *Signs* 10 (1985): 477–94; Kolenda, "Woman as Tribute, Woman as Flower: Images of 'Woman' in Weddings in North and South India," *American Ethnologist* 11 (1984): 98–117; Lamphere, "From Working Daughters to Working Mothers: Production and Reproduction in an Industrial Community," *American Ethnologist* 13 (1986): 118–30; Leacock, "Women's Status in Egalitarian Society: Implications for Social Evolution," *Current Anthropology* 19 (1978): 247–55, 268–75; Lever, "Honor as a Red Herring," *Critique of Anthropology* 16, no. 3 (1986): 83–106; Mathews, "We Are Mayordomos: A Reinterpretation of Women's Roles in the Mexican Cargo System," *American Ethnologist* 12 (1985): 285–301; Messick, "Subordinate Discourse: Women, Weaving, and Gender Relations in North Africa," *American Ethnologist* 14 (1987): 210–25; Millar, "On Interpreting Gender in Bugis Society," *American Ethnologist* 10 (1983): 477–93; Mintz, "Men, Women, and Trade," *Comparative Studies on Society and History* 13 (1971): 247–69; Molnar, "Women and Politics: Case of the Kham Magar of Western Nepal," *American Ethnologist* 9

(1982): 485–502; Moses, "Female Status, the Family, and Male Dominance in a West Indian Community," *Signs* 3 (1977): 142–53; Murphy, *Women of the Forest;* Netting, "Women's Weapons: The Politics of Domesticity among the Kafyar," *American Anthropologist* 71 (1969): 1037–45; Norkunas, "Women, Work, and Ethnic Identity: Personal Narratives and the Ethnic Enclave in the Textile City of Lowell, Massachusetts," *Journal of Ethnic Studies* 15, no. 3 (1987): 27–40; Rogers, "Female Forms of Power and the Myth of Male Dominance: A Model of Female-Male Interaction in Peasant Society," *American Ethnologist* 2 (1975): 727–56; Strathern, "Comments on Leacock," *Current Anthropology* 19 (1978): 267.

Class 19   An Indian anthropologist presents her research on women in India and describes how they were affected by the values of the British and by changes in the law.

Class 20   *Asian-American women.* Lecture on Southeast Asian values related to gender in Southeast Asia and in the United States. Professor's own research on Southeast Asia and on Southeast Asian–Americans.

Class 21   *Southeast Asians speak for themselves.* Interviews on gender with a Laotian Buddhist monk and nun about values in their culture.

Class 22   Value maintenance and value change; adjustments to a new society; the refugee experience. Lecture.

Class 23   *Workshops on Asian and Asian-American women.* Students select *one* of the following readings. The class is divided into three workshops for reports and discussion. One student from each group will report to the entire class following these separate workshops. Readings: Burki, *Cambodian and Laotian Mothers and Daughters in Chicago* (1987); Haines, *Refugees in the United States: A Reference Handbook* (1985); Hossain, Zakir, and Punnipa, "Occupation Adjustment of Laotian Women in the United States Labor Force" (on reserve); Keefe, *Negotiating Ethnicity: The Impact of Anthropological Theory and Practice* (1989); McIntosh and Alston, "Religion and the New Immigrants: Initial Observations Concerning Lao Refugees in Houston, Texas" (1988); Sen, *The Lao in the United States since Migration: An Anthropological Inquiry* (1978); Shepherd, "Coping in America: Contextual Variables in the Adaptation of Female Refugees and Immigrants," *SDI* (1987); Tepper, *Southeast Asian Exodus:*

From Tradition to Resettlement, Understanding Refugees from Laos, Kampuchea, and Vietnam in Canada (1980); Haines, Rutherford, and Thomas, "Family and Community among Vietnamese Refugees," *International Migration Review* (1981); Huyck and Fields, "Impact of Resettlement on Refugee Children" *International Migration Review* (1981); Keyes, "Mother or Mistress but Never a Monk: Buddhist Notions of Female Gender in Rural Thailand," *American Ethnologist* (1985); Stein, "The Refugee Experience: Defining the Parameters of a Field of Study," *International Migration Review* (1981); Muir, *The Strongest Part of the Family;* Muecke, "Resettled Refugees: Reconstruction of Identity: Lao in Seattle," *Urban Anthropology* (1987); Mortland and Ledgerwood, "Secondary Migration among Southeast Asian Refugees in the United States," special issue ("Southeast Asian Refugees in the United States"), *Human Organization and Studies of Cultural Systems and World Economic Development* (1987); Zaherlick and Brainard, "Demographic Characteristics, Ethnicity, and the Resettlement of Southeast Asian Refugees in the United States," *Human Organization* (1987); Scott, "The Hmong Refugee Community in San Diego: Theoretical and Practical Implications of Its Continuing Ethnic Solidarity," *Anthropological Quarterly* (1982).

Class 24   Film: *Blue Collar and Buddha*, a film on cultural contact and value conflict among Lao refugees and blue-collar Americans.

Class 25   Lecture: value conflicts and change; problems of cultural contact and change and of different value systems within the same society. Readings: Keefe, ed., *Negotiating Ethnicity: The Impact of Anthropological Theory and Practice;* Bodley, *Victims of Progress;* Schuster, *The New Women of Lusaka.*

Class 26   *Review. Term papers due.*

SEX, DISCRIMINATION, AND THE DIVISION OF LABOR

Cecilia A. Conrad Department of Economics
Barnard College
New York, NY 10027

Required Text

Blau, Francine, and Marianne Ferber. *The Economics of Women, Men, and Work.* Prentice-Hall, 1986.
Required readings were placed on reserve.

Syllabus

I. Introduction

A. Women in the U.S. Economy and the Economic Woman
Blau and Ferber, chaps. 1 and 2.
B. The Debate over Women's Economic Status—An Overview
Bergman, B. "Does the Market for Women's Labor Need Fixing?" *Journal of Economic Perspectives* 3, no. 1 (Winter 1989): 43–60.
Fuchs, V. "Women's Quest for Economic Equality," *Journal of Economic Perspectives* 3, no. 1 (Winter 1989): 25–42.
Lazear, E. "Symposium on Women in the Labor Market," *Journal of Economic Perspectives* 3, no. 1 (Winter 1989): 3–8.
Smith, J., and M. Ward. "Women in the Labor Market and the Family," *Journal of Economic Perspectives* 3, no. 1 (Winter 1989): 9–24.

II. The Male-Female Wage Gap and Occupational Segregation

A. Historical Overview
  Goldin, Claudia. *Understanding the Gender Gap: An Economic History of American Women,* chap. 3. Oxford University Press, 1992.
  Jones, J., *Labor of Love, Labor of Sorrow,* 199–221, 235–68. Random House, 1986.
  Matthaei, Julie. *An Economic History of Women in America,* part 2, chaps. 9–12. Schocken, 1982.
  (Optional)
B. The Economic Theories

Blau and Ferber, chaps. 6, 7, and 8.

Blaxall, M., and Barbara Reagan. *Women and the Workplace*, part 3. University of Chicago Press, 1976.

C. The Economic Evidence, part 1: Statistical Studies

Corcoran, M., and G. Duncan. "Work History, Labor Force Attachment and Earnings Differences between the Races," *Journal of Human Resources* 14 (Winter 1979): 3–20.

Gunderson, M. "Male-Female Wage Differentials and Policy Responses," *Journal of Economic Literature* (March 1989): 46–53.

U.S. Civil Rights Commission. *The Economic Status of Black Women: An Exploratory Investigation.* Government Printing Office, 1990.

D. The Economic Evidence, part 2: Case Studies

Freeman, Richard, and Jonathan Leonard. "Union Maids: Unions and the Female Work Force," in *Gender and the Workplace*, ed. Clair Brown and Joseph Pechman. Brookings Institution, 1987.

Reskin, Barbara F., and Heidi Hartmann, eds. *Women's Work, Men's Work: Sex Segregation on the Job.* National Academy Press, 1986.

Schwartz, Felice. "Management Women and the New Facts of Life," *Harvard Business Review* 89 (Jan.–Feb. 1989): 65–76.

Stober, Myra, and Carolyn Arnold. "The Dynamics of Occupational Segregation among Bank Tellers," in *Gender in the Workplace*, ed. Clair Brown and Joseph Pechman. Brookings Institution, 1987.

E. The Economic Evidence, part 3: Comparative Studies

Abraham-Van der Mark, E. "The Impact of Industrialization on Women: A Caribbean Case," in *Women, Men and the International Division of Labor*, ed. J. Nash and M. P. Fernandez-Kelly. SUNY Press, 1984.

Anker, Richard, and Catherine Hein. "Sex Inequalities in Third World Employment: Statistical Evidence," in *Sex Inequalities in Urban Employment in the Third World*, ed. Richard Anker and Catherine Hein. St. Martin's Press, 1986.

F. Legal Protections and Affirmative Action

Blau and Ferber, chap. 8, 262–68.

Goldin, Claudia. *Understanding the Gender Gap*, chaps. 6 and 7.

Gunderson, M. "Male-Female Wage Differentials and Policy Responses," *Journal of Economic Literature* (March 1989): 53–72.

"Johnson Controls," unpublished materials on reserve.

Leonard, Jonathan. "Women and Affirmative Action," *Journal of Economic Perspectives* 3 (Winter 1989): 61–76.

G. Comparable Worth

Aaron, Henry J., and Cameron Lougy. *The Comparable Worth Controversy.* Brookings Institution, 1986.

III. The Sexual Division of Labor in the Home and Female Labor Supply

A. Historical Overview

   Matthaei, Julie. *An Economic History of Women in America,* chaps. 3, 5, 6, and 8.

B. Neoclassical Theory of the Household

   Blau and Ferber, chap. 3.

   Leibowitz, A. "Women's Work at Home," in Cynthia Lloyd, *Sex, Discrimination and the Division of Labor.*

   Sawhill, I. "Economic Perspectives on the Family," *Daedalus* (Journal of the American Academy of Arts and Sciences) 106 (Spring 1977): 115–25. Reprinted in Alice Amsden, *The Economics of Women and Work,* chap. 5.

C. Female Labor Supply

   Blau and Ferber, chap. 4.

   Jones, Barbara. "Black Women and Labor Force Participation: An Analysis of Sluggish Growth Rates," in *Slipping through the Cracks: The Status of Black Women,* ed. M. Simms and J. Malveaux. Transaction, 1986.

   Reimers, C. "Cultural Differences in Labor Force Participation among Married Women," *American Economic Review* 75 (May 1985): 252–55.

   Wallace, P. *Black Women in the Labor Force.* chaps. 2 and 3.

D. Alternative Perspectives

   Folbre, Nancy. "Cleaning House: New Perspectives on Households and Economic Development," *Journal of Development Economics* 22 (June 1986): 5–40.

   Sen, Gita. "The Sexual Division of Labor in the Working Class Family," *Review of Radical Political Economics* (Summer 1980): 76–86.

E. Marriage and Fertility

   Conrad, Cecilia. "The Changing Age Distribution of Births in the United States," Ms.

   Ellwood, Daniel T., and Jonathan Crane. "Family Changes among Black Americans: What Do We Know?" *Journal of Economic Perspectives* 4 (Fall 1990): 9–24.

   Wilson, William J., and Kathryn M. Neckerman. "Poverty and Family Structure: The Widening Gap between Evidence and Policy Issues," in *Fighting Poverty: What Works and What Doesn't,* ed. Sheldon Danzinger and Daniel H. Weinberg. Harvard University Press, 1986.

IV. The Impact of the Sexual Division of Labor on Economic Well-Being

A. Child Rearing and Public Policy

Hartmann, Heidi, and Roberta Spalter-Roth. "Working Parents: Differences and Similarities," Ms, 1991.

Kamerman, Sheila B., and Alfred J. Kahn. "Innovative Parenting Policies and Gender Equity," Ms, 1991.

B. Women and Divorce

Dornbusch, Sanford M., *Feminism, Children, and the New Families,* chap. on "Divorce" by Lenore Weitzman. Guilford Press, 1988.

C. The Feminization of Poverty

Durbin, Elizabeth. "The Vicious Cycle of Welfare: Problems of Female Headed Households in New York City," in Lloyd, *Sex, Discrimination and the Division of Labor.*

Goldberg, Gertrude Schaffner, and Eleanor Kremen, eds. *The Feminization of Poverty: Only in America?* Praeger, 1990.

Sawhill, I. "Poverty in the United States: Why Is It So Persistent?" *Journal of Economic Literature* 26 (Sept. 1988): 1073–19.

D. Women and National Income Accounting

Waring, Marilyn. *If Women Counted: A New Feminist Economics,* chap. 1. Harper, 1988.

ETHNICITY IN THE AMERICAN CITY

C. Cindy Fan Department of Geography
University of California
Los Angeles, CA 90024

Course Description and Objective

This course is one of nine elective courses in the concentration "Spatial Demography and Social Processes in the City" offered by the Department of Geography. The syllabus was developed in the FEW Interdisciplinary Seminar and later revised using some materials from the FEW seminar "The Americas: Crossing Borders, Crossing Cultures." Although it is an upperdivision course, the contents are basic and include introductory materials to the study of ethnicity. Gender and ethnicity are interwoven throughout the course and special attention will be given to women of color in the United States.

The objective of the course is to encourage and facilitate critical thinking about geographical aspects of ethnicity in the United States. To this effect the historical and geographical background of contemporary issues about people of color will be introduced. The course focuses specifically upon the African-American, Native American, Hispanic, and Asian-American populations. Current debates as well as case studies (particularly in California) will be employed to explain the changing distribution; dynamics in the social, economic, and political dimension; and adjustment problems confronted by these groups and their impacts upon the American landscape.

Syllabus

Class 1

Introduction: Ethnicity in America
a. What is ethnicity?
b. What is a minority?
c. Nature of minority-majority relations
d. Overview of course
McKee, Jesse O., ed. 1985. "Introduction." *Ethnicity in Contemporary America: A Geographical Appraisal.* Dubuque, Iowa: Kendall/Hunt.

Sollors, Werner. 1989. "Introduction: The Invention of Ethnicity." In *The Invention of Ethnicity*, ed. W. Sollors, ix–xx. New York: Oxford University Press.

Class 2   *Historical and Geographical Background*
a. Geographical background of minorities
b. Nature of migration: forced versus voluntary; causes of migration as related to international political and economic relations
c. Are minorities migrants?
d. U.S. immigration policy

García, Philip. 1985. "Immigration Issues in Urban Ecology: The Case of Los Angeles." In *Urban Ethnicity in the United States*, ed. Lionel Maldonado and Joan Moore. Beverly Hills, Calif.: Sage Publications.

McKee, *Ethnicity*, chapter 1: "Humanity on the Move."

Mangiafico, Luciano. 1988. *Contemporary American Immigrants*, chapter 1: "The Ebb and Flow of Immigration to the United States." New York: Praeger.

Walker, Robert, and Michael Hannan. 1989. "Dynamic Settlement Processes: The Case of U.S. Immigration." *Professional Geographer* 41, no. 2: 172–83.

Class 3   *Demography and Spatial Distribution*
a. Population estimates and projections
b. Fertility and mortality
c. Age structure
d. Variations between and within ethnic groups

Lin Fu, Jane S. 1988. "Population Characteristics and Health Care Needs of Asian Pacific Americans." *Public Health Reports* 103, no. 1: 18–27.

McHugh, Kevin E. 1989. "Hispanic Migration and Population Redistribution in the United States." *Professional Geographer* 41, no. 4: 429–39.

McKee, *Ethnicity*, chapter 2: "The Native American"; chapter 3: "The Evolving Spatial Pattern of Black Americans: 1910–80"; chapter 4: "Mexican Americans"; chapter 5: "The Cuban Americans"; chapter 8: "Japanese Americans"; chapter 9: "The Chinese in America."

Mangiafico, chapter 2: "Sociodemographic Characteristics of U.S. Immigrants."

Momeni, Jasmid A. 1984. *Demography of Racial and Ethnic Minorities in the United States: An Annotated Bibliography with Review Essay*. Westport, Conn.: Greenwood Press.

Class 4   *Migration, Mobility, and Population Redistribution*

a. Interregional migration patterns
b. Intraregional migration patterns
c. Population shifts of minorities in relation to national population and capital movements
d. Explanation of migration patterns
Same readings as 3; and
Wekerle, G. R., and B. Rutherford. 1989. "The Mobility of Capital and the Immobility of Female Labor: Responses to Economic Restructuring." In *The Power of Geography: How Territory Shapes Social Life*, ed. Jennifer Wolch and Michael Dear. Boston: Unwin Hyman.

Class 5
Spatial Assimilation, Ethnic Pluralism, and Ethnic Segregation
a. Theories
b. Models
c. Case studies
Darden, Joe T. 1985–86. "Asians in Metropolitan Areas of Michigan: A Retest of the Social and Spatial Distance Hypothesis." *Amerasia* 12, no. 2: 67–77.
Fernández, Ricardo R., and William Vélez. 1985. "Race, Color, and Language in the Changing Public Schools." In Maldonado and Moore, *Urban Ethnicity*.
McKee, *Ethnicity*, chapter 12: "Urban Ethnic Islands"

Class 6
Housing and Residential Patterns
a. Ghettoization
b. Ethnic enclaves
c. Ethnic neighborhood succession
d. Los Angeles case study
Denton, Nancy A., and Douglas S. Massey. 1988. "Residential Segregation of Blacks, Hispanics, and Asians by Socioeconomic Status and Generation." *Social Science Quarterly* 69, no. 4: 797–817.
Pearlstone, Zena. 1990. *Ethnic L.A.* Beverly Hills: Hillcrest Press.
Schreuder, Yda. 1989. "Labor Segmentation, Ethnic Division of Labor, and Residential Segregation in American Cities in the Early Twentieth Century." *Professional Geographer* 41, no. 2: 131–43.

Class 7
Ethnic Labor Markets and Entrepreneurship
a. Ethnic minorities and the U.S. economy
b. Labor market activities
c. Self-employment and entrepreneurial activities
d. Economic ties with foreign and home countries

e. Los Angeles case study

Carlson, Leonard A., and Caroline Swartz. 1988. "The Earnings of Women and Ethnic Minorities." *Industrial and Labor Relations Review* 41, no. 4: 530–46.

Chai, A. Y. 1983. "Coping with the Oppressions of Gender, Class and Race." *Engage/Social Action* 92: 56–62.

Nelson, K. 1986. "Labor Demand, Labor Supply and the Suburbanization of Low-Wage Office Work." In *Production, Work, Territory: The Geographical Anatomy of Industrial Capitalism*, ed. Allen J. Scott and Michael Storper. Boston: Allen and Unwin.

Soja, Edward W. 1989. "It All Comes Together in Los Angeles" and "Taking Los Angeles Apart: Towards a Postmodern Geography." *Postmodern Geographies: The Assertion of Space in Critical Social Theory*, 190–248. London: Verso.

Tienda, Marta, and Ding-Tzann Lii. 1987. "Minority Concentration and Earnings Inequality: Blacks, Hispanics, and Asians Compared." *American Journal of Sociology* 93, no. 1: 141–65.

Class 8   *Interethnic Discrimination, Conflict, and Competition*
a. Employment
b. Political, legal, and judicial
c. Education (school segregation)
d. Racially and ethnically motivated violence

Johnson, James H., and Melvin L. Oliver, eds. 1988. *Ethnic Dilemmas in Comparative Perspective.* Proceedings of the Conference on Comparative Ethnicity. Los Angeles: Institute for Social Science Research.

Lambert, Richard D. 1981. "Ethnic/Racial Relations in the United States in Comparative Perspective." *Annals of the American Academy of Political and Social Science* 454: 189–205.

Class 9   *Current Policy Issues*
a. Access to economic opportunity
b. Affirmative action
c. Participation in the political process
d. Ethnic minorities in an aging society

Lee, Jik-Joen. 1986. "Asian American Elderly: A Neglected Minority Group." *Journal of Gerontological Social Work* 9, no. 4: 103–16.

Sandefur, Gary D., and Marta Tienda. 1988. *Divided Opportunities: Minorities, Poverty and Social Policy.* New York: Plenum Publishers.

Class 10

Shrestha, Nanda R., and DeWitt Davis, Jr. 1989. "Minorities in Geography: Some Disturbing Facts and Policy Measures." *Professional Geographer* 41, no. 4: 410–21.
Ethnic Women's Perspectives
a. Women and work
b. Feminist consciousness
Chow, Esther Ngan-Ling. 1987. "The Development of Feminist Consciousness among Asian American Women." *Gender and Society* 1, no. 3: 284–99.
Clark-Lewis, Elizabeth. 1987. " 'This Work Had an End': African-American Domestic Workers." In *To Toil the Livelong Day*, ed. Carol Groneman and Mary Beth Norton, 196–212. Ithaca, N.Y.: Cornell University Press.
Ruiz, Vicki L. 1989. " 'And Miles to Go . . .': Mexican Women and Work, 1930–1985." In *Western Women, Their Land, Their Lives*, ed. Lillian Schissel, Vicki Ruiz, and Janice Monk, 117–36. Albuquerque: University of New Mexico Press.

Other References

1. Proceedings of the conference on "California Immigrants in World Perspective," UCLA, 26–27 April 1990
2. Population Reference Bureau publications
O'Hare, William P. 1992. "American Minorities—The Demographics of Diversity." *Population Bulletin* 47, no. 4.
O'Hare, William P., and Judy C. Felt. 1991. "Asian Americans: America's Fastest Growing Minority Group." *Population Trends and Public Policy* no. 19.
O'Hare, William P., Kelvin M. Pollard, Taynia L. Mann, and Mary M. Kent. 1991. "African Americans in the 1990s." *Population Bulletin* 46, no. 1.
Valdivieso, Rafael, and Cary Davis. 1988. "U.S. Hispanics: Challenging Issues for the 1990s." *Population Trends and Public Policy* no. 17.
3. Videos
a. *In the Heart of Big Mountain.* Consequences of government decrees to relocate Navajos in order to make way for energy development projects
b. *Through Strength and Struggle* Eighteen-month citywide fight to win the legal right to job retraining and placement waged by Chinese seamstresses in Boston

INTRODUCTION TO U.S. GOVERNMENT AND POLITICS

David Camacho Department of Political Science
Northern Arizona University
Flagstaff, AZ 86011

Course Objectives

This course is designed to introduce students to U.S. political processes and governmental institutions primarily as viewed at the national level. The course assumes no prior knowledge of the subject matter, although it is presumed that students are self-motivated as well as interested in U.S. politics. The course is not comprehensive. As much as one might want it otherwise, it is simply impossible to cover all of the important topics concerning U.S. politics over the fifteen weeks of the term.

The selection of topics we will deal with has been guided by three objectives the instructor has for this course:

The first is the acquisition by students of basic knowledge concerning the basic processes and institutional structures of the U.S. government and the development of practical political skills by students, that is, of critical capacities useful in understanding and critiquing research concerning political phenomena.

An interdisciplinary approach is applied to gain some sense of the phenomena that make up the study of U.S. government and politics. Anthropological, economic, historical, and social-psychological evidence complement the political analysis at the center of our investigation. Constitutional and moral questions are explored, for they interact with political and economic policies that help determine the social fabric of our republic.

For a more explicit understanding and application of the major concepts dealt with in this course, we will review the experiences of women of color in the United States. The injustices that women of color have endured have been a point of discussion for more than two centuries. A second objective of this course, then, is to understand why the injustices committed against women of color were committed. To this end we will critically analyze the concepts of race, gender, class, and power.

The intent is not to dismiss as trivial the long struggle against several forms of discrimination by Anglo women. Instead, it is suggested that in the contemporary period the "dilemma" that our democratic republic finds itself in significantly revolves around the treatment endured by women of color. This dilemma arises from divergence between professed ideal and actual practice. A third objective of this course, then, is to gain some sense of the democratic nature of our republic. Accordingly, a central theme of this course deals with "democracy."

Required Texts

Gloria Anzaldúa, ed., *Making Faces, Making Soul:* Haciendo Caras.
Bettina Aptheker, *Woman's Legacy: Essays on Race, Sex, and Class in American History.*
Lewis Lipsitz and David Speak, *American Democracy,* 2d ed.
Steven Lukes, *Power: A Radical View.*
Cherríe Moraga and Gloria Anzaldúa, eds., *This Bridge Called My Back: Writings by Radical Women of Color.*
Pietro S. Nivola and David H. Rosenbloom, *Classic Readings in American Politics,* 2d ed.
In addition to the required readings, students are strongly encouraged to read regularly one of the leading daily newspapers *(Wall Street Journal, New York Times, Los Angeles Times, Washington Post)* or weekly newspapers *(Christian Science Monitor, Washington Post Weekly)* to keep current on major events. Much of the discussion will draw on current events.

Course Requirements

Three analyses will consist of critical reviews of the assigned readings. An important part of these written analyses is to integrate the issues raised in lecture into the papers topics. While lectures include themes from the readings, they will be keyed to themes that reach beyond the readings. Indeed, there are some ponderous issues involved in understanding U.S. government and politics, issues that can only be dealt with responsibly on the basis of personal values. It is through class discussion that some of the most useful ways of coming to terms with these issues and values are formed. The critical analyses will likely be from eight to twelve pages in length.

Syllabus

Week 1   *What is politics? What is democracy? Politics, power, and democracy. Foundations in U.S. government and politics.* Lipsitz and Speak, intro. and chapter 1; Lukes, entire book; Nivola and Rosenbloom, sec. 1

Week 2	*The Constitution as a political-economic document. Federalism and the separation of powers.* Lipsitz and Speaks, chapters 2–3; Nivola and Rosenbloom, sec. 2
Week 3	*Public rights or private liberties?* Lipsitz, chapters 4–5
Week 4	*The political economy of rights: the case of African-American women.* Aptheker, entire book
Week 5 *Analysis 1*	Paper topic: Recount the experiences of African-American women within the framework of democracy. What contradictions do you encounter between what is professed and what is real? What is the political nature of the African-American woman's experience? How might the structure of government help explain differences between reality and what is professed?
Week 6	*Political socialization. Ideology.* Lipsitz and Speaks, chapter 6; Moraga and Anzaldúa, 7–57
Week 7	*Political development and behavior.* Anzaldúa, secs. 1–3
Week 8	*Interest group politics. Elections and the media. The politics of protest.* Lipsitz and Speaks, chapters 7–10; Nivola and Rosenbloom, secs. 3 and 4
Week 9	*Women of color and the politics of protest.* Anzaldúa, secs. 4–5; Moraga and Anzaldúa, 105–92
Week 10 *Analysis 2*	Paper topic: How does political socialization help explain political development and behavior? Why is protest viewed as "unconventional politics"? Why is protest usually unsuccessful? Support your discussion through the application of the political development and behavior of women of color. Does the socialization of women of color help explain their political agenda? How might the political successes and failures of women of color be explained?
Week 11	*Institutional foundations of U.S. government and politics.* Nivola and Rosenbloom, secs. 5–8
Week 12	*The democratic nature of U.S. political institutions.* Lipsitz and Speaks, chapters 11–14
Week 13	*The policy process. Institutional and systemic agendas. The political economy of public policy.* Lipsitz and Speaks, chapters 15–16; Nivola and Rosenbloom, sec. 9.

Week 14	*Public policy and women of color. Mobilization efforts by women of color: limitations and strategies.* Anzaldúa, secs. 6–7; Moraga and Anzaldúa, 61–101 and 195–220
Week 15 Analysis 3	Paper topic: This analysis attempts to integrate course topics within a framework of public policy. How do power and politics help explain institutional and systemic agendas? How do "separation of powers" inhibit mobilization efforts by women of color? What other structural impediments inhibit mobilization efforts by women of color? How does "mainstream ideology" contribute to the political development and behavior of women of color?

INTRODUCTION TO AMERICAN NATIONAL GOVERNMENT

Stephanie Greco Larson Department of Political Science
George Washington University
Washington, DC 20052

The goal of integrating literature by and about women of color into the undergraduate curriculum is, in part, to get students to see the world in new ways and to increase empathy as well as information. Expanding reading lists to incorporate new authors and viewpoints and diversifying the subject matter through new lectures are the ways we traditionally approach this task. While these steps are essential to curriculum reform, they should not be the final steps taken, since they allow the students to view the material passively and possibly not internalize it. Course discussion and essay exams assist the student in interacting with the material, but they too may not be enough. I believe that it is also essential to devise assignments that force students to confront their preconceptions and their lack of awareness actively. By adding a new assignment to my Introduction to American Government course, I tried to heighten students' involvement with the material about women of color while also acquainting them with the political process. This course is the basic course for lower-division undergraduates. It serves as a departmental requirement for political science majors and is one of the classes that fulfills the social science university requirement for undergraduate majors in the college.

The task of incorporating literature about women of color into the political science class holds particular problems because the discipline has long focused on institutions of power. To the extent that women of color have been excluded from these institutions, first by legal discrimination and now through other mechanisms, they are naturally excluded from the study of the institutions. The challenge becomes how to alter an American government course in a way that does not misrepresent the discipline. Part of this can be done by expanding the definition of *politics* in ways that are less traditional by recognizing the "power of the people." Another approach is to provide the students with a vehicle by which they can see how women of color are excluded from institutional power. By focusing on elitism in U.S. governmental structures and looking for approaches that individuals can take within these constraints to facilitate change, the student is exposed to both actual and potential power. This keeps the lesson both realistic and hopeful.

The assignment used for this class was one that utilized role playing. Role playing requires the students to try to see things through someone else's eyes. Students were required to write a paper from the perspective of a person who, based upon her or his institutional and economic position, would not be thought of as having political power. Rather than give the students the choice of identifying individuals to role-play, which might still result in women of color being excluded, they were randomly assigned roles that I devised. For a class of sixty-three I had twenty-one different roles, each given to three students. Of the twenty-one roles seven were women of color (e.g., a Native American woman living on a western reservation), two were women whose race was not identified (e.g., a lower-middle-class single mother), two were people of color whose gender was not identified (e.g., a recent immigrant from Central America), and nine made no race or gender distinctions (e.g., a physically handicapped office clerk).

The assignment was for the students to identify a political problem that would be of concern to the person they were assigned. This choice needed to be justified for its relevance and practicality. Next the issue needed to be discussed in terms of the status quo, the changes that the person would want made, and the political debate that surrounds the issue. It was necessary for the student to discuss ways that the person could try to exert influence on the issue, making sure to explain coalitions and government jurisdiction. The students were required to use at least one piece of written material and one interpersonal experience when writing the paper. By interpersonal experience I meant that they should attend a lecture, observe a congressional hearing or meeting, attend a court session, interview someone, or contact an interest group or government agency that would help them understand either the person, the problem, or the process.

Because my university is located in Washington D.C., the interpersonal experiences were easy to come by; they included interviews with people from the National Clearinghouse for Bilingual Education, the Gay and Lesbian Task Force, the Bureau of Indian Affairs, the Joint Center for Political Studies, the National Farm Union, and the Department of Defense. Students also used resources on campus such as a lecture by African-American sociologist Joyce Ladner and interviewing an African-American ROTC student. Some students contacted organizations such as the National Coalition of Hispanic Health and Human Services and the Environmental Protection Agency. Many students identified these experiences as the most useful part of the paper. As one student wrote, "[a black female staff sergeant] described to me typical examples of discrimination and the current status of discrimination on a typical army base. . . . As a previously 'discrimination-ignorant' white male, I perhaps value my interpersonal experience with her the most. For one of the few times in my life, I feel like I understand what it is like to be in someone else's shoes."

Most students evaluated the assignment favorably at the end of the semester. On a scale of 1 to 7, with 1 being "Worthless" and 7 being "Extremely worthwhile," the average was a 5.2. Fifty-three percent of the class rated the assignment a 6 or 7, with only 14 percent saying 1 or 2. This is only slightly lower than their evaluations of the first assignment, which involved discussing their own political socialization and attitudes. A few students made additional comments on the assignment which were also favorable and spoke to its ability to have students see outside their own experiences, such as, "I thought the role playing assignment was the best idea. It really allowed me to realize the frustration and complications that people go through." Of course, reactions were not unanimously favorable. One student, who evaluated all of the readings that related to women of color as "worthless" and none of the other readings this low, felt the same way about the assignment and added that it was "silly."

Overall, the assignment seemed to be a success. It allowed the students flexibility in selecting topics and research materials while still forcing them to look at things from a perspective that most of them were unfamiliar with. Although many students identified organizations that could be used by their assigned individuals and various efforts that could be taken, frustration at the lack of power an individual has in changing policy usually prevailed. The assignment often resulted in an increased awareness about inequality in U.S. society and an appreciation for how it is systemically maintained. One student ended his paper with this observation, "If a nation can be judged by the way it treats its poorest citizens, then American must be judged harshly for its treatment of the poor urban black woman."

Course Description

Although you are probably familiar with some of the governmental structures, political actors, and history of the United States, much of this class's material will be new. Do not assume that a high school civics class or a college-level American history course will provide you with enough information to pass this class. We do not stress current events, historical trivia, or structural details. Instead, we will see how the scientific method has been used to predict behavior of political actors such as voters (prior to the midterm examination) and government officials (after the midterm).

This course has been redesigned with a Ford Foundation grant to support the integration of material about women of color into the undergraduate liberal arts curriculum.

Voices and Viewings

"Voices" is a new addition to this class which will allow you to hear relevant statements that go beyond the books and lecture structure. I will be reading (very briefly) political reflections of various origin which relate to the day's rather straightforward lecture. These reflections will be from politicians (i.e., the founding fathers, Justice Benjamin Cardozo, Representatives Tip O'Neil, Bill Nelson, and Patricia Saiki), journalists and writers (i.e., Chris Matthews, bell hooks, Kurt Vonnegut, and Douglass Adams), social scientists (i.e., E. E. Schattsneider, Robert Lane, V. O. Key, and Stacey Yap), and citizens (such as Celia Fire Thunder of the Assembly of California Indian Women). You will be adding your own voices to this political patchwork during discussion group meetings, in which you may persistently adhere to certain ideas but must also be respectful of attitude diversity.

"Viewings" are tapes that can be watched in the library's audiovisual center. The viewing covered on the midterm examination is: *Eyes on the Prize: America's Civil Rights Years.* The viewings covered on the final are: "Frontline: So You Want to Be President" and *Gideon's Trumpet.*

Required Readings

The Irony of Democracy is the core text in this class. The authors argue that the United States is elitist and demonstrate evidence for this interpretation by examining political institutions and actors. I hope that this theoretical perspective will challenge your preconceived notions about democracy and stimulate you to rethink some of them. You should also be critical of the arguments made by the authors. The additional readings will help you do this by providing you with alternative points of view and more intensive examinations of political questions.

James David Barber, "The Presidential Character: With a Special Focus on the Reagan Presidency," in *American Government: Readings and Cases,* ed. Peter Woll
Paul Burstein, "Elections, Lobbying, and Leadership," *Discrimination, Jobs, and Politics*
Thomas R. Dye and Harmon Zeigler, *The Irony of Democracy,* 7th ed.

Paula Giddings, "SNCC: Coming Full Circle," *Where and When I Enter: The Impact of Black Women on Race and Sex in America*

Anthony Lewis, chapter 14, *Gideon's Trumpet*

David M. O'Brien, "The Reagan Judges: His Most Enduring Legacy?" in *The Reagan Legacy: Promise and Performance*, ed. Charles O. Jones

James P. Pfiffner, "Moving the President's Legislative Agenda," *The Strategic Presidency: Hitting the Ground Running*

Larry Sabato, *The 1988 Elections in America: The Change That Masks Continuity*

Wendy Sarvasy, "Reagan and Low-Income Mothers: A Feminist Recasting of the Debate," in *Remaking the Welfare State: Retrenchment and Social Policy in America and Europe*, ed. Michael K. Brown

Barbara Sinclair, "Leadership Strategies in the Modern Congress," in *Congressional Politics*, ed. Christopher J. Deering

Carlos G. Velez-I., "The Nonconsenting Sterilization of Mexican Women in Los Angeles," in *Twice a Minority: Mexican American Women*, ed. Margarita B. Melville

Syllabus

Class 1	*Welcome to Class* Irony 1
Class 2	*Political Science: Why is it called a science?* This includes a discussion of the scientific method and techniques used to collect data. Irony 2
Class 3	*Political Science: What is political?* The different definitions used by elitists and pluralists are provided as well as a description of each school of thought. Irony 3
Class 4	*Government Structure:* How are American political institutions structured, and why? The founding fathers' fear of factions is discussed. Irony 4
Class 5	*Public Opinion:* How do we form our political attitudes and evaluations? We will see how children are typically socialized toward the political system and how these orientations are different based on gender, class, and race.
Class 6	*Public Opinion:* What orientations are common in our political culture? Are Americans trusting, efficacious, and tolerant? Irony 5

Class 7	*Public Opinion:* How useful is ideology in structuring public opinions? What is ideology, and how it is measured? Read Sarvasy
Class 8	*Political Participation:* How do people try to influence government? We will see how socioeconomic status predicts levels of participation and the exception of black women. Irony 6
Class 9	*Political Participation:* How are social movements organized, and what impact do they have on government? The welfare mothers movement will be used as an example. Irony 15
Class 10	Read Giddings
Class 11	*Political Participation:* How are political parties used to influence and organize government? Irony 7
Class 12	*Political Participation:* How do voters choose between presidential candidates? Realignments are discussed as a time when this participation is most meaningful. Irony 8
Class 13	*Political Participation:* How do interest groups attempt to influence government? Irony 9
Class 14	*Midterm Examination*
Class 15	*Presidential Election Campaigns:* What steps are taken when a candidate runs for the presidency? Read Sabato
Class 16	*Presidential Election Campaigns:* How has media coverage looked in recent presidential campaigns? Irony 10
Class 17	*Presidential Personality:* How is James Barber's typology used to characterize presidents? Read Barber
Class 18	*Presidential Power:* What is the difference between the constitutional powers of the president and his actual power in office? The importance of public support and the factors that influence it are discussed. Read Pfiffner
Class 19	*Presidential Power:* What powers does the president have to lead the nation? The president's influence on the bureaucracy and·Congress is discussed. Irony 11

Class 20	*Congressional Elections:* What is the incumbency advantage, and why does it exist? The minimal influence of presidential coattails in congressional races is also discussed.
	Irony 12
Class 21	*Congressional Structure:* How is Congress organized? The centrality of committees is illustrated.
Class 22	*Congressional Structure:* What impact does Congress's organizational structure have on decision making?
	Read Sinclair
Class 23	*Congressional Decision Making:* What factors influence how closely a member of Congress represents her or his district when voting? The process of cue taking is explained.
	Read Burstein
Class 24	*Judicial Branch Structure:* How are the courts organized? Special attention will be paid to the selection of judges.
	Read O'Brien
Class 25	*Supreme Court Procedures:* How do cases get to the Supreme Court? The steps a case goes through from filing to opinion writing are described.
	Irony 13
Class 26	*Supreme Court Decision Making:* How do justices decide whether to reverse a lower court's decision? The political nature of these choices is emphasized.
	Read Lewis
Class 27	*Supreme Court Decisions:* What can we learn about the Court's power by looking at key decisions? Various freedom of speech, procedural rights, and civil rights cases are described.
	Read Velez-I.
Class 28	*Final Examination*

PSYCHOLOGY OF LANGUAGE AND GENDER

Nancy M. Henley Department of Psychology
University of California
Los Angeles, CA 90024

Course Objectives

Although this course is psychologically and empirically based, it necessarily draws from the broad spectrum of fields contributing to the interdisciplinary study of language and gender. These include linguistics, sociology, literature, anthropology, communication studies, women's studies, and gay/lesbian studies. The course focuses on U.S. (and British) English but recognizes that there are many speech communities within American English (including speakers of Black English, bilingual Spanish-English speakers, etc.) and seeks to represent some of this diversity. The particular readings listed here are not meant as the best selection but, rather, one of a number of selections I have used over the years; the list is still in development.

The course begins with the classical division into two concerns that have dominated much of the literature in this field: (1) How do females and males use language differently? and (2) How do speakers use language differently when referring to females and males? It soon moves beyond these, however, to raise questions of conversational strategies and how gender is constructed and maintained through language.

A number of contrasts are deliberately built in to the readings:

1. Jespersen's 1922 delineation of characteristics of "women's language" is juxtaposed to Lakoff's 1973 one for comparison and contrast of both identified features and underlying theories. At the same time, these are put into their historical and cultural contexts.
2. Lakoff's (and Jespersen's) ideas based on contemplation of European-descent people (English and American) are contrasted with ideas and studies by/of women of color (e.g., Stanback, Zentella, Valdés-Fallis, Nichols, Goodwin, Grant), especially African-American women, who typically challenge the ideas that women are dominated linguistically by men or are more conservative linguistically than men.
3. Themes prominent in writings of women and men of color are compared with themes raised by lesbians and gay men, for example, issues of gender and cultural identity and self-worth through language, self-labels and la-

bels by others, and of assimilation versus maintaining one's cultural and linguistic heritage.

4. Lakoff's interpretation of (white) "women's language" as a gender-socialized weaker style than (white) men's is contrasted with revisionist interpretations by McMillan (that female/male difference is explained by variables of interpersonal sensitivity and relative power) and O'Barr (that "women's language" is really powerless speech, characteristic of different powerlessness groups and situations of powerlessness). This latter interpretation particularly expands the discussion from within-group gender difference to socially structured linguistic interaction.

5. A traditional interpretation of (white) men's language style as tragically inexpressive because of male role socialization (Balswick and Peek) is contrasted with three alternative views: Sattel's, that male inexpressiveness flows from power and effects control; Philipsen's, that among white, working-class men talkativeness varies with situation and relationship to interlocutor; and Abrahams's, that not all men are inexpressive—African-American men, for example, make their way through life on the strength of their verbal adeptness.

6. Typical views of Black English Vernacular (BEV) and verbal performance as practiced almost solely by men are challenged by studies of African-American women, who demonstrate adeptness at BEV verbal styles equal to men's.

7. Gardner's (white) feminist analysis of men's street remarks to women is contrasted with Kochman's cultural interpretation of male-female interaction as differing greatly between blacks and whites.

The great advantage that comes from taking diverse viewpoints in this course is in seeing the broad set of issues that arise as involving gender, which largely do not come out of literature on white women's and men's language. Besides the issues listed in (3), these include: alienation from and ambivalence toward "mainstream" white society and "standard" English, bilingualism and code switching, generational differentiation and change. Perhaps the greatest challenge they pose to much of (white) language and gender studies is: Who are to be counted as women? Are not Latina, Asian-American, Native American, and African-American women, women also?

But, in addition, these studies throw new light on the issues already identified in this field, such as language proficiency versus deficiency, conservatism versus innovation, and status, power, and silencing. They show that there is commonality as well as diversity in the issues we face as women and men of different colors and cultures.

Written Assignments

Comment Paper

Two to three pages commenting on one or more of the readings. Comment on the reading, don't summarize it (though it should be clear you have read the reading and thought about it). You do not have to agree with the author on whose work you are commenting, nor with the instructor.

Observational Study of Language or Nonverbal Behavior Relating to Gender

I. Choosing a Topic

Choose a topic that is of interest to you and that is clearly related to the content of this course; a good way to do that is to pick something that is mentioned in your course reading or in class (you may want to look ahead in your text for ideas). Most topics are expected to concern verbal language, but you may observe nonverbal communication if you wish. Examples of possible topics are listed below, but the list is not meant to be exhaustive—you can think of many more!

Choose something that there is previous research or theoretical support for (see Hypothesis, below). This will likely be derived from your reading in this course but can be derived from outside reading.

Choose an aspect that is not too broad. Don't try to watch three things at once; do a good job on one.

Choose an aspect of language that occurs frequently enough to be studied sufficiently; you may wish to make some practice observations to make sure this is the case. (Above all, don't wait until the last minute to learn you can't find enough examples of the behavior you want to study!)

Examples of Possible Topics

Sex differences in speech: Do women use the intensifier *so* or tag questions more than men? Do women use more polite forms than men do?

Use of obscenities: I would prefer that you not observe something already well known, like whether men use taboo words more than women (unless you just don't believe they do). But you could check this sex difference out for age differences or observe all-female groups for use of taboo words or observe differences in same-sex and mixed-sex groups.

Compare different genders on their use of certain language forms in written material, such as novels, biography, and plays (e.g., look at first-person use versus other persons; color words, numbers, different parts of speech, politeness forms). Or observe ways women and men are referred to in different writings (e.g., from fifty years ago versus today).

Black English: Are there gender differences in the kinds or extent of BEV forms used? How frequent is code switching (switching from "standard" to BEV or vice versa) in different sexes (and maybe generations or classes)? Do Stanback's observations hold?

Spanglish: When bilingual speakers mix Spanish and English, are there sex, age, or other group differences in which parts of speech or other types of words are likely to be said in Spanish, which in English? (You might listen to radio disk jockeys for this.)

"Valley talk": Do both females and males use it? If so, do they use it differently?

Language variation in general: How do Lakoff's or Jespersen's observations hold up when applied to other specific speech communities (e.g., Japanese-American, Korean, or Arab immigrant)? What hypotheses of sex difference in language use are suggested by specific history, language, or circumstances of a particular group?

If you work with the public, check out ways people address you—ask questions, give orders. Are there gender (and ethnic, age, class / location of store) differences, for example, in politeness or use of aggravated versus mitigated directives (see Goodwin)?

Language development: If you have access to children, record and classify the vocabulary of a child/children over a day or more, noting whether the different genders have started to take on gender-differentiated characteristics of adult speech.

Which characteristics of adults' speech to children differ by speaker or addressee gender? How is this affected by child's age?

Conversational interaction: What verbal turn-taking signals or verbal turn-holding mechanisms are used, with what frequencies, in what circumstances, by which gender of speaker and/or person spoken to? Which sex interrupts more, in same- or mixed-sex conversations, or who yields the floor or holds onto it more when interrupted?

II. Doing the Research

The study must be empirical: that is, it must report data you have gathered (e.g., it cannot be an essay or literature review paper). This should be an observational study. You want to see what happens in some real-life (or culturally depicted) situation, not an artificially created one, so don't go manipulating real life. (Exceptions: permission for manipulating real life may be given by the instructor, for an executable plan.) Your exploratory question or hypothesis may be derived from your reading in this course or from outside reading or experience.

Formulate a hypothesis. While you may do an exploratory study, that is, without having a particular hypothesis, it is helpful to think about what you may find, especially on the basis of what you have learned in the course, and decide what you expect to happen—that is, to formulate a hypothesis. Then you collect the data to test the hypothesis. Nothing is held against you if your hypothesis is not supported by the data, so don't think you need to fudge the results or write the hypothesis after you've gathered the data.

Define your terms and procedures. Make sure you have a clear idea of exactly what you are looking for: write out definitions of key concepts and terms, for example, if you want to observe the politeness of women's versus men's requests, tell how you will determine politeness—such as use of question versus statement syntax and/or intonation, use of compound requests, number of words in the request, use of modal forms (*could, would*), use of *please* and *thank you*, et cetera. Don't use fuzzy ideas like "I will just listen to how polite people's language is when they order burgers."

For many ideas you may want to compare different situations or categories of persons, but don't make a comparison, such as "Girls in my study used more obscenity than boys do" or "Women's speech is more assertive than it used to be," unless you have the data or information to back up the comparison (e.g., you have observed both sexes or have data from another time).

Keep careful records. You will need to count and report the number of occurrences of whatever you are looking at in your research, along with the relevant circumstances of the research (e.g., who is being observed, TV show analyzed, or year that historical material was written). Take a notebook or pad marked with the aspects of the behavior you are observing, as well as other things you want to note in the situation (e.g., sexes, ages, occupations, settings, length of time, etc.), and note carefully in it every instance of what you are observing, at the time it happens (don't try to recollect). Needless to say, position yourself where the behavior to be observed is most likely to occur (for door-opening behavior, in front of frequented doors; for tag questions, where you can hear people conversing).

Even though you may have a hypothesis, be absolutely open to observe just what happens—don't miss or reinterpret disconfirming events or be swayed by your expectations or hopes into recording what you want to find.

How many subjects or observations, or whatever, do you need? This is hard to tell in advance; as a rough rule of thumb, aim for about forty subjects or observations of a particular variable; or expect to spend three to five hours collecting data.

III. Writing the Paper

Be sure to report your results in numerical terms. Reporting is often best done in a table that breaks your data down by meaningful variables and shows the amount of occurrences for each variable. You do not need to use statistical tests; if, however, you do know how to use them, feel free to do so and report the results. You will not be given more credit for using a statistical test correctly nor demoted for using one incorrectly; do it for your own interest.

Format and length: the paper should be brief, typically three to four pages. Use the following format, which will guide both those who have had practice in the psychology style and those who have not:

Name

Date

Title of paper

Abstract (a brief summary of the research and its findings; one paragraph of a few sentences is usually enough)

Introduction (background of research, such as a claim or finding in a reading, general stereotypes or beliefs, reason to explore this topic)

Hypothesis (or purpose if exploratory study; be very clear—this need take only one, two, or three sentences, usually)

Method (here you tell what subjects and settings, or what materials, were used, and how many; your research definitions and procedures; be thorough)

Results (report exactly what you found, using numbers; here is where tables of results go—make sure they are clearly labeled)

Discussion (here discuss what you found in your experiment and what you think it means, given your hypothesis; does it support or contradict research or theory that was described in the course? You may speculate a little on what the results might mean if more extensive research bore them out; and on anything else you learned from the research.)

Exams

There will be two exams, each composed of multiple choice, short answer, and essay items.

Reading List

Books

David Graddol and Joan Swann (G&S), *Gender Voices* (Oxford: Basil Blackwell, 1989).

Robin Lakoff (LAK), *Language and Woman's Place* (New York: Harper and Row, 1975).

Barrie Thorne, Cheris Kramarae, and Nancy Henley (TKH), eds., *Language, Gender, and Society* (New York: HarperCollins, 1983).

Reserved Reading (RR)

Otto Jespersen, "The Woman." Chapter 13 of *Language: Its Nature, Development, and Origin*, 237–54 (1922; reprint, New York: Norton, 1964).

Marsha H. Stanback, "Language and Black Woman's Place: Evidence from the Black Middle Class," in *For Alma Mater*, ed. P. A. Treichler, C. Kramarae, and B. Stafford, 177–96 (Urbana: University of Illinois Press, 1986).

Ana C. Zentella, "Language and Female Identity in the Puerto Rican Community," in *Women and Language in Transition*, ed. J. Penfield, 167–79 (Albany: SUNY Press, 1987).

Guadalupe Valdés-Fallis, "Code-Switching among Bilingual Mexican-American Women: Towards an Understanding of Sex-Related Language Alternation," *International Journal of the Sociology of Language* 17 (1978): 65–72.

Joseph J. Hayes, "Lesbians, Gay Men, and Their 'Languages,'" in *Gayspeak: Gay Male and Lesbian Communication*, ed. James W. Chesebro, 28–42, 317–19 (New York: Pilgrim Press, 1981).

William M. O'Barr and Bowman K. Atkins, "'Women's Language' or 'Powerless Language?'" in *Women and Language in Literature and Society*, ed. S. McConnell-Ginet et al., 93–110 (New York: Praeger, 1980).

Julie R. McMillan, A. Kay Clifton, Diane McGrath, and Wanda S. Gale, "Women's Language: Uncertainty or Interpersonal Sensitivity and Emotionality?" *Sex Roles* 3 (1977): 545–59.

Jacqueline Sachs, "Cues to the Identification of Sex in Children's Speech," in *Language and Sex: Difference and Dominance*, ed. B. Thorne and N. Henley, 152–71 (New York: HarperCollins, 1975).

Caroline Henton, "Vocal Discord," *UC-Davis Magazine* (November–December 1988): 18–21, 28.

Eleanor Maccoby and Carol Jacklin, "Verbal Abilities." Excerpt from *Psychology of Sex Differences*, 75–85 (Stanford: Stanford University Press, 1974).

Marianne Engle, "Family Influences on the Language Development of Young Children," *Women's Studies International Quarterly* 3 (1980): 259–66.

Marjorie H. Goodwin, "Directive-Response Speech Sequences in Girls' and Boys' Task Activities," in *Women and Language in Literature and Society* ed. S. McConnell-Ginet et al., 157–73 (New York: Praeger, 1980).

Jack O. Balswick and Charles W. Peek, "The Inexpressive Male: A Tragedy of American Society, *Family Coordinator* 20 (1971): 363–68.

Gerry Philipsen, "Speaking 'Like a Man' in Teamsterville: Culture Patterns of Role Enactment in an Urban Neighborhood," *Quarterly Journal of Speech* 61 (1975): 13–22.

Roger D. Abrahams, "Black Talking on the Streets," in *Explorations in the Ethnography of Speaking*, ed. R. Bauman and J. Sherzer, 240–62 (New York: Cambridge University Press, 1974).

Don H. Zimmerman and Candace West, "Sex Roles, Interruptions and Silences in Conversation," in *Language and Sex: Difference and Dominance,* ed. B. Thorne and N. Henley, 105–29 (New York: HarperCollins, 1975).

Linda Grant, "Black Females' 'Place' in Desegregated Classrooms," *Sociology of Education* 57 (1984): 98–111.

Carol B. Gardner, "Passing By: Street Remarks, Address Rights, and the Urban Female," *Sociological Inquiry* 50 (1981): 328–56.

Thomas Kochman, "Male and Female Interaction: The First Phase," chapter 5 of *Black and White Styles in Conflict,* 74–88 (Chicago: University of Chicago Press, 1981).

Nancy Henley and Jo Freeman, "The Sexual Politics of Interpersonal Behavior," in *Women: A Feminist Perspective,* 4th ed., ed. Jo Freeman, 457–69. Palo Alto, Calif.: Mayfield, 1989).

Nancy M. Henley, "Gender Hype" (review of Goffman, gender advertisements), *Women's Studies International Quarterly* 3 (1980): 305–12.

Nancy M. Henley, "Molehill or Mountain? What We Know and Don't Know about Sex Bias in Language," in *Gender and Thought: Psychological Perspectives,* ed. M. Crawford and M. Gentry, 59–78 (New York: Springer-Verlag, 1989).

Julia P. Stanley, "When We Say 'Out of the Closets!'" *College English* 36 (1974): 385–91.

Julia Penelope [Stanley], "The Agents Within." Chapter 9 of *Speaking Freely: Unlearning the Lies of the Fathers' Tongues,* 144–79.

Suzette Haden Elgin, "A Sampler from Láadan" (and another brief excerpt). From *A First Dictionary and Grammar of Láadan,* 34–36, 93–95 (Madison, Wis.: Society for the Furtherance and Study of Fantasy and Science Fiction, Inc. [SF3], 1985).

Cheris Kramarae and Paula A. Treichler, "Menopause," "Menstruation," "Needed Words," "Pregnancy." Excerpts from *A Feminist Dictionary,* 266–67, 268–71, 296–99, 354–55 (Boston: Pandora Press, 1985).

American Psychological Association, "Consideration of the Reader." Excerpt from *Publication Manual,* American Psychological Association, 43–49, 3d ed. (Washington, D.C.: Author, 1983).

Course Outline and Reading Schedule

Class 1
I. Introduction and Overview
Language and the conception and surrounding edifice of gender are two (perhaps *the* two) central constructions of human cultures. Why has their intersection come under examination in recent years? What are the questions in this field of study? What have we found out? Are there really a "women's language" and a "men's language" in American English? Do women speak a "powerless" lan-

guage, and, if so, ought they to change to speak more like men? Do lesbians and gay men speak differently from each other and differently from straight men and women, and, if so, should they change? Does one's relation to language vary according to one's gender, race, and culture? How are our identities tied into language by factors of gender variation?

Class 2   A. *Using and Being Used by the Language*
G&S: Chapter 1, Introduction
RR: Jespersen, "The Woman"

Class 3   LAK: Part 1: "Language and Woman's Place"
Recommended: TKH Bibliography:
    I. Comprehensive Sources
    III. Stereotypes and Perceptions of Language Use

Class 4   B. *Language, Gender, Culture, and Identity*
RR: Stanback, "Language and Black Woman's Place"
RR: Zentella, "Language and Female Identity in the Puerto Rican Community"
RR: Valdés-Fallis, "Code-Switching among Bilingual Mexican-American Women: Towards an Understanding of Sex-Related Language Alternation"
RR: Hayes, "Lesbians, Gay Men, and Their 'Languages' "
Recommended: TKH Bibliography:
    IV. Sex Differences and Similarities in Language Use: Linguistic Components
    F. Bilingualism; G. Other Languages
    VIII. Language Varieties in American English

Class 5   *II. Gender-Based Differences in Language Usage*
What are the differences between men's and women's voices? Are these differences "natural" or learned? What language forms do men and women actually use differently? Are these differences the same across cultures? How do they develop when language is first learned? How does adults' use of language to children shape their behavior by gender? Are "sex differences" in language really power differences? Is women's language more polite than men's? What underlies gender differentiation in language?
A. *Phonology*
RR: Sachs, "Cues to the Identification of Sex in Children's Speech"
TKH: McConnell-Ginet, "Intonation in a Man's World"
RR: Henton, "Vocal Discord"

Class 6   G&S: Chapter 2, "The Voice of Authority"

	Comment paper due
	Recommended: TKH Bibliography:
	IV. Sex Differences and Similarities in Language Use:
	Linguistic Components
	A. Theoretical Issues; C. Phonetic Variants; D. Supra-
	segmentals
Class 7	B. *Usage*

TKH: Nichols, "Linguistic Options and Choices for Black Women in the Rural South"

G&S: Chapter 3, "Accents of Femininity? Gender Differences in Language Use"

Recommended: TKH Bibliography:
IV. Sex Differences and Similarities in Language Use: Linguistic Components
B. Word Choice and Syntactic Use

Class 8   C. *Language Development*

RR: Maccoby and Jacklin, "Verbal Abilities"

RR: Engle, "Family Influences on the Language Development of Young Children"

TKH: Gleason and Greif, "Men's Speech to Young Children"

RR: Goodwin, "Directive-Response Speech Sequences in Girls' and Boys' Task Activities"

Recommended: TKH Bibliography:
IV. Sex Differences and Similarities in Language Use: Linguistic Components
E. Verbal Ability
VII. Children and Language

Class 9   D. *"Women's Language" or ???*

LAK: Part 2, "Why Women are Ladies"

RR: McMillan et al., "Women's Language: Uncertainty or Interpersonal Sensitivity and Emotionality?"

RR: O'Barr and Atkins, " 'Women's Language' or 'Powerless Language'?"

Class 10   *Midterm exam*

Class 11   *III. Conversational interaction*

How does our conversational interaction differ by gender? Are men harmed by cultural pressures to be emotionally inexpressive? Ought they to change? How do class, race, and ethnicity interact with gender in speaking styles? What are conversational politics, and how do we use them? Is our nonverbal behavior gendered: Do we walk, stand, sit, touch, gesture, nod, look, and use space and time differently as women and men? Are women's nonverbal signals weak and men's strong? Can we change our body language by trying, and, if so, should we?

A. *Being a Man Linguistically*

RR: Balswick and Peek, "The Inexpressive Male: A Tragedy of American Society"

TKH: Sattel, "Men, Inexpressiveness, and Power"

RR: Philipsen, "Speaking 'Like a Man' in Teamsterville: Culture Patterns of Role Enactment in an Urban Neighborhood"

RR: Abrahams, "Black Talking on the Streets"

Recommended: TKH Bibliography:

   V. Conversational Interaction

   A. General References; F. Variation by Setting

   VI. Genre and Style

   A. Speech Genres

Class 12   B. *Conversational Interaction and Interruption Patterns*

TKH: Fishman, "Interaction: The Work Women Do"

RDR: Zimmerman and West, "Sex Roles, Interruptions, and Silences in Conversation"

TKH: West and Zimmerman, "Small Insults: A Study of Interruptions in Cross-Sex Conversations between Unacquainted Persons"

Class 13   G&S: Chapter 4, "Conversation: The Sexual Division of Labor"

RDR: Grant, "Black Females' 'Place' in Desegregated Classrooms"

Recommended: TKH Bibliography:

   V. Conversational Interaction

   B. Amount of Speech; C. Interruption; D. Conversational Topics; E. Control of Topics; H. Other Languages

Class 14   C. *Interaction on the Street*

RR: Gardner, "Passing By: Street Remarks, Address Rights, and the Urban Female"

RR: Kochman, "Male and Female Interaction: The First Phase"

Class 15   D. *Nonverbal Interaction*

RR: Henley and Freeman, "The Sexual Politics of Interpersonal Behavior"

RR: Henley, "Gender Hype"

In class: Slide presentation on Body Politics

Observational study due

Recommended: TKH Bibliography:

   IX. Nonverbal Aspects of Communication

Class 16	IV. *Gender Marking and Gender-Based Bias in Lexicon, Prescription, and Usage*

What kinds of bias are represented in the words and grammar of a language and in the ways people choose to use them? Are women and men equally stereotyped and maligned in the English language? Is the use of the masculine as a generic form (as in "mankind," "the student . . . he") anything more than a linguistic convention, and is it demanding of our attention? Does this form cause any real, measurable damage?

A. *Excluding, Defining, Derogating—and Their Effects*
G&S: Chapter 5, "Is Language Sexist?"

Class 17   TKH: Martyna, "Beyond the He/Man Approach: The Case for Nonsexist Language"
Recommended: TKH Bibliography:
II. Gender Marking and Sex Bias in Language Structure and Content
A. General and Comprehensive; B. Historical; D. Generics; E. Gender Marking, Naming; F. Terms of Address; G. Institutional Support; H. Critiques and Proposals
B. *Psycho- and Sociocultural Factors*
TKH: MacKay, "Prescriptive Grammar and the Pronoun Problem"
RR: Henley, "Molehill or Mountain? What We Know and Don't Know about Sex Bias in Language"

Class 18   RR: Stanley, "When We Say 'Out of the Closets!' "
G&S: Chapter 6, "Language, Communication, and Consciousness"

Class 19   RR: Penelope, "The Agents Within"
Recommended: TKH Bibliography:
II. Gender Marking and Sex Bias in Language Structure and Content
C. Linguistic Gender; J. Other Languages and Cultures
V. *Toward Change*
Are people and institutions changing their usage of biased forms, and, if so, how? Is a neutral pronoun possible? Are gender-biased language and gender difference in language usage two different things, or is there a link between how the language uses us and how we use the language?
RR: Elgin, "A Sampler from Láadan" (and other excerpt)
RR: Kramarae and Treichler, "Menopause," "Menstrua-

tion," "Needed Words," "Pregnancy" (excerpts from *A Feminist Dictionary*)

RR: American Psychological Association, "Consideration of the Reader"

Class 20   TKH: Penelope and Wolfe, "Consciousness as Style; Style as Aesthetic"

G&S: Chapter 7, "Linguistic Intervention"

Recommended: TKH Bibliography:

V. Conversational Interaction

G. Changing the Ways We Speak

VI. Genre and Style

B. Literary Style; C. Seizing the Language

ANALYZING SOCIETY

Rolf Kjolseth Department of Sociology
University of Colorado
Boulder, CO 80309

Course Objectives

This is a general liberal arts course with the triple objectives of (1) offering a partial introduction to the approach of social science (concepts, methods, and topics); (2) providing a survey of U.S. and other societies in historical and comparative perspectives; and (3) developing students' abilities in critical thinking on controversial issues. The course draws students with very diverse interests, most of them non–social science majors. It is a very large class with approximately one thousand students. Each week students attend two large lectures and a small-group session directed by one of twelve teaching assistants. Concern for gender and ethnic issues are interwoven throughout the semester in addition to receiving separate emphasis in some of the syllabus segments. For example, students may be asked to analyze how the nature of the data in specific studies was affected by the gender, age, and ethnicity of the researcher.

Prior to the start of the semester the instructor and all twelve teaching assistants participate in the university's three-day "Fall Intensive Teacher Training Program," which emphasizes gender and cultural issues. Throughout the semester the instructor and teaching assistants meet in a weekly teaching seminar to discuss and evaluate all aspects of the course. Frequently, outside consultants (such as from the University Multicultural Counseling Center) are invited to assist in these evaluations. Two basic texts are used in this course. One, Vander Zanden's *Sociology: The Core,* is a concise treatment of concepts and methods which is sensitive to gender and ethnic issues and emphasizes comparative Europe-U.S. stratification, that is, inequality—a recurring theme I use as an "umbrella" for gender issues and those affecting people of color. The second text is a collection of classic, contemporary, and cross-cultural articles (e.g., Macionis, *Seeing Ourselves*), over one third of which deal with different aspects of gender and issues related to class, race, and ethnicity.

Required Texts

John J. Macionis, *Seeing Ourselves: Classic, Contemporary, and Cross-Cultural Readings in Sociology*
James W. Vander Zanden, *Sociology: The Core*

Syllabus

V = Vander Zanden; all other readings from Macionis

Class 1	*Course Overview*
Class 2	C. Wright Mills, "The Promise of Sociology"; Peter Berger, "Invitation to Sociology"
Class 3	V: "Developing a Sociological Consciousness"
Class 4	Horace Miner, "Body Ritual among the Nacirema"; Maureen Giovannini, "Female Anthropologist and Male Informant: Gender Conflict in a Sicilian Town"
Class 5	V: "Culture and Social Structure"
Class 6	Dianne F. Herman, "The Rape Culture"; Karl Marx and Friedrich Engels, "Manifesto of the Communist Party"
Class 7	V: "Socialization"
Class 8	George Herbert Mead, "The Self"; John R. Coleman, "Homeless on the Streets of New York"; Erving Goffman, "The Presentation of Self"
Class 9	V: "Social Groups and Formal Organizations"
Class 10	Arlie Russell Hochschild, "The Managed Heart"; William Ouchi, "Decision Making in Japanese Organizations"
Class 11	V: "Deviance and Crime"
Class 12	David L. Rosenhan, "On Being Sane in Insane Places"; Elliott Currie, "Crime in World Perspective"
Class 13	V: "Social Stratification"
Class 14	Michael Harrington, "The New American Poverty"; Mary Romero, "Day Work in the Suburbs: The Experience of Chicana Private Housekeepers"
Class 15	Karl Marx, "Alienated Labor"; Studs Terkel, "Working, Jobs and How People Feel about Them"; Julianne Malveaux, "You Have Struck a Rock: A Note on the Status of Black Women in South Africa"
Class 16	Robert N. Butler, "The Tragedy of Old Age in America"; Daniel Callahan, "Setting Limits: Medical Goals in an Aging Society"
Class 17	V: "Inequalities of Race, Ethnicity, and Gender"

Class 18	William Julius Wilson, "The Black Ghetto Underclass"; Nijole V. Benokraitis and Joe R. Feagin, "Subtle and Covert Forms of Sex Discrimination"
Class 19	V: "Political and Economic Power"
Class 20	C. Wright Mills, "The Power Elite"; Herbert J. Gans, "Deciding What's News"
Class 21	V: "Marriage, Family, and Alternative Life Styles"
Class 22	Suzanne K. Steinmetz, "The Violent Family"; David Popenoe, "The Changing Swedish Family"
Class 23	V: "Religion, Education, and Medicine"
Class 24	Samuel Bowles and Herbert Gintis, "Education and Inequality"; Max Weber, "The Protestant Ethic and the Spirit of Capitalism"; Peter Downs, "Your Money or Your Life!"
Class 25	V: "Ecology, Population, and the Urban Environment"
Class 26	Paul R. Ehrlich and Anne H. Ehrlich, "World Population Crisis"; Frances Moore Lapp, Rachel Schurmann, and Kevin Danaher, "U.S. Food Aid: Weapon against Hunger?"
Class 27	V: "Social Change, Collective Behavior, and Social Movements"
Class 28	Louis Wirth, "Urbanism as a Way of Life"; Claude S. Fischer, "Toward a Subcultural Theory of Urbanism"
Class 29	Neil Smelser, "A Theory of Collective Behavior"; Norris R. Johnson, "The Who Concert Panic"; Marion Grfin Dnhoff, "The ANC Challenges to White South African Government"
Class 30	Georg Simmel, "The Metropolis and Mental Life"; Barbara R. Bergmann, "A Policy Agenda for the Sex-Role Revolution"

INTRODUCTION TO SOCIOLOGY

Yaffa Schlesinger Department of Sociology
Hunter College, City University of New York
New York, NY 10021

Course Description

This introductory course is, in the words of the sociologist Peter Berger, an invitation to sociology. Our goal is to understand the sociological perspective and its unique method of inquiry, including some of the basic concepts, propositions, and theories.

Two large themes run through every topic. The first is *continuity* and *change* (technology, ideology, and social organization); particular attention is paid to the changing role of women. The second theme is *cultural diversity*, which looks at different memories, values, and norms of ethnic groups that make up U.S. society. Special attention will be paid to women of color. These two themes reflect conflict between tradition and change among ethnic groups.

Each chapter has its own oral and written assignments based on the text and on your imagination. The assignments will be handed in and graded in the middle of the semester and at the end. Most of the students follow the assignments because they are short and manageable and because class discussion becomes more meaningful.

Course Requirements

Final short essay: Distinguish between technological and ideological changes (giving examples of each) and how they have affected the changing role of women of color. Select one ethnic group and describe a woman belonging to that ethnic group: her peculiar characteristics, style, values, and norms and how her role has been changing.

A quiz based on the readings

A final exam

Required Texts

Beth Hess et al., *Sociology*, 3d ed. (Macmillan)
Toni Morrison, *Sula* (Penguin)
Richard Rodríguez, *Hunger of Memory* (Bantam)

Course Outline

Part 1: The Sociological Perspective

Chapter 1   *What Is Sociology?*
Using C. Wright Mills's advice that the sociological imagination links biography and history, personal troubles and public issues (5), conduct an interview with your grandmother. Remember to link her life to the time and place in which it happened. Ask her about her grandmother.

Chapter 2   *Doing Sociology*
In the piece "Undocumented Community" Rodrigues studied the Hispanic life of migrants in Houston (38). What was his question? What method did he use? What did he find out?

Chapter 3   *The Cultural Context*
Give two examples of ethnocentrism and cultural relativism related to women of color. What did you learn from reading "Experience of Miscarriage" (54–55)? What does Arlie R. Hochschild mean by "commercialization of human feelings"? Why are women more vulnerable than men?

Chapter 5   *The Social Self*
How do gender, ethnicity, and social class shape the social self? Write an essay on: What person has influenced your life greatly, and in what ways?

Chapter 6   *Principles of Stratifications and Theoretical Perspectives*
Write an essay on "The Working Class Female," after reading "The Working Class Men" (177–78), reflecting on the particular problems of working-class women.

Chapter 8   *Sex and Gender*
How is the National Organization of Changing Men related to the changing role of women? Would you belong to this organization? Would you recommend it to the men in your family? Explain.

Chapter 10   *Racial, Ethnic, and Religious Minorities*
Summarize the models of integration and barriers to integration. What did you learn from "The Asian Success Story" (265)? What did you learn from the Mexican-American migration (268)?

Part 2: Social Institutions

Chapter 11   *Courtship, Marriage, and the Family*
Based upon your readings and upon your experience, write an essay on "The Future of the Family." Note the important social changes that affect the family and the diversity in American family (298–99).

Chapter 12   *The Economic System and the World of Work*
Using data of the Bureau of Labor Statistics, present a table of labor force participation by ethnicity and gender (note, e.g., that in New York people of color make up the majority part of the labor force). What does the table show? Can you suggest some problems based on studying the table?

Chapter 13 *Power, Politics, and Militarism*
Briefly explain the differences between Marx and Weber as they view the concept of power. How do C. Wright Mills (the power elite) and David Riesman (veto groups) view the American political system? How can women participate in the political system?

Chapter 14 *Education*
Write a critique (two pages) on the American educational system, noting its uniqueness, its achievements, and its failures.

Chapter 15 *Religions and Ideologies*
Marx's view of religion and the economy. Weber's view of religion and the economy. Black churches in America (411). Women in the pulpit (415). Civil religion.

INTRODUCTION TO SOCIOLOGY

Karen Pugliesi Department of Sociology and Social Work
Northern Arizona University
Flagstaff, AZ 86011

Course Objectives

Two broad purposes underlie the content of this course: to introduce you to the field of sociology and to explore diversity in the lives of people in the United States. We will begin with an overview of sociology: its history, perspective, methodology, and the important concepts and theories sociologists use to describe and analyze human societies. Our study of these topics will provide the foundation for an exploration into the various ways that social structure and social forces affect the lives of subgroups and individuals within a society (what sociologists sometimes call "macro-micro links").

In particular, we will use sociological "tools" to examine the work, family, and personal experiences of several subgroups in the United States: the "working class," married dual career couples, Chicanos employed in the food processing industry, African Americans, and those employed in the electronics manufacturing industry of California. The theme that will guide our inquiry into the lives of these groups is the interrelationship between work (the structure of the economy and what each of us does for a living) and personal and family life (our "life-styles," opportunities, concerns, and perspectives). Through this exploration you should achieve a better understanding of the structure and dynamics of human societies and the diverse peoples of the

United States and of the field of sociology. I also expect that you will develop greater insight regarding your own lives.

A variety of instructional approaches will be utilized in the course, including lecture, discussion, class exercises, individual out-of-class exercises and assignments, and group presentations. The first section of the course will rely most heavily on lectures. The second section will involve few lectures; student presentations and discussion exercises will dominate the last section of the course. Throughout the semester a high level of student preparation and participation will be expected.

Course Requirements

1. Course grades will be based on the following: two exams, one paper, one group presentation, and class participation. There will be two exams during the first section of the course (the overview of sociology). These exams will cover lecture, class activities, and the Charon text.
2. Each student will also write a paper that will involve an analysis of one of the assigned books. Detailed instructions for the paper will be given in class.
3. Students reading the same book will be required to participate in the preparation of a group presentation. The presentations will involve analysis of the material using sociological concepts and theories. Evaluation of each student's contribution to the group presentations will be based on peer evaluations and my assessment.

Required Texts

Joel M. Charon, *The Meaning of Sociology.* Englewood Cliffs: Prentice-Hall, 1990.

Dennis Hayes, *Behind the Silicon Curtain: The Seductions of Work in a Lonely Era.* Boston: South End Press, 1989.

Jacqueline Jones, *Labor of Love, Labor of Sorrow: Black Women, Work and the Family, From Slavery to the Present.* New York: Vintage, 1985.

Lillian Rubin, *Worlds of Pain: Life in the Working Class Family.* New York: Basic Books, 1969.

Patricia Zavella, *Women's Work and Chicano Families: Cannery Workers of the Santa Clara Valley.* Ithaca, N.Y.: Cornell University Press, 1987.

Additional selections appear in the course syllabus.

Syllabus

Week 1	*Introduction* Charon, chaps. 1 and 13
Week 2	*The Sociological Perspective and Methodology* Charon, chap. 2; Mills, "The Sociological Imagination"
Week 3	*Social Organization: Structure* Charon, chaps. 3–4, 7–8; Zimbardo, "The Pathology of Imprisonment"; Horwitz, "Honor and Reputation in the Chicano Gang"
Week 4	Exam 1 *Social Organization: Power and Inequality* Charon, chaps. 5 and 10; Ehrenreich, "Is the Middle Class Doomed?"; Phillips, "Reagan's America" Simulation: Starpower
Week 5	*Stratification: Class, Gender, and Race* National Committee on Pay Equity, "The Wage Gap: Myths and Facts"
Week 6	*Culture and Socialization* Charon, chaps. 6 and 11; Miner, "Body Ritual among the Nacerima"; Lever, "Sex Differences in the Complexity of Children's Play and Games"
Week 7	*Deviance and Social Change* Charon, chaps. 9 and 12; Rosenhan, "On Being Sane in Insane Places"
Week 8	Exam 2
Week 9	*Diversity in the United States: Macro-Micro Links* Baca Zinn, "Families in America"
Week 10	Group Presentation and Discussion of Worlds of Pain Kohn, "Social Class and Parental Values"; Hochschild, excerpts from *The Second Shift: Working Parents and the Revolution at Home*
Week 11	Group Presentation and Discussion of Jones, *Labor of Love, Labor of Sorrow* Wilson, "The Black Community in the 1980s: Questions of Race, Class, and Public Policy"
Week 12	Group Presentation and Discussion of Zavella, *Women's Work and Chicano Families* Farley, "Mexican Americans"
Week 13	Group Presentation and Discussion of Hayes, *Behind the Silicon Curtain* Gilbert and Kahl, "Social Class, Occupation, and Social Change"

SOCIOLOGY OF SEX AND GENDER

Ruth Wallace Department of Sociology
George Washington University
Washington, DC 20052

Course Description

This course examines the gendered nature of virtually all social relations, in-stitutions, and processes. We will explore the causes of gender inequality from three levels of analysis: social institutions; daily interactions; and indi-vidual perceptions, beliefs, and emotions. We will also identify some of the consequences of gender inequality and explore strategies for change. This course is one of a number at George Washington University which has been revised with the support of a Ford Foundation grant to integrate materials about women of color into the undergraduate curriculum. Thus, in the final segment of the course we will examine the interaction of race, class, and gen-der in the lives of women of color. The course will consist of lectures, class discussions, films, and guest speakers. The films and discussion sessions will supplement and integrate that lectures and reading materials.

Course Requirements

1. Personal journal: to relate course lectures and readings to personal expe-riences, to review and comment on newspaper articles (including the school newspaper) on gender themes, and to record observations of stu-dent behavior and campus incidents that illustrate gender issues. Students are encouraged to clip and enclose articles of particular relevance to the course.

    Journal entries should be dated and recorded a minimum of twice weekly. Journals will be collected, unannounced, twice during the semes-ter and at the last class. Periodically students will be asked, on a volunteer basis, to share journal entries with the class. Journals will be evaluated on the regularity and thoughtfulness of entries. Insight will be valued over verbosity. Assessments of Satisfactory +, Satisfactory, and Unsatisfactory may be earned.
2. Discussion groups
3. Two papers and a final examination

    Students are required to complete two of these three assignments. If all three of these assignments are completed, the lowest grade will be de-leted.

Paper 1

Choose *one* of the following topics. You do not need to do any extra reading for this paper, but I expect references to your assigned reading and to class notes.

1. Choose a group of which you are an active member or have been so in the recent past (e.g., family, work group, religious or voluntary organization, club or team, friendship group). Describe and analyze the impact of gender on how that group is structured, how it normally functions, any conflicts that arise (or why they fail to arise), et cetera.
2. Analyze your own life in terms of the impact gender has had on your social roles, choices, priorities, self-concept, major events, et cetera. For students who are over thirty, include an analysis of how gender-related changes since the 1960s have affected you or why they have not.
3. Interview your same-sex parent, grandparent, or someone who is over fifty concerning the impact of gender on her or his life. Describe and analyze similarities and differences between their experiences and yours.
4. Interview someone who is different from you on one of the following dimensions: sex, race, ethnicity, national origin, sexual preference; and proceed as in 3 above.

Paper 2

You will need to do some extra reading for this paper, and references to your readings should be included in the paper. Choose *either* 1 or 2.

1. Select a problem associated with gender inequality. (You may choose to elaborate on a topic covered in class.) Define your problem; use your readings to explain why the problem exists; recommend two strategies for solving or lessening the problem and speculate on the impact of your recommendations on the larger society.
2. Describe and analyze *two* recent (post-1980) studies about gender published in sociology journals. Some examples of such journals are: *American Sociological Review, American Journal of Sociology, Gender and Society, Sociological Inquiry, Social Problems, Social Forces, Symbolic Interaction, Sociological Analysis*, and *Journal of Contemporary Ethnography*. Your paper should include the following: (1) a brief description of each study, including the sample, the method of data collection, and the major findings; (2) present proof for your argument that the authors have analyzed some aspect of gender at the macro, micro, and/or subjective level; (3) an evaluation of the articles, wherein you assess both the strengths and weaknesses.

Final Examination

Answer questions 1, 2, and 3. Then answer one more, chosen from the remaining questions. Each question will contribute one fourth of the final exam grade.

1. Discuss the importance of the subjective, micro, and macro levels of sociological analysis with respect to gender inequality.
2. Define feminism and discuss the various types of feminism. Explain how the types of feminism differ with respect to the causes of gender inequality and the strategies for change.
3. Give at least one example of each of the following concepts from Anne Moody's autobiography: race, class, gender, meaning, and power.
4. Define three consequences of gender inequality and then recommend at least one strategy for solving or lessening each one.
5. Discuss at least five of the laws and ordinances in the United States which were designed to create and maintain the privileges of upper-class white males.
6. Define blatant (or overt), subtle, and covert sex discrimination and give examples of each.

Required Texts

Patricia M. Lengermann and Ruth A. Wallace (L/W). *Gender in America: Social Control and Social Change.* Prentice-Hall, 1985.
Anne Moody. *Coming of Age in Mississippi.* Dell, 1976.
Laurel Richardson and Verta Taylor, eds. (R/T). *Feminist Frontiers II: Rethinking Sex, Gender, and Society.* Random House, 1989.

Recommended Texts

Paula Gunn Allen. *The Sacred Hoop: Recovering the Feminine in American Indian Traditions.* Boston: Beacon Press, 1986.
Maya Angelou. *I Know Why the Caged Bird Sings.* New York: Random House, 1969.
Gloria Anzaldúa. *Borderlands / La Frontera.* San Francisco: Spinsters/aunt lute, 1987.
Paula S. Rothenberg. *Racism and Sexism: An Integrated Study.* New York: St. Martin's, 1988.
Margarita B. Melville, ed. *Twice a Minority: Mexican American Women.* St. Louis: C. V. Mosby, 1980.

Syllabus

Class 1	*Introduction to Course*
Class 2	*The Social Construction of Gender*
	L/W: chaps. 1, 2
Class 3	*Causes of Gender Inequality: Macro*
	L/W: chap. 5
Class 4	*Discussion Groups*
	R/T: 1, 13
Class 5	*Causes of Gender Inequality: Micro*
	L/W: chap. 4
Class 6	*Discussion Groups:* American History Museum Exhibits ("From Parlor to Politics" and/or "Costume, Gender, and Power")
Class 7	*Causes of Gender Inequality: Subjective*
	L/W: chap. 3
Class 8	*Discussion Groups*
	R/T: 6, 9, 20
	First Paper Due
Class 9	*Consequences of Gender Inequality: Rape*
	R/T: 41, 42
	Film
Class 10	*Discussion Groups*
	R/T: 39, 44
Class 11	*Consequences: Domestic Violence*
	R/T: 45, 24
Class 12	*Discussion Groups*
	R/T: 3, 46
Class 13	*Consequences: The Second Shift*
	R/T: 17
Class 14	*Discussion Groups*
	R/T: 18, 21
Class 15	*Explaining Social Change*
	L/W: chap. 6, 8
Class 16	*Discussion Groups*
	R/T: 28, 50
Class 17	*Strategies for Change: Macro, Micro*
	L/W: chaps. 9, 10
	Film: *Wilmar 8*
Class 18	*Discussion Groups*
	R/T: 23, 2
	Second Paper Due
Class 19	*Strategies for Change: Subjective*
	L/W: chap. 7

Class 20	*Discussion Groups* R/T: 48, 22
Class 21	*Women of Color: Early Socialization* Moody: pt. 1
Class 22	*Discussion Groups* R/T: 15, 16
Class 23	*Women of Color: Formal Education* Moody: pts. 2, 3
Class 24	*Women of Color: Their Contributions* Moody, pt. 4
Class 25	*Discussion Groups* R/T: 19, 33
Class 26	*The Future: Constraints and Resources* L/W: chap. 11, 12
Class 27	*Discussion Groups* R/T: 53
Class 28	*Final Examination*

SOCIOLOGY OF THE FAMILY

Terry Arendell Department of Sociology
Hunter College, City University of New York
New York, NY 10021

Course Description

This survey course explores central issues in the sociological study of the American family, in both historical and contemporary contexts, with the primary emphasis given to the contemporary family. Two central questions serve as the overall framework for the course: "What is going on in families?" and "Why is this going on?" Two broad facets of sociological study of the family are emphasized: (1) the family as a major social institution in relationship to other major social institutions, particularly the industrial capitalist economy and the liberal democratic polity, and (2) the family as a primary social group and a unit of intense interpersonal relationships. Recognized and assessed throughout the course are the socially structured inequalities in American society based on wealth and income and race, ethnicity, and gender; these are recognized and developed as being the primary factors in the diversity of family forms, experiences, and relations, both within family units and between the family and other social institutions. In seeking to gain a more objective and critical understanding of the institution of the family and family interactional processes, ideological assumptions and persistent myths about "the American family" and its variations and place in society are considered and critiqued. Various theoretical frameworks for examining and understanding the family are considered; primary among these are feminist and conflict perspectives with some assessment of the traditional use of functionalist theory. The course format consists of lectures, discussions, readings, films, and assigned written papers and essay exams.

Required Texts

Because this is a survey course, the reading assignments for this course are extensive.

Family in Transition, 6th ed., A. Skolnick and J. Skolnick (S&S)
Families in Peril, M. Edelman
Nation: Special Issue on the Black American Family
Brown Girls, Brownstones, P. Marshall
The Joy Luck Club, A. Tan
Mothers and Divorce, T. Arendell
As We Are Now, M. Sarton

Additional selected readings are on reserve in the library and available as handouts to the class, as indicated on the reading schedule.

Syllabus

Weeks 1, 2	*Introduction to the Course; Introduction to the Sociological Study of the Family*
	Readings: S&S, Introduction, 1–21
	S&S, 1: Gough, "Origin of the Family"
	S&S, 2: Hareven, "American Families in Transition"
	S&S, 3: Schwartz Cowan, "Twentieth-Century Changes in Household Technology"
	S&S, 5: Uhlenberg, "Death and the Family"
	S&S, 40: Lasch, "The Family as a Haven in a Heartless World"
	Thorne, "Feminist Rethinking of the Family"

The Family and Social Inequalities

Weeks 3, 4   *The Family in an Industrial Capitalist Society: Class Inequalities*
Readings: Edelman, *Families in Peril*
Thornton Dill: "The Means to Put My Children Through"
Tillie Olsen, "I Stand Here Ironing"

Week 5   *The Family and Racial Stratification—African Americans: Historical Overview and Contemporary Patterns*
Film: *Black Mother, Black Daughter*
Readings: *Nation*, special issue
S&S, introduction to part 5
S&S, 35: Staples and Mirande, "Racial and Cultural Variations among American Families"
excerpt, Stack, *All Our Kin*

Weeks 6, 7   *The Family and Racial Stratification—Hispanic Americans: Historical Overview and Contemporary Patterns; Immigration*
Readings: Marshall, *Brown Girl, Brownstones*

Weeks 7, 8   *The Family and Racial Stratification—Asian Americans: Historical Overview and Contemporary Patterns; Immigration*
Readings: Tan, *The Joy Luck Club*
In-Class Midterm Examination

The Family as an International Unit: Issues of Gender and Parent-Child Relations

Weeks 9, 10   *Contemporary Marriage: Trends, Analyses, and the Ideal of Companionate Marriage*
Film: *A Death in the Family*
Readings: S&S: Introduction to part 2
S&S, 11: Bernard, "The Good Provider Role"
S&S, 12: Goode, "Why Men Resist"
S&S, 14: Rosenblum, "The Conflict between and within the Genders"
S&S, 15: Rubin, "Blue-Collar Marriage and the Sexual Revolution"
S&S, 16: Cancian, "Gender Politics"
S&S, 19: Spanier, "Cohabitation in the 1980s"
S&S, 20: Blumstein and Schwartz, "American Couples"
S&S, 21: Cuber and Haroff, "Five Types of Marriage"

	S&S, 22: Hertz, "More Equal than Others"
Week 10	*Divorce and Remarriage American Style*
	Readings: Arendell, *Mothers and Divorce*
	S&S, 27, Ahrons and Rodgers, "The Remarriage Transition"
	Recommended:
	S&S, 6, Cherlin, "The Trends"
	S&S, 7, Norton and Moorman, "Current Trends in Marriage and Divorce among American Women"
Weeks 11, 12	*Parenting and Childhood*
	Readings: S&S, 28, Zelizer, "Pricing the Priceless Child"
	S&S, 30, Kay, "Reproductive Technology and Child Custody"
	S&S, 31, Rossi, "Transition to Parenthood"
	S&S, 32, Fein, "Research on Fathering"
	S&S, 33, Mednick, "Single Mothers"
Weeks 12, 13	*Domestic Violence*
	Guest lecturer and film: *Doloree*
	Readings: S&S, 4, Gordon, The Politics and History of Family Violence"
	S&S, 23, Straus, Gelles, and Steinmetz, "The Marriage License as a Hitting License"
	excerpts from *Worldwatch*
Week 13	*Lesbian and Gay Parenting: Alternative Family Forms*
	Film: *We Are Family*
	Readings: excerpt from Audre Lorde; excerpts from Adriene Rich
Week 14	*Families and the Aged; Families and Health Crises*
	Readings: S&S, 10, Cherlin and Furstenberg, "The Modernization of Grandparenthood"
	Sarton, *As We Are Now*
	excerpts on grandmothers serving as foster parents; excerpts on AIDS and the family
Week 15	*Family Policy and the Politics of the Family*
	Readings: S&S, 38, Luker, "Motherhood and Morality in America"
	S&S, 39, Bowers vs. Hardwick: "Do Homosexuals Have a Right to Privacy"
	S&S, 41, Bane, "Here to Stay: Parents and Children"
	S&S, 42, Bellah et. al., "Habits of the Heart"
	S&S, 43, Cancian, "The History of Love: Theories and Debates"

MODERN SOCIOLOGICAL THEORY

Rubén Martínez Department of Sociology
University of Colorado
Colorado Springs, CO 80933

Course Objectives

The purpose of this course is to examine sociological theories by focusing on the theoretical frameworks of thinkers representing the different "schools" of thought. Beginning with the views of Comte and Marx the course moves to the ideas of Durkheim, Weber, and Simmel. The focus then shifts to the emergence of sociology in the United States. Contemporary theoretical frameworks and recent developments within each are also examined. This includes works in neofunctionalism, critical theory, symbolic interactionism, and feminist theory.

The course concludes with an examination of minority perspectives within the broad area of sociological theory. Particular emphases are placed on critiques of the epistemological and ontological assumptions of mainstream sociological theory.

Course Requirements

Students will write three short papers and take three essay examinations. In the papers students will compare the basic views and perspectives of two thinkers or two theoretical frameworks. The exams will occur, on the average, every five weeks of the semester.

Required Texts

George Ritzer, *Sociological Theory*, 3d ed.
Jonathan H. Turner, Leonard Beeghley, and Charles H. Powers, *The Emergence of Sociological Theory*, 2d ed. (Turner et al.)

Reserve Materials

Tomás Almaguer, "Toward the Study of Chicano Colonialism"
Maxine Baca Zinn, "Sociological Theory in Emergent Chicano Perspectives"
Ruth Bleier, ed., *Feminist Approaches to Science*
Ketayun Gould, "Feminist Principles and Minority Concerns: Contributions, Problems, and Solutions"
Maurice Jackson, "Toward a Sociology of Black Studies"

Wendy Luttrell, "Working-Class Women's Ways of Knowing: Effects of Gender, Race, and Class"

Marcia Millman and Rosabeth Moss Kanter, eds., *Another Voice*

Alfredo Mirande, "Chicano Sociology: A New Paradigm for Social Science"

Jonathan H. Turner, *The Structure of Sociological Theory*, 5th ed.

Patricia Zavella, "The Problematic Relationship of Feminism and Chicana Studies"

Syllabus

I. Introduction

Class 1   *Introduction to the Course*

Class 2   *The Role of Theory in the Scientific Research Process.*
Turner, "Sociological Theory: Diversity and Disagreement"

II. Europe and the Founding of Sociology

Class 3   *The Early Years.*
Ritzer, "A Historical Sketch of Sociological Theory: The Early Years"

Class 4   *Sociology and Auguste Comte.*
Turner et al., "August Comte and the Emergence of Sociological Theory"

Classes 5, 6 *Dialectics and Karl Marx.*
Ritzer, "Karl Marx"; Turner, et al., "The Sociology of Karl Marx"

Classes 7, 8 *Social Facts and Emile Durkheim.*
Ritzer, "Emile Durkheim"; Turner et al., "The Sociology of Emile Durkheim"

Classes 9, 10 *Rationalization and Max Weber.*
Ritzer, "Max Weber"; Turner et al., "The Sociology of Max Weber"

Classes 11, 12 *Forms of Interaction and George Simmel.*
Ritzer, "George Simmel"; Turner et al., "The Sociology of George Simmel"

III. Early American Sociological Theory

Classes 13, 14 *The Early Years.*
Ritzer, "A Historical Sketch of Sociological Theory: The

Later Years"; Turner et al., "The Emergence of Modern Theoretical Perspectives"

IV. Contemporary Schools of Sociological Theory

Classes 15, 16   *Varieties of Functionalism.*
                  Ritzer, "Structural Functionalism, Neofunctionalism, and the Conflict Theory Alternative"
Classes 17, 18   *Neo-Marxian Thought.*
                  Ritzer, "Varieties of Neo-Marxian Sociological Theory"
Classes 19, 20   *Contemporary Symbolic Interactionalism.*
                  Ritzer, "Symbolic Interactionism"
Classes 21, 22   *Phenomenology and Ethnomethodology.*
                  Ritzer, "Phenomenology and Ethnomethodology Sociology"
Classes 23, 24   *Exchange Theory.*
                  Ritzer, "Exchange Theory and Behavioral Sociology"
Classes 27, 28   *Feminist Theory.*
                  Ritzer, "Contemporary Feminist Theory"; Elizabeth Fee, "Critiques of Modern Science . . . ," in Bleier; Sue Rosser, "The Relationship between Women's Studies and Women in Science," in Bleier; Daniels, "Feminist Perspectives in Sociological Research," in Millman
Classes 29, 30   *Minority Views and Critiques.*
                  Jackson, "Toward a Sociology of Black Studies"; Mirande, "Chicano Sociology: A New Paradigm for Social Science"; Baca Zinn, "Sociological Theory in Emergent Chicano Perspectives"
Class 31   *Sociological Theory and Minority Women.*
                  Zavella, "The Problematic Relationship of Feminism and Chicana Studies"; Gould, "Feminist Principles and Minority Concerns . . ."; Luttrell, "Working Class Women's Ways of Knowing . . ."
Class 32   *Metatheory and Sociological Theory.*
                  Ritzer, "Metatheory and a Metatheoretical Scheme for Analyzing Sociological Theory"
Class 33   *Course Review and Recapitulation*

AMERICA'S PEOPLES: POPULATION AND SOCIAL STRUCTURE IN THE UNITED STATES

Lawrence Carter Department of Sociology
University of Oregon
Eugene, OR 97403

Course Description

This course, America's Peoples: Population and Social Structure in the United States, will explore how the size, composition, and distribution of the diversity of ethnic and racial subpopulations that constitute the American people have shaped the dynamics of social structure, culture, and change in the United States. We will trace these developments historically and contemporaneously to understand them as forces that help mold society with attendant advantages and disadvantages for its peoples. Primary attention will be given to the demographic forces, fertility, mortality, and migration, to show how they dictate what the population will look like and the sociocultural dynamics that result from that complexity.

The population of the United States is composed mostly of people of European stock. The second largest component has been people of African heritage. Social contact has resulted in cultural change. Accordingly, American culture and society had been largely rooted in Europe with adaptations from Africa. As this culture has become more homogenized, it is less identifiable with the distinctive contributions of European nationality–based cultures or of those specific to regions of Africa. Cultural differences, where observable, more clearly follow lines stratified by class and race, often in instances in which race becomes synonymous with class. Under these circumstances major infusions of change are now coming from non-European parts of the world, largely Latin America and Asia. The major source of these infusions is the "new new migration" of peoples from the Third World.

A characteristic demographic feature of developed societies is that they experience decelerated natural increase, that is, declining excess of births over deaths. Thus, their growth slows appreciably over time. The United States is one such country. As such, when labor is needed and it is not produced indigenously, then migration is the source of recruitment. The major historical source of labor, Europe, is deplete of stock for the same demographic reason. The Third World maintains a surplus of labor due to high rates of natural increase. The underdeveloped countries, then, are increasingly the major suppliers of new immigrant labor to the United States.

Migrants are culture bearers. When a "critical mass" of migrants becomes established in a receiving country, their culture also becomes rooted in that country. How the receiving country adjusts to the stresses and strains of those infusions often shapes the circumstances of the life-style of the culture bearers, the migrants. This dynamic also produces irrevocable social change in the society at large. What makes this "new new migration" so intriguing is that it consists of peoples of color, highly visible with visibly different life-styles. How will they be absorbed?

The new new migrants have higher birthrates than does the receiving population, so, as a component of population, they will grow faster. Consequently, the racial composition of the United States can expect to change markedly in the future. Given this strong blend of racial and cultural complexity, American society may shift further from its European and traditional American roots. How this dynamic may be played out and how it augurs for the future of the society are issues to be examined in the course.

Concurrently, with the influx of the new new migrants, there is an accelerating transformation of gender roles in U.S. society. To some extent both changes are responses to common structural changes in the society. At times the changes are complementary, while at others they are conflictual. These outcomes will be addressed in the course.

Course Objective

Our goal is to study U.S. population phenomena within a sociological framework used to analyze historical, contemporary, and anticipated population conditions and trends as they are connected to social situations and the organization of U.S. society. As such, the course will be centered around three major areas:

1. historical and theoretical perspectives on population analysis;
2. exploration of the three demographic variables: birth, death, and migration; and
3. exploration of the impact of population change on the social structure of the United States.

Required Readings

Gill, R. T., N. Glazer, and S. A. Thernstrom, *Our Changing Population*
Population Reference Bureau, *1993 U.S. Population Data Sheet*
Steinberg, Stephen, *The Ethnic Myth*
Selected readings

Syllabus

Week 1   *The Population Revolution: Demography and Historical Demography*
Gill et al., *Our Changing Population:* Chapter 1, Introduction: The Demographic Revolution, 1–6; chapter 2, Our Historic War against Mortality, 19–35; chapter 3, The Flight from Fertility, 36–53; chapter 4, America on the Move, 54–74.
Robey, Bryant, and Cherry Russell, "How America Is Changing," *American Demographics* (July–August 1982): 16–27.

Week 2   *An Aging Population and the Older Generations: Complications of Successful Economic and Demographic Survival*
Gill et al., *Our Changing Population:* chapter 5, The Aging Society, 75–91; chapter 6, Is There a Crisis in Social Security? 92–108; chapter 7, To Work or to Retire, 109–24; chapter 8, Health Care and the Elderly, 125–40.

Week 3   *Subnations: Race, Ethnicity, and Community*
Petersen, William, *Population:* chapter 4, Subnations, 99–143.
Steinberg, Stephen, *The Ethnic Myth:* Introduction—The New Ethnicity in Historical Perspective, 3–4; chapter 1, The Ignominious Origins of Ethnic Pluralism in America, 5–43; chapter 2, The Ethnic Crisis in American Society, 44–81.
Thernstrom, Stephen, ed., *Harvard Encyclopedia of American Ethnic Groups:* Gleason, Philip, "American Identity, 31–58; Petersen, William, "Concepts of Ethnicity," 234–42.

Week 4   *The Colonial Period, 1607–1790*
Jacobs, Wilber R., "The Tip of an Iceberg: Pre-Columbian Indian Demography and Some Implications for Revisionism," 123–32.
Thernstrom, Stephen, ed., *Harvard Encyclopedia of American Ethnic Groups:* Spicer, Edward H., "American Indians," 58–65; Erickson, Charlotte, "English," 319–24; Holt, Thomas C., "Afro-Americans," 5–10.

Week 5   *The Complexities of Racial Diversity in the United States*
Bogue, Donald, "Color-Nativity-Race Composition," in Mam, ed., *Population and Society,* 378–94.
Thernstrom, Stephen, ed., *Harvard Encyclopedia of American Ethnic Groups:* Holt, Thomas C., "Afro-

Americans," 11–23; Lai, H. M., "Chinese," 217–34; Erickson, Charlotte, "English," 324–36; Kitano, Harry L., "Japanese," 561–71.

Midterm Examination

Week 6   *The Historical Process of the Settlement and Racial and Ethnic Diversification of the United States*
Gill et al., *Our Changing Population:* chapter 13, Black America—Two Steps Forward, 213–32; chapter 18, Immigration Old and New, 311–28; chapter 19, Through the Golden Door, 329–46; chapter 20, Have We Decided to Control Our Borders? 347–63; chapter 21, The Hispanics: Is the Pot Still Melting? 364–83.
Ward, David, "Immigration: Settlement Patterns," in Thernstrom, *Harvard Encyclopedia of American Ethnic Groups,* 496–508.

Week 7   *The Historical Transformation of Sex Roles and American Family Structure*
Gill et al., *Our Changing Population:* chapter 9, The "Traditional" American Family, 143–60; chapter 10, A Tale of Two Generations, 161–77; chapter 11, Working Wives and Mothers, 178–95; chapter 12, The American Male—Liberated or on the Run? 196–212.
Hareven, Armada K., and John Model, "Family Patterns," in Thernstrom, *Harvard Encyclopedia of American Ethnic Groups,* 346–54.

Week 8   *The Changing Status of Children in American Society*
Gill et al., *Our Changing Population:* chapter 14, The Changing Worlds of Childhood, 235–52; chapter 15, Children in Poverty, 203–70; chapter 16, Who's Watching the Children, 271–88; chapter 17, Educating the Next Generation, 289–308.

Week 9   *The Entanglement of Race, Ethnicity, and Social Class during the Middle Period*
Steinberg, Stephen, *The Ethnic Myth:* Introduction—The New Darwinism, 77–81; chapter 3, The Myth of Ethnic Success: The Jewish Oration Lager Story, 82–105; chapter 4, The Culture of Poverty Reconsidered, 106–27; chapter 5, Education and Ethnic Mobility: The Myth of Jewish Intellectualism and Catholic Anti-Intellectualism, 128–50; chapter 6, Why Irish Became Domestics and Italians and Jews Did Not, 151–68; revised introduction—The Iron Law of Ethnicity, 169–72; chapter 7, The

Reconstruction of Black Servitude after the Civil War, 173–200; chapter 8, Racial and Ethnic Conflict in the Twentieth Century, 201–21; chapter 9, The "Jewish Problem" in American Higher Education, 222–54.

Weeks 10, 11   *The Present Currency of Race, Ethnicity, and Gender in the 1990s: Prologue to Chaos or Cohesion?*

Bumpass, Larry, "What's Happening to the Family? Interactions between Demographic and Institutional Change," in *Demography* 27(A): 483–98.

Eckart, A. Roy, *Black-Woman-Jew: Three Wars for Human Liberation:* chapter 7, Double Jeopardy: Racism and Sexism, 51–62.

Gill et al., *Our Changing Population:* chapter 22, Can We Live Long and Live Well, 389–406; chapter 23, Does the Family Have a Future, 407–23; chapter 24, Will the Poor Always Be with Us? 424–43; chapter 25, The United States and the World Population Explosion, 444–73.

Kanter, Rosabeth M. "Token Women in the Corporation, 100–108.

Levine, Art, "The Birth Dearth Debate," in *U.S. News and World Report* 108: 64–65.

Steinberg, Stephen, *The Ethnic Myth:* chapter 10, Dilemmas and Contradictions of Ethnic Pluralism in America, 253–62; epilogue—Ethnic Heroes and Racial Villains in American Social Science, 263–302.

Wattenberg, Ben J., "The Birth Dearth: Dangers Ahead," in *U.S. News and World Report* 108: 56–63.

THE SOCIOLOGY OF SOCIAL MOVEMENTS: AN ANNOTATED BIBLIOGRAPHY OF COURSE MATERIALS ON WOMEN OF COLOR

Val **Burris** Department of Sociology
University of Oregon
Eugene, OR 97403

A. The Industrial Workers' Movement

Bardacke, Frank. 1988. "Watsonville: A Mexican Community on Strike." In *Reshaping the U.S. Left: People's Struggles in the 1980s*, ed. Mike Davis and Michael Sprinker, 149–82. New York: Verso.
    This article recounts the events surrounding a strike by mostly female

Mexican-American workers at a frozen food plant in Watsonville, California, in 1985–86. It discusses the historical background of the strike, the legacy of racial oppression experienced by the workers, and the importance of national pride as a mobilizing theme. Can be used by itself or as a complementary text for the film *Watsonville on Strike*.

Byerly, Victoria. 1986. *Hard Times Cotton Mill Girls: Personal Histories of Womanhood and Poverty in the South*. Ithaca, N.Y.: ILR Press.

Oral histories based on interviews with about twenty female textile workers, both black and white. Most of the autobiographical sketches are very brief and focus on personal and family issues. There is some good material on women's involvement in trade union struggles, working conditions in the mills, and the mobilization of workers around the issue of brown lung disease. Very interesting and enjoyable to read.

Duron, Clementina. 1984. "Mexican Women and Labor Conflict in Los Angeles." *Aztlan* 15, no. 1: 145–61.

Documents a strike by Mexican-American garment workers in Los Angeles in 1933. This was one of the first major strikes by Mexican-American women and did much to dispel the stereotype of Chicanas as passive and unresponsive to trade union appeals. An interesting case study, although presented in a very dry fashion and without much analysis.

Fernández Kelly, María Patricia. 1983. *For We Are Sold: Women and Industry in Mexico's Frontier*. Albany: SUNY Press.

Examines the situation of female factory workers, most of them employees of U.S. corporations, along the U.S.-Mexican border, in Ciudad Juarez. Especially recommended are chapter 4 ("Maquiladoras and the International Division of Labor"), which provides a theoretical perspective on the rise of border industries, and chapter 6 ("Maquiladoras: The View from the Inside"), an ethnographic account of factory workers' experience based on participant observation and interviews with workers. (Chapter 6 is also reprinted in *My Troubles Are Going to Have Trouble with Me: Everyday Trials and Triumphs of Women Workers*, ed. Karen B. Sacks and Dorothy Remy, 229–46. New Brunswick, N.J.: Rutgers University Press.)

Fuentes, Annette, and Barbara Ehrenreich. 1983. *Women on the Global Assembly Line*. Boston, Mass. South End Press.

A good text for showing the impact of U.S. multinational corporations on the lives of women (especially women of color) around the world. Very well written. Can be used in conjunction with the video *Global Assembly Line*. For a shorter, more journalistic piece by the same authors, see Barbara Ehrenreich and Annette Fuentes, "Life on the Global Assembly Line," *Ms.*, January 1981, 53–59. Highly recommended.

Glenn, Evelyn Nanako. 1985. "Racial Ethnic Women's Labor: The Intersection of Race, Gender, and Class Oppression." *Review of Radical Political Economics* 17, no. 3: 86–108.

Examines the work and family situations of black, Mexican-American, and Chinese-American women from the mid-nineteenth century to the present in light of Marxist-feminist and colonial labor system theories. Argues that the experiences of women of color do not fit many of the assumptions of existing theories. Examines such specific topics as the public-private split, the relative importance of domestic versus paid labor, the family as a locus of women's oppression, and the nature of reproductive labor. Recommended.

Global Assembly Line. Video recording. 1986. Los Angeles: Educational TV and Film Center.

This documentary, filmed in electronic assembly and garment factories, examines the exploitation of female workers in the free trade zones of developing countries. A good film for showing the international dimension to the exploitation and struggles of women of color. Can be used in conjunction with Fuentes and Ehrenreich, *Women on the Global Assembly Line,* or with any of the writings on the Maquiladoras (e.g., Fernández Kelly, *For We Are Sold*). Recommended.

Janiewski, Dolores E. 1985. *Sisterhood Denied: Race, Gender, and Class in a New South Community.* Philadelphia: Temple University Press.

A study of working-class women in Durham, North Carolina, based on oral history interviews, documents, and statistical data. The book is modeled after E. P. Thompson's approach to working-class history, emphasizing the cultural dimension of class formation. Especially good material on the union struggles of the 1930s. Provides an insightful analysis of both the successes and failures to achieve black-white unity. The key arguments are summarized in chapter 8, which could be read on its own. Highly recommended.

Katz, Naomi, and David S. Kemnitzer. 1984. "Women and Work in Silicon Valley: Options and Futures." In *My Troubles Are Going to Have Trouble with Me: Everyday Trials and Triumphs of Women Workers,* ed. Karen B. Sacks and Dorothy Remy, 209–18. New Brunswick, N.J.: Rutgers University Press.

This article examines the darker side of the high-tech female economy of Silicon Valley. It is based on a study of female blue-collar production workers in the Santa Clara area, most of them newly arrived Asian immigrants. Situates the growth of subcontracting and home work within the context of changes in the international economy and the corporate offensive against health and safety regulation. Raises some interesting issues concerning the relative underdevelopment of workplace activism among Asian women, compared with their high level of community activism. Recommended.

Lamphere, Louise. 1984. "On the Shop Floor: Multi-Ethnic Unity against the Conglomerate." In *My Troubles Are Going to Have Trouble With Me: Everyday Trials and Triumphs of Women Workers,* ed. Karen B. Sacks and Dorothy Remy, 247–63. New Brunswick, N.J.: Rutgers University Press.

This article examines the day-to-day processes of shop floor resistance among female workers in a New England garment factory. The focus is on the potentially divisive ethnic split among the workers and the manner in which women mobilize informal social networks to build multiethnic unity and enhance their resistance to exploitation by the company. Useful for raising the question of whether and how working-class women's forms of resistance may differ from those traditionally associated with male workers.

Lynd, Alice, and Staughton Lynd, eds. 1988. *Rank and File: Personal Histories by Working Class Organizers*, 2d ed. New York: Monthly Review Press.

This book presents a collection of interviews and personal statements by rank-and-file activists in the trade union movement. Pages 1–25, 59–80, and 103–21 tell the stories of Christine Ellis, Stella Nowicki, and Sylvia Woods, the three women interviewed in the film *Union Maids*. Not as engaging as the film but still useful as course reading.

Nash, June, and María Patricia Fernández Kelly, eds. 1983. *Women, Men, and the International Division of Labor.* Albany: SUNY Press.

This collection includes several articles on the employment of Mexican women along the U.S.-Mexican border: María Patricia Fernández Kelly, "Mexican Border Industrialization, Female Labor Force Participation, and Migration"; and Jorge A. Bustamante, "Maquiladoras: A New Face of International Capitalism in Mexico's Northern Frontier." Neither of these are ideal choices for required course readings, but both provide useful background information.

Peña, Devón Gerardo. 1980. "Las Maquiladoras: Mexican Women and Class Struggle in the Border Industries." *Aztlan* 11, no. 2: 159–229.

Examines questions of trade union strategy and class consciousness among Maquiladoras workers. Very theoretical and, for that reason, not ideal as an assigned reading but useful as a background reference for instructors.

Ruiz, Vicki L. 1987. *Cannery Women, Cannery Lives: Mexican Women, Unionization and the California Food Processing Industry, 1930–1950.* Albuquerque: University of New Mexico Press.

This book examines the trade union struggles of Mexican and Mexican-American women in the canning industry in the 1930s and 1940s. Based on interviews with former cannery workers. A good complement to works such as *Rank and File* and the film *Union Maids*. Recommended.

Ruiz, Vicki L., and Susan Tiano, eds. 1987. *Women on the U.S.-Mexican Border: Responses to Change.* Boston: Allen and Unwin.

This collection of articles examines the social situation of Mexican and Mexican-American women on both sides of the U.S.-Mexican border. Particularly useful for a social movements class are the articles by Gay Young ("Gender Identification and Working-Class Solidarity among Maquila Workers in Ciudad Juarez"), Devón Peña ("Tortuosidad: Shop Floor Struggles of Female Maquiladora Workers"), and Kathleen Staudt ("Programming Women's Empowerment: A Case from Northern Mexico").

Salt of the Earth. Motion picture. 1954. Independent Productions Corporation and the International Union of Mine, Mill, and Smelter Workers.

A somewhat didactic, but nevertheless powerful, semidocumentary drama of a strike by predominantly Mexican-American workers at a New Mexico mine. Much of the plot revolves around the efforts of the workers' wives to involve themselves more equally in the strike and the resistance that this provokes among the traditionally patriarchal male workers. An excellent film for bringing together issues of race, class, and gender. A classic.

Union Maids. Motion picture. 1976. Franklin Lakes, N.J.: New Day Films.

This documentary includes interviews with three women who were active as union organizers during the 1930s. Sylvia Woods, the African-American woman among the three, recounts her political development, beginning with her early childhood participation in the movement of Marcus Garvey. The exploitation of black women and their resistance to that exploitation is documented in her discussion of her own experiences in organizing female laundry workers. The three women interviewed in this film are also included among those interviewed in *Rank and File,* edited by Alice Lynd and Staughton Lynd, which provides a useful complementary text.

Watsonville on Strike. Video recording. 1989. Watsonville, Calif.: Migrant Media Productions.

Documents a strike by Mexican-American frozen food workers in Watsonville, California, in 1985–86. Many of the workers and union leaders are Mexican-American women. The film documents the solidarity of the Chicano community behind the strikers and how this influenced the outcome of the strike. English subtitles can be hard to read on a TV monitor.

Wilson, Michael, and Deborah Silverton Rosenfelt. 1978. *Salt of the Earth.* Screenplay by Michael Wilson. Commentary by Deborah Silverton Rosenfelt. New York: The Feminist Press.

This book provides an excellent companion volume to the film *Salt of the Earth.* The commentary by Deborah Rosenfelt examines the feminist themes of the film, provides us with historical background on the New Mexico mining region where the film was made, and profiles the Mexican-American women who participated in the film. The book also discusses the making of the film in the context of McCarthy-era blacklisting and the efforts to suppress the film once it was made. Don't show *Salt of the Earth* in your classes without reading this work. Also useful (but less insightful in my opinion) is Herbert Biberman, *Salt of the Earth: The Story of a Film* (Boston: Beacon Press, 1965).

Wong, Diane Yen-Mei, with Dennis Hayashi. 1989. "Behind Unmarked Doors: Developments in the Garment Industry." In *Making Waves: An An-*

thology of Writings by and about Asian American Women, ed. Asian Women United of California, 159–71. Boston: Beacon Press.

This article examines the working conditions and unionization struggles of Asian-American women in the garment industry, particularly in the San Francisco Bay area. Discusses the role of subcontracting in perpetuating sweatshop conditions and the special vulnerability of new Asian immigrants. Some interesting material, although the article is purely descriptive and somewhat rambling.

Zavella, Patricia. 1987. *Women's Work and Chicano Families: Cannery Workers of the Santa Clara Valley.* Ithaca, N.Y.: Cornell University Press.

An ethnographic account of Chicana cannery workers and their families, based on in-depth interviews with twenty-four women and participant observation in California canneries. Highly readable with lots of good quotes from the cannery women about the difficulties they face in the workplace and the family. Recommended.

B. The Civil Rights Movement

Cantarow, Ellen, and Susan Gushee O'Malley. 1980. "Ella Baker: Organizing for Civil Rights." In *Moving the Mountain: Working Women for Social Change,* Ellen Cantarow et al., 52–93. New York: The Feminist Press.

Presents a biography and interview with civil rights leader Ella Baker. Discusses her early work with the National Association for the Advancement of Colored People (NAACP) in the 1940s and 1950s, her association with Martin Luther King, Jr., as the executive secretary of the Southern Christian Leadership Conference, and the important role she played in the founding of the Student Nonviolent Coordinating Committee (SNCC). The personal recollections of Baker are interspersed with sections by the editors which provide historical background for the student. This reading provides a good complement to *Eyes on the Prize,* parts 3 and 5, which cover the founding of SNCC, the Mississippi voter registration drive of 1964, and the Mississippi Freedom Democratic Party. Highly recommended.

Carson, Clayborne. 1981. *In Struggle: SNCC and the Black Awakening of the 1960s.* Cambridge, Mass.: Harvard University Press.

This is the definitive work on the Student Nonviolent Coordinating Committee (SNCC), one of the most important organizations of the black civil rights movement. Covers the activities of many of the key female activists of the civil rights movement, including Ella Jo Baker, Fannie Lou Hamer, Ruby Doris Robinson, and Diane Nash. Recommended.

Eyes on the Prize: America's Civil Rights Years, 1954–1965. Video recording. 1986. Alexandria, Va.: PBS Video.

An excellent classroom resource. Covers the civil rights movement from the early 1950s through the passage of the Voting Rights Act of 1965. The role of black women is featured in part 1 (which covers Rosa Parks and the women who organized the Montgomery bus boycott), part 3 (which covers the sit-in movement, including an interview with Diane Nash), and part 5 (which covers the role of women such as Ella Baker and Fannie Lou Hamer in the Mississippi Freedom Democratic Party). Highly recommended.

Giddings, Paula. 1984. *When and Where I Enter: The Impact of Black Women on Race and Sex in America.* New York: William Morrow.

A sweeping narrative on the political activism of black women from emancipation through the 1970s. Covers such important figures as Mary Church Terrell, Ida B. Wells-Barnett, Frances Ellen Harper, Fannie Barrier Williams, Mary McLeod Bethune, and Ella Baker. Very well written. An excellent text for students.

Hamer, Fannie Lou. 1965. "Life in Mississippi." Interview by Jack O'Dell. Originally appeared in *Freedomways* magazine. Reprinted in *CALC Report* (October 1988): 8–12.

Interview with a key female leader in the civil rights movement about her upbringing in Mississippi and her activities with the Mississippi Freedom Democratic Party. A good short piece to read in conjunction with *Eyes on the Prize*, part 5.

Hampton, Henry, and Steve Fayer, with Sarah Flynn. 1990. *Voices of Freedom: An Oral History of the Civil Rights Movement from the 1950s through the 1980s.* New York: Bantam Books.

This book is an outgrowth of the *Eyes on the Prize* documentary series. It includes extended excerpts from interviews that were conducted for the film but not included in the final cut. Each chapter has a brief historical introduction by the editors, followed by the interview material. The chapter on the Montgomery bus boycott highlights the role of Jo Ann Robinson, and the chapter on the sit-in movement highlights the activities of Diane Nash. These chapters are good readings to go along with parts 1 and 3 of *Eyes on the Prize*.

McAdam, Doug. 1988. *Freedom Summer.* New York: Oxford University Press.

A history of the Mississippi voter registration campaign of the summer of 1964, based on extensive interviews with many of the participants. Particularly recommended for classroom use is chapter 3, which discusses the personal experiences and reflections of participants in the campaign. The book provides only limited detail on the role of black women within the campaign; however, there is excellent material on the broader issue of sexism within the civil rights movement and the tensions created within the movement by the intersection of racial and gender divisions. Highly recommended.

Neverdon-Morton, Cynthia. 1978. "The Black Woman's Struggle for Equality in the South, 1895–1925." In *The Afro-American Woman: Struggles and*

Images, ed. Sharon Hartley and Rosalyn Terborg-Penn, 43–57. Port Washington, N.Y.: Kennikat Press.

This article discusses the women and the women's organizations whose activities laid the foundations for the civil rights movement of the 1950s and 1960s. The article emphasizes the struggles of black women to improve educational opportunities for black students and explores some of the tensions between black and white women's groups.

Payne, Charles. 1989. "Ella Baker and Models of Social Change." *Signs* 14, no. 4: 885–99.

A thumbnail biography of Ella Baker, an influential figure in the civil rights movement. Discusses her early upbringing and her work with the NAACP, the Southern Christian Leadership Conference, and the Student Nonviolent Coordinating Committee. The article stresses Baker's distinctive approach to movement organization, which emphasized group participation and development over centralized leadership. Highly recommended.

Robinson, Jo Ann Gibson. 1987. *The Montgomery Bus Boycott and the Women Who Started It.* Ed. David J. Garrow. Knoxville: University of Tennessee Press.

The Montgomery bus boycott of 1955–56 is often heralded as one of the opening campaigns of the civil rights movement and is probably most famous for catapulting Martin Luther King, Jr. into the national spotlight. This book draws our attention to the unsung heroines of the boycott, the women of the Montgomery Women's Political Council and their leader, Jo Ann Gibson Robinson, whose organizing efforts paved the way for the Montgomery boycott and were indispensable to its success. Includes many great photos and documents. Excellent on showing the important resources that women's church and social networks provide for movement organizing. Highly recommended.

SNCC Freedom Singers, Fannie Lou Hamer et al. 1980. *Voices of the Civil Rights Movement: Black American Freedom Songs, 1960–1966.* Audio recording. Washington, D.C.: Smithsonian Institution.

Music is an important cultural resource for many protest movements. If you want to explore that topic, I recommend this recording.

West, Guida. 1981. *The National Welfare Rights Movement: The Social Protest of Poor Women.* New York: Praeger.

This study examines the National Welfare Rights Organization (NWRO) from its formation in 1966 until its demise in the late 1970s. The NWRO was made up mainly of poor black women, although middle-class blacks and some whites played important roles as leaders or allies. West presents a detailed analysis of the conflicts created by racial, class, and gender divisions within the NWRO. In discussing the internal conflicts within the organization, she highlights a number of important issues concerning movement strategy and resource mobilization. A massive study, probably not well suited for class assignment but useful as a background resource.

Williams, Juan. 1987. *Eyes on the Prize: America's Civil Rights Years, 1954–1965*. New York: Viking.

The companion volume to the *Eyes on the Prize* documentary videos. Filled with photos and interviews with participants in the civil rights movement. Chapter 3 includes an interview with Jo Ann Robinson about the Montgomery bus boycott. Chapter 5 includes an interview with Diane Nash about the student sit-in movement in Nashville. Plenty of other good material. Reads a bit like a high school civics textbook, but nevertheless recommended.

Wilson, William Julius. 1987. *The Truly Disadvantaged: The Inner City, the Underclass, and Public Policy*. Chicago: University of Chicago Press.

A good text for addressing the issue of what the civil rights movement failed to achieve, particularly in economic terms. Wilson's book is excellent as a course text. It is well written, free of jargon, and includes a good review of the literature and concise summaries at the end of each chapter. Chapter 3 ("Poverty and Family Structure") is particularly good at addressing the issues of black female poverty. Wilson effectively rebuts the notion that the increase in black female-headed households is due to welfare dependency. Highly recommended. (If you want a shorter reading to assign, a brief presentation of Wilson's thesis can be found in William Julius Wilson et al., "The Ghetto Underclass and the Changing Structure of Urban Poverty," in *Quiet Riots: Race and Poverty in the United States*, ed. Fred R. Harris and Roger W. Wilkins.

C. The Chicano Movement

Mirande, Alfredo, and Evangelina Enríquez. 1979. *La Chicana: The Mexican American Woman*. Chicago: University of Chicago Press.

A classic work on Mexican-American women. Tends to romanticize the Chicano family and is rather uncritical in its defense of machismo, but very readable and packed with historical and sociological information. Chapters cover the history of the Mexican-American people as it has affected the situation of Chicana women, women's role in the family and the workplace, and images of Chicana women in literature. Chapter 7 on Chicana feminism has a lot of good historical material on Chicana political activists.

Mora, Magdalena, and Adelaida R. Del Castillo. 1980. *Mexican Women in the United States: Struggles Past and Present*. Los Angeles: UCLA Chicano Studies Research Center.

A collection of articles on female activists in the Chicano student movement, the labor movement, and other struggles. Includes profiles of

Chicana activists and statistics on the socioeconomic situation of Mexican-American women. Particularly useful for a social movements class are the article by Patricia Hernández ("Lives of Chicana Activists"), which profiles two student activists at San Diego State University, and the article by Laurie Coyle, Gail Herschatter, and Emily Honig ("Women at Farah: An Unfinished Story"), which examines the 1972–74 strike at the Farah apparel manufacturing company in El Paso, Texas.

Pierce, Jennifer. 1984. "The Implications of Functionalism for Chicano Family Research." *Berkeley Journal of Sociology* 29:93–117.

A feminist critique of Mirande and Enriquez's classic work, *La Chicana*. Mirande is criticized for idealizing the sexual division of labor in Chicano families, for glossing over the oppressive aspects of machismo, and for relying too heavily on cultural explanations. A well-argued critique.

Sánchez, Rosaura, and Rosa Martínez Cruz, eds. 1977. *Essays on La Mujer.* Los Angeles: UCLA Chicano Studies Center.

An interesting collection of articles on Chicana women, although by now a bit dated. The most useful for a social movements class is the article by Sonia A. López ("The Role of the Chicana within the Student Movement").

D. The Farm Workers' Movement

Baer, Barbara, and Glenna Matthews. 1976. "The Women of the Boycott." In *America's Working Women: A Documentary History,* Rosalyn Baxandall, Linda Gordon, and Susan Reberly, 363–72. New York: Vintage Books.

An article based on interviews with Chicana women, including Dolores Huerta, vice president of the United Farm Workers of America (UFW). Huerta discusses her life and work with the UFW, both in organizing workers and promoting the grape boycott. Very readable. Recommended.

Cantarow, Ellen. 1980. "Jessie Lopez de la Cruz: The Battle for Farmworkers' Rights." In *Moving the Mountain: Working Women for Social Change,* Ellen Cantarow et al., 94–151. New York: The Feminist Press.

Presents a biography and interview with Jessie Lopez de la Cruz, an early organizer and leader of the United Farm Workers of America (UFW). The personal recollections of de la Cruz are interspersed with sections by the editors which provide historical background for the student. Good material on the general plight of farm workers in the United States and the social and economic situation of Chicana women in particular. Highly recommended.

New Harvest, Old Shame. Video recording. 1990. Alexandria, Va.: PBS Video.

This PBS "Frontline" documentary follows a family of Mexican-American migrant farm workers as they travel from Florida to the Midwest and back in the course of the harvest season. Comparisons with

Edward R. Morrow's classic 1960 documentary, *Harvest of Shame,* are used to show that the situation of farm workers has improved little during the last quarter-century. Examines the age and sexual division of labor within farm worker families and the special hardships and concerns of migrant women. Highly recommended.

Troubled Harvest. video recording. 1990. Available from Center for the Study of Women in Society, University of Oregon.

This locally produced video documents the hardships of Mexican farm workers in the Pacific Northwest. The video focuses on the dangerous effects of pesticide use in the fields, including their effects on female workers. Well made but tends to present farm workers purely as victims without giving sufficient attention to their struggles of resistance. For that reason I prefer either *New Harvest, Old Shame* or *Wrath of Grapes* for a social movements class.

Wrath of Grapes. Video recording. 1988. United Farm Workers of America.

This documentary by the United Farm Workers (UFW) illustrates the dangers of pesticide use in the production of grapes and other commercial crops. Includes interviews with Mexican-American women about their health problems induced by pesticides. The film emphasizes the dangers to children and pregnant women from exposure to pesticides and calls for tighter regulation and support for the UFW grape boycott. Recommended.

E. The Women's Movement

Collins, Patricia Hill. 1989. "The Social Construction of Black Feminist Thought." *Signs* 14, no. 4: 745–73.

Collins argues that black women in America have developed a distinctive consciousness regarding their oppression, based on their own unique experience. She shows how, in the course of struggle, black women have developed a different view of themselves and their world than that offered by the established social order. The paper then sketches the contours of what Collins calls an "Afrocentric feminist epistemology." These themes are developed in greater detail and more concretely in Collins's book, *Black Feminist Thought.*

———. 1990. *Black Feminist Thought. Knowledge, Consciousness, and the Politics of Empowerment.* Boston: Unwin Hyman.

Examines a number of feminist issues from the perspective of how well feminist theory addresses the situation of black women. The topics include women's work, the family, domestic labor, sexual politics, patriarchal ideology, and lesbian rights. Particularly useful for a social movements course is chapter 7 ("Rethinking Black Women's Activism"), which argues that the activism of black women often takes forms that are ignored by traditional social movement theory—for example, community building, teaching, and church work.

Davis, Angela. 1983. *Women, Race, and Class.* New York: Vintage Books.

Davis traces the history of the relationship between the women's movement, the black struggle, and the working-class movement in America. With regard to the contemporary women's movement, she shows how a number of goals that white feminists take for granted (e.g., the campaign against rape or the promotion of birth control) appear somewhat differently from the perspective of black women. Recommended.

Evans, Sarah. 1979. *Personal Politics: The Roots of Women's Liberation in the Civil Rights Movement and the New Left.* New York: Vintage Books.

Examines the important role that women played in the civil rights movement and the New Left and how the disillusionment they experienced within those male-dominated movements led to the rise of the women's liberation movement. Evans focuses mainly on the experience of white women, although the book also touches on the role of black women within the student wing of the civil rights movement. An excellent book for any course that deals with both civil rights and the women's movement.

García, Alma M. 1989. "The Development of Chicana Feminist Discourse, 1970–1980." *Gender and Society* 3, no. 2: 217–38.

Discusses the development of Chicana feminism in relation to the ideology of cultural nationalism, the dominant ideology of the Chicano movement. Garcia examines the obstacles to Chicana feminist organizing created by the emphasis on national unity, feminist bashing within the Chicano movement, and the problematic relationship between Chicanas and the white feminist movement. Also includes comparisons with the experience of Asian-American and African-American feminists.

Gonzales, Sylvia. 1977. "The White Feminist Movement: The Chicana Perspective." *Social Science Journal* 14, no. 2: 67–76.

This article discusses the unique cultural factors that inhibit feminist organizing among Chicana women as well as the tendency of white feminist organizations to marginalize Chicana women and their concerns. Well written but not much depth to the analysis. Consuelo Nieto ("The Chicana and the Women's Rights Movement") covers the same issues much better, in my opinion.

hooks, bell. 1984. *Feminist Theory: From Margin to Center.* Boston: South End Press.

This book surveys a wide range of issues in contemporary feminist theory from the perspective of a black feminist. hooks raises many good points concerning feminist theory and feminist strategy, although the sharpness of her critique makes this a less-than-ideal text for students who are new to feminism and feminist debates.

King, Deborah K. 1988. "Multiple Jeopardy, Multiple Consciousness: The Context of Black Feminist Ideology." *Signs* 14, no. 1: 42–72.

An excellent article that raises questions about the "multiple oppression" model of class, race, and gender for its essentially additive approach to understanding the oppression of black women. King argues that we must look more closely at the interaction between different forms of oppression and the tensions that these create with different social movements. This theme is developed concretely by examining the history of black women's relationship to the civil rights movement, the feminist movement, and the labor movement. Recommended.

Lewis, Diane K. 1977. "A Response to Inequality: Black Women, Racism, and Sexism." *Signs* 3, no. 2: 339–61.

This article examines the reasons for black women's initial tendency to reject identification with the women's movement as well as the factors that eventually led to a more favorable reaction to feminism. Lewis argues that black feminism was encouraged by the fact that black women did not share equally in the gains of the civil rights movement.

Nieto, Consuelo. 1974. "The Chicana and the Women's Rights Movement: A Perspective." *Civil Rights Digest* 6, no. 3: 36–42.

An early article that discusses the problems of enlisting Chicana women in the feminist movement. Nieto discusses issues of the Mexican-American family, the Catholic church, the perception of feminism as divisive within the Chicano community, and the feelings of marginality among Chicanas active in the women's movement. Recommended.

Sacks, Karen Brodkin. "Toward a Unified Theory of Class, Race, and Gender." *American Ethnologist* 16, no. 3: 534–50.

This article by a leading feminist theorist examines the weaknesses of traditional (Marxist) concepts of class and explores the possibilities for more adequately dealing with issues of race and gender within class theory. Sacks reviews a wide range of contemporary feminist writings, especially those of Marxist- or socialist-feminists. She argues that the concept of the working class must be reformulated to encompass both waged and unwaged work and the community relations within which these take place. A provocative article, but it may be a bit abstract for most students.

Terborg-Penn, Rosalyn. 1978. "Discrimination against Afro-American Women in the Woman's Movement." In *The Afro-American Woman: Struggles and Images*, ed. Sharon Hartley and Rosalyn Terborg-Penn, 17–27. Port Washington, N.Y.: Kennikat Press.

This article examines the important role that black women played within the early women's movement as well as the discrimination they experienced within the movement. Touches on such important figures as Sojourner Truth, Frances Ellen Harper, Mary Church Terrell, and Ida B. Wells-Barnett. Brief but informative.

Focus on Puerto Rican Studies

AN INTERDISCIPLINARY GUIDE FOR RESEARCH AND CURRICULUM ON PUERTO RICAN WOMEN

Edna Acosta-Belén, Christine E. Bose, and Barbara R. Sjostrom

INTRODUCTION

An Interdisciplinary Guide for Research and Curriculum on Puerto Rican Women has been developed as part of the project "Integrating Puerto Rican Women into the Curriculum and Research," funded with a grant from the Ford Foundation Mainstreaming Minority Women's Studies program and a grant from the New York State United University Professors Labor-Management Committees, awarded to the Center for Latin America and the Caribbean (CELAC) and the Institute for Research on Women (IROW) at the University at Albany, State University of New York (SUNY). The guide contains information on issues, strategies, and priorities for integrating class, race, ethnicity, and gender into the curriculum and research based on a two-day conference on the topic, followed by a two-day SUNY Faculty Development Seminar on Puerto Rican women held at the University at Albany in June 1991.

These activities centered on efforts to provide a theoretical and methodological framework for developing and/or revising curriculum and formulating research projects dealing with women of color in general and Puerto Rican women in particular in the Humanities and Social Sciences. The overall focus of the University at Albany project was to provide the knowledge and strategies to translate theory into practice.*

This guide utilizes the single-group approach to curriculum integration,

Edna Acosta-Belén is Distinguished Service Professor in the Department of Latin American and Caribbean Studies at University at Albany, SUNY. Christine E. Bose is Associate Professor in the Department of Sociology at University at Albany, SUNY. Barbara R. Sjostrom is Associate Professor in the Department of Curriculum and Instruction at Rowan College of New Jersey.

with a primary emphasis on Puerto Rican women. The basic principles and strategies that serve as a framework to this guide can, however, be applied across disciplines and groups. As such, the guide is intended to be exemplary rather than all encompassing. In other words, the information contained herein includes *samples* of concepts, objectives, activities, and resources and does not purport to be exhaustive.

It is our hope that the guide will serve as a blueprint for revising and reconceptualizing courses or developing new ones, and in promoting or facilitating research that reflects some of the included themes. The unique feature of the current guide is its emphasis on the actual process of curriculum revision/development and knowledge transformation rather than a focus on content information about Puerto Rican women.

PURPOSE OF THE GUIDE The objectives of *An Interdisciplinary Guide for Research and Curriculum on Puerto Rican Woman* are twofold: (1) to assist Humanities and Social Science faculty in the development and/or revision of courses that integrate the dialectics of class, race, and gender or content material on Puerto Rican women; and (2) to facilitate this integration in the formulation of research proposals and projects.

In this guide we take our departure from the notion that, in order to approach the process of curriculum and research inclusion and knowledge transformation about women of color, information and a basic understanding of the following concepts is required:

- colonialism/neocolonialism
- content-specific curriculum
- culture contact/acculturation
- decolonization
- exclusion versus omission
- gender diversity
- hegemony/subordination
- linguistic diversity
- multicultural diversity
- otherness/alterity
- patriarchy
- universality/particularism

Within the stated broad goals three major questions framed the University at Albany project:

1. In what ways has the new scholarship on women and people of color questioned, challenged, or modified concepts, theories, and methods that have been used traditionally in a particular discipline?
2. What resources and strategies have been used successfully to formulate

research and revise curricula to integrate gender, class, race, and ethnicity in higher education?
3. How can theoretical and methodological approaches be used, or revised, to promote curriculum integration on Puerto Rican women or people of color in general across the disciplines?

STRUCTURE OF THE GUIDE The basic structure of the guide consists of nine thematic units derived from: (1) a review of the literature and curricular materials in various disciplines; (2) topics from a content analysis of syllabi and research projects, including those submitted by faculty members who participated in the SUNY Faculty Development Seminar at the University at Albany; and (3) a format including key concepts, objectives, discussion questions, suggested instructional strategies and activities, resources, and a tenth unit of demographic data profiles for use across the disciplines.

STEPS FOR THE DEVELOPMENT/REVISION PROCESS OF COURSE SYLLABI

The first step in the curriculum integration process is to review curricular offerings in the Humanities and Social Sciences and determine which courses would be appropriately targeted. Several considerations should be kept in mind. The first is that we are looking for the integration of issues related in this case to Puerto Rican women throughout the curriculum. Therefore, it is important to avoid selecting only those courses in which the content deals specifically with women or Puerto Rican women. Second, it is important to stress the *interdisciplinary* nature of the process. Therefore, selection should not be limited to courses that primarily focus on the targeted group(s) (e.g., Latino Cultures, Introduction to Women's Studies). Also, keep in mind that integration is applicable to many different groups and disciplines, and, while this guide is about Puerto Rican women, the process described herein is transferable across groups and disciplines.

Once appropriate courses have been selected the second step of the development/revision process calls for gathering and reviewing information on the group itself. This can be accomplished by referring to the Demographic Data section of this guide as well as to the recommended readings and materials bibliographies provided for each unit.

The third step involves the development/revision of a course syllabus that integrates information about Puerto Rican women according to the particular discipline. This entails writing a course description with key concepts, objectives, discussion questions, instructional strategies and resources. (Refer to units for sample format.)

The last step entails planning for course implementation and evaluation. This guide will facilitate the process by providing: (1) basic statistical information on Puerto Rican women; (2) an interdisciplinary bibliography with books, articles, films, and other sources; and (3) innovative instructional strategies that represent current trends for assessing student outcomes (e.g., portfolios, reflective journals, film reviews, ethnographic interviews, photographic essays, participatory videos, oral histories, role playing, cultural identity profiles, diaries, reaction papers, cooperative learning projects).

ALBANY PR-WOMENET DATABASE

Under the initiative of CELAC and IROW, the University at Albany now holds the PR-WOMENET Database, a major interdisciplinary bibliographic source on Puerto Rican women's research. A printed edition of *Albany PR-WOMENET Database: An Interdisciplinary Annotated Bibliography on Puerto Rican Women*, by Edna Acosta-Belén and Christine E. Bose, with Anne Roschelle (Albany: CELAC/IROW, 1991), is available to the public and updated annually. This volume represents the most complete reference tool on Puerto Rican women to date.

UNIT 1   THE DIALECTICS OF CLASS, RACE, ETHNICITY, AND GENDER

Disciplinary Area: Social Sciences

Key Concepts:

- colonization
- discrimination
- feminist theory
- gender roles
- knowledge transformation
- machismo
- marianismo
- *mestizaje*
- migration
- oppression
- prejudice
- race relations
- racism
- socialization
- stratification

General Objectives

1. To analyze the relationship between gender, race, class and ethnicity/ nationality as related to Puerto Rican women in the United States and on the Island
2. To analyze the different meanings of race and ethnicity for the U.S. and Island contexts
3. To explore the impact of Spanish and U.S. colonization on the Puerto Rican people
4. To compare and contrast gender roles for Puerto Rican women throughout various periods of history
5. To discuss the impact of commuter migration on the status of Puerto Rican women
6. To analyze the issue of race as a compounding element to Puerto Rican women's oppression within the context of U.S. society
7. To examine the socioeconomic status and productive roles of Puerto Rican women in both the U.S. and Island contexts

8. To examine the changing stratification system in Puerto Rico over time and women's place in it
9. To study the evolution of feminist theory and its impact on scholarship about Puerto Rican women
10. To analyze the impact of feminist theory on transforming knowledge about women of color in general.

Discussion Questions

1. Using the concepts of machismo and marianismo, discuss the nature of women's roles in contemporary Puerto Rican society and the United States. Include changes in roles during the past few decades for women in general and Puerto Rican women in particular.
2. What influence has the colonial status of Puerto Rico had on the status of women? Use the work of Acosta-Belén, Azize, Rivera, and Ríos to guide the discussion (see Recommended Readings at the end of each unit).
3. What impact do mass migration from Puerto Rico to the United States and the prevalent commuter migration pattern have on Puerto Rican male and female sex roles?
4. How have the racial definitions used in the United States added a compounding element to Puerto Rican women's oppression?
5. How has social class shaped different forms of women's activism in the United States and on the Island?
6. What has been the impact of feminist theory on the transformation of knowledge regarding Puerto Rican women? Use Minnich's book as a broad theoretical framework for the discussion.

Instructional Strategies

1. *Film Review:* Have students review a film with a theme that centers on differential treatment of people based on gender, social, or racial/ethnic status. Students will then prepare a film review that addresses a series of structured questions.

   The format for the film review includes: (a) a brief synopsis of the plot; (b) an overview of the film's major themes; (c) an analysis of how a particular character was treated differently because of race, age, ethnicity, sexual preference, et cetera; (d) a reaction to the film from the student's own perspective as a cultural being; and (e) an analysis of what was gained from viewing the film from a multicultural perspective.

   Sample guide questions to facilitate the activity include: (a) Does the film offer a positive or negative image of cultures or groups portrayed? (b) Does it illustrate basic commonalities across all groups of people without making value judgments? (c) Does it appear to present factual information objectively? (d) Does it portray one segment of the population and their activities as representative of the entire culture or country? (e) Does it present information in a balanced and unambiguous way? (f) Does it explore intergroup conflict and tension in a balanced and objective manner? (Adapted from J. N. Hawkins and J. Maksik, *Teacher's Resource Handbook for African Studies* [Los Angeles: UCLA, 1976].)

2. *Critical Essay:* Summarize the essence of feminist phase theory to develop a gender-balanced multicultural curriculum using the essay by Thompson Tetreault. Select the model with which you are most comfortable and explain why this model appeals to you and how you could apply it in your own work.

or

Analyze the works of Minnich, Collins, or Giddings. Outline their major contributions to the field of feminist theory and how these could be applied to the study of Puerto Rican women.

or

Write an essay that highlights the milestones in the evolution of feminist theory. Include some of the obstacles encountered and how these were dealt with. Finally, discuss the progress made and its impact on contemporary scholarship on Puerto Rican women in the United States and on the Island.

Recommended Readings

Acosta-Belén, Edna. Forthcoming. *In the Shadow of the Giant: Colonialism, Migration, and Puerto Rican Culture.* Philadelphia: Temple University Press.

———. 1986. "Puerto Rican Women in Culture, History, and Society." In *The Puerto Rican Woman: Perspectives on Culture, History, and Society,* ed. Edna Acosta-Belén, 1–29. New York: Praeger.

Amott, Teresa, and Julie Matthaei. 1991. *Race, Gender, and Work: A Multi-Cultural Economic History of Women in the United States.* Boston: South End Press.

Azize Vargas, Yamila. 1990. "The Roots of Puerto Rican Feminism." *Radical America* 23, no. 1: 71–80.

Banks, James A., and Cherry A. McGee Banks, eds. 1986. *Multicultural Education: Issues and Perspectives.* Boston: Allyn and Bacon.

Butler, Johnnella E. 1986. "Transforming the Curriculum: Teaching about Women of Color." In *Multicultural Education: Issues and Perspectives,* ed. James A. Banks and Cherry A. McGee Banks, 145–63. Boston: Allyn and Bacon.

Centro de Estudios Puertorriqueños History Task Force. 1979. *Labor Migration under Capitalism.* New York: Monthly Review Press.

Collins, Patricia Hill. 1990. *Black Feminist Thought.* Boston: Unwyn Hyman.

Duley, Margot I., and Mary I. Edwards, eds. 1986. *The Cross Cultural Study of Women.* New York: The Feminist Press.

Giddings, Paula. 1984. *When and Where I Enter . . . : The Impact of Black Women on Race and Sex in America.* New York: William Morrow.

Hull, Gloria T., Patricia Bell Scott, and Barbara Smith, eds. 1982. *All the Women Are White, All the Blacks Are Men, but Some of Us Are Brave.* New York: The Feminist Press.

Jorge, Angela. 1986. "The Black Puerto Rican Woman in Contemporary American Society." In *The Puerto Rican Woman: Perspectives on Culture, History, and Society,* ed. Edna Acosta-Belén, 180–88. New York: Praeger.

Minnich, Elizabeth Kamarck. 1990. *Transforming Knowledge.* Philadelphia: Temple University Press.

Ortiz, Altagracia. 1988. "The Labor Struggles of Puerto Rican Women in the Garment Industry of New York City, 1920–1960." *Cimarrón* 1, no. 3: 39–59.

———. 1989–90. "The Lives of the Pioneras." *Centro de Estudios Puertorriqueños Bulletin* 2, no. 7: 41–47.

Ríos, Palmira. 1983. "Women under Colonialism: The Case of Puerto Rico." *TransAfrica Forum* 2, no. 1: 9–20.

Rivera, Marcia. 1986. "The Development of Capitalism in Puerto Rico and the Incorporation of Women into the Labor Force." In *The Puerto Rican Woman: Perspectives on Culture, History, and Society,* ed. Edna Acosta-Belén, 30–45. New York: Praeger.

———. 1980. "Educational Policy and Female Labor." In *The Intellectual Roots of Independence,* ed. Iris Zavala and Rafael Rodríguez, 349–53. New York: Monthly Review Press.

Rodríguez, Clara. 1989. *Puerto Ricans Born in the U.S.A.* Boston: Unwyn Hyman.

———. 1984. "Prisms of Race and Class." *Journal of Ethnic Studies* 12:99–120.

———. 1979. "Economic Factors Affecting Puerto Ricans in New York." In *Labor Migration under Capitalism,* Centro de Estudios Puertorriqueños History Task Force, 197–222. New York: Monthly Review Press.

———. 1973. *The Ethnic Queue in the United States: The Case of Puerto Ricans.* San Francisco: R&E Research Associates.

Sánchez Korrol, Virginia. 1983. *From Colonia to Community: The History of Puerto Ricans in New York City, 1917–1948.* Westport, Conn.: Greenwood Press.

Stevens, Evelyn P. 1973. "Marianismo: The Other Face of Machismo in Latin America." In *Female and Male in Latin America,* ed. Ann Pescatello, 89–101. Pittsburgh: University of Pittsburgh Press.

Thompson Tetreault, Mary Kay. 1986. "Integrating Content about Women and Gender into the Curriculum." In *Multicultural Education: Issues and*

Perspectives, ed. James A. Banks and Cherry A. McGee Banks, 124–44. Boston: Allyn and Bacon.

Vázquez Calzada, José L. 1979. "Demographic Aspects of Migration." In *Labor Migration under Capitalism*, Centro de Estudios Puertorriqueños History Task Force, 223–38. New York: Monthly Review Press.

UNIT 2   RESTORING WOMEN IN HISTORY: THE ISLAND AND U.S. EXPERIENCES

Disciplinary Area: Humanities/Social Sciences (History)

Key Concepts:

• colonization
• industrialization
• labor movement
• migration
• patriarchy
• slavery
• suffrage movement
• women's organizations

General Objectives

1. To explore the impact of various cultures (e.g., African, European, and Indian) on Puerto Rican society
2. To study the history of the feminist, women's, and suffrage movements in Puerto Rico
3. To study women's contributions to the formation and development of the U.S. Puerto Rican community
4. To explore the impact of socialization and U.S. colonialism on the Island on the definition of gender roles for Puerto Rican women in the domestic, agricultural, and industrial labor force
5. To study the evolution of Puerto Rican women's/feminist organizations in Puerto Rico and the United States and explore their impact on issues of women's rights and equity
6. To examine the role of Puerto Rican women activists in the labor movement for the U.S. and Island contexts.

Discussion Questions

1. How did Spanish and U.S. colonialism in Puerto Rico affect women both in the domestic sphere and wage labor force during various periods of history?
2. What impact did the U.S. takeover of Puerto Rico have on the overall status of women on the Island?
3. What trends developed in the suffrage movement in Puerto Rico along class lines, and who were the key proponents?
4. What was significant about the suffrage movement in Puerto Rico as compared to the United States, and what changes did it bring about for women?
5. What have been the role and goals of women's organizations in contemporary Puerto Rican society?

Instructional Strategies

1. *Essays, diaries, or letters:* Have students read an essay by Luisa Capetillo or by another female Puerto Rican writer. Then have them do a content analysis of its themes within the context of women's and workers' rights, feminism, or women's position in society. It is useful to have structured guide questions for students from which they can analyze the texts.
2. *Role playing:* Have students assume the position of a notable Puerto Rican woman in history (e.g., Lolita Lebrón). They should read about her life first and focus on a salient theme (e.g., women's involvement in political movements). Then have students select an article from the *New York Times* or other newspaper on the topic in question. Have them respond to the article the way they believe the person selected would have. Finally, have them write an editorial to the newspaper on behalf of that figure.

Recommended Readings

Acosta-Belén, Edna. 1986. "Puerto Rican Women in Culture, History, and Society." In *The Puerto Rican Woman: Perspectives on Culture, History, and Society,* ed. Edna Acosta-Belén, 1–29. New York: Praeger.

———. 1980. "Women in Twentieth Century Puerto Rico." In *Puerto Rico and Puerto Ricans,* ed. Adalberto López, 273–82. Cambridge, Mass.: Schenkman.

Andreu Iglesias, César, ed. 1984. *Memoirs of Bernardo Vega.* Trans. by Juan Flores. New York: Monthly Review Press.

Azize Vargas, Yamila. 1990. "The Roots of Puerto Rican Feminism: The Struggle for Universal Suffrage." *Radical America* 23, no. 1: 71–80.

Baerga, María del Carmen. 1984. "Wages, Consumption, and Survival:

Working-Class Households in Puerto Rico in the 1930s." In *Households and the World Economy*, ed. Joan Smith, Immanuel Wallerstein, and Hans-Dieter Evers, 233–51. Beverly Hills: Sage.

Barceló Miller, María de F. 1991. "Colonialism, Party Politics, and the Women's Suffrage Movement in Puerto Rico in the 1920s." Paper presented at Seminar on "Integrating Puerto Rican Women into the Curriculum and Research," SUNY-Albany, June.

Bean, Frank D., and Marta Tienda. 1987. *The Hispanic Population of the United States*. New York: Sage.

Benmayor, Rina, Ana Juarbe, Celia Alvarez, and Blanca Vázquez. 1987. *Stories to Live By: Continuity and Change in Three Generations of Puerto Rican Women*. New York: Centro de Estudios Puertorriqueños.

López, Alfredo. 1987. *Doña Licha's Island: Modern Colonialism in Puerto Rico*. Boston: South End Press.

Meléndez, Edwin, Clara Rodríguez, and Janis Barry-Figueroa, eds. 1991. *Hispanics in the Labor Force: Issues and Policies*. New York: Plenum Press.

Ortiz, Altagracia. 1989–90. "The Lives of the Pioneras: Bibliographic and Research Sources on Puerto Rican Women in the United States." *Centro de Estudios Puertorriqueños Bulletin* 2, no. 7: 41–47.

Picó, Isabel. 1980. "The History of Women's Struggle for Equality in Puerto Rico." In *Sex and Class in Latin America*, ed. June Nash and Helen I. Safa, 202–13. South Hadley, Mass.: Bergin Publishers.

Rivera, Marcia. 1980a. "The Incorporation of Women into the Wage Labor Force during the First Decades of the Twentieth Century." In *The Intellectual Roots of Independence*, ed. Iris Zavala and Rafael Rodríguez, 344–48. New York: Monthly Review Press.

———. 1980b. "Puerto Rican Women in the Economic and Social Processes of the Twentieth Century." In *The Intellectual Roots of Independence*, ed. Iris Zavala and Rafael Rodríguez, 337–43. New York: Monthly Review Press.

Sánchez Korrol, Virginia. 1990. "In Search of Unconventional Women: Histories of Puerto Rican Women in Religious Vocations before Mid-Century." In *Unequal Sisters: A Multicultural Reader in U.S. Women's History*, ed. Carol DuBois and Vicki L. Ruiz, 322–32. New York: Routledge.

———. 1986. "The Forgotten Migrant: Educated Puerto Rican Women in New York City." In *The Puerto Rican Woman: Perspectives on Culture, History, and Society*, ed. Edna Acosta-Belén, 170–79. New York: Praeger.

———. 1980. "Survival of Puerto Rican Women in New York before WWII." In *The Puerto Rican Struggle: Essays on Survival in the United States*, ed. Clara Rodríguez, Virginia Sánchez Korrol, and José Alers, 47–57. Maplewood, N.J.: Waterfront Press.

———. 1979. "On the Other Side of the Ocean: The Work Experiences of Early Puerto Rican Migrant Women." *Caribbean Review* 8, no. 1: 22–28.

Silvestrini, Blanca. 1986. "Women as Workers: The Experience of Puerto Rican Women in the 1930s." In *The Puerto Rican Woman: Perspectives on Culture, History, and Society,* ed. Edna Acosta-Belén, 59–74. New York: Praeger.

Valle, Norma. 1986. "Feminism and Its Influence on Women's Organizations in Puerto Rico." In *The Puerto Rican Woman: Perspectives on Culture, History, and Society,* ed. Edna Acosta-Belén, 75–87. New York: Praeger.

UNIT 3   POLITICAL ECONOMY: WOMEN AND WORK

Disciplinary Area: Social Sciences

Key Concepts:

- demographics
- division of labor
- feminization of poverty
- fertility
- head of household
- income
- inequality
- poverty
- socioeconomic status
- sterilization
- stratification
- work force

General Objectives

1. To explore the socioeconomic status and productive roles of Puerto Rican women both on the Island and in the United States
2. To examine the occupational profile for Puerto Rican women in the United States and on the Island and the similarities and/or differences between both
3. To analyze the impact of migration on the inclusion of Puerto Rican women in traditional or nontraditional roles in the labor force on the Island and in the United States
4. To examine how the demographic patterns of Puerto Rican women (e.g., marital status, age, education, fertility) in the United States and Island work force are related to the variables of income and the occupational or household division of labor

5. To examine the impact of changing household structures on women's income and poverty in the United States and on the Island
6. To analyze the impact of discrimination on Puerto Rican women in the work force (e.g., overrepresentation in particular occupations).

Discussion Questions

1. What has been the impact of capitalist development on the structural placement of women?
2. What has been the impact of industrialization on Puerto Rican women's labor force participation in Puerto Rico as compared with the United States?
3. How has women's productive work in the home or in the informal economy been analyzed by economic theory?
4. How has the contemporary women's movement influenced gender politicization for Puerto Rican women in the United States and on the Island?
5. How has mass sterilization had an impact on Puerto Rican women within the political and economic spheres?
6. How have political and economic spheres influenced sterilization policies?
7. How have different economic conditions in Puerto Rico and various parts of the United States influenced women's migration for jobs?

Instructional Strategies

1. *Photographic Essay:* Select a theme (e.g., street vendors, women in the garment industry) and either collect or take photographs representative of the theme. You can choose a particular historical period or focus on contemporary society as a point of reference. Write a description of each photograph and an essay that explains the theme. Include a brief description of the theme, the context variables, a summary and analysis of the events, findings, and conclusions.
2. *Oral Histories:* Select an example of the oral history of a Puerto Rican woman (e.g., coffee picker, tobacco stripper, garment worker). The oral histories are meant to sketch women's lives in the home, workplace, or community in order to provide a better understanding of their functions and experiences in their particular milieu. (See Benmayor et al., *Stories to Live By: Continuity and Change in Three Generations of Puerto Rican Women.*)

    Study the format and content of the oral history. Then identify someone with extensive experience in a particular occupation and develop that person's oral history. Use a structured interview format to collect data.

Recommended Readings

Acevedo, Luz del Alba. 1990. "Industrialization and Employment: Changes in the Patterns of Women's Work in Puerto Rico." *World Development* 18, no. 2: 231–55.

Barry Figueroa, Janis. 1991. "A Comparison of Labor Supply Behavior among Single and Married Puerto Rican Mothers." In *Hispanics in the Labor Force: Issues and Policies*, ed. Edwin Meléndez, Clara Rodríguez, and Janis Barry Figueroa, 183–202. New York: Plenum Press.

Benmayor, Rina, Ana Juarbe, Celia Alvarez, and Blanca Vázquez, eds. 1987. *Stories to Live By: Continuity and Change in Three Generations of Puerto Rican Women*. New York: Centro de Estudios Puertorriqueños.

Bose, Christine E. 1986. "Puerto Rican Women in the United States: An Overview." In *The Puerto Rican Woman: Perspectives on Culture, History, and Society*, ed. Edna Acosta-Belén, 147–69. New York: Praeger.

Colón, Alice. 1991. "Industrial Restructuring or Shattering Developmentalist Illusions: Employment, Joblessness, and Poverty among Puerto Rican Women in the Island and the Middle Atlantic Region." Paper presented at Seminar on "Integrating Puerto Rican Women into the Curriculum and Research," SUNY-Albany, June.

Petrovich, Janice, and Sandra Laureano. 1986–87. "Towards an Analysis of Puerto Rican Women in the Informal Economy." *Homines* 2, no. 10: 70–81.

Presser, Harriet. 1980. "Puerto Rico: Recent Trends in Fertility and Sterilization." *Family Planning Perspectives* 12, no. 2: 102–6.

Ramírez de Arellano, Annette, and Conrad Seipp. 1983. *Colonialism, Catholicism, and Contraception: A History of Birth Control in Puerto Rico*. Chapel Hill: University of North Carolina Press.

Santana Cooney, Rosemary, and Alice Colón Warren. 1980. "The Recent Struggle of Puerto Rican Females." In *The Puerto Rican Struggle: Essays on Survival in the United States*, ed. Clara Rodríguez, Virginia Sánchez Korrol, and José Alers, 58–73. Maplewood, N.J.; Waterfront Press.

Weller, Robert H. 1968. "A Historical Analysis of Female Labour Force Participation in Puerto Rico." *Social and Economic Studies* 17, no. 1: 60–69.

Recommended Films

Manos a la Obra: The Story of Operation Bootstrap (1983; color documentary; 59 mins.). Distributed by the Cinema Guild, 1697 Broadway, New York, NY 10019; (212) 246-5522. An in-depth analysis of the impact of the industrialization program "Operation Boostrap" undertaken in Puerto Rico in the 1950s. The model, which was the cornerstone of the colonial Commonwealth government and was primarily dependent on U.S. capital, has been used by the United States as a development showcase for other Third World countries. The film tries to discern between the government's propaganda and the socioeconomic realities of Puerto Ricans on the Island and those who have migrated to the United States.

Puerto Rico: Paradise Invaded (1987; color documentary; 30 mins.). Distributed by the Cinema Guild. This documentary examines the historical and contemporary colonial relationship between Puerto Rico and the United States and the socioeconomic, cultural, and political impact of U.S. control of the Island. The views of workers and proponents of independence are also presented through interviews.

UNIT 4 FAMILY AND GENDER ROLES

Disciplinary Area: Social Sciences (Sociology, Psychology)

Key Concepts:

- child rearing
- divorce
- family
- gender roles
- head of household
- heterosexism
- household division of labor
- religion
- sexual orientation
- socialization

General Objectives

1. To describe traditional and changing gender roles for Puerto Rican women on the Island and in the United States
2. To analyze the family structure for Puerto Ricans on the Island and in the United States in relation to the economic structure and women's participation in it
3. To analyze the significant increase of Puerto Rican women as heads of household both on the Island and in the United States
4. To analyze the influence of traditional gender roles on attitudes toward homosexuality and lesbianism in Puerto Rico and the United States
5. To explore issues related to sexual orientation for Puerto Rican women in the United States and on the Island

6. To examine the importance of Catholicism, Protestantism, and alternative religious practices such as *santería* and *espiritismo* on Puerto Rican women

7. To examine how development and industrialization correlates with increases in sterilization, divorce, and a decline in fertility for Puerto Rican women.

Discussion Questions

1. What are the traditional gender roles for Puerto Rican women on the Island and in the United States?
2. How do the gender roles historically ascribed to Puerto Rican women influence child-rearing practices on the Island and in the United States?
3. What are the similarities and/or differences in Puerto Rican women's roles in the United States as compared with the Island?
4. How do the attitudes toward or the experience of homosexuals and lesbians differ between Puerto Rico and the United States?
5. What are the primary religions practiced by Puerto Ricans on the Island and in the United States? Have there been changes in the religious orientation in light of U.S. domination on the Island and migration patterns?

Instructional Strategies

1. *Reflective Journal:* Have students read materials related to family and gender roles over the course of the semester. Then have them reflect on the materials using the following format: (a) a brief summary of the content of materials dealing with this topic; (b) questions or ideas generated by the materials; (c) any new concepts that surfaced from the materials; (d) subjective reactions to the content; and (e) comments on what they learned from the process of keeping a thematic journal.

2. *Timeline:* Have students develop a historical timeline that traces the evolution of gender roles for Puerto Rican women from the precolonial period to the present. On the timeline they will highlight major changes (e.g., women's suffrage). To facilitate the project students should group issues by period, conduct a content analysis of information gathered, and decide what to include. Timelines should represent history in abbreviated form.

Recommended Readings

Comas-Díaz, Lillian. 1988. "Mainland Puerto Rican Women: A Sociocultural Approach." *Journal of Community Psychology* 16, no. 1: 21–31.

Hidalgo, Hilda, and Elia Hidalgo Christensen. 1979. "The Puerto Rican Cultural Response to Female Homosexuality." In *The Puerto Rican Woman:*

Perspectives on Culture, History, and Society, ed. Edna Acosta-Belén, 110–23. New York: Praeger.

Miranda King, Lourdes. 1979. "Puertorriqueñas in the United States: The Impact of Double Discrimination." In *The Puerto Rican Woman: Perspectives on Culture, History, and Society,* ed. Edna Acosta-Belén, 124–33. New York: Praeger.

Muñoz Vázquez, Marya. 1986. "The Effects of Role Expectations on the Marital Status of Puerto Rican Women." In *The Puerto Rican Woman: Perspectives on Culture, History, and Society,* ed. Edna Acosta-Belén, 110–19. New York: Praeger.

Ramos, Juanita, ed. 1987. *Compañeras: Latina Lesbians.* New York: Latina Lesbian History Project.

Rodríguez Cortés, Sonia. 1986–87. "Socio-Cultural Religious Background of Puerto Rican Women." *Homines* 10, no. 4: 277–88.

Santana Cooney, Rosemary, Lloyd H. Rogler, Rosemarie Hurrell, and Vilma Ortiz. 1982. "Decision Making in Intergenerational Puerto Rican Families." *Journal of Marriage and the Family* 44: 621–31.

Tienda, Marta, and Jennifer Glass. 1985. "Household Structure and Labor Force Participation of Black, Hispanic, and White Mothers." *Demography* 22, no. 3: 381–94.

Zambrana, Ruth, ed. 1982. *Work, Family, and Health: Latina Women in Transition.* New York: Hispanic Research Center.

UNIT 5   THE PSYCHOLOGY OF WOMEN

Disciplinary Area: Social Sciences (Psychology)

Key Concepts:

- cultural identity
- enculturation
- manipulation strategies
- marginalization
- personal autonomy/assertiveness
- prejudice
- race relations
- self-concept
- socialization
- stereotypes
- stress
- value orientations

General Objectives

1. To study the enculturation and socialization processes as they affect Puerto Rican women's development
2. To analyze self-concept as it evolves for Puerto Rican women as members of a triple minority in terms of gender, race, and ethnicity
3. To explore the dynamics of prejudice, discrimination, and stereotypes as they relate to Puerto Rican women within the context of race relations in the United States and Puerto Rico
4. To study the evolution of cultural identity and consciousness among Puerto Rican women writers in the United States and on the Island
5. To explore the means by which Puerto Rican women have made gains toward personal autonomy or liberation during the past two decades.

Discussion Questions

1. What are prevalent female stereotypes, and how do they lead to prejudice or discrimination against women in general and Puerto Rican women in particular?
2. How does racial prejudice affect self-concept and cultural identity for Puerto Ricans within the Island colonial context?
3. What are some of the ways in which the racial definitions and attitudes within Puerto Rican and U.S. societies influence women's self-concept?
4. What are appropriate strategies for minimizing stereotypes regarding Puerto Rican women?

Instructional Strategies

1. *Cultural Identity Essay:* Have students write an essay on their own cultural identity using the microcultures of gender, ethnicity/nationality, race, socioeconomic status, sexual preference, et cetera. Define subjective culture and cultural identity as a framework for the assignment. Students will describe the impact of any or all of the microcultures on their development, describe any incidents of differential treatment they received which they perceive as related to the microcultures, and write an analysis of the impact of cultural identity on how they have evolved as individuals.

   The following guidelines should be given to students to facilitate the essay development: (a) operationalize a definition of cultural identity as applicable to you; (b) describe your cultural background with a discussion of significant features of your own enculturation (e.g., religion, gender) and discuss why you think these were influential; (c) give examples of events or experiences in school or other institutions which you feel were significant in your development as a cultural being; (d) provide background on your family and its traditions as these relate to your cultural development;

(e) describe any differential treatment you or a family member or friend has experienced which you attribute to gender issues; (f) list strategies you would utilize in relating to people who come from a cultural background markedly different from your own.

2. *Social Justice Meditation:* Have students select a single theme (e.g., prejudice, self-concept, gender bias) and do a series of readings from newspaper or magazine articles related to the topic. At three intervals during the semester have students write a short essay in which they reflect on the topic selected. Encourage them to document both a specific domestic and international incident related to the topic.

Provide a series of guide questions to facilitate their analysis. At the end of the semester students will have a class discussion of the topics selected within the overall context of social justice.

Recommended Readings

Amott, Teresa, and Julie Matthaei. 1991. *Race, Gender, and Work: A Multi-Cultural Economic History of Women in the United States.* Boston: South End Press.

Betances, Samuel. 1972–73. "The Prejudice of Having No Prejudice in Puerto Rico." *The Rican: Journal of Contemporary Puerto Rican Thought,* 1:41–54, 3:22–37.

Comas-Díaz, Lillian. 1989. "Puerto Rican Women's Cross Cultural Transitions: Developmental and Clinical Implications." In *The Psychosocial Development of Puerto Rican Women,* ed. Cynthia García Coll and María Lourdes Mattei, 166–99. New York: Praeger.

García Coll, Cynthia, and María Lourdes Mattei, eds. 1989. *The Psychosocial Development of Puerto Rican Women.* New York: Praeger.

Ginorio, Angela. 1987. "Puerto Rican Ethnicity and Conflict." In *Ethnic Conflict: International Perspectives,* ed. Jerry Boucher, Dan Landis, and Karen Arnold Clark, 182–206. Newbury Park, Calif.: Sage.

Rivera Ramos, Alba Nydia. 1991. "The Psychological Experience of Puerto Rican Women at Work." Paper presented at Seminar on "Integrating Puerto Rican Women into the Curriculum and Research," SUNY-Albany, June.

Rodríguez, Clara. 1989. *Puerto Ricans Born in the U.S.A.* Boston: Unwyn Hyman.

Safa, Helen I. 1988. "Migration and Identity: A Comparison of Puerto Rican and Cuban Migrants in the United States." In *The Hispanic Experience in the United States,* ed. Edna Acosta-Belén and Barbara R. Sjostrom, 137–50. New York: Praeger.

Sánchez Korrol, Virginia. 1988. "Latinismo among Early Puerto Rican Migrants in New York City." In *The Hispanic Experience in the United States,* ed. Edna Acosta-Belén and Barbara R. Sjostrom, 151–62. New York: Praeger.

Sjostrom, Barbara R. 1988. "Culture Contact and Value Orientations: The Puerto Rican Experience." In *The Hispanic Experience in the United States*, ed. Edna Acosta-Belén and Barbara R. Sjostrom, 163–86. New York: Praeger.

UNIT 6   REPRODUCTIVE RIGHTS AND HEALTH ISSUES

Disciplinary Area: Social Sciences (Public Policy)

Key Concepts:

- aging
- AIDS
- birth control
- child care
- domestic violence
- mental health
- poverty
- reproductive rights
- sexual violence
- sterilization

General Objectives

1. To analyze the impact of socioeconomic status on the reproductive rights on women in general and Puerto Rican women in particular
2. To explore the effects of industrialization in Puerto Rico on the reproductive rights of Puerto Rican women
3. To compare the rural and urban experiences of Puerto Rican women in the United States and on the Island regarding birth control, sterilization, and reproductive rights
4. To study the incidence and nature of family violence toward Puerto Rican women and their children in the United States and on the Island
5. To compare and contrast the aging process for Puerto Rican women in the United States and on the Island
6. To ascertain health needs of and services available and utilized by Puerto Rican women in the United States and on the Island.

Discussion Questions

1. What has been the impact of family violence on legislation in Puerto Rico and the United States?
2. How do value orientations compare regarding the reproductive rights of Puerto Rican women in the United States and Puerto Rico?
3. What role does the church and/or other institutions in Puerto Rico play on issues related to women's reproductive rights?
4. What information and services are available to Puerto Rican women in the United States and Puerto Rico regarding health issues such as: AIDS, venereal disease, birth control, childhood diseases, and family violence?
5. How do Puerto Rican family patterns influence attitudes and practices toward the elderly?

Instructional Strategies

1. *Debate:* Students from the class will be assigned randomly to two different groups. Each group will assume one position regarding a topic such as birth control. They will research the topic and present the supporting arguments for the position and their reasons for defending the position. It is important to emphasize the research dimension of the process.
2. *Participatory Video:* Have students select an issue (e.g., aging, poverty, child care). They will also select an agency that deals with this issue in the community. They will interview clients and personnel working in the area and do a video that illustrates environmental services, interaction patterns, and how people feel about their particular roles. This technique has been used frequently in journalism and cultural anthropology courses whereby a video of domestic workers, for example, or a shelter for abused spouses served as the unit of analysis.

Recommended Readings

Angueira, Katherine. 1988. "To Make the Personal Political: The Use of Testimony as a Consciousness-Raising Tool against Sexual Aggression in Puerto Rico." *Oral History Review* 16, no. 2: 65–93.

Comas-Díaz, Lillian. 1982. "Mental Health Needs of Puerto Rican Women in the United States." In *Work, Family, and Health: Latina Women in Transition,* ed. Ruth Zambrana, 1–10. New York: Hispanic Research Center.

Comas-Díaz, Lillian, and J. W. Duncan. 1985. "The Cultural Context: A Factor in Assertiveness Training with Mainland Puerto Rican Women." *Psychology of Women* 9, no. 4: 463–76.

García Coll, Cynthia, and María de Lourdes Mattei, eds. 1989. *The Psychosocial Development of Puerto Rican Women.* New York: Praeger.

Mahard, Rita E. 1989. "Elderly Puerto Rican Women in the Continental United States." In *The Psychosocial Development of Puerto Rican Women*, ed. Cynthia García Coll and María de Lourdes Mattei, 243–60. New York: Praeger.

Ramírez de Arellano, Annette, and Conrad Seipp. 1983. *Colonialism, Catholicism, and Contraception: A History of Birth Control in Puerto Rico*. Chapel Hill: University of North Carolina Press.

Rodríguez-Trías, Helen. 1984. "The Women's Health Movement: Women Take Power." In *Reforming Medicine*, ed. Victor Sidel and Ruth Sidel, 107–26. New York: Pantheon Books.

Vázquez Nuttall, Ena. 1978. "Coping Patterns of Puerto Rican Mothers Heading Single Family Households." *Interamerican Journal of Psychology* 12, no. 1: 5–13.

Zambrana, Ruth, ed. 1982. *Work, Family, and Health: Latina Women in Transition*. New York: Hispanic Research Center.

Zambrana, Ruth, and Marsha Hurst. 1984. "The Interactive Effect of Health Status on Work Patterns among Urban Puerto Rican Women." *International Journal of Health Services* 14, no. 2: 265–77.

Recommended Films

La Operación (color documentary; 60 mins.) Using Puerto Rico as a case study, this documentary describes the use of mass sterilization in Puerto Rico during the 1950s and 1960s as a population control tool and a way to increase the availability of women's labor for new U.S. industries on the Island. It also emphasizes how the colonial status of Puerto Rico allowed it to become a testing laboratory for new birth control drugs.

UNIT 7 WOMEN'S LITERATURE AND ART

Disciplinary Area: Humanities (Literature, Art)

Key Concepts:

- artistic expression
- feminist criticism
- images of women
- literary canon
- stereotypes
- women's writing

General Objectives

1. To examine artistic works by Puerto Rican women and place them within the context of feminist criticism
2. To analyze the artistic expression of Puerto Rican women in the United States and on the Island as a form of social protest
3. To analyze the images of women as portrayed in Puerto Rican literature and popular cultural expressions (e.g., music)
4. To review criticism on the works of Puerto Rican women in the United States and on the Island
5. To analyze the criteria utilized for the inclusion and omission of certain authors in the traditional Puerto Rican literary canon
6. To study the literary works of Puerto Rican women written in Spanish and English as reflections of the colonial and migrant experience of Puerto Ricans and of women's condition.

Discussion Questions

1. Who are the principal female Puerto Rican writers and artists, and what have been their major contributions?
2. How is art as social expression manifested in the works of Puerto Rican women in the United States and on the Island?
3. What obstacles have been encountered by female Puerto Rican writers who write in English about the Puerto Rican experience?
4. What have been the major criteria for deciding which works or authors constitute the Island's literary canon?
5. How have Puerto Rican women been portrayed in literary works during various historical periods?
6. How are women portrayed in popular music and the visual media?

Instructional Strategies

1. *Portfolio:* Have students compile samples of their assignments related to this unit during the semester. Toward the end of the semester have students reflect on what they have learned and detail the process using the work they have compiled. For example, students frequently find that their views on a particular topic as reflected in early assignments vary from later ones. It is helpful to provide a matrix or set of structured questions for students to use in analyzing their work and reflecting on the process. This type of project facilitates students' documentation of their own cognitive processes and development in analysis, synthesis, and application of course material.
2. *Reaction Paper:* Students will read literary works by female Puerto Rican writers (e.g., *Nilda* by Nicholasa Mohr or *The Line of the Sun* by Judith

Ortiz Cofer). They will then present various viewpoints regarding the inclusion of these works as part of the literary canon, present their own views on the topic, and explain their reasoning.

Recommended Readings

Acosta-Belén, Edna. 1990. "Puerto Rican Literature in the United States." In *Redefining American Literary History,* ed. A. LaVonne Brown Ruoff and Jerry W. Ward, 373–80. New York: MLA.

————. 1986. "Ideology and Images of Women in Contemporary Puerto Rican Literature." In *The Puerto Rican Woman: Perspectives on Culture, History, and Society,* ed. Edna Acosta-Belén, 120–46. New York: Praeger.

Algarín, Miguel, and Manuel Piñero, eds. 1975. *Nuyorican Poetry: An Anthology of Puerto Rican Words and Feelings.* New York: Murrow.

Azize, Yamila. 1989. "A Commentary on the Works of Three Puerto Rican Women Poets in New York." In *Breaking Boundaries: Latina Writers and Critical Readings,* ed. Asunción Horno-Delgado et al., 146–65. Amherst: University of Massachusetts Press.

Cortés, Félix, Angel Falcón, and Juan Flores. 1976. "The Cultural Expression of Puerto Ricans in New York City." *Latin American Perspectives* 3, no. 3: 117–50.

Fernández Olmos, Margarite. 1982a. "From the Metropolis: Puerto Rican Women Poets and the Immigration Experience." *Third Woman* 1, no. 2: 40–51.

————. 1982b. "Sex, Color, and Class in Contemporary Puerto Rican Women Authors." *Heresies* 4, no. 3: 46–47.

Flores, Juan, Juan Attinasi, and Pedro Pedraza. 1982. "La Carreta Made a U-Turn: Puerto Rican Language and Culture in the United States." *Daedalus* 110, no. 2: 193–213.

Mohr, Eugene. 1982. *The Nuyorican Experience: Literature of the Puerto Rican Minority.* Westport, Conn.: Greenwood Press.

Mohr, Nicholasa. 1985a. *Rituals of Survival: A Woman's Portfolio.* Houston: Arte Publico.

————. 1985b. *Nilda.* Houston: Arte Publico.

Monteflores, Carmen de. 1989. *Cantando bajito/Singing Softly.* San Francisco: Spinsters/aunt lute.

Ortiz Cofer, Judith. 1989. *The Line of the Sun.* Athens: University of Georgia Press.

Rodríguez Laguna, Asela, ed. 1987. *Images and Identities: The Puerto Ricans in Two World Contexts.* New Brunswick, N.J.: Transaction.

Turner, Faythe, ed. 1991. *Puerto Ricans at Home in the U.S.A.: An Anthology.* New York: Open Hand Publishing.

Vélez, Diana. 1989. "Cultural Constructions of Women by Contemporary

Puerto Rican Authors." In *The Psychosocial Development of Puerto Rican Women,* ed. Cynthia T. García Coll and María de Lourdes Mattei, 31–59. New York: Praeger.

———, ed. 1988. *Reclaiming Medusa: Short Stories by Contemporary Puerto Rican Women.* San Francisco: spinsters/aunt lute.

Recommended Films

Birthwrite (1988; color documentary; 60 mins.). Distributed by Hispanic Research Center. Arizona State University, Tempe, AZ 85287. This documentary includes dramatizations from prose fiction works and poetry readings by well-known Latino writers in the United States. It also includes interviews about their experiences growing up in America and how their writings reflect the particular experiences of each of their respective groups.

Plena Is Work, Plena Is Song (1989; color documentary; 37 mins.). Distributed by the Cinema Guild. The cultural and political history of the *plena,* a Puerto Rican musical blend of African and Spanish traditions. It emphasizes its working-class origins, its widespread popularity (during the 1920s through 1950s), and its various functions in expressing the personal, cultural, and political realities of the Puerto Rican people, both on the Island and in the U.S. migrant communities.

UNIT 8   MIGRATION

Disciplinary Area: Social Sciences (Sociology, Anthropology, History)

Key Concepts:

• acculturation
• colonization
• demographic patterns
• language contact
• syncretism
• transnational sociocultural systems
• value orientations

General Objectives

1. To learn the differences between the terms *migration, emigration,* and *immigration*
2. To explore the dynamics of global mass movements of people from developing to industrialized countries and from rural to urban areas in terms of socioeconomic and political variables and how these affect family structure in general and women in particular
3. To study Puerto Rican migration to the United States as a commuter migration within the context of Puerto Rico's Commonwealth status
4. To analyze the phenomena of language and culture contact vis-à-vis the processes of acculturation and cultural maintenance among Puerto Rican migrants.

Discussion Questions

1. How have changing demographic patterns affected Puerto Rican women in the areas of education, child rearing, women's roles, labor, and housing both on the Island and in the United States?
2. What has been the impact of the mass migration of Puerto Ricans to the United States in the 1950s and the reverse migration to Puerto Rico in the 1970s on gender roles and family structure?
3. How have assimilationist and pluralistic viewpoints been applied to the experience of Puerto Ricans in the United States?
4. How do the experiences of the first- and second-generation Puerto Ricans in the United States compare regarding the issues of culture shock, marginalization, acculturation, national/ethnic consciousness, and biculturalism, and what are the implications for Puerto Rican women?
5. How do the cultural expressions of Puerto Ricans in the United States reflect the straddling of two cultures and other class and race considerations?

Instructional Strategies

1. *Cooperative Learning Activity:* Divide the class into several groups. Each group will study one set of statistics (e.g., income, fertility rates). They will then develop either a piece of legislation or a community-based program to address the needs identified by their individual group. In order for a cooperative learning activity to work effectively, each member of the group has a particular role (e.g., recorder, timekeeper, speaker, discussant).
2. *Immigrant Interview:* This strategy consists of a structured ethnographic interview with an immigrant who came to the United States as an adolescent or adult. A series of structured questions eliciting information on the following areas is helpful: (a) family background in country of origin in-

cluding religion, socioeconomic status, education, and occupations; (b) reasons for leaving; (c) migration/immigration experience itself; (d) expectations for experience in the United States; (e) ways in which the experience was positive or negative; (f) comments on the adaptation process in the United States; (g) response from the student interviewer regarding the process of conducting the interview, including what was learned about the immigrant experience.

Recommended Readings

Andreu Iglesias, César, ed. 1984. *Memoirs of Bernardo Vega: A Contribution to the History of the Puerto Rican Community in New York City.* Trans. by Juan Flores. New York: Monthly Review Press.

Centro de Estudios Puertorriqueños History Task Force. 1979. *Labor Migration under Capitalism.* New York: Monthly Review Press.

Colón, Jesús. 1982. *A Puerto Rican in New York and Other Sketches.* New York: International Publishers.

Hernández Alvarez, José. 1967. *Return Migration to Puerto Rico.* Berkeley: University of California Press.

Maldonado, Rita. 1976. "Why Puerto Ricans Migrated to the United States in 1947–63." *Monthly Labor Review* 99, no. 9: 7–18.

Rodríguez, Clara. 1989. *Puerto Ricans Born in the U.S.A.* Boston: Unwyn Hyman.

Recommended Films

Los dos mundos de Angelita (The Two Worlds of Angelita) (1983; color film; 73 mins.). Distributed by First Run/Icarus Films, 153 Waverly Place, New York, NY 10014; (212) 727-1711. This film captures the transition of a nine-year-old Puerto Rican girl and her family, who migrate from a small rural town in Puerto Rico to New York's Lower East Side. It focuses on issues of cultural conflict, gender roles, economic hardship, and discrimination.

Los sures (1983; color documentary; 58 mins.). Distributed by the Cinema Guild. This documentary explores life in the primarily Hispanic (Puerto Rican) community of Williamsburgh, Brooklyn (known as Los Sures), one of New York's poorest neighborhoods. The film focuses on the personal stories of five families surviving in the inner city.

UNIT 9   WOMEN AND EDUCATION

Interdisciplinary (Sociology, Philosophy, History, Psychology, Anthropology, Education, Women's Studies, Ethnic/Racial Studies)

Key Concepts:

- bias in testing
- bilingualism
- cognitive styles
- cultural identity and cognition
- cultural literacy
- knowledge transformation
- learning styles
- melting pot
- multiculturalism/diversity
- self-fulfilling prophecy
- sexist language
- teacher expectations
- tracking

General Objectives

1. To analyze the phenomenon of multiculturalism within the context of the United States as a nation of immigrants with an overall "melting pot" ideology
2. To study the concepts of language attitudes and norms, language proficiency, bilingualism, language shift, and language contact as these affect the experience of Puerto Ricans on the Island and in the United States
3. To analyze differential discourse patterns between Puerto Rican men and women and discuss the function of these patterns
4. To explore the link between language, culture, and cognition in the formation of cultural identity for Puerto Rican women on the Island and in the United States
5. To explore the existence of cultural biases in tests administered to Puerto Ricans
6. To analyze the phenomenon of tracking as it affects the education and career choices of Puerto Rican women
7. To study the impact of teacher expectations and the self-fulfilling prophecy on the educational experiences of Puerto Rican women.

Discussion Questions

1. What are the dynamics of teacher expectations as they relate to Puerto Rican children's achievement, and how are they differentiated by gender? (Use Rosenthal et al., *Pygmalion in the Classroom* [New York: Holt, Rinehart and Winston, 1968] as a point of departure for the discussion.)
2. What is the impact of standarized testing on Puerto Rican women? Use a sample of questions from standardized tests (e.g., Graduate Record Examination [GRE]) and analyze from a culturally pluralistic perspective.
3. How could Freire's theory on cultural literacy be applied to the experience of Puerto Ricans?
4. What are the implications of Minnich's book *Transforming Knowledge* (Philadelphia: Temple University Press, 1990) for the education of Puerto Ricans?

Instructional Strategies

1. *Vignettes of Experience:* In this activity students are asked to reflect upon two significant learning experiences (positive or negative) which have had a lasting impact on their own development. One can provide a context by referring to some of the key concepts in the unit such as tracking, teacher expectations, sexist language, or bias in testing. Have students describe the specific learning experiences related to the key concepts, discuss their impact, and evaluate how these experiences better prepared them to interact in a multicultural setting.
2. *Activity File:* Have students choose one key concept from the unit and compile an article file throughout the semester. Once they have completed article collection, have them conduct a content analysis of recurrent themes from the articles and present a position paper that represents their viewpoint on the topic. Finally, have them reflect on how their positions relate to the particular experience of Puerto Rican women.

Recommended Readings

Andersen, Margaret. 1988. *Thinking about Women: Sociological Perspectives on Sex and Gender.* New York: Macmillan.

Andersen, Margaret, and Patricia Hill Collins, eds. 1991. *Race, Class, and Gender: An Anthology.* Belmont, Calif.: Woodsworth.

Banks, James A., and Cherry A. McGee Banks, eds. 1989. *Multicultural Education: Issues and Perspectives.* Boston: Allyn and Bacon.

Butler, Johnnella E. "Transforming the Curriculum: Teaching about Women of Color." In *Multicultural Education: Issues and Perspectives,* ed. James A. Banks and Cherry A. McGee Banks, 145–63. Boston: Allyn and Bacon.

Ferdman, Bernardo. 1990. "Literacy and Cultural Identity." *Harvard Educational Review* 60, no. 2: 181–203.

Freire, Paolo, and Donaldo Macedo. 1987. *Literacy: Reading the Word and the World.* South Hadley, Mass.: Bergin and Garvey.

Freire, Paolo, and Ira Schor. 1987. *A Pedagogy for Liberation: Dialogues on Transforming Education.* South Hadley, Mass.: Bergin and Garvey.

Minnich, Elizabeth K. 1990. *Transforming Knowledge.* Philadelphia: Temple University Press.

Schmitz, Betty. 1985. *Integrating Women's Studies into the Curriculum: A Guide and Bibliography.* New York: The Feminist Press.

UNIT 10   DEMOGRAPHIC DATA

In this section recent data on the overall status of Puerto Rican women on the Island and in the United States are presented and described. The material provides a background on the general social and economic situation of Puerto Rican women, in order to contextualize discussions in any discipline, course, or substantive area. We have organized the information into topics that parallel some of the areas covered in earlier units: education; marital status and family structure; employment, income, and poverty; and health and reproduction. In many cases a historical overview is provided as well.

In presenting this socioeconomic profile, we want to both compare and contrast the situation of women on the Island and in the United States, keeping in mind that circular (or commuter) migration patterns mean that many women are likely to have experienced both contexts. Where possible, we also contrast the situation of Puerto Ricans in the United States with that of other Latinas.

Education

In 1988 Puerto Ricans in the United States had attained a median education level of 12.0 years, which falls in the middle of other Latino groups: Mexicans averaged 10.8 years and Cubans and Central and South Americans averaged 12.4 years. At the same time, the non-Latino population had a median education of 12.7 years. (These figures are for people over twenty-five years of age, who are presumed to have completed most of their education. Note also that we will use the terms *Latino or Latina* interchangeably with Hispanic, which is the U.S. census official term.)

Since a general description can mask any gender differences, note that in 1988 Puerto Rican men's median education was 12.1 years, with 53.1 percent of them completing high school, while Puerto Rican women averaged 11.8

years of education and had 48.8 percent completing high school. These are not large differences, and all age groups of men and women between twenty-five and forty-four report an average education between 12.0 and 12.6 years. In fact, the only point at which there appears to be a larger gender gap in education is among those forty-five to sixty-four years old, where men average 10.4 years and women 8.5 years of education. Thus, the gender difference in median education is primarily caused by this older group. In fact, among younger groups aged fifteen to twenty-four, Puerto Rican women have a slightly higher educational level than Puerto Rican men.

Nonetheless, the rates of high school completion for both men and women are relatively low. Among other Latino men 64.9 percent graduate from high school, compared with 53.1 percent of Puerto Rican and 45.8 percent of Mexican men over age twenty-five. While 62.1 percent of other Latina groups graduate, only 48.8 percent of Puerto Rican and 43.3 percent of Mexican women do so. Since the United States' national high school completion rate is 76.9 percent, high school dropout rates are still relatively high for Puerto Ricans (and Mexicans).

When we turn to the Island it is harder to find comparable data. Historical statistics show a similar narrowing gender gap in median education, however, for those over twenty-five years of age, as shown in table 1.

TABLE 1   MEDIAN YEARS OF EDUCATION, BY GENDER, IN PUERTO RICO

Year	Men	Women
1950	4.1	3.3
1960	4.8	4.3
1970	7.5	5.9
1980	9.7	9.2

Source: Junta de Planificación de Puerto Rico 1990, A-1, table 1.

Unfortunately, 1988 median data were not available. Yet, since we know that Puerto Rican women's average education in the United States in 1978 was 9.9 years, and it has now increased to 11.8 years, it is probably fair to assume that their median education on the Island has risen as well. We know that between 1970 and 1980 the percentage of women who graduated from high school (*escuela superior*) increased from 24.3 to 32.8 percent, and the numbers of female college and university graduates increased from 11.3 to 18.3 percent of all women. In fact, in the 1987–88 academic year 65 percent of the postsecondary degrees conferred in Puerto Rico went to women.

Marital Status and Family Structure

Among Latinos in the United States, for men and women combined, marital status was distributed in 1988 as shown in Table 2.

TABLE 2   MARITAL STATUS OF LATINOS IN THE UNITED STATES, 1988

Marital Status	Puerto Rican	Mexican	Cuban	Non-Hispanic
Never married	34.7	31.9	24.8	25.8
Married	52.5	58.0	58.5	59.3
Widowed	4.3	3.5	7.6	7.4
Divorced	8.4	6.6	9.1	7.5
Total, 15 years and older	100.0%	100.00%	100.0%	100.0%

Source: Schick and Schick 1991, 35, table C1-1.

FIGURE 1   DIVORCE RATES FOR PERSONS FIFTEEN AND OVER, BY HISPANIC SUBGROUP, 1985

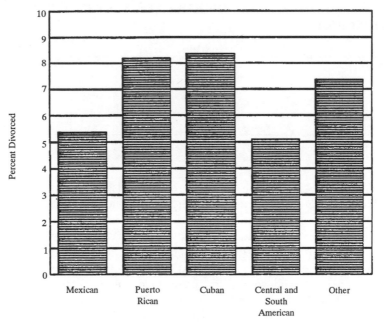

Source: Schick and Schick 1991, 47, table C1-15.

As compared with other Latino groups and non-Latinos, Puerto Ricans have a relatively low percentage of married couples and a slight overrepresentation of never-marrieds. As figure 1 shows, both Cubans and Puerto Ricans in the United States have comparatively high divorce rates.

In Puerto Rico we can provide both historical and contemporary marriage data separately, for men and women fifteen years of age or older. At least in 1980 both marriage and widowhood rates were a little higher on the Island than in the United States. Over time we see rising marriage rates that leveled off in 1950, combined with lowered rates of singlehood, but continually increasing divorce rates that appear similar to those in the United States.

TABLE 3   MARITAL STATUS OF MEN AND WOMEN IN PUERTO RICO, OVER TIME

Year	Single	Married	Widowed	Divorced
Men				
1899	48.4	46.9	4.7	—
1910	43.7	52.3	3.9	0.1
1920	41.9	53.5	4.3	0.3
1930	43.2	52.6	3.9	0.3
1940	42.4	53.3	3.8	0.5
1950	38.6	57.0	3.6	0.8
1960	34.6	61.1	3.1	1.2
1970	33.6	61.7	2.9	1.8
1980	31.3	62.5	2.7	3.5
Women				
1899	43.7	44.0	12.3	—
1910	38.0	51.1	10.7	0.2
1920	34.0	53.4	12.0	0.6
1930	33.8	54.0	11.3	0.9
1940	31.4	55.4	11.6	1.6
1950	27.3	59.4	11.2	2.1
1960	25.6	61.4	10.3	2.7
1970	26.8	60.0	9.3	3.9
1980	24.7	58.7	9.3	7.3

Also includes consensual unions and separations.

Source: Junta de Planificación de Puerto Rico 1990, A-14, table 13 (original table appears in Spanish).

Largely as a result of the increasing divorce and high widowhood rates, we are seeing a rising rate of female-headed households on the Island. In 1970 15.9 percent of family heads were women, and in 1980 the figure increased to 21.3 percent.

The rates of female-headed households, however, are much higher for Puerto Ricans in the United States. In 1988, while 51.6 percent of Puerto Rican families were headed by a married couple and 4.3 percent were headed by a man with no spouse, fully 44.0 percent of all families were headed by a female householder. A female householder does not necessarily have children, but 35.5 percent of all Puerto Rican households are headed by women with children aged eighteen or younger. This may be because the largest increase in Puerto Rican female-household heads has been among women aged twenty to twenty-nine—the women most likely to have resident young children. The large numbers of female-headed households include both those headed by women who have not married and those who have been divorced. These high rates are more similar to those for African Americans than to those for Mexicans, who report only 18.5 percent of families with a female head.

Employment, Income, and Poverty

Jobs and income are always key to survival, and in this section we review several different economic aspects. We begin by examining employment and unemployment rates. These are not opposite statistics: you can only be counted as unemployed if you are looking for work and thus are part of the labor force. This definition often results in an undercounting of women's unemployment, since they are often "discouraged workers" who would seek jobs only if they believed any were available in their neighborhood or if child care were a possibility.

Tables 4 and 5 show that Puerto Rican women's labor force participation rates are increasing both in the United States and on the Island; however, their employment rates are consistently higher in the United States. For example, in 1988 the U.S. rate was 40.9 percent, and the island rate in 1989 was 31.9 percent. In contrast, Puerto Rican women in the United States have labor force participation rates that are more than ten percentage points lower than for any other Latina group and fifteen percent lower than for non-Hispanics. Thus, they are more likely to work than Puerto Rican women on the Island but less likely to do so than many other U.S. resident groups.

TABLE 4   CIVILIAN LABOR FORCE PARTICIPATION RATES OF THE HISPANIC POPULATION AGED SIXTEEN YEARS AND OVER BY SEX, 1980 TO 1988

	Non-Hispanic Persons	All Hispanics	Mexican	Puerto Rican	Cuban	Other Hispanic
		Percentage in Labor Force				
Male						
1980		79.9	82.8	72.2	NA	NA
1982	74.8	80.5	83.6	71.5	NA	NA
1984	74.1	79.0	80.4	70.9	77.7	80.6
1986	74.0	79.0	81.1	67.8	78.2	79.0
1988	73.9	78.9	80.4	68.6	77.2	80.6
Female						
1980		48.0	49.6	35.0	NA	NA
1982	52.3	48.7	49.7	35.6	NA	NA
1984	53.4	49.6	50.1	36.8	55.1	55.6
1986	55.2	48.9	49.1	37.8	53.9	53.7
1988	56.2	52.1	52.4	40.9	53.6	57.6

Source: Schick and Schick 1991, 152, table G1-3.

TABLE 5   LABOR FORCE PARTICIPATION RATES, BY GENDER, IN PUERTO RICO (BY PERCENTAGE)

Year	Male	Female
1971	70.7	27.9
1975	65.7	27.2
1980	61.1	27.5
1985	58.4	27.8
1986	58.5	28.3
1987	59.9	29.9
1988	60.4	31.2
1989	61.3	31.9

Source: Junta de Planificación de Puerto Rico 1990, A-21–A-22, tables 20–21.

Labor force participation rates also vary by age, as shown in figure 2 for women on the Island, giving comparative employment rates in 1971 and 1989 for differing age groups. The rates have risen considerably for women between the ages of twenty-five and sixty-four but have dropped for those under twenty-four who may be staying in school longer.

FIGURE 2   LABOR FORCE PARTICIPATION RATES FOR WOMEN, BY AGE, IN PUERTO RICO

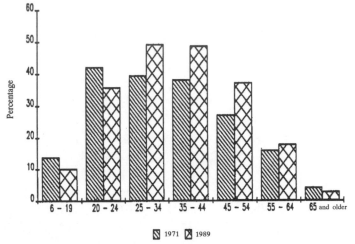

Source: Junta de Planificación de Puerto Rico 1990, 11, fig. 14. (Original graph appears in Spanish; this is a translation).

When we turn to unemployment several features are notable:

1. Comparing men and women in similar geographic settings, we find that in Puerto Rico men's unemployment rates are consistently higher than women's; while in the United States, the rates fluctuate considerably, and it is not unusual for Puerto Rican women to have higher unemployment than the men.
2. Comparing men's opportunities, we find that their unemployment rates are consistently and considerably higher in Puerto Rico than in the United States, while for women unemployment rates in both settings appear comparable. This feature implies that men may have more economic reason to migrate to the United States than do women.
3. Comparing Latinas in the United States, Puerto Rican women always have the highest unemployment, while Cuban women have the lowest.

For further details see table 6 and figures 3 and 4.

TABLE 6   UNEMPLOYMENT OF THE HISPANIC POPULATION, AGED SIXTEEN YEARS AND OVER, 1980 TO 1988

	Non-Hispanic Persons	Percentage of Labor Force Unemployed				
		All Hispanics	Mexican	Puerto Rican	Cuban	Other Hispanic
Male						
1980	—	8.3	8.4	11.5	NA	NA
1982	10.1	13.3	13.0	20.8	NA	NA
1984	8.4	11.6	12.6	11.8	8.6	8.9
1986	7.5	11.3	11.7	16.4	6.3	9.2
1988	6.1	9.5	11.0	8.2	4.1	7.4
Female						
1980	—	10.5	11.8	13.0	NA	NA
1982	8.7	13.5	13.9	11.7	NA	NA
1984	7.5	11.6	11.9	15.6	4.8	11.5
1986	7.0	9.5	10.3	14.1	4.1	7.3
1988	5.4	7.0	7.7	10.5	1.7	5.2

Source: Schick and Schick 1991, 176, table G4-7.

FIGURE 3   UNEMPLOYMENT RATES FOR HISPANIC WOMEN, BY HISPANIC SUBGROUP, 1978 TO 1986 (BY PERCENTAGE)

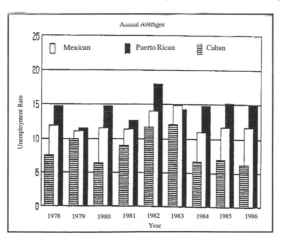

Source: Schick and Schick 1991, 175, fig. G4-6.

FIGURE 4   UNEMPLOYMENT RATES BY GENDER IN FIVE YEARS IN PUERTO RICO

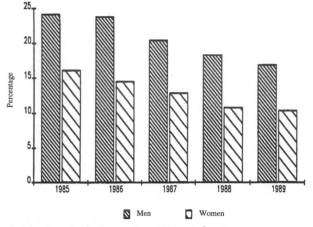

Source: Junta de Planificación de Puerto Rico 1990, 11, fig. 13.

Thus far, we have examined unemployment and employment rates but said little on the types of occupations in which people are working. As table 7 shows, Puerto Rican women in the United States are most likely to be working in technical, sales, or clerical work/administrative support (43.3 percent), with professional work (20.0 percent) and service work (18.1 percent) the next most frequent types of jobs. Factory work, which was more common in earlier years, only represents 15.7 percent of the occupations of employed Puerto Rican women. In contrast, Puerto Rican men are about equally likely to work in the technical/sales field, service work, precision production and craft jobs, or as operators/laborers (22.3, 21.2, 20.2, and 25.4 percent, respectively). Note, however, that Puerto Rican women are twice as likely as men to work in managerial or professional jobs.

While the occupational categories used for Puerto Rico are a little different than those in table 7 and therefore not entirely comparable, we see that women's most frequently held jobs are clerical (27.7 percent), followed by professional or technical work (23.3 percent), craft workers and foremen (17.8 percent), and other service workers (15.7). Historically, women's representation has been increasing in all of these jobs except as foremen and craft workers, where they have declined from 49.9 percent of the female labor force in 1940 to 17.8 percent in 1989. Presumably, this represents the decline in the needlework and tobacco industries in that period.

In spite of any minor differences in job distribution between Puerto Rico and the United States, it is clear that the occupational segregation by gender is similar. In both places approximately two-thirds of all women work in the combined fields of professional, technical, managerial, clerical, and sales,

TABLE 7 OCCUPATIONS BY GENDER FOR LATINOS IN THE UNITED STATES, 1989 (BY PERCENTAGE)

	Puerto Ricans		Mexicans		Cubans	
Occupation	Women	Men	Women	Men	Women	Men
Managerial and professional	20.0	10.6	12.8	8.7	22.3	25.2
Technical, sales, admin. support	43.3	22.3	36.8	12.0	43.1	25.3
Service	18.1	21.2	24.6	17.7	17.1	10.2
Farming, fishing	—	0.3	1.9	11.1	0.8	1.6
Precision prod., craft, repair	2.9	20.2	3.0	19.8	2.4	15.2
Operators and laborers	15.7	25.4	20.9	30.7	14.3	22.5
Total	100	100	100	100	100	100

Source: Schick and Schick 1991, 186–87, table H1-3.

while only 42 percent of Puerto Rican men on the Island and 33 percent of men in the United States do so.

Given the gender differences in occupation, we might also expect to find differences in earnings among the employed as well as differences in income (for all persons age fifteen and older) from all sources. Table 9 summarizes this data.

In general, we find that both Latina's and non-Latina's total income in the United States is about half of men's, although the figure rises to 63 percent for women in Puerto Rico. Both Mexican and Puerto Rican women have incomes that are lower than among Cubans or the non-Latino population, presaging upcoming figures on poverty.

When we focus only on the median occupational earnings of the employed, the absolute dollar figures generally go up. We also see that, once employed, Puerto Rican women have earnings equivalent to the average for all women in the United States. Unfortunately, they have a relatively low employment rate, thus lowering the overall population income figures. It is only because Latino men earn comparatively less than non-Latino men that the female-to-male earnings ratio for Puerto Ricans, Mexicans, and Cubans is relatively high (above 67 percent in all cases as compared with 53 percent for non-Latinos).

Thus, the earnings effect of occupational segregation can be described in two ways. On the one hand, women's earnings are not impacted greatly by ethnicity, while men's earnings do vary considerably according to ethnic group. On the other hand, women's earnings are affected by their gender, and, while most Latina groups earn incomes similar to non-Latinas, that figure is always lower than men's income.

Figures on income become even more dramatic when one examines the

TABLE 8 PERCENTAGE OF EMPLOYEES, BY OCCUPATION AND SEX, IN PUERTO RICO (BY PERCENTAGE)

Women	1940	1950	1960	1980	1989
Farm owners/admin.	2.4	0.6	0.3	0.1	0.0
Farm workers	2.3	2.4	1.4	0.5	0.4
Professional/tech.	6.0	9.9	15.6	18.9	23.3
Managers/officials	1.6	2.7	4.2	3.5	7.6
Sales	2.1	2.8	4.7	5.4	5.7
Clerical	4.2	9.5	16.9	23.6	27.7
Craft and foremen	49.9	40.0	28.9	25,8	17.8
Laborer, nonfarm	0.3	0.6	0.8	1.1	0.3
Domestic service	27.6	22.8	13.4	4.9	1.5
Other service work	3.4	8.3	12.2	13.1	15.7
Total	99.8	99.6	98.4	96.9	100
Men					
Farm owners/admin.	11.7	8.3	4.2	2.0	2.5
Farm workers	45.8	40.0	26.2	8.5	3.3
Professional/tech.	2.0	3.4	5.4	8.9	12.8
Managers/officials	5.8	7.2	8.8	8.8	14.1
Sales	2.8	3.4	4.8	7.3	7.4
Clerical	5.9	6.1	6.8	8.4	7.6
Craft and foremen	7.1	9.7	14.6	20.3	20.1
Operatives	7.3	9.9	13.8	16.6	14.5
Laborer, nonfarm	6.8	6.8	8.4	9.0	6.2
Domestic service	1.1	0.8	0.3	0.2	0.0
Other service work	3.7	4.4	6.7	10.0	11.4
Total	100	100	100	100	99.9

Source: Junta de Planificación de Puerto Rico 1990, A-23, table 22.

overall distribution, and not only the averages. Usually, we are most concerned with the lower end of that distribution or with the rates of people living below the poverty line. In Puerto Rico 19.3 percent of female household heads lived below the poverty level in 1970, and that figure rose to 23 percent in 1980. The figures for the United States, however, are even more dramatic. As shown in figure 5, fully 65 percent of Puerto Rican female-headed households and 38 percent of Puerto Rican families lived below the poverty level in 1987. At the same time, the respective national averages for non-

TABLE 9   INCOME AND EARNINGS IN THE UNITED STATES AND PUERTO RICO

	Mean Income (1987)		Median Earnings (1988)	
	Women	Men	Women	Men
Puerto Ricans	$8,819 (54%)	$16,233	$11,241 (70%)	$16,122
Mexicans	$8,833 (59%)	$14,888	$8,110 (67%)	$12,107
Cubans	$11,155 (52%)	$21,520	$11,966 (68%)	$17,572
Non-Latina/os	$11,571 (50%)	$23,196	$11,245 (53%)	$21,267
	Mean Income (1980)			
	Women	Men		
Puerto Rico	$3,866	$6,100 (63%)	—	—

Sources: Schick and Schick, 186–87, table H1-3; and Junta de Planificación de Puerto Rico 1990, A-17, table 16.

FIGURE 5   U.S. FAMILIES BELOW POVERTY LEVEL, BY RACE OR ETHNIC GROUP, 1987

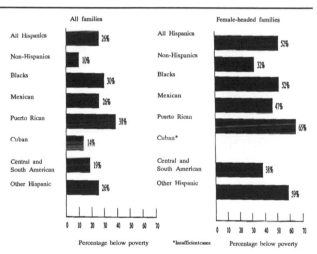

Source: Schick and Schick 1991, 221, fig. H3-10.

Latinos were 32 percent and 10 percent. Not surprisingly, only 11 percent of Puerto Rican families in the United States earned more than $50,000 in 1988.

Health and Reproduction

Before discussing health and reproduction, it is important to look at age distributions, which can help predict both fertility and infirmities. Puerto Ricans and Mexicans in the United States average eight to ten years younger than non-Latinos. In contrast, Cubans in the United States, as mostly political migrants, tend to be five to seven years older than average.

TABLE 10   MEDIAN AGE BY GENDER AND ETHNICITY IN THE UNITED STATES, 1988

	Women	Men
Puerto Rican	25.7	23.8
Mexican	23.9	23.9
Cuban	40.9	36.9
Non-Latinos	33.8	31.9

Source: Schick and Schick 1991, 17, table A5-6.

The median age of Puerto Ricans on the Island is relatively similar to that in the United States. In 1980 women averaged 25.5 years and men 23.6 years, and they had life expectancies in 1986 of 78.9 and 70.7 years, respectively.

Given the youth of the Puerto Rican population, fertility and childbirth are obviously important features. In the United States in 1987 the fertility rates per one thousand women aged fifteen to forty-four were: Mexicans, 94.5; Puerto Ricans, 67.7; and Cubans, 51.1. The average fertility rate was 68.5; thus, Puerto Rican women are actually having slightly fewer children than the norm. Some concern has been expressed, however, over the percentage of these births that are to teenage or unmarried mothers.

TABLE 11   PERCENTAGE OF BIRTHS THAT ARE TO TEENAGE OR UNMARRIED MOTHERS, UNITED STATES, 1987

	Births to Teen Mothers	Births to Unmarried Mothers
Puerto Rican	20.5	53.0
Mexican	17.3	28.9
Cuban	6.2	16.1
National average	12.4	24.5

Source: Schick and Schick 1991, 103, table E1-2.

While their rates of teenage motherhood are only 8 percent higher than average, Puerto Rican women are becoming unmarried mothers at a rate that is twice the national average. This obviously poses important questions for how such families will be supported, since women generally earn less than men and since Puerto Rican female household heads are not more likely to be employed than other women. Of course, one needs to know more about their living arrangements and the availability of other income sources before creating any social policy focused on this issue. In fact, this is an area in which more research is needed.

When we look at specific fertility rates in Puerto Rico for women aged fifteen to forty-four we find that births per woman have dropped dramatically over time (see table 12).

TABLE 12 FERTILITY RATES FOR WOMEN, AGED FIFTEEN TO FORTY-FOUR, IN PUERTO RICO

Year	Births per Woman (Puerto Rico)
1940	5.79
1950	5.37
1960	4.77
1970	3.35
1980	2.78
1986	2.38

Source: Junta de Planificación de Puerto Rico 1990, A-15, table 14.

This quick decline in birth rates was principally caused by the large numbers of Puerto Rican women who have been sterilized. In 1950 only 16 percent of reproductive-age women were sterilized, but by 1982 39 percent of all such women and fully 43 percent of all mothers were sterilized. This rate is the highest in the world and the cause of much research on sterilization abuse.

In the early years of the 1950s factories would offer jobs only to women who could prove they would have no more children, thus causing many women to have "*la operación.*" More recently, the rapid rise in caesarean births from 25.6 percent in 1981–82 to 29.6 percent in 1986–87 is the major cause of choosing sterilization. Women cite this type of birth experience as being more significant in their choosing sterilization than their total number of children. It is important to note that Puerto Rico also has the highest caesarean section rate in the world, even higher than the 22.3 percent rate in the United States. Again, we appear to see a health abuse in need of further investigation. This is undoubtedly one of the reasons that physical and mental health is a major area of research on Puerto Rican women.

Statistical Data Sources for This Unit

Boletín Informativo: Oficina de Estadísticas de Salud. 1989. "Nacimientos Por Cesárea en Puerto Rico, Años 1981–82 al 1986–87." Vol. 4, ser. D-1, no. 1 (16 June 1989).

Bose, Christine E. 1986. "Puerto Rican Women in the United States: An Overview." In *The Puerto Rican Woman: Perspectives on Culture, History, and Society*, ed. Edna Acosta-Belén, 147–69. New York: Praeger.

del Pinal, Jorge H., and Carmen De Navas. 1990. *The Hispanic Population in the United States: March 1989*. U.S. Bureau of the Census, Current Population Reports, ser. P-20, no. 444. Washington, D.C.: U.S. Government Printing Office.

Junta de Planificación de Puerto Rico. 1990. *Indicadores Socioeconómicos de la Situación de las Mujeres en Puerto Rico*. San Juan: Junta de Planificación de Puerto Rico.

Schick, Frank, and Renee Schick. 1991. *Statistical Handbook on U.S. Hispanics*. Phoenix: Oryx Press.

Vázquez Calzada, José. N.D. "Estadísticas Demográficas de la Población Feminina de Puerto Rico." MS, Graduate School of Public Health, University of Puerto Rico, Río Piedras.

AFTERWORD
Women of Color in the Curriculum

Beverly Guy-Sheftall

The most significant reforms in American higher education over the past three decades have come as a result of the development of black studies, ethnic studies, and women's studies. Paradoxically, women of color fell through the cracks in each of these new disciplines, and black women's studies emerged in the 1970s as a corrective to the invisibility, in particular, of women of African descent. In 1982 The Feminist Press published the first interdisciplinary anthology in the field, *All the Women Are White, All the Blacks Are Men, But Some of Us Are Brave*, which was edited by Gloria T. Hull, Patricia Bell-Scott, and Barbara Smith, all three of whom were solid black studies scholars. I am reminded of the rationale for this ground-breaking book, which would set in motion subsequent critiques by women of color[1] about the lack of attention to ethnic, class, cultural, and racial difference and result in the much needed reform of women's studies itself:

> Women's studies courses . . . focused almost exclusively upon the lives of white women. Black studies, which was much too often male-dominated, also ignored Black women. . . . Because of white women's racism and Black men's sexism, there was no room in either area for a serious consideration of the lives of Black women. And even when they considered Black women, white women usually have not had the capacity to analyze racial politics and Black culture, and Black men have remained blind or resistant to the implications of sexual politics in Black women's lives. (*All the Women*, xx–xxi)

Beverly Guy-Sheftall is director of the Women's Research and Resources Center at Spelman College and a consultant for the Ford Foundation.

The founding of *SAGE: A Scholarly Journal on Black Women* a year later signaled the "coming of age" of black women's studies.

Women of color continued to argue passionately throughout the 1980s that womanhood is not a monolithic category and that the concept of global sisterhood based on universal female oppression is misleading or even mythic. Johnnella Butler, who codirected one of the first curriculum development projects that attempted collaborative efforts between women's studies and ethnic studies, asserted:

> White women function both as women who share certain similar experiences with women of color and as oppressors of women of color. . . . White women share with White men an ethnicity, an ancestral heritage, a racial dominance, and certain powers and privileges by virtue of class, race, and ethnicity, by race and ethnicity if not class, and always by virtue of White skin privilege. ("Transforming the Curriculum," 69–70)

These kinds of critiques provided the catalyst for serious self-examination on the part of women's studies practitioners and resulted in a new wave of scholarship and pedagogy, which I believe has reinvigorated the field and is finding its way into the core curriculum of many colleges and universities throughout the country.

When the history of the women's studies movement in the United States is written, I am certain that the Ford Foundation will be central to the narrative of the development of women's studies in the academy and changes in its complexion. To be sure, Ford's Mainstreaming Minority Women's Studies Initiative (MMWSI) has been critical to the reform of women's studies by providing funds for the incorporation of scholarship on American ethnic minority women into undergraduate liberal arts curricula. The project's focus on collaborations with black studies and ethnic studies around issues of race, ethnicity, class, and gender will, I hope, result in much needed reforms within these disciplines as well.

Women of Color and the Multicultural Curriculum is a testament to the capacity of women's studies to transform itself by acknowledging that gender is only one variable in analyses of the female experience and that white, middle-class women represent only a part of that experience. The "Interdisciplinary Guide for Research and Curriculum on Puerto Rican Women" provides a useful model for curriculum development efforts focusing on other groups of women both within the United States and beyond, and it reminds us of the necessity of making visible *all* women.

This publication also reminds me that our educational institutions themselves are in need of serious transformation. We have failed in fundamental ways to prepare students for the multicultural world of the twenty-first century in which they will live and work. White students, male and female, need an inclusive curriculum and a culturally diverse environment in which to learn as much as students of color, male and female, do. It is intellectually incorrect and dishonest to ignore culture, race, ethnicity, gender, class, and sexuality in the structure of the undergraduate curriculum if our main objective is to broaden students' understanding of the social, cultural, and political realities of the human condition over time and throughout the world. I think it is the responsibility—some would say burden— of the academy, with support from other institutions, to "lend its talents to the cause of justice, compassion, and enlightenment in a world in urgent need of those blessings."[2]

Derek Bok raised the questions: "What social purpose can an American university claim to have at the end of the twentieth century? What contributions can we make to society that will justify the benefits we receive and inspire the students who come with us to learn?" Part of the answer for me is that acknowledging cultural diversity in the curriculum, which focusing on women of color enables us to do, will bring students face to face with the plight of millions on our planet and, I hope, encourage all of us to develop strategies that will make this beleaguered world of ours a better place to live for women and men of all colors.

NOTES

1. For a discussion of the emergence of the term *women of color,* see Johnnella E. Butler, "Transforming the Curriculum: Teaching about Women of Color," *Multicultural Education: Issues and Perspectives,* ed. James A. Banks and Cherry M. Banks (Boston: Allyn and Bacon, 1989); reprinted in *Transforming the Curriculum: Ethnic Studies and Women's Studies,* ed. Johnnella E. Butler and John C. Walter (Albany: SUNY Press, 1991). Subsequent references to Butler's article are from the reprint. The term *women of color* has also been problematized; see *Third World Women and the Politics of Feminism,* ed. Chandra Talpade Mohanty, Ann Russo, and Lourdes Torres (Bloomington: Indiana University Press, 1991), for a discussion of the term.

2. In his parting commencement address at Harvard, June 1991, President Derek Bok spoke movingly about the "social responsibilities of American universities."

The Feminist Press at The City University of New York offers alternatives in education and in literature. Founded in 1970, this nonprofit, tax-exempt educational and publishing organization works to eliminate stereotypes in books and schools and to provide literature with a broad vision of human potential. The publishing program includes reprints of important works by women, feminist biographies of women, multicultural anthologies, a cross-cultural memoir series, and nonsexist children's books. Curricular materials, biographies, directories, and a quarterly journal provide information and support for students and teachers of women's studies. Through publication and projects, The Feminist Press contributes to the rediscovery of the history of women and the emergence of a more humane society.

NEW AND FORTHCOMING BOOKS

The Answer/La Respuesta: The Restored Text. Including a Selection of Poems, by Sor Juana Inés de la Cruz. Critical Edition and Translation by Electa Arenal and Amanda Powell. $12.95 paper, $35.00 cloth.

Australia for Women: Travel and Culture, edited by Susan Hawthorne and Renate Klein. $17.95 paper.

The Castles of Pictures: A Grandmother's Tales, by George Sand. Translated by Holly Erskine Hirko. $9.95 paper, $19.95 cloth.

Challenging Racism and Sexism: Alternatives to Genetic Explanations, Genes & Gender VII, edited by Ethel Tobach and Betty Rosoff. $14.95 paper, $35.00 cloth.

Folly, a novel by Maureen Brady. Afterword by Bonnie Zimmerman. $12.95 paper, $35.00 cloth.

Japanese Women: New Feminist Perspectives on the Past, Present, and Future, edited by Kumiko Fujimura-Fanselow and Atsuko Kameda. $15.95 paper, $35.00 cloth.

Shedding and Literally Dreaming, by Verena Stefan. Afterword by Tobe Levin. $14.95 paper, $35.00 cloth.

The Slate of Life: More Contemporary Stories by Women Writers of India, edited by Kali for Women. Introduction by Chandra Talpade Mohanty and Satya P. Mohanty. $12.95 paper, $35.00 cloth.

Songs My Mother Taught Me: Stories, Plays, and Memoir, by Wakako Yamauchi. Edited and with an Introduction by Garrett Hongo. Afterword by Valerie Miner. $14.95 paper, $35.00 cloth.

Prices subject to change. *Individuals:* Send check or money order (in U.S. dollars drawn on a U.S. bank) to The Feminist Press at The City University of New York, 311 East 94th Street, New York, NY 10128. Please include $3.00 postage and handling for the first book, $.75 for each additional. For VISA/MasterCard orders call (212) 360-5790. *Bookstores, libraries, wholesalers:* Feminist Press titles are distributed to the trade by Consortium Book Sales and Distribution, (800) 283-3572.